THE
OUTER
TEMPLE
OF
WITCHCRAFT

ABOUT THE AUTHOR

Christopher Penczak (New Hampshire) teaches classes throughout New England on witchcraft, meditation, reiki, crystals, and shamanic journey. He is the author of *City Magick* and *Gay Witchcraft*, and writes for several local and national metaphysical magazines.

THE OUTER TEMPLE OF WITCHCRAFT

CIRCLES, SPELLS, AND RITUALS

CHRISTOPHER PENCZAK

Llewellyn Publications

Woodbury, Minnesota

First Edition
Sixteenth Printing, 2020

Book design by Donna Burch
Cover background © 2002 from Photodisc
Cover design by Lisa Novak
Editing by Tom Bilstad
Interior Illustrations by Llewellyn Art Department and © 2004 by Mary Ann Zapalac on pages 124, 236–237, 300, and 310
Llewellyn is a registered trademark of Llewellyn Worldwide Ltd.

Library of Congress Cataloging-in-Publication Data
Penczak, Christopher.
        The outer temple of witchcraft: circles, spells, and rituals / Christopher Penczak.—1st ed.
                p.   cm.
        Includes bibliographical references (p.) and index.
        ISBN 13: 978-0-7387-0531-6
        ISBN 10: 0-7387-0531-4
        1. Witchcraft.   I. Title

        BF1566.P45 2004
        133.4'3--dc22

                                                        2004044201

Llewellyn Publications
A Division of Llewellyn Worldwide Ltd.
2143 Wooddale Drive
Woodbury, MN 55125-2989
www.llewellyn.com

 Printed in the United States of America on recycled paper

Other Releases by Christopher Penczak

City Magick: Urban Spells, Rituals, and Shamanism

Spirit Allies: Meet Your Team from the Other Side

The Inner Temple of Witchcraft: Magick, Meditation, and Psychic Development

The Inner Temple of Witchcraft CD Companion

Gay Witchcraft: Empowering the Tribe

The Outer Temple of Witchcraft: Circles, Spells and Rituals

The Outer Temple of Witchcraft CD Companion

The Witch's Shield: Protection Magick and Psychic Self-Defense

Magick of Reiki

The Temple of Shamanic Witchcraft: Shadows, Spirits and the Healing Journey

The Temple of Shamanic Witchcraft CD Companion

Sons of the Goddess

Instant Magick: Ancient Wisdom, Modern Spellcraft

Mystic Foundation

Ascension Magick: Ritual, Myth and Healing for the New Aeon

The Temple of High Witchcraft: Ceremonies, Spheres and the Witches' Qabalah

The Temple of High Witchcraft CD Companion

The Living Temple of Witchcraft Volume One: The Descent of the Goddess

The Living Temple of Witchcraft, Volume One CD Companion

The Living Temple of Witchcraft Volume Two: The Journey of the God

The Living Temple of Witchcraft, Volume Two CD Companion

The Witch's Coin: Prosperity and Money Magick

The Witch's Heart: The Magick of Perfect Love & Perfect Trust

Special thanks to Steve, Rosalie, and Ronald for all your love and support.
Thanks to all my teachers, and to all my students who are my greatest teachers,
for asking all the questions that are answered in this book.
Thanks to Leandra Walker for her input.
A very special thanks to Scott Cann, Edward Newton, Ginella Cann, Laura Davis,
Alan R. White, Derek O'Sullivan, Mark J. Gracy, and Charles Dizon-Gracy.

CONTENTS

LIST OF EXERCISES

LIST OF FIGURES

Whenever you have need of anything,
once in the month
and
better it be when the
Moon is full,
you shall assemble in some secret place
and
adore the spirit of
Me,
Who is Queen of all the Wise.

—from "The Charge of the Goddess"

Introduction

WHAT IS THE OUTER TEMPLE?

I got involved with witchcraft because I wanted to do spells. I didn't believe in them, not at first, but that didn't stop my curiosity. I did believe in the power of the mind. I did believe in unseen forces that were not yet measurable by science, but at heart I was a skeptic. Believe it or not, to a certain extent, I still am. But my yardstick is not scientific data anymore. Personal experience has become my greatest measure of the truth, for I have come to discover that although there may be many universal truths existing, it's my interpretation of them, my personal truth, that affects my life the most.

So I had a friend who was involved in the craft and spellwork, and spoke with such a personal conviction, I was curious. She gave me an opportunity to do a spell. And it worked beyond my wildest dreams. It was a healing spell for another, and the recipient of this magick, along with her newborn child, had a miraculous recovery. But my skeptical mind of course jumped to the most logical conclusion: coincidence. It was exciting to think that I had such influence and connection to the universe, but I was probably delusional. It really had nothing to do with the ritual a group of witches did on the Full Moon. She simply had good doctors and was lucky. But somehow, I couldn't believe that completely. My doubt was now on the side of logic and science. I felt something happen that night under the Moon. I knew something happened. I just couldn't believe it.

So, as the budding little scientist I presumed myself to be, I sought to settle the matter once and for all. The only way to do that was to collect more data. So I began training in the science and art of the witch. I tried my best to divorce it from its third definition—a religion. Some don't like that word, so they choose "spiritual path," but I wasn't going for either definition. It was strictly a science at first. I approached it methodically, trying to understand the concepts and philosophies involved. And my teachers had me study everything from fringe quantum physics to ancient Hermetic philosophy. People around me would often stress how it wasn't a religion for them, but a science. As I practice the craft, no matter my protests to the contrary, I found that there is no way to divorce witchcraft entirely from the spiritual because, by its very nature, it is a training of spiritual transformation.

Thankfully, I was a very fortunate man. It would have been quite easy for me to get so wrapped up into the methodical techniques and ideas that I would never have discovered the gifts the practice of witchcraft had to offer me. It would have also been very easy to get trapped in the quest for power—the power to make change in the world through spellwork. For I had discovered the more spells I did, the more they came true. My thoughts of coincidences were overruled by events beyond the bounds of the law of averages. All these successful spells could not just be lucky coincidences. Something more was at play. Although the science helped my logical mind, it would have been very easy indeed to become almost intoxicated with the feeling of power. Coming from a feeling of powerlessness, like my life was out of my control, the ability to create changes in the world through magick can act like a drug. I grew up somewhat the shy, lonely bookworm/artist in an all-boys Catholic school of jocks. I felt like much of my life was planned out for me, and had a hard time truly being myself. Although I had a very loving and supportive family, I struggled with my place in the world and felt terrible pressure and nervousness.

Many people come to the craft from a place of feeling powerless and are drawn to magick because of the sense of power and control it seems to convey. Most teachers and books start with ritual and spellcraft, like a cookbook. If you follow these directions, with these specific words and ingredients, you will do a successful spell. The feeling is great and empowering, but many never learn why they used such words or ingredients, or how the spell worked in the bigger scheme of things. The immediate need is taken care of, without a thought to the spiritual path, the larger picture in the ways of the witch. And for some, that is where it begins, remains, and ends. I find that sad, but everyone is on a different path.

I was fortunate because my first serious teacher was a true wise woman. After studying with friends and doing lots of study and research on my own, I started taking very basic classes with a famous and public witch in Massachusetts named Laurie Cabot. Though our time together was short, just two one-week series of classes spread apart over a few months, Witchcraft As a Science I and II, they were life-changing. My mother, best friend, and I took it as a lark initially. We wanted something together and we were curious if witchcraft was real. The most perplexing yet transformative part of the process was the first few classes. We didn't start with magick. We didn't start with ritual. We didn't learn spells. We started with meditation. We started by learning to create in the inner world first. If we can't create in our inner space, why should we claim the power to create in the outer world? The power of our thoughts, both fully consciousness and subconscious, was stressed. We create from both, so we must become self-aware. We must have mental discipline. We must create consciousness with our magick. And most importantly, we must create from self-esteem and self-love. Only then do we learn the mysteries of spellcraft.

Wow. Well, I didn't have a lot of those qualities. I just wanted to do more spells. No one told me it was going to be this hard. I almost gave up. But I followed the wise woman's advice, and the ability to meditate and find inner guidance has served me just as much as ritual and spellcraft. Both are complementary and needed.

The first book in this series, *The Inner Temple of Witchcraft*, is a manual of this inner work. If you are not familiar with inner work and meditation, I suggest you pick it up. Much of the history, definitions, and philosophical concepts are covered in detail in it. The second course, *The Outer Temple of Witchcraft*, focuses on the application of the rituals and much of the artistic expression of the craft. If you don't have *The Inner Temple of Witchcraft*, the essential techniques and concepts that are needed for this book will be reviewed before the true lessons begin. If the first book is referenced in this work, it will be abbreviated as ITOW, with whatever chapter number or exercise cited. But in essence, this is a complete course on its own, and can be done if you have not completed the inner temple. In fact, it may inspire you to go back and do the first course.

The Outer Temple of Witchcraft is a course similar to the first. Starting with preliminary chapters and basic exercises to prepare you for the work ahead, the remainder of the book is divided into twelve lessons that can be completed over a year, along with exercises, rituals, and homework to be done. Traditional training in witchcraft is a year and a day, so you can plan your schedule accordingly. With twelve chapters, you can tackle one lesson a month, but realize some lessons are longer and more challenging than others. And each student will find certain aspects more challenging than others. If you have difficulty with meditation and quieting your mind, the inner experiences at the beginning of the course may be harder for you. If you are unsure of your will, spellcraft can be more difficult. Some find ritual easy to execute, while others are unsure when moving and speaking, even in the privacy of their own home. You will discover your balance of elements, and your relationship to those inner aspects represented by the elements. Things you would not think would be a challenge often are, revealing your true strengths and weaknesses. Revelations are blessings on the path. They bring greater awareness and that can only help our magick, though the experience is not always fun.

If you are experienced with both inner and outer workings of Wicca, then there is no reason you cannot use this book as a reference, taking the information, spells, rituals, and meditations that you are drawn to do. I do that with many books myself. But this is a foundation book, and if you don't have a strong, confident foundation in this material, or if your training has been very different and has not focused at all on the inner experience, then perhaps you should build that foundation by following the lessons step by step. It could simply confirm that you are as grounded as you think, or open new areas of personal development and learning.

The course culminates in a self-test and self-initiation ritual to the second degree of witchcraft in a five-degree system, each based on the elements. The second degree is the arena of the priestess and priest. Here all the rites and rituals are not only learned, but their meanings and mysteries truly explored. A good priestess and priest not only knows the rituals, but also understands them on the deepest levels.

One does not necessarily have to identify with the word "witch" to practice this material, although it is taught in the traditions of modern witchcraft. When recently interviewed by a grad student researching "modern" religions, she said, "I do so much of what you are talking about. Perhaps not the same words and rituals, but at the heart of it, I believe and practice many of the same things. Would you consider me a witch?" That is not for me to say. Personally I feel whenever one is honoring the earth and sky, the cycles of nature, taking personal power and personal responsibility, and creating through intention, one is practicing the heart of witchcraft, regardless of the word chosen. Would it be considered modern Wicca? Probably not. But I feel many magicians, mages, shamans, healers, priestesses, and the like are doing the same work that I am, even without the same name.

The Outer Temple of Witchcraft is based on my own Witchcraft Two: Building the Outer Temple class, and I must admit that as many non-witches have taken my witchcraft classes as those who identify themselves as witches or pagans. I've had those who are mystical Christians, Hindus, Buddhists, and the like, who felt drawn to the material. Many claim no identity or label, and are just seekers or practitioners. Personally, I feel a great responsibility to reclaim the word "witch" as something sacred and healing since it has been maligned for so many years. People tell me I should choose another word because "witchcraft" comes with so much cultural baggage, but I am a witch and what I do is witchcraft. Those who feel the magick in those words and traditions find each other. When I teach other classes with different names, they never have the same interest as classes in the craft. So I'd rather heal the misinformation and perform an act of sacred alchemy to transform the word "witch" back into its proper meaning. But in the end, it is up to you how you identify yourself and what you choose to do with the material.

The element of earth is the focus of *The Outer Temple of Witchcraft*. While in the first level we connected to fire, our inner will, light, and guidance, the purpose of the second level is to bring that sacredness, that magick from the inner world to the outer world, into the material plane embodied by the element of earth. *The Outer Temple of Witchcraft CD Companion*, like the first, is available to guide you on your journey. Subsequent works in the series will explore the mysteries of water, air, and spirit through the various branches of witchcraft.

On this earthy level we see the sacred in all things: in nature, in the seasons, in animals, plants, stones, stars, and most importantly, ourselves and each other. Spirituality is in everything, and in every moment. Unlike other religions and philosophies, witches live a sacred life every moment. We don't relegate divinity to only a particular day of the week or certain building. The Goddess and God are ever present in everything and we strive to carry that awareness in every moment. Through the outer temple, we learn to create sacred space through ritual. We honor the sacred space that is all around us, in the forest and in our living room. We create a temple between the worlds, where our inner sacredness comes out into the outer world.

Not only do we see the sacredness of all things in the world, but we grow to realize that our intentions affect everything because we are all connected through a web of life. We must be responsible and walk lightly on the web. We learn we are always creating in the physical. Our body is always re-creating itself as cells divide and we continue the life process. We also create on many other levels, and must take a conscious, active role in the creation. We learn to manifest as we honor the cycles. This is spellcraft. This is ritual. We must partner with the divinity of the world to continually create the lives that are most correct and healthy for ourselves and for all others. When we define the word *wicca* as "to bend or shape" this is the bending and shaping we are talking about—bending, shaping, partnering with the divine forces to flow with them and create, rather than constantly struggle, fight, and swim upstream against the tides of life. We can only do this through partnership with the divine forces of the world. The world, the earth and sky, Sun, Moon, and stars—all that we see is divinity in manifestation.

Be well,

Christopher Penczak

Sacred Space and the Circle

If you enter the heart of the teachings of witchcraft, at the core you will find the power of sacred space. When I started, "sacred space" was just words in a ritual. No one really explained the true meaning of that term to me. "Sacred space" was just a buzzword. But as I kept saying it as a part of the rituals, I learned. Eventually, the layers of the mystery were revealed to me. I finally understood what sacred space was all about.

Looking back on it, it seems so obvious, but the teachings I initially received didn't emphasize the sacred aspects of the craft. Everyone around me was so afraid of using the word "religion" or "spirituality"; so much was kept to the technical and philosophical. And at the time, that's what I needed. My emphasis wasn't on the sacred. Now, in my own teachings, I have a hard time divorcing myself from talking about the spiritual path of witchcraft, because it is all part of what led me to my spiritual path. At the moment, if you are like I was, you might not appreciate this. In fact, I can describe it at length and with my own personal stories and meanings, but until you seek spirituality out and start to experience it yourself, my words are meaningless.

I've contemplated not sharing these things, but letting my students figure it out for themselves, as I did. I decided not to for one simple reason. For many people, the craft of the witch becomes so focused on spellwork or memorizing rituals that even the concept of the greater meanings and mysteries never cross their minds. The possibility is not contemplated and explored because, for so many, it is unknown. Students will still have to figure it out on their own, truly, because it must experienced.

All I hope to do is plant a small seed of awareness, and give you the means to be your own gardener, the means to care for and nurture that seed. You can always choose to grow something else. You can save the seed of truly understanding sacred space for a later time, like I did. Or, you can grow it and make it flourish right now. The choice is up to you.

Perfect Love and Perfect Trust

Sacred space is simply honoring the sacredness, the divinity, found in all things everywhere. Through the ritual of the witch's circle, we mark a territory, a circle that can be out in nature or in our bedroom, and recognize its sacredness. We acknowledge that this space exists not only in the physical, but also in all worlds, and opens the doorway between the worlds, to be in conscious communion with the sacredness on all levels of reality. Our temple is said to stand not in any one world, but between the worlds, and in all worlds. In our sacred space, there is no separation. Through it we partner with all that is seen and unseen, through perfect love and perfect trust.

"Perfect love and perfect trust" were other buzzwords I heard in circle. Some traditions used them. Others didn't. But no one really explained to me what these important words meant, other than saying "sacred space" or "love and trust." I knew the "perfect" was a big key to this mystery, but at the time, I was focused on the Moon, and picking the right time to do my spells, rather than really understanding what I was saying. I was told to say "perfect love and perfect trust," so I did, but didn't know why and didn't really dwell on it.

Only once I ventured out of my safe world of Wicca did I really come to understand these five important words. I developed a very eclectic view of the witch, looking to all traditions, not just Celtic. I studied shamanism, energy healing, Kabalah, yoga, reiki, flower essences, and herbs, purposely looking outside the pagan view. Witchcraft became a vast umbrella for all these disciplines, since its philosophies gave me a great grounding that I noticed many in the "New Age" world didn't have. As the craft of the wise, I saw all these disciplines as part of witchcraft, though I soon found out many did not.

Through this exploration of new techniques and philosophies, I found a common thread: unconditional love. I wasn't big on the word "love." I thought it misused. So many people say the word "love" but never really back it up with any meaning or intent. As a songwriter, I thought of all the trite songs using the word "love," and how it has lost its value. So I avoided the word in my creative work. Even in my Witchcraft I class experience, I thought of self-love as self-confidence, assurance, and esteem. But here the word "love" kept on popping up. I thought these New Age practices a holdover from the 1960s, with vague concepts of free love and spiritual love, and started to question if I was learning anything of real value. Then I felt the love.

Through various meditation workshops, one in particular about awakening the heart chakra to unconditional love, I really felt it. I really awakened it. Like all things, I entered a skeptic, but from the first moment, I felt heaviness in my chest. As the day went on, it melted away and I left the weekend course dazzling, light, and with an open heart. Not only did I feel this nebulous unconditional love coursing through me, I had a sense that I am the love, too. Everyone is.

While reflecting on that experience in my Book of Shadows journal, I skimmed through my notes and realized that the first time I felt this type of love was in the witch's circle. It wasn't the same because I was not taught to really focus on it as a witch. In the workshop, that was the purpose of the entire weekend. But it was present in the first magickal circle, even if I had my eyes closed to it. I traced the teaching of this unconditional love back, and the start of my personal thread was in witchcraft classes, through perfect love and perfect trust.

Slowly on the intellectual level, I began to distinguish the difference between what my society had been calling love, what I would later call personal love, and what the mystics call unconditional love. Witches call it perfect love. Unconditional love is just that: perfect, unattached, without limits and restraints. This love simply is, and to me it is the binding force of the universe. In the ITOW, we covered the Hermetic principle called the Principle of Mentalism, stating "We are all thoughts in the divine mind," meaning we are all part of a greater whole. I wish there was another principle stating we are all pulses within the divine heart, because it is through this heart we truly feel the unity, even though the mind can intellectually know it. With unconditional love, you are loved simply because you exist. You are love.

With personal love, that is our relationship love, be it familial, romantic, or friendship. There are often conditions to it and it sometimes seems to come with a struggle. The dichotomy between unconditional love and personal love, what mainstream society simply refers to both as love, pushed me to avoid the concept altogether. Unfortunately, English often lacks the subtleties of other languages, particularly on the spiritual concepts. Many other languages have separate words for differing kinds of love.

Perfect trust is a divine sense of knowing and security with the creative spirit, the Goddess and God. We work actively to partner with the divine ones, through our magick and meditations, realizing that we are all part of that divine mind. But when things seem confusing, when our guidance isn't clear, when our magick isn't working as we planned, and when we are suffering tragedy, we have a trust in the divine through our knowing of being unconditionally loved. It isn't logical or rational, but when we truly experience and know it, no personal challenge will ever be viewed the same way again.

Perfect trust runs both ways. As we have it through this unconditional love for the divine, we know the Goddess and God have it for us. They trust us to fulfill our parts of the pattern. We have infinite choices and freedom as to how we serve the large pattern and fulfill our parts, but we trust that all actions can serve the greater spiraling pattern of the universe.

Through practicing the rituals of perfect love and perfect trust, through creating sacred space, we grow in our sense of connection and love. Even if we don't initially feel it, it is there, growing and expanding in our awareness, until we are ready. We best manifest our desires, our magick, through truly feeling our connection to the Goddess, the God, and all the universe. We connect and create sacred space through the perfect love and perfect trust the divine has for us, and we have for them. If everything is sacred, all the time, and we simply do our rituals to open the door to a partnership with the sacred, everything is therefore filled with this unconditional love, this perfect love and perfect trust. All we have to do is open our eyes to it, in and out of our rituals.

The challenge we have, as those walking the spiritual path of witchcraft, is to inject more and more perfect love and perfect trust, or sacredness, to all thoughts and actions in our life, bringing it to every relationship and exchange. No small feat to accomplish, but this is the path of enlightenment, taken one step at a time. As overused as the saying may be, it truly is the journey, and not the destination, when walking the witch's road.

The most important lesson I've learned in applying perfect love and perfect trust to the world is that unconditional love doesn't mean unconditional relationships. You can hold a sacred love for someone in your heart, and honor that person as a living being, as a spiritual soul, but you can draw a boundary for your own health and well-being. Unconditional love doesn't mean you encourage others to walk all over you and hurt you. As the witch's circle casts a boundary of sacred space, I think it is an important reminder that we, too, while in the physical plane, have appropriate boundaries of our own space, health, and well-being.

RETURN TO THE INNER TEMPLE

Before we go forward in our work, we should reflect on the inner temple. In ITOW, the lessons focused on finding a sacred space within yourself, on the inner planes of reality. Only through finding the sacredness on the unseen planes can you truly open the doorways between worlds and create a temple of sacred space intersecting with the physical world through the rituals of witchcraft.

A key lesson of this previous work was to gain the discipline to enter a meditative state, a level of altered consciousness where you can perceive energy more easily and direct it with your will. In the ritual state, you will not go as deep as in meditative, but understanding how to enter both levels of consciousness, easily at anytime, is a measure of a truly well-trained witch. Laurie Cabot used to say to my class that you should be able to enter alpha state while riding a crowded subway train. I don't recommend it, since that might blind you to the dangers of urban travel, but in theory, you should be able to do it.

The discipline aspect bothers some students. Feeling witchcraft is light, spacy, and free, they don't understand the need for discipline. Discipline is one aspect of the craft, but an important one. It is the earthy foundation upon which all other free and ecstatic practices are built. It is easy to get distracted, physically or magickally, and proper discipline lets us keep our focus clear regardless of distractions or surprises.

When in the sacred space, all thoughts become thoughts of creation. Without mental discipline, you might create something you don't want. There are all sorts of precautions built into the rituals for this reason, but the best precaution is self-aware-ness. When I first started in Wicca, I was untrained in my first circle. Although it was a very magickal experience on all levels, I couldn't help but have distracting thoughts: "Is this real? I feel silly wearing a robe. Wow, the Moon came out from behind the clouds when she called it."

I even had thoughts from my previous years of Catholicism, thinking, "Uh oh, per-haps I was wrong about this witchcraft thing. Perhaps God is mad at me for this and we are going to Hell." Not the best thoughts to be having in a sacred space, but per-fectly understandable. I had them flash in my mind, and hear many first-time witches feel the same thing, but feel embarrassed to admit it. Thankfully none of us created from those thoughts, but the circle space can intensify all feelings. Some people feel overwhelmed in the sacred space. They are usually people who are undisciplined or ungrounded in themselves and their own self-image and self-esteem. Such energy can be overwhelming even to one fully aware, depending on the ritual.

The key to fully integrate into the sacred space and be open to the most magickal of experiences is the ability to clear the mind, enter an altered state, and tune into the sacred energies within you and the circle, to bring balance and harmony. Some people can do it naturally without any training, but the best way I've found to teach it to oth-ers is to learn the discipline of meditation.

Altered States

To work magick and meditation, you must be able to enter an altered state, often called gnosis. In magick, an altered state is any level of brain activity that is different from normal waking activity that helps you process energy, will, and intuition.

Our states of consciousness are based on brain wave activity. The four states we are more concerned about are beta, alpha, theta, and delta. Beta is normal waking consciousness, at thirteen to sixteen hertz, or cycles, per second. Alpha is the magickal state most people talk about, a light meditative state clocking in at eight to thirteen cycles per second. When we visualize creatively, daydream, meditate, and enter a light hypnotic state, we are in alpha. Theta is a deeper state, ranging from four to eight hertz. The lowest state is delta, at four or less hertz.

Alpha is the state we are most involved in for this book. Light states of alpha are called ritual consciousness. You must be open and aware to energy and intuition, but not so deep that you are immobile. During rituals you still need to speak, light candles, read spells, and perform other actions. In group rituals, you need to be aware of silent cues and group dynamics while still maintaining your magickal awareness. On the deeper levels of alpha, moving toward theta, we enter a more immobile, deeper awareness, tuning into the inner planes. Some totally block out the physical world, while others are true walkers between the worlds, aware of both the inner reality and outer world simultaneously. I've had both experiences, depending on my own times of personal power and awareness. Neither is better than the other, as long as it works for you.

Learn this technique to enter a meditative state. Use only the first countdown when needing to enter ritual consciousness. Do the complete countdown for deeper meditation and journeying.

EXERCISE 1

Entering an Altered State

1. Get into a comfortable position. If you are going into an inner meditative experience, make sure you are sitting comfortably, either feet flat on the floor, or cross-legged on the floor. If you are getting into ritual consciousness, simply stand with feet apart to give you balance and support.

2. Take a few deep breaths and relax your body. Bring your awareness to the top of your body, starting at the head, and give yourself permission to relax. As you breathe, release the tension. Move from your head and neck into the shoulders and arms. Relax and feel all the tension melt away. Relax your chest and back. Feel waves of relaxation move down your spine. Relax your abdomen, lower back, and hips. Relax your legs down to your ankles and feet. Feel the waves of relaxation sweep all that doesn't serve your highest good out through your fingers and toes, grounding and neutralizing this unwanted energy into the Earth, transforming it like the earth turns fallen leaves into new soil.

3. Relax your mind. Release any unwanted thoughts and worries as you exhale. Relax your heart and open it to the love of the Goddess and God. Relax your soul and follow your inner light, guidance, and protection.

4. Visualize a giant screen before you, like a blackboard or movie screen. This is the screen of your mind, or what is called your mind's eye. Whenever you visualize or recall anything, remember a person's face or anything else, you project it onto this screen. Anything you desire will appear on the screen.

5. On the screen of your mind, visualize a series of numbers, counting down from 12 to 1. With each number, you get into a deeper meditative state. The numbers can be any color you desire, drawn as if writing them, or appearing whole.

   Now visualize 12, see the number 12 on your screen, 12.

   11, see the number 11 on your screen, 11.

   10, see the number 10 on your screen, 10.

   9, see the number 9 on your screen, 9.

   8, see the number 8 on your screen, 8.

   7, see the number 7 on your screen, 7.

   6, see the number 6 on your screen, 6.

   5, see the number 5 on your screen, 5.

   4, see the number 4 on your screen, 4.

   3, see the number 3 on your screen, 3.

   2, see the number 2 on your screen, 2.

   1, see the number 1 on your screen, 1.

6. You are at your ritual consciousness. Everything done at this level is for your highest good, harming none.

7. You are now counting down to a deeper, more focused meditative state. Count backward from 13 to 1, but do not visualize the numbers this time. Let the numbers gently take you down. 13, 12, 11, 10, 9, 8, 7, 6, 5, 4, 3, 2, 1. You are now at your deepest meditative state, your magickal mindset, in complete control of your magickal abilities. Say to yourself,

   "I ask the Goddess and God to protect and guide me in this meditation."

8. From this point, you can continue on to other exercises and experiences, or meditate at this level for a bit and bring yourself up, counting from 1 to 13 and then 1 to 12. Gently start to wiggle your fingers and toes, and slowly move to bring your awareness back to the physical.

9. Take both hands and raise them up over your head, palms facing your crown. Slowly bring them down over your forehead, face, throat, chest, abdomen, and then groin, and "push out" with your palms facing away from you. This gives you clearance and balance, releasing any harmful or unwanted energies you might pick up during your magickal experiences. Tell yourself:

> "I give myself clearance and balance. I am in balance with myself. I am in balance with the universe. I release all that does not serve me."

10. Ground yourself as needed. You can ground yourself back into the physical state by pressing your hands down onto the floor and releasing excess energy to the Earth. You can also visualize your feet and toes as roots digging deep into the earth. When all else fails, activate your digestive system by drinking a full glass of water or eating something to bring your energy back to your body.

The following meditation is the most important experience from ITOW. Called the Inner Temple meditation, it is to help a witch find the sacred within her- or himself. If you have already experienced this or a similar meditation, try it again. Visiting your own inner sacred space regularly is an important part of the practice of witchcraft.

EXERCISE 2

The Inner Temple

1. Start Exercise 1: Entering an Altered State to get into your meditative mind-state.

2. In your mind's eye, visualize the great World Tree, a gigantic tree reaching up to the heavens and deep below the earth, larger than any tree you have ever seen. It is a sacred tree and you may recognize it as oak, ash, pine, willow, or

any other tree that has meaning for you. If you don't visualize anything, sense the tree with your other psychic senses. Hear the wind through its branches. Smell the earth where its roots dig in. Feel the texture of the bark. Simply know the tree is there and it will be. The tree is ever present and everywhere.

3. Imagine the screen of your mind's eye is like a window or doorway, a portal you can easily pass through. Step through the screen and stand before the World Tree. Look up and feel its power. Touch the tree and place in it the intention of visiting your inner temple.

4. Look around the base of the giant tree, in the roots, and search for a passageway. It may be a hole or tunnel, or even a pool of water that gives you entry into the tree. As you enter, you find yourself in a tunnel, winding and spiraling to your inner temple.

5. At the end of the tunnel you see a light, and you move toward that light and step out into your inner temple. Look around. Take stock of all you see. Notice all the fine details of your sacred space. Let the images come to you. The inner temple can be a place you have visited in the physical world, or an amalgam of sacred sites and shrines from your deepest inner knowing.

6. Explore your inner temple. You will find a variety of sacred objects for your use. Usually there is a reflective surface, such as a mirror or pool of water for gazing. Gardens, plants, altars, crystals, and a variety of tools will be found. Gateways leading to other energies and levels of consciousness can also be found. Your inner temple is like your launching pad for deeper journeys.

7. If there is anything about your temple you do not like, you can change it now by doing some inner spiritual decorating. Your temple will reflect your own inner being. Usually it responds to your will, and reflects your state of inner awareness. If something will not change, it is usually a message that you need to change something in your physical life to make the inner change a reality.

8. Once done, return through the World Tree tunnel that brought you to this place and stand before the World Tree. Step back through the screen of your mind's eye and let the World Tree gently fade from view.

9. Return yourself to normal consciousness, counting up, giving yourself clearance and balance. Do any necessary grounding.

More detailed instruction in basic meditation and the inner temple can be found in the ITOW, chapter 6 and chapter 14, respectively.

BRINGING SACRED SPACE INTO YOUR LIFE

A universal technique found in so many cultures and spiritual paths is altar building. It is a simple but very effective way to bring sacred space into your home, office or other living area. In ITOW, we built a meditation altar. For the outer temple, the altar will grow as we grow with our understanding of the elements and our tools. An altar constantly reminds us of the sacred cosmos it represents. It is a microcosm for our sacred space, which is a symbol for the universe itself.

I've had a lot of people complain that they don't need an altar, that it is stupid or archaic, and, as modern witches, we don't need to use tools of the past. I understand the sentiment. I felt the same way as a "scientific witch" myself. I didn't want to be superstitious, and not understand the reasons behind my actions or tools. But the ancients did know a thing or two. There is a reason why altar building is found in so many cultures. I don't know of any other technique that is as simple, yet profoundly powerful, to remind the aspiring practitioner of sacred space every day.

It reminds a witch that everything is sacred. It represents what the witch is working on, in the inner and outer worlds. If you leave a candle burning for a current spell, that is where your sacred attention is focused. If you put something on it to represent your inner learning, such as a particular herb or stone, you are emphasizing those lessons in your own inner sacred world. You see it every day, and every day, you rededicate yourself to the spiritual path simply by acknowledging it. By making a space for it in your home, you are symbolically making a space for the life of a witch in your life. Every action is powerful and symbolic, not only affecting our subconscious mind, but also energetically affecting us and our environment for the better.

To start, create an altar in your home where you can do meditative and ritual work. Ideally, you want to have an altar you can keep out and see often, but some of us don't have that luxury. I know witches who hide their altar in an empty closet, or have designed it in such a way that it closes so no one else can see it. One clever witch used an empty Victrola box she could close when company came over. Others have to dismantle and reassemble the altar when any magickal work is done. Do what is best for your situation.

Traditionally, altars are supposed to face either north or east. As you learn about the circle, elements, and directions, you will learn the ideas behind those directions, but all directions are magickal. Use what your intuition calls you to do, and what your space allows. You can always face the altar in another direction to fit the room, and face whatever direction is appropriate for the ritual you are doing.

For now, simply place a candle on the altar, any color you desire. You can place an altar cloth beneath it. Traditional colors are black and white, but again, follow your own intuition and tastes. If you have gathered any "power objects" but are unsure as to their properties and qualities, such as feathers, stones, incense, crystals, shells, and the like, feel free to add them to this embryonic altar. If you are familiar with altar setup and desire to make a traditional altar, then so do. As we go through the various lessons, you will collect or make ritual tools to be used and place them on the altar. For now, if you are uncertain, don't worry about it.

CASTING A CIRCLE OF LIGHT

One of the most universal symbols in creating sacred space, found in earth-honoring cultures around the world, is the symbol of the circle. The circle is the symbol of life, like the ouruborous, the serpent devouring its own tail; it has no beginning and no ending, but continues on in various forms. The circle is the symbol of the Earth itself, as well as the Moon and Sun. The circle is the cycles of life between the planet and heavens, as embodied by the changing seasons. It is the egg of creation, brimming with all potentials and possibilities. The circle is sacred.

Tribal cultures often met in a circle, for both political and religious reasons. In the circle, everyone has a voice. Everyone has importance. Elders and teachers are respected, but the hierarchy is not apparent. As in nature, everyone is valued. Everyone has their place. A monkey is not valued by the Goddess more than an ant in the circle of life. They simply have a different role to play.

The circle is a symbol of boundaries. The circle marks a space and territory when cast, creating a temple. It is a method of bringing the inner sacredness out into the world. We resonate with the circle because we live inside a sphere. Our aura, our energy field, is often viewed as an egg or sphere stretching out a bit beyond our arm's length. Around us in the four directions, we perceive this personal energy field as a circle of personal space, and our sense of boundaries is defined by how healthy this field, this circle, is. When we come together in a group, it is as if our circles merge to a larger field. Inside it we share the intimacy of sacred space and perfect love.

Because of the boundary associations, redefining the circle around us is a technique of protection. When we emphasize it, we not only strengthen our own energy fields, but we create a space that is more centered, quiet, and powerful for ourselves. You don't have to be a witch to do this technique. Many spiritualists do this. I know a few "psychic investigators" who use the circle technique for protection in difficult circumstances when investigating harmful energies or entities.

Although you can draw this circle of light around you at any time, for any reason, in modern witchcraft there is an emphasis on starting either in the north or the east. The north relates the magnetic north pole, and is emphasized when in the Northern Hemisphere, since it is the closest magnetic pole to you. If you were in the Southern Hemisphere the emphasis might be in the south. Practitioners with a strong Earth/ Goddess focus feel a strong affinity to the north, and it plays a role in many mythologies. I focus on the north, and feel it as the greatest source of natural power to connect with when casting a circle. It is like a well of energy freely giving itself to the witch for the creation of sacred space.

Those with an emphasis in the east might focus more on the solar aspects of power, since the Sun rises in the east and the day starts there. Both north and east work, and in fact, any direction is okay, but those are the two most powerful and traditional.

Witches will sometimes carry a magnetic compass to find magnetic north when casting a circle where the directions are unknown to them, particularly when indoors and the Sun's rising and setting cannot be used as a marker, although magnetic north is a bit different from directional north.

I have found the use of a compass is not necessary. Like bird and other animals, people can tune into the magnetic field of the Earth and find it for direction. I do the following experiment in class and it almost always works. Even if it is tough the first time around, the more you practice it and get a feel for what you are looking for, the better you become at it.

Close your eyes and spin around until you are a bit dizzy and don't know what direction you face. Take a moment to center yourself and get your balance, without opening your eyes. Then raise your arms. Some will raise only their receptive hands, usually your nondominant hand. So if you are right-handed, your left hand is your receptive hand. I use both, and simply raise my arms at a ninety-degree angle from my body, with my wrists bent up and palms facing forward, to feel the energy. Then make a slow, clockwise circle, and notice the different sensations in your hands. Try to feel the strongest source of energy. Make several circles if you need to, and find the highest point of power. It can feel like a magnetic pull or push, or feel like a temperature change or "pins-and-needles" tingle. Everyone describes it differently because everyone processes energy differently. Once you find it, open your eyes, and if need be, check it with a compass. You most likely have found north, or pretty close to it.

If you didn't, there are several reasons. If you are solar oriented, then you might have found east, or the direction where the Sun is currently. If the time is near sunset, you might be pointing toward the west. Strong electromagnetic fields can also screw up this exercise. So if you live near an electrical generator station, or have high-powered electrical or computer equipment near you, you might get a "false" signal. But most of the time, it does work.

Once you find your directions, decide if you want to start in the north or east, and do the following exercise. It can be done for fun and practice, or to set a space before meditation, ritual work, divination, and or any other psychic experience.

Exercise 3

The Circle of Protection

1. Start Exercise 1, but only enter your ritual consciousness state, not a full meditative state.

2. Think of your own inner power. Think of the feeling you have while visiting the inner temple. Re-create that feeling in your body, heart, mind, and soul. Acknowledge your own sacredness and the sacredness of the space around you, no matter if you are indoors or outdoors.

3. Point to your power direction with your energetically projective hand, or dominant hand, and trace a clockwise circle of light around you. You can physically move your hand and body clockwise, eyes open, or you can do this in your mind, with your eyes closed. Experiment with both as you practice this exercise. The color of the light is traditionally blue, violet, or white, but use any color that you feel intuitively drawn to use.

4. Trace a second circle, over the first to strengthen it. The color might change naturally, or you can choose to change it.

5. Create a third circle, over the second, as before the color can change.

6. Feel the shift in energy and vibration inside the circle. Notice the changes in your inner and outer perceptions.

7. When done, release the circle. There are two ways to do this. Both start by retracing the circle backwards. Begin by pointing at the direction you have chosen and trace a counterclockwise circle, again either in your mind, or physically moving to trace the circle.

   For the first technique, imagine as you move the circle counterclockwise that you are opening a curtain, and when you complete the circle, you are pushing out the curtain ring. The effect is like a pebble dropped in a puddle of water. The ring of light expands infinitely outward.

   The second technique consists of using your hand like a vacuum cleaner. You are "sucking up" the ring of light through your finger, and then imagining grounding the light through your body, legs, feet, and into the Earth. You don't have to ground it, but if you don't, you might feel lightheaded or over-energized, so I suggest you ground the excess energy. Personally, I prefer the first technique.

8. Return yourself to normal consciousness, counting up and doing any necessary grounding.

The circle is drawn clockwise, what witches call deosil. A Celtic scholar friend of mine said that regardless how the word looks, and how most modern pagans pronounce it phonetically, a more accurate pronunciation of the word would be "jed-sil." Clockwise is the direction of the Sun, and symbolizes the creation of life and the growth process. When witches create, they move Sun-wise. When in ritual space and doing spellwork or healing, always move clockwise in the circle if possible.

The circle is released counterclockwise, also called widdershins. Moving against the movement of the Sun is to release and decrease.

When creating the circles of light, they can take on a variety of effects. My friend Claire describes her circles like lariats spinning around her in the air. When my friend Erik did this exercise, the circles rotated independently of each other, like a gyroscope, creating a sphere-like impression around him. Another student described the three rings braiding together like Celtic knots. Once you create the circles with your intent, notice how you perceive them. Circles are like people; each is individual to that moment and time. Your circles can have a particular "flavor" to them that people recognize, or they can change with the day and time as you create them. Pay attention to the changes. They can have messages for you on the path.

Once the circle is created, you can feel a variety of changes. To many, the sense of boundary and temple is so complete that the air seems to be still, even if it is breezy outside the circle. The temperature could change, usually rising with the containment of energy. Other shifts may be within your own body and mind. Feelings of peacefulness, stillness, energy, and even nervousness and lightheadedness are common. Those less-wanted reactions, such as lightheadedness or agitation, usually pass when one becomes used to the intense energy of some circles. The more rooted you are in your own sacredness, the less you will experience such distractions.

Later we will be using ritual words and the wand, a tool used to create this sacred space, but it is important to remember that you have all the tools you need inside you, wherever you go. Ritual tools help and have great energy to contribute, but they are not the only means necessary to create a ritual. Always remember, the sacredness of life is always ever present, in you and around you, permeating all of creation.

Foundations of Magick

The Outer Temple of Witchcraft is a manual of outer magick, an instructional course teaching you how to tap your inner resources to partner with nature and shape the world around you. The root of the word "witchcraft" is often traced to the word "wicca," meaning "to bend or shape." The bending or shaping refers to bending the natural forces of energy, to create change. This is magick. In fact, the modern revival of the religion of witchcraft is often referred to as Wicca. This active partnership with nature through your own personal awareness and energy is the heart of the craft. Through understanding the patterns and energies of the world around us, we learn to partner with the patterns within us, to find balance on all levels, and in all worlds. This act of partnership and transformation is called magick.

Before we delve into the "cookbook" of spell recipes and rituals, I find it extremely beneficial, as modern people living in the scientific age, to understand the mechanics of magick and how it works as part of a rational universe. (For a more intensive look at the intersection of science and magick, review ITOW, chapters 7 and 8.)

What is Magick?

Magick is the art and science of creating change in accord with your will. That simply means you learn the techniques to project your intentions out to the universe and the universe responds in kind by manifesting your intentions. The universe responds to our thoughts, feelings, and words all the time. In mystical communities, adepts say we create our own reality. Everyone does, through the energies we put out into the universe. The universe responds through simple laws of cause and effect, called magickal theory. They are the spiritual laws of the universe found in many mystical cultures, just as science defines the physical laws of the universe. They are not mutually exclusive. In fact they are complementary. Science, through the study of quantum physics and other "fringe" theories, is bordering more and more on the mystical.

The difference between one who does magick—a witch, magician, shaman, or sorcerer—and anyone else is that the magickal practitioner knows she or he creates from thought, emotion, and word. Most people are not aware of it, and think things happen to them randomly. A witch creates consciously and learns the best techniques to create. When something "bad" happens to you—an illness, an injury, or any other unfortunate occurrence—part of you is creating it, though you are probably not be aware of it. It can be an unconscious part, repressed and forgotten, or a higher, wiser, divine part that is showing you something for growth. A witch strives to get conscious and partner with both the unconscious and the divine to better understand these experiences, to transform them into blessings. Meditation, magick, and introspection are all ways of getting more conscious of these parts. Then the witch learns to actively partner with these parts and partner with the forces of nature all around.

The key word is "partner," not "dominate." You are going to create your life anyway, based on the sum of all your thoughts, words, intentions, and feelings. Would you rather create unconsciously and feel disconnected, or become aware and create from a place of knowing love and, hopefully in time, wisdom? I choose to create consciously! Most witches do.

Magick is simply manifestation through energy and intent. What I call magick has many other names, particularly in this modern world. So many people are afraid of the word "magick" itself, but when you call it something else, they are happy with it and realize they are already doing a form of magick. Creative visualization, positive thinking, manifestation, and affirmations are all forms of magick that can be found in many corporate retreats and self-help books. They shy from the "m" word because it has so many connotations that are deemed superstitious. In actuality, there is a science behind it. Prayer can be a form of magick and is probably the most popular form. When you connect with your notion of the divine and ask the divine to fulfill your intent, you are doing magick. Unfortunately, most people don't know how to pray effectively because their methods of prayer don't really help them connect and partner with the divine. Many modes of prayer encourage people to feel separate and disconnected from the divine, begging for forgiveness and feeling as though they have to give up aspects of life they enjoy to receive a blessing. These forms of prayer conjure the antithesis of the consciousness that magick needs—separation. Magick is about connection. But there are those in traditional faiths that do feel love and connection when praying, and they are often doing magick, even if they don't know it.

HISTORY OF MAGICK

You wouldn't know it by the last two thousand years of history, but magick has been a part of most cultures, dating back to the dawn of civilization. We don't live in a particularly magickal culture at the moment, so such concepts are not given serious attention, and are relegated to the realm of superstition and folktale. But there is both a history and science underlying the concepts of magick.

I find it strange that our culture relies too much on concepts of the Western civilization founded in the Greco-Roman traditions. Their histories, philosophies, logic, math, and poetry are still taught in fine learning institutions around the world. They were ancient pagan cultures, and the concepts of the gods, magick, mysticism, meditation, and ritual were a strong force in their culture, shaping their philosophies. We have divorced ourselves from those ideas that modern man finds unpalatable, and in the process divorced ourselves from great spiritual truths that run in many cultures and religions. The history of magick is the history of humanity. Without it, we would not have our arts and sciences, our religions and culture. Magick is as much a part of human nature as eating, drinking, building, and loving.

The story of magick starts with the Stone Age people across the world. As we developed into tribes, there are those who discovered an aptitude for working with the unseen forces, what we call spirits, psychic abilities, and magick. They became the first witches, the first shamans. They are beyond name, but are truly all our ancestors.

These first walkers between the worlds brought back their experiences in the spirit realm, which became our first story, our first mythology. They brought back the first symbols and languages, dabbing their petroglyphs on cave walls. They sang their spirit songs and beat their drums, giving us the first music. All art and all culture was at first sacred art. Through their intuition and nature inquisitiveness, these world walkers became the first healers, using herbalism and basic first aid. As guides and counselors, they saw the need for rituals, holidays, and rites of passage. They helped connect the first people to the world, yet knew the touch of the spirit realm. All acts of creation, healing, and celebration were acts of magick, for they kept the tribe in touch with the forces of life. They did rituals for the bounty of the land, the hunt, and the fertility of the people, so that the line may survive. We know much about these people because many tribal indigenous cultures, with similar rites and rituals, still exist in remote pockets of the world, holding on to the old ways. In part, they have inspired modern man's return to the magickal realms.

As our Stone Age ancestors moved from the hunter-gatherer realm and into the agricultural, small towns developed and then grew into civilizations. Mud huts gave way to stone temples and the development of the first technologies. And our shamans survived, growing in number and forming the orders of priests and priestesses in these ancient worlds. Here developed the Sumerian, Egyptian, and Greek mystery schools. These priestesses and priests of the pagan gods became the guardians of magick for the ruling class and common people alike. Although building and writing developed for a number of reasons, they developed in part for religious reasons. The first languages were sacred languages. We spell words, and we do spells for magick because language and magick are so interconnected. The first philosophers, scientists, doctors, architects, artists, musicians, and astronomers were involved in the sacred arts.

Some of the magick wielders were not a part of the building of the ancient cradles of civilization, but remained tribal, forming different yet no less beautiful and complex cultures. Most notable are the Druids of the Celtic tribes and the seers, shamans, and rune masters of the Teutonic people. They later intermingled with the Greek and Roman civilizations in their mutual migrations across Europe. They kept the traditions of tribal magick alive, and created great poetic forms of magick through an intricate oral tradition.

Although most witches credit the rise of Christianity with the ending of the ages of magick, that is not necessarily the case. True, they seem to coincide, but the paradigm shift really came with the advent of institutional Christianity, not Christianity itself. Many persecutions and demonization of witches began in the Roman Empire. The Roman Christian church seemed to simply inherit them and take them to a more disturbing level.

The Judeo-Christian traditions have a long history of mysticism. The first forms of Christianity could be called magickal. The Jewish traditions keep their mystical lore in the form of the Tree of Life, the Kabalah. Even in the early church, Christian magick was deemed a miracle or blessing. It was only as the church became more institutionalized did other religions and forms of magick become associated with harm and evil. Even now, rituals such as faith healing in the Christian tradition and the sacrament of communion in Catholicism can be considered forms of ritual magick. I come from a Catholic family, and when discussing witchcraft with hostile members of my former faith, I have made comparisons to lighting candles in church with lighting candles on my altar. Both are using the same principles, just in a different place, with a different framework. Both are magick.

For good or for ill, the tools and traditions of pagan magick went underground in Europe when the institutional church began to persecute those who wielded power, along with any social or political dissidents that did not fit its new world order. Propaganda painting the witch as the servant of Satan began, even though ancient pagans and witches had no belief or even concept of Satan in their worldview. The Devil as the ultimate source of evil is a Christian concept.

Folk magick survived in the kitchen tools and in the royal courts of Europe. Alchemy and astrology were hidden with the court advisors. There it remained until the revival of magick and occultism at the end of the nineteenth century. Eastern concepts, including meditation, yoga, chakras, and psychic abilities, made their migration to the West. The well-to-do in Europe revived ancient Hermetic traditions, fusing it with the Hebrew Tree of Life, astrology, and the tarot to create the modern traditions of ceremonial magick, such as the Order of the Golden Dawn, neither exclusively pagan, Jewish, or Christian, yet reminiscent of the old orders of priests and priestesses of Egypt and Greece.

They, in turn, inspired a revival of pagan magick and religion in the twentieth century without the Christian influences, focusing on the divine as both Goddess and

God, female and male. These neopagan movements, including modern Wicca, also looked to the shamanic traditions of the Americas and Siberia to rediscover their own European shamanic roots and the possibility of the Stone Age Goddess cultures. All became associated, at least in large bookstores, with the New Age, and the variety of ancient and reinterpreted information encouraging the seeker to build a personal understanding and relationship with the divine powers. That personal relationship, in essence, is magick, and it has always been, always is, and always will be with us. The history of magick is the history of life.

How Does It Work?

I have studied witchcraft because starting out in a scientific modality, I wanted to find the most efficient and effective method to harness this energy of manifestation. In my experience, from my initial discovery to now, nothing has come close to the rituals of witchcraft in creating such a powerful connection and sense of oneness to do magick for the highest good.

Granted, in retrospect, I have to qualify this statement. It is the most powerful technique for me. Though many agree (since many students have had the same experience as myself), I have found that everyone needs to make a personal connection, and no matter how powerful the technique, if it doesn't resonate with you, if it doesn't touch your heartstrings, then it will not work effectively for you. Witchcraft resonates deep within my soul. It took me a long time to embrace it, but I am a witch. I have been before, and I will probably be again. I have a broad definition of the word "witch," encompassing the wisdom of the world, but witchcraft is in my heart. The theory, words, and foundation of it resonate with and have guided all my other studies and experiences. If you are afraid of witchcraft, and can't get over that fear, it might never resonate with you and your experience will not be as moving.

The wonderful draw of modern witchcraft to me is the adaptability of it. We are all our own priestesses and priests, and, when in a personal tradition, can adapt the rituals to suit our own tastes as long as we keep the foundation points in mind and our rituals are backed by solid theory and understanding. You can change the words, mythology, and structure to suit the song of your own heart. Not many religions and spiritual paths give you such a freedom. You can't do your own Catholic Mass or do it your way.

I suppose you could, but the Catholic church would not be too pleased with you. Witchcraft, on the other hand, encourages you to find your own voice and spread your own wings. No one can do it for you. So if you resonate with the ideas of witch-craft, but not the particular ritual exactly the way it was shown to you, once you un-derstand the ritual you can change it. The true test will be if it works.

It is my fervent hope that you will not use this manual to follow my rituals by rote. My rituals change as I do. I hope you build a strong foundation of magickal experi-ence and create your own rituals and traditions. That is the true power of the witch.

But before you start writing your own rituals and spells, you should understand those key foundation stones that are at the core of all successful magick. The first cri-terion is a clear intention. You must be very clear in the outcome of your magick. This is the difference between conscious and unconscious creation. Notice now I said "out-come." When we focus on an act of magick, we should always focus on the outcome, not necessarily the way it comes to us. Always "spell" for the final result, not the way you think it should come to us. Part of the partnership with the divine is to acknowl-edge that the universe is ever abundant and how we can conceive a spell as human be-ings is limited. The Goddess and God have numerous and possibly more efficient means of granting our spell. If we envision only one path to us, then we close all other doors. We ask the final result be "correct," "harming none," or "for the highest good," but we don't close any other doors that could bring us our desired result.

For example, so many witches do spells for money, but not the use of the money. Witchcraft is a path of balance, and rarely do we desire money just for money's sake. Prosperity spells are often for the resources to go on vacation, get a new car, buy a home, or fulfill any other need or desire. Instead of focusing on money, focus on the result. Do a spell for the vacation, car, or home of your dreams. You could still get the money for it, or you could win it in a contest, have it willed to you, get it as a bonus from work, or any number of other possibilities beyond our imagination. You never know how a spell will fulfill itself, and it's not always from what seems like the most likely source. That is a spell of clear intent.

When we do magick in a spirit of the highest good, the divine matches need to need, to fulfill the result of the spell. That is how the universe is ever abundant. We think in material terms of supply and demand, and in limited resources, but when we are spiritually aware, our needs can be taken care of by synchronistically getting us the things we need and at the same time, helping another by fulfilling their intents. The universe has no spare parts.

One of the things that really threw me about magick was how much synchronicity plays a part in it. Synchronicity is defined as two events that are unrelated by conventional mechanisms, yet are somehow related when viewed through the right lens, particularly the psychic lens. Synchronicity played a big part in Carl Jung's work in psychology, particularly in regard to divination techniques such as tarot and I-Ching. Spells often result in actions that seem like coincidences. In fact, it is easy to write them off as such, and not as magick.

We have to follow our spells up with real-world action, and be ready to take the opportunities, the open doors, that come to us. If we do a spell for a new job, it is important to be available for interviews and send out résumés. The perfect job could fall on our front step, but if we don't answer the door, we will never get it. It is tempting to say, "I would have gotten that job without the spell anyway, and that magick isn't real." I've had many people say that to me. But I know so many people who have done such a job spell. Before, they may have searched for a job for months with no luck. Then, within a matter of days to weeks after the spell, they land a perfect job. It seems like a coincidence, but in reality, it isn't. It is the unseen hand of the Goddess and God, not only guiding your actions, but also guiding the universe for the door to open to you. But you have to be willing to walk through it. No one will force you to accept the blessings of magick.

As you do more magick, you will be able to see that it isn't the power of coincidence at work. The law of averages starts to break when all these seeming "coincidences" come your way and your life dramatically changes. I stopped believing in luck and coincidence long ago. All things are connected. Everything happens for a reason, and often that reason is the energy we send out through our thoughts, words, and intentions.

The second criterion is strength of will. You must have the desire for the result to be made into reality. If you don't care, the universe won't care. Many people never receive the fruits of their spellwork because they don't want to claim them. In the end, fear wins out over desire. Not only must you desire it, but also as you exercise your personal will, you learn to connect with your divine will, or higher will. That is the essence of magick, true will. When we ask for a spell to be for the highest good, and it fails, we have to reflect on whether we did the spell incorrectly, or it was not for our higher good. If not, why did we want it, if our highest, divine aspect does not want it? Why are we out of partnership with our divine self? That is the true wisdom of magick.

Lastly, even if you have a clear intention and will, you need a method to raise and direct energy to fulfill your intention. Here is where the rituals of witchcraft come in so powerfully. There are many techniques to raise and direct energy, from visualization and prayer to spoken word. They are all rituals in their own way, a repeated action that directs conscious energy with your will and intent. But the combination of forces in witchcraft, the specific combination of techniques and the wide palette of tools to work with, and aspects of nature to partner with, make it by far the hands-down winner for me in regard to consciously creating my life. This manual is a step-by-step plan in the arts of spellcraft and partnership, and all the rituals and techniques needed to successfully do spellwork will be explored.

WHY DO WE DO MAGICK?

Recently a student asked me a question I was hard pressed to answer. She asked, "Why do we do magick? There are other spiritual traditions that don't really do magick, and they are still mystical and personal. Why do witches?" I was stumped. My immediate reaction was, "We just do. That's what witches do. That's what I was taught, and that is what I am teaching." But that is not the answer. I think all witches know it intuitively, but it was the first time I was forced to put it into words.

We do magick to truly know, beyond a shadow of a doubt, that all things are connected, that all things are one. We have the Hermetic principle, "We are all thoughts in the divine mind." But that is only a principle. That's a nice idea, but until we experience it, it doesn't seem real. At least it didn't to me.

Witchcraft is a religion of experience. We don't take anything on faith. We don't need faith, really, because we have a personal experience and relationship with the divine. We experience what we learn directly, and require no prophet or ultimate intermediary. We learn to connect in our own way.

As we start in the craft, we do spells for a sense of personal empowerment. We want to express this connection, to feel empowered, and, honestly, to see if it really works. We do it to make our life easier and to help those around us. Some focus strictly on that stage, either becoming afraid of the power and not practicing, or obsessing over the power and forgetting the spiritual path. But you can't continue to do magick, healing, and meditation without reflecting on how and why it works.

Doing magick consistently and reliably first shows us how powerful our thoughts, words, and actions are, and how they can be our helpers or our own personal traps. We observe the differences between those who live a conscious life and an unconscious life. The web of life becomes ever apparent to us, as we notice how the smallest actions can affect those very far from us. In science, they have coined the term "butterfly effect," speculating if the air generated by a butterfly on one side of the world can contribute to the hurricane developing much later on the other side. All things are connected, and through magick, though our failures as well as our successes, we learn that truth. We learn the power all humans carry in the world, and hopefully develop a great respect for this powerful connection, and for ourselves.

Through magick, unlike other forms of manifestation and prayer, we partner with the divine in nature, through the elements, animal spirits, herbs, stones, colors, Sun, Moon, planets, and stars. We learn everything is alive. Everything has a consciousness. They might be different from us, but everything contains a spirit and is a part of the pattern of creation. We must learn to partner with creation, to truly live in the world and be with it, rather than destroying it.

We learn to be caretakers and helpers in the world. We learn a path of service. Ultimately witches are servants to the divine, and to the community. They are healers, counselors, and mediators. They are religious leaders and guides. Because of this deep awareness of our connections, you cannot help but develop compassion for others, for it is compassion for yourself. You cannot help but to help others, because you are helping yourself and the greater world. When you heal yourself, you contribute to the overall healing of the world. When you help someone else heal, you are contributing to your own healing. Both processes must go hand in hand.

Ultimately through magick, we learn by our experience that we are not only all connected, but we are all one. One spirit with many different expressions, as nature is one. We are a part of nature. We are a part of the divine. Both are simultaneous and not exclusive. But without the experience, it is only philosophy. We do magick to know we are all one. This is the spiritual truth of magick.

The Ethical Witch

I am always staggered by the number of people who think witches can do anything they want. Those outside the craft really have no idea of the strong ethical philosophy that is involved in magick. And unfortunately, in some cases, many who are involved in the craft don't understand the ethical philosophy involved and the historic function of the witch as wise one. They perpetuate the "anything goes," power-tripping stereotype.

Wiccans and Witches and Pagans

The calling to be a witch has historically been one of great responsibility. Witches in the truest sense of the word are those who use their sacred knowledge and connection in service to others, the tribe, the world, and the highest good. That's no easy task. The craft starts as a personal exploration and calling, but even when you heal and help yourself to a better life through magick, you are helping contribute to the overall health and happiness of the entire world. If we are all connected, all our thoughts, feelings, and actions contribute to the overall world health.

A witch has many definitions. A witch is a walker between worlds, serving to connect the spirit world and the material world, acting as a bridge, mystic, and visionary.

The practice of witchcraft is one of the priestess and priest. Many people practice the heart of witchcraft without using the name Wiccan. "Wicca," with a capital *W*, rather than the root word "wicca," refers to the modern revival of the religion of witchcraft. Technically, it is a fairly new religion in its current form, but its practice stretches back through the ages. Some consider the word to apply only to those initiated in a formal tradition of Wicca, such as Gardnerian or Alexandrian witchcraft, but many informal practitioners refer to themselves as Wiccans. Some prefer it because it is a less scary word than "witch." Others opt for different words all together, like "mage," "sorcerer," or "seer," and avoid any "w" words.

The word "pagan," or technically "neopagan" in the modern context (being new pagans), refers to those practicing a revival of the ancient Earth-based religions, but do not necessarily identify with the word "witch." Most who are involved in the revival of the ancient ways, particularly those traditions and myths of pre-Christian Europe, Egypt, and the Middle East, can be considered pagans. All witches and Wiccans are pagans, but not all pagans consider themselves witches or Wiccans. Many witches and Wiccans think of themselves as the ministers, the priests and priestesses of the overall pagan community, feeling they have more of a mystical inclination than others who follow the Earth paths, but most pagans I know don't feel the same way about it. They see themselves as just as mystical. I've used all three words to describe myself in various times and situations.

In the end, they are all names and labels, and you have to find the ones that serve you the best on this Earthwalk. Some words will help you with self-identity, while others don't. For me, and many others, it was just important to confess to myself that yes, I am a witch. That's me. That's what I am about. It's a label, but it is as much a part of my identity as male, gay, white, or musician. It is an integral part of me, and the admission of it in a less-than-supportive society was life changing. I am a witch.

For some, witchcraft becomes a vocation of healing, teaching, and counseling others, even if only "part-time." Witches on the spiritual path become role models whether they realize it or not. People first came to me to study witchcraft not because of any great interest in Wicca, but because I seemed to change my life for the better and they wanted to know my "secret." They wanted to know how to change and become happier, self-confident, and more fulfilled. Many expected quite literally a "magick pill" or potion, a quick fix. But a few realized it was a lifelong practice—a change of lifestyle and a change of how to be in the world. It takes a dedication and a discipline like any other path. And that is when I started sharing what simple knowledge I had gathered from my teachers, and, ever so informally, began teaching.

ONLY TWO RULES

Witchcraft at its heart is simple. Though there are complex philosophies, rituals, spells, and systems associated with it, they are all the trappings of the craft. The actual practice is infinitely simple to understand, but can be extremely hard to follow. We live in a society that regulates and regiments what we can do and can't do. It is defined by laws written into books and we find freedom or prison in the exact way the language is written. Lawyers find loopholes to move around such laws, and technicalities give us exceptions to the law all the time.

The universe has no exceptions. Universal law is not written in a book to be erased and revoked at a later date. It is immutable, although its execution can appear mysterious. Just because someone wrote "What goes up, must come down" to define gravity, doesn't mean that gravity didn't exist before that was written. Spiritual, universal mechanics function the same way. The codes of witchcraft are not necessarily moral codes, but are commonsense understanding of how to live in balance with the universe for the mutual health and benefit of everyone.

The first "law" of witchcraft is the Law of Three. Everything comes back to you threefold. Every thought, intention, emotion, and, most particularly, every action returns to you stronger than when it first came from you. This is how spells work. You put out an intent full of energy, and it returns to you stronger, more manifested. It leaves you as an idea, and returns as a reality. I imagine the energy bouncing back from an imaginary wall at the end of the universe, recoiling stronger than when I threw it, gaining momentum to reach me.

Well, this law works all the time, intentionally when doing magick, and when doing anything. People think of it as the Law of Karma, but the concept of karma is a bit more complex than this, particularly when involved with the concepts of reincarnation. Think of the Law of Three, sometimes called the Law of Return, as a principle in physics. It simply is. There is no moral standard to it, but it can feel that way. When we put out joy, we often receive joy back. When we put out pain, we often receive pain back. But the return time can be different under different circumstances. Many report it is instantaneous. Others wait quite a while, and even feel it catches up with us in future lifetimes.

The second "rule" in witchcraft is not so universal in nature, but is really a suggestion as to how to deal with this universal rule. It's known among witches as the Wiccan Rede, or simply the Rede. A rede is a credo, or suggestion, not an ironclad rule, but most witches realize sooner or later, through their own actions or from those around them, why it is such a good idea to follow this rede. The Wiccan Rede in its most basic form is "Do what thou will, and let it harm none." Another popular version is "An' it harm none, do what ye will."

Seems real easy, doesn't it? The execution can be more difficult than you think. Unlike moral codes such as the Ten Commandments, you have no real guide as to what is acceptable behavior and what isn't. Each situation, like each moment in time, is unique and individual. Each individual must weigh the actions and results. When you do "no harm," that means to yourself, too. Wicca is not the religion of self-sacrifice or martyrdom. You are free to live your life, but do not cause harm to others or yourself, because you will return that harm. Ultimately the decision and responsibility lies with you. It always does, even in more regulated societies and traditions, but in witchcraft the tradition actually says "No, we can't decide for you. You must live your life and live by the consequences of your actions." There is no perfect score. You live your life and learn from your mistakes, and realize that many of those mistakes are great teachers and blessings, even if they don't necessarily feel good at the time. They reveal us to ourselves, so that we can grow and transform.

So contrary to popular belief, witches do not do curses or cast evil hexes on unsuspecting people. I'm sure some people do this with their knowledge, but they have a different definition of the word "witch" than most witches I know, and unfortunately they harm the reputation of us all. There are no true satanic witches. The Devil, as the Prince of Evil, is a Christian concept and plays no part in witchcraft. Neither do Satanic spells, Black Masses, or ritual sacrifice. "Witches" involved in these titles or practices are not witches in the same sense of the word. Some are educated and openly state they are different from the neopagan movement following their own path, while others are simply confused and mix elements of Wicca with Hollywood horror movie stereotypes. Just as there are those who call themselves Christians who do not love others as their neighbors, who harm, maim, and kill, there are those who use the word "witch" but do not live up to the true spirit of the tradition as wise one, healer, and visionary. They do not live by the Wiccan Rede anymore than the supposed Christians live by the Christian rules "Love your neighbor as yourself" and "Do unto others as you would have done onto you." In essence, they are not so different than witchcraft.

The highest aspect of the Rede deals with not only our will, desires, needs, and wants, but also our higher will. Often the word "will" is capitalized in the various forms of the Rede, to denote true magick, and life is about merging your personal will and need with the higher need. When you have these two forces aligned, all your magickal working will take a quantum leap forward. Each act of magick is an opportunity to practice this merger one spell at a time. When you really merge the two on deeper and deeper levels in all parts of your life, you are walking the spirit road of the witch.

Below is an extended version of the simple Rede. This is but one version of many possibilities passed among witches.

Extended Wiccan Rede
Bide the Wiccan laws we must
In perfect love and perfect trust
Live and let live,
Fairly take and fairly give.
Cast the circle thrice about
To keep all evil spirits out.
To bind the spell every time,
Let the spell be spake in rhyme.
Soft of eye and light of touch,
Speak little, listen much.
Deosil go by the waxing Moon,
Singing out the witches' rune.
Widdershins go by the waning Moon,
Chanting out the baneful rune.
When the Lady's Moon is new,
Kiss thy hand to her, times two.
When the Moon rides at her peak,
Then your heart's desire seek.

Heed the north wind's might gale,
Lock the door and trim the sail.
When the wind comes from the south,
Love will kiss thee on the mouth.
When the wind blows from the east,
Expect the new and set the feast.
When the wind bows from the west,
Departed souls will have no rest.
When the west wind blows o'er thee
Departed spirits restless be.
Nine woods into the cauldron go,
Burn them fast and burn them slow.
Elder be your Lady's tree,
Burn it not or cursed ye'll be.
When the Wheel begins to turn,
Let the Beltane fires burn.
When the Wheel has turned to Yule,
Light the log, the Horned One rules.
Heed ye flower, bush, and tree,
By the Lady, blessed be.
Where the rippling waters flow,
Cast a stone and truth ye'll know.
When ye have and hold a need,
Hearken no to other's greed.
With a fool no season spend,
Nor be counted as his friend.
Merry meet, merry part,
Bright the cheeks and warm the heart.
Mind the Threefold Law ye should,
Three times bad and three times good.
When misfortune is anow,
Wear the blue star on the brow.
True in love ever be,

Unless thy lover's false to thee.
Eight words to the Wiccan Rede fulfill
An' it harm none, do what ye will.

Figure 1: *Extended Wiccan Rede*

Personal Honor

Since the craft is sparse in determining a universal code of behavior, it puts the burden of creating a personal code of ethics on the practitioner. This is simply for you and no others. What is right for you might not be right for anyone else, and through witchcraft we realize this. Every witch, consciously or not, starts to develop a personal code of ethics and honor, for both magick and everyday life. We create our own boundaries and definitions, and must learn to explore them and redefine them as needed. They are not set in stone, but based on our beliefs, thoughts, feelings, and experiences.

Some of the common boundaries revolve around spellwork. A common boundary, which I highly recommend, is not doing spellwork for others without their permission. If you can get the person's conscious permission for the spell, that is the best situation for the working. They should be actively engaged in the process and following up the spell with real-world action. You can word your request however you like. Some witches simply ask to "pray in my own way" for the person and receive permission. When you can't physically reach the person to ask permission, some witches ask permission of the recipient's higher self, going into deep meditation, asking to connect with the divine essence of the recipient, and then getting a feel of a yes or no. Some use methods of divination such as the pendulum or muscle testing. (See ITOW, chapters 13 and 15, for more information on these techniques.) In any case, the work is done for the highest good of the recipient. It is considered at the very least in extremely bad form to do magick for someone who has not given permission, would be averse to someone using witchcraft, or has out-and-out declined.

Witchcraft is the magick of love, and love must be freely offered. If it is forced without regard to someone's free choice, it is no longer love. Then it becomes what many in Hollywood witchcraft refer to as black magick. I don't use that term. If it is harmful, unloving magick, I simply call it harmful or unhealthy magick. I don't use a color to denote it. White magick is not necessarily good magick. I know many people who claim to do white magick, and to pray for others, for results against their wishes. These white witches feel they know what is best, regardless of free choice. And I know many dark, gothic witches, worshiping the gods and goddesses of the Underworld, who are very loving and healing and would never strive to do any harm, magickal or otherwise.

One of my personal boundaries goes even further than getting permission. With the exception of healing work, I almost never do a spell for someone else. It's not that I'm selfish, or uncaring. I won't do it for someone, because for me that is disempowering. The most transformative aspect of the craft for me was the empowerment, of taking responsibility for my own action and creating my own life. I don't want people to transfer their authority from one institution or religion onto me.

I will do a spell with others. I will teach them how to do it and guide them the whole way. I will give them the tools and guidance to do it on their own if they prefer, but I don't simply fix things for others. I say almost because each situation is unique and there have been exceptions, but as a rule, I find the conscious engagement of the person to be most vital to the process.

When you are a public witch, you field strange requests from family, friends, and strangers to do magick for them. But many don't even want to take the time to be present when you do the spell. How can they really want it, if they don't want to put any time into it? I ask people to be involved to weed out those looking for the quick fix from the local witch to get exactly what they want, rather than a reflective process to understand and change. If I did every spell request I was given without engaging the recipient to be involved, I would be doing spells for others all the time, with no time for my own personal work and journey. "Do no harm" means you must help yourself to happiness as well as helping others.

New witches often get trapped into this pattern. They desire to serve and help others, but don't draw a boundary as to when it is appropriate to use a spell and when it is not. If the person can't be bothered to be involved, to light a candle, to read a spell, to simply be present and focus on the intent, then I can't be bothered either. Sounds unfair to some, but the gods help those who help themselves. Those who act create change. Those who wait, wait for a long time.

This is how I got involved in teaching in the first place. People came to me to learn to do spells or have psychic readings. I did that for a while, and still do, but then I got more interested in helping others get their own answers in meditation and do their own spellwork. That is the true empowerment. I am no more special than anyone else. If you truly desire to walk the path, put the time and effort into understanding and practicing the craft, as then your magick and meditations will lead you to the happiness, healing, and spirituality you crave.

As time goes on, you will find yourself creating a personal code of honor, an internal practice of spiritual truths that you will not deviate from without deep reflection and inner guidance. Some write it out and reflect on it over time. Others carry it with them, with no need to put it into words. Again, there are no easy answers. The final decision, and consequence of all your decisions, is up to you. It has been, it is, and it always shall be this way.

MOTIVATION

After reading up on the ethics of the craft, would-be witches often get discouraged. "You mean it's not easy? You mean I can't turn my ex into a toad? You mean I can't curse someone who crossed me?" Yes, that's exactly what I mean. I don't teach that style of witchcraft. It is a path of wisdom, not curses. If that is why you decided to become a witch, then think long and hard because what you do will return to you.

Thinking about your motivation to study witchcraft, magick, and spellwork is an important exercise. Why do you want to do this? What is the reason and motivation behind it? I'm not discouraging you or encouraging you by your motivations. My motivations certainly changed as I changed. I wanted to do spells. I found a wonderful power in spellwork. I couldn't believe spells worked, but they did, and I wanted to experience more of magick, to study it and know why. I didn't have any grand spiritual aspirations. I thought I was studying witchcraft as a science, not a religion. But the two intertwined. I would do anything to do spellcraft on a deeper level. When my teachers said you have to learn meditation, psychic awareness, and healing before going on to spells, I did just that. And the process of both developing those skills and actually doing deeper spellwork opened me up to the spiritual path.

It's easy for me to dismiss others starting on the path as not interested in the spirituality. Some seem scary because they are fascinated with spells, and spell books are so readily available. I might have seemed that way when I started out, too, so I never judge or dismiss someone by his or her motives unless the beginner purposely wants to do harm with it. You can never know how a teaching will affect and change someone. This manual is not just another spell book, but a guide to a deeper unfolding, wherever it may take you on your personal path.

For me, it's been highly beneficial to remember my first motivations for entering the craft, so I understand better when people enter it. I can remember my excitement and nervousness about it. This following exercise is important because it will not only serve you right now, but far into the future.

EXERCISE 4

Motivation

Think about what first drew you to the witchcraft, including spells and magick. What was your focus? Were you drawn to spells? Some are not, and are actually afraid of spellwork, or even revolted by it, but are still drawn to witchcraft as a path. What are your thoughts and feelings on the matter? Contemplate your motives for this choice on the path.

Write a short paragraph or two describing your motives, in whatever level of detail you would like, in your Book of Shadows or journal. Put it someplace you will keep it and see it years from now.

Do not go on to Lesson One before completing this exercise.

THE ROLE OF A
PRIESTESS AND PRIEST

The second degree of witchcraft usually bestows the title of priestess or priest upon the initiate. At this time, the initiate moves beyond the basic understanding of the craft and moves into the rituals to create sacred space. Truly all witches, in every tradition, are considered priests and priestesses if they do rituals to experience the love of the Goddess and God. We are all our own clergy. As mystics on a personal path of enlightenment, no one can do it for you. No one can really be your intermediary with spirit. Teachers, elders, and High Priestesses and High Priests can guide you and help you, but they only truly help you if they teach you the skills to help yourself. In the end, no one can experience this for you.

Most traditions of witchcraft have three levels. A new student starts as an initiate, and after a year and a day of training and reflection progresses to the first initiation and becomes a witch. Such witches take part in rituals, learning the craft of the witch through spell and ceremony. The second degree is for one who learns to create sacred space, cast a magick circle, and lead a ritual, privately or in group. These witches take a more active role in their coven or community. At the third degree, a group confers the honor of High Priestess or High Priest, and that witch either takes a more active role in teaching and leading the group, or will leave the group to start their own coven. When someone has had four or more covens "hive off" after initiating four High Priest/esses, that witch is often called a Witch Queen or Witch King in some traditions. Most modern witches I know shy away from these titles.

One does not have to be in a formal coven to study the ranks. Many solitary and eclectic witches consider themselves priestesses and priests, and rightly so. I think anyone who has studied the craft to hold ritual and build a relationship with the divine through nature is a priestess or priest.

In my own system of teaching, the course material is based on five levels of study, each based on one of the five elements. The second degree is still the path of the priestess and priest. *The Outer Temple of Witchcraft* is the course material of this level, based on the element of earth. Through our experiences in the world, through nature, through magick, and through our rituals, we can connect with the divine, as priestesses and priests, at this level of study.

What Does It Mean to Be a Priestess or Priest?

Being a priestess or priest is an individual practice, just as witchcraft is. But the core concept is to become your own clergy. No one is your intermediary. You have all the knowledge, tools, and experience to hold your own ceremonies, to make your own prayers, to do your own magick. In fact, others may come to you to help them make a connection to the spiritual worldview.

Being your own clergy comes with a measure of responsibility. When you take on such a role, it's hard to go back to a worldview where others must do things for you. Becoming clergy, even in traditional covens, means you become your own leader, rather than a follower. You are not just a member of the congregation. In witchcraft, the congregation is clergy. We gather in a circle because all voices are heard. All views have weight and importance. In the circle we honor those with knowledge and experience, but all of us are practitioners on the path. All of us can hold ritual. There is not just one leader and all the rest are followers. Some run their groups in such a way, but when truly exploring the mysteries of witchcraft, this is not so. We all stand side by side in the magick circle.

A part of this responsibility comes from our magickal awakening to the unseen, and our relationship with nature. Once you understand the majesty of nature, it's hard to go back to the old way of doing things, the old way of thinking and being. Suddenly everything comes alive. Everything and everyone is luminescent and filled with the love of the Goddess and God. Even those things and people we don't like, we learn to love by seeing the Goddess and God in each and every one. With this awakening comes a sense of caretaking, or stewardship. Witches seek to partner with the world and preserve it.

Much of the craft of the witch, ancient and modern, is in taking care of others. Witches were the first doctors, nurses, and midwives, all rolled into one. They were the first ministers and counselors. They were the first religious leaders. But they also guided hunting and agriculture. Later, as the ancient priests and priestesses, they guided the construction of temples and cities. Those in the craft of the wise have guided their people, their tribe and civilization, with their knowledge and insight of the energetic worlds. Is it any surprise that as our Western culture wiped out the witches, pagans, and other indigenous cultures, the world is left is a state of spiritual and ecological turmoil at the beginning of the twenty-first century? Witches realized the symbiosis of the world around them with humanity.

Modern witches have reclaimed this sense of stewardship for the Earth. We do not own the world. We are caretakers, and we have not been doing a good job. Pagans and witches in the new century seek to change that. We no longer have such an individual sense of tribe and people. We live in the modern world, with the tribe of the world, the global village, as some call it. We are all connected. Our mythology, history, music, literature, science, and philosophy are all intermingling. Spiritual seekers need to see the wisdom in all cultures, and apply that to the world.

Activism abounds in modern paganism. Some of us are involved in political and social movements of environmentalism, animal rights, and basic human rights. Others work on a one-on-one basis, hoping to change the thoughts and beliefs of things one person at a time, using ritual, herbalism, and meditation to shift other people's worldview when they are ready. Many do one of the most important jobs, simply living a spiritual, balanced life, and modeling that way of life for others to see in a quiet, non-threatening way. Both energetically and personally they are changing the world.

Through this course, find how you connect with nature, and apply this spiritual wisdom to your daily life. Learn to live a magickal life, seeing the luminescent in everything around you, in each moment. Study nature, magickally, philosophically, and scientifically. As we study the patterns, seasons, and cycles of the Earth, we see them reflected within our own souls, hearts, minds and bodies. The Hermetic Principle of Correspondence says "As above, so below." It also means that what you find in the outside world, you find in the inside world, too. (For more on Hermetic principles, look to ITOW, chapter 8.)

One of the prime ways witches at this level of education study the cycles internally and externally is through the celebration of the Wheel of the Year and the path of the Moon. The priestesses and priests officiate the rituals, solitary or in group, to celebrate the mysteries. Through celebrating these rituals, one has a greater understanding of the patterns of creation. Celebration brings in the joy and love of magick, and only through this greater understanding of creation can we truly be partners and caretakers of the Earth while living here, with her, in body.

Being a priestess or priest doesn't make you better than anybody else in paganism or in other religions. We each have our own path to walk, and each claim the roles and responsibilities that are best for us. I know many people who uphold the highest ideals of a priestess, but are not even pagan. But they are on the mystical path and see the divine in everything, holding their own communion with the Earth, and creating their own magick, even if they would not call it magick.

Ultimately, priestesses and priests are servants to the greater good, to the cycles of nature, to the community, and to the divine. All our acts, be they personal or altruistic, help the overall world if done in perfect love and perfect trust. Even opening yourself to the idea of magick changes the world for the better. I'm sure many of you might not even believe in magick yet, if you have not experienced it. That's fine. I didn't. But keeping an open mind and exploring stimulates the consciousness of the world, and allows others to feel comfortable keeping an open mind and exploring the unknown world. Only then do we experience the connection of all things. That is a service to the divine. You might already be a priestess or priest, and not even know it!

YEAR-AND-A-DAY RITUAL

Customarily, each level of training for a witch is a year and a day, coming from the Celtic myths where quests would be undertaken for a year and a day. This course is laid out in the same manner. Twelve lessons are contained within, where each one can be done in the span of a month. Some lessons are longer than others, so look ahead and see how much work you are allotting yourself in each monthly span. The end of the course results in a self-initiation ceremony, for you to claim the role of priestess or priest, and to live it in your day-to-day life.

If you complete the lessons early, you can reflect on each, putting it into practice before moving on to the next. Or, you can move from lesson to lesson and have time to reflect at the end of the cycle. If you find your own personal pace takes longer than a year, it is far better to take your time with it and truly master and embody the lessons than to rush and walk away with little understanding. Part of studying the cycles is learning our own cycles and habits.

For myself, I'm a goal-oriented person and will commit to something if I write it down on my calendar, so I write down my personal deadlines, realistically so, and have them in front of me. This is a constant reminder to walk my talk. If you have a friend to study with, the two of you can keep each other on track. Although solitary work is very rewarding, there is something magickal about sharing the path with another, and being able to discuss, practice, laugh, and learn together. My first experiments, my first coven, was my mother and our good friend Laura. We all had equal experience and were exploring together, but had each other as a support group and safety net. Having a partner for this course is not mandatory though. It can be done equally as well alone.

Whenever undertaking a new venture or training, I think it is very important to prepare your energy and intention. I do this through ritual. So your first step on this path is to create a dedication ritual, to declare your intentions to complete this study, and dedicate yourself to this aspect of the craft for a year and a day. If you studied the ITOW, then this type of ritual will be familiar to you.

EXERCISE 5

Intention Ritual

1. Since at this level you will be working with the four elements, have four simple symbols of the elements of earth, fire, air, and water. You can use a stone, candle, incense, and a chalice, cup, or bowl, respectively. Have a white candle for spirit in the center. Place them on your workspace. Don't worry about directions and orientations on your space. Put them wherever it feels right. If you have a meditation altar, use it. If not, clear a space in a spot that is quiet to do this work, where others will not disturb you. You will also need paper and black thread.

2. On a small piece of paper, write out your intentions for this level of study. Here is an example:

   "I, *(state your name)*, ask in the name of the Goddess and God for aid in my studies of this level of witchcraft. I intend to become a priest/ess of witchcraft. I intend to complete this work successfully within one year if this is correct and for my highest good. I ask to be open to all experiences and understand all lessons given to me. So mote it be."

3. Light your fire candle and the incense. Leave the spirit candle unlit.

4. Do Exercise 3 and envision yourself in a safe, sacred space.

5. Say this or something similar, "I ask for the love and guidance of the four elements, earth, fire, air, and water, and the love and guidance of the Goddess and God. Hail and welcome." Feel the presence of the divine. Know it, even you don't feel anything different. The universe will always reach out to help those who sincerely call to it.

6. Hold the white spirit candle. Think about your spirituality and the path of the witch. Invite the Goddess and God to be fully present in your life, however you envision the divine. Light the candle.

7. Spend a few moments reflecting on the meaning of the priestess and priest. Reflect on the path you are taking. Even if you think you don't want to be a priestess or priest for the community, you are one for yourself, and through this ritual, you acknowledge and seek to deepen that role.

8. Read your intention slip out loud. Then roll it up like a scroll and tie it with the black thread, binding it together and sealing your intention. Keep the paper safe for use in the initiation ritual at the end of the year's time.

Record the experience in your Book of Shadows. A Book of Shadows originally was a book of spells and rituals passed on from High Priest/ess to new witch, hand copied very carefully. Today, a BOS (as it is abbreviated) is a combination of spell/ritual book, journal, experiment log, and dream journal. I used to separate all these sections in a binder for my Book of Shadows. I had separate books for a while. Then I did my BOS on the computer, though some traditionalists would be aghast at having sacred information on a computer. They have all blended together now, so find a method and medium of recording your experiences, meditations, dreams, and rituals that works best for you.

Homework

- Reflect on what it means to be a priestess or priest of witchcraft.

- Complete Exercises 1–4 if you haven't already done so. Record your experiences in your journal/Book of Shadows.

- Complete Exercise 5, recording your impression and experience. Prepare your course of study schedule for the next year and a day.

- Keep a regular journal, as either a part of your BOS or separately. Record your magickal experiences, dreams, and day-to-day life. See how your magick becomes a part of your daily life.

LESSON ONE
WHO ARE THE GODS?

Who are the gods? Who are the goddesses? And more importantly, what are they? For those of us living in the modern world, usually raised in the background of the modern Judeo-Christian traditions, these questions aren't easy. In the resurrection of ancient beliefs, the concepts of the goddesses and gods are not as clear-cut and ever present as they were in the ancient pagan world. We must remember that ancient pagans of all lands were culturally raised not only with the concept of their own gods and goddesses, but with the general concept of plural divinity. Their stories, myths, and culture reflected this way of thinking. I don't know about you, but I was not raised with such concepts.

Now, the concept of the gods and goddess has become a powerful aspect of my own spirituality, but when I started, I just didn't get it. I remember my friend Laura asking our teacher, "But really, what are the gods?" She never got a satisfactory answer. The teacher was frustrated because ultimately the gods are a mystery to be explored by each individual, and no written or oral description can do the experience justice. I can empathize with my teacher, but it didn't help me at the time. I began my search of witchcraft as a scientific pursuit. Do a particular ritual and you get a result. Explore a meditation or psychic ability, and grow in your aptitude. I didn't understand how the gods fit into it all. I thought the concept an archaic throwback, and if I was washing my hands of such concepts as Father, Son, and Holy Ghost, why would I go back to Artemis, Cernunnos, and Freya? I wanted to see the divine as this amorphous divine mind, the creative spirit beyond shape and form. People call it God, Goddess, Tao, or anything else, but it was beyond all those words. And I was half right.

In paganism, in fact any religion that honors the forces of nature, all things are alive. All things have spirit and presence, even a form of consciousness to them. Through partnering with these forces we create magick. As the vast universe has this vast guide and creative presence guiding it, what I call the Great Spirit or divine mind, every aspect of creation has an aspect of that vast creative spirit guiding it. In the ITOW, we learned about the divine mind through the Hermetic principles. But we also learned about the Laws of Polarity and Gender. One could say the primary form of creation is manifested through two primal forces. To witches, these two forces are the Great Goddess, mother of all, and the Great God, the father of creation. Through their love, all the other aspects of creation are manifested and guided. Ancient peoples personified all these guiding forces of creation as gods and goddesses. They guided natural phenomenon, such as the Moon, Sun, Earth, sky, mountains, storms, oceans, rivers, animals, and forests as well as concepts of life, such as love, war, wisdom, death, creativity, magick, and healing.

Some Native American tribes have a great story to describe this. The whole world is a dream. The Great Dreamer dreamed the world into existence, but wanted to share the joy of creation. So the Great Dreamer created many other dreamers, who dreamed up the rest of creation. There was a dreamer of rocks, a dreamer of birds, a dreamer of clouds, a dreamer of corn, a dreamer of the Moon, and so on. Together, the Great Dreamer and the little dreamers keep the world turning and ever changing through their new dreams.

These aspects of creation are almost universal. You will find the same concepts from a variety of cultures. In psychology, these repeated themes and images are called archetypes, but to me, that word resigns something very magickal into a mundane psychological expression. If we are going to use that well-known word, I prefer the term "archetypal being." It conveys the meaning of the word, but brings it alive. These archetypal beings are not merely images, but living beings of vast power and creative force. Just because they are not physical, or strictly physical, doesn't mean they are not alive on other levels of consciousness.

You find them as the Earth Mother, Sky Father, God of the Dead, God of War, Goddess of Love, Goddess of Wisdom, and the gods of magick. Each is a manifestation of the great Goddess and God. Their similarities abound in cultures that have had contact with each other, such as the Egyptian, Greek, and Roman, but similarities can be found across the world, in Central and South America, or in the East. There is something far larger and universal involved with archetypal beings. They reveal themselves to each culture. Even in our culture that does not typically recognize them, these beings come out in our movies, music, pop culture, and literature if we simply look for their new faces.

Now as each of these beings reveals itself, each culture interprets the archetypal being differently. Although there are many similarities, each culture has a different language, personal symbol system, mythology, values, customs, and economy. Those factors influence the culture's interpretation of the archetype. This wisdom is first revealed to the mystics, the shamans, seers, priestesses, priests, and witches, who then transform their visionary experiences in the other worlds into the myths and stories of the culture. They are passed on through an oral tradition, changing and adapting as they are retold, to reflect the changing culture. So many cultures have a vision of a Mother or Earth Goddess, but they each have a different name for her, a different image and different rituals to connect with her. They are all talking to the spirit of the Earth, the one planet, but they each give her a different voice, a different form. These different interpretations of the archetypal powers are called godforms. The godforms are the various names of deities we learn in mythology.

Artemis, Diana, Isis, and Arianrhod are all godforms of the Moon Goddess. Hermes, Mercury, Odin, Thoth, Nabu, and Oghma are all godforms of the Magician/Messenger God. Hecate, Ereshkigal, Morgan, Cerridwen, and Kali are all godforms of the Underworld/Crone/Destroyer Goddess. Osiris, Tammuz, Dionysus, and even Jesus Christ can be viewed as godforms of the Sacrificed/Resurrected God. And as each culture has a variety of godforms to interpret the archetypal energies, one godform can embody more than one archetype. Isis, for example, is a multifaceted goddess, as the goddess of the Moon, magick, life, the fertile land of the Nile, and justice. She embodies many creative forces simultaneously.

THE DIAMOND OF DIVINITY

Technically this belief of many deities is called polytheism, as opposed to monotheism, the belief in one god. Ancient pagan beliefs, and their revivals, are typically classified as polytheistic. Those raised in the mainstream Western world were most likely raised in a monotheistic culture, even if you were not raised in a religious manner. The concepts of monotheism are all pervading in this culture. People exclaim "Oh my God!" not "Oh my gods!" Our money often says "In God We Trust." When people talk about God, everyone has a general agreement of the idea, but if you talk about gods, people look at you funny.

Judaism, Christianity, and Islam are the big three monotheistic religions. But even they have a variety of interpretations of monotheism. They all believe in the one God of the good books, but Christians have a trinity: Father, Son, and Holy Ghost. Early Christians may have called the Holy Spirit aspect the Holy Sophia, possibly recognizing the feminine at some point. Catholics recognize the feminine through Mary, and recognizes the saints as intermediaries. In old translations of the book of Genesis, recognized by all three faiths, the word we normally view as "God" is actually "Elohim," a plural word more accurately translated by some scholars as "creative gods." So even the monotheistic religions have some polytheistic elements, whether the average practitioner knows it or not.

As modern people, we do not live in a world exclusively monotheistic or polytheistic. Both concepts are possible, though many people feel they must choose between the two. As a witch, defined as a walker between the worlds, I fall between the two. People have told me I have a very Hindu approach to divinity. I actually intuitively feel that there is a great ancient connection between the traditions of the Indus Valley. Some cultures migrated into Europe, such as the Celtic tribes, while others became what we now consider the Hindu culture. If you compare the art, myth, and some philosophies, there are striking similarities, along with major differences. I know modern pagans who call upon Hindu gods, and American Hindus who find kinship in paganism. The two are not that different, but I've been accused by more militant pagans of not really understanding paganism or polytheism as the ancients did. I don't live in an either/or world, but can hold both views simultaneously, and I think perhaps some of the ancient pagans did as well. It is only through our modern, mostly monotheistic lens that we create the absolute division between polytheism and monotheism, when in reality, each camp is simply emphasizing a different point. I hold both concepts simultaneously through the image of a diamond.

To me, divinity is like a beautiful, multifaceted, multilayered diamond reflecting the light of creation. The search for spirituality is the search for the diamond. There are many different ways of looking at the diamond, since it is so vast and complex. The light can be so bright it is hard to know. Details are hard to grasp. The entire thing seems overwhelming, so we create views to take in this vast and unknowable light.

Some seekers are attracted to a few facets of the crystal. Each facet is like a different goddess or god. Each one is brilliant in its own right, reflecting the light of creation in its own way. Certain seekers focus on one particular facet that catches their attention, and bring all their energy to that particular deity. Other are fascinated by a patch of facets, representing a group of gods, perhaps the gods of a particular culture, called a pantheon.

Other seekers are overwhelmed by the details, and only focus on the great bright light of the diamond, seeing only one light, and only one divinity. If anyone tries to point out the many aspects of divinity, they cannot see it because there is only the one light.

The wise ones see the diamond is both one solid shape in its entirety, whole and complete, yet with many facets that lead to the center light. The wise one can switch between each paradigm because both are true, yet neither fully encompasses the mystery of the divine. The diamond is just a symbol. And the important thing to remember is that this diamond is multilayered, and we are facets in the whole diamond, too, we simply don't recognize that fact often enough. The closer you go to the center of the diamond, the bigger the "facets" get, leading to the archetypal beings, the great Goddess and God, and finally the vast Great Spirit or divine mind, that is the center, the light, and the entire diamond simultaneously.

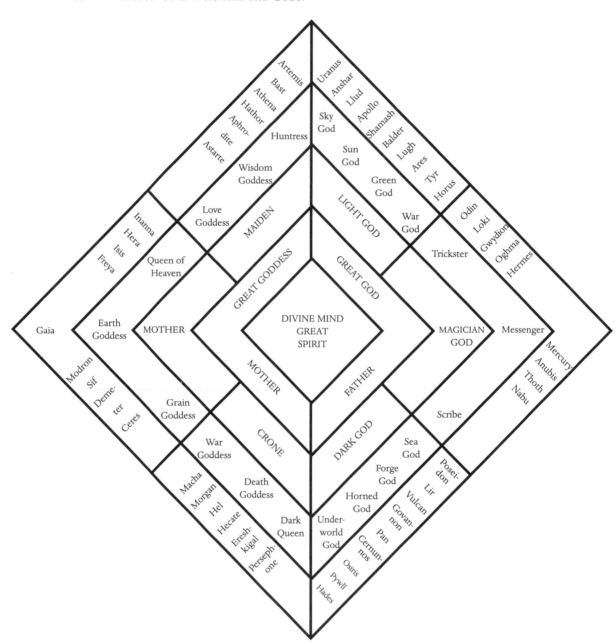

Figure 2: *Diamond of Divinity*

Another image is that the various deities are shadows all cast from the same flame. They all come from the same source. The dreamer story is another symbol of this truth. If the world is the Great Dreamer and the little dreamers, we are dreamers of a sort, too, with the power of creation. When myths say we are made in the gods, or God's image, it's not physical or gender, it is the power of creation we share. We are partners with the divine to create the universe. We share in it. That is true magick.

Lately I've been attracted to the word "monism" rather than "polytheism." Monism can be defined as a worldview where there is one whole. Monism sounds like the divine mind. Sounds like the image of the hologram, used in science and spirituality, where every part contains the whole pattern (ITOW, chapter 7). In the monist view, there can be the appearance of individual parts, but in essence, everything is part of the greater whole. We are all thoughts in the divine mind. We are all connected by the web of life, by the one spirit running through all things. I am you and you are me, but for practical purposes, I perceive myself as different than you for this Earthwalk. I pay my bills. You don't. I make my own choices, you don't. Spirituality is learning to see these connections, and to live and act by them, yet walk your own path.

WHY SHOULD I KNOW THE GODS?

These are all interesting theories, images, and ideas, but so what? What is their purpose? I had been involved in witchcraft for so long, I started to lose touch with newness of these ideas. While teaching this course, my very sharp and wise student Sheryl said something like, "I understand what you are saying, but why do we look to the gods and goddesses now? What is the purpose?" And I was stunned because it is such a big part of my life, but it was such a beautiful question. I had the same one, but never put it so bluntly when I started.

The variety of archetypal beings and godforms help us personally connect with the divine. They are each individual in their energy, and some will resonate with us more than others, becoming gateways to the center of the diamond, to the heart of magick. People will often ask why not go to the source, the Great Spirit, but like the light of the diamond, it can seem so vast, so distant and so remote, creating problems when wanting to cultivate a personal relationship with the divine.

Ever notice that many monotheistic religions have a very distant, authoritarian figure as the center, remote and sometimes punishing? Any personal relationships are done through another figure, such as a savior, saint, prophet, or angelic image. People rarely report visions of Yahweh, but many people are touched by Christ, Mary, or an angel. Those that don't focus on these emissaries often feel untouched by God, wondering why things happen, speaking to God but waiting for an answer, wondering if he is listening. That is why so many people are not interested in spirituality, because they feel unconnected in any personal way, and this has resulted in the breakdown of some very basic truths for most people.

There are those monotheists that can connect directly to the Creative Spirit, or an aspect of it, without focusing on a facet. They just choose to let in a little of the light, as much as they can handle. Others find more connection through the emissaries. These divine beings, like the gods, act as portals to the vast creative energy to the center. Grant Morrison, in his groundbreaking mystical comic *The Invisibles,* implies the gods are masks for the divine during one character's shamanic initiation, and I think that is a powerful image to work with.

In this wise-one view, the divine is both personal and impersonal. The impersonal aspect of the divine is like nature, unconditional, neither good nor evil. It just is, and acts on fundamental principles: physical, energetic, and spiritual. The light of the diamond shines on all if you look at it. But in this view, the divine is also personal, manifesting through the aspects of creation with which our soul resonates. We each are attracted to different elements of nature and human consciousness, be it the ocean, forest, lightning, art, music, or healing. They lead us to our own personal understanding of the mysteries.

Those on a path to enlightenment ask me why are the gods so petty in so many myths, particularly Greek and Roman mythology. Why do they do these "unspiritual" things? Why are they so human? Are they not role models for enlightenment? Of course they are! They show us that our "humanity" and our highest traits, along with our lowest, are a part of divinity. The monotheistic visions of the divine have distant, perfect, cold images of the divine at times, lacking anything humanly relatable. The pagan mythologies do not. At the core, these ancient and shining ones are not petty or cruel, but our understanding of them is through the lens of human experience, and it doesn't make them any less divine. If you study the cycles of myths in any culture, you will notice how the myths change. Early Greek myths hold versions of the story we never hear, with a softer, more feminist view. As the culture became more patriarchal, the goddesses were still honored, but the stories changed, becoming more violent or pettier at times. Older versions of the myth of Persephone have the maiden seduced by the lord of the Underworld. In later versions, she is raped and kidnapped. Each version is a truth, not the only truth. Each version is the truth viewed through the lens of the Greek culture at that time. But remembering our human traits, and seeing them in the divine, opens us up to the divinity that dwells within our entire being.

When I say the gods are portals, gateways, or masks, I do not mean to imply the gods are not animated by their own presence, will, and personality. In fact, that is one of the advantages of cultivating a relationship with them. They can act as spiritual guides or teachers to an aspiring witch. They will often offer their love, healing, and protection. They will guide the priestess and priest on the path, as defined by their own particular characteristics. Those whose gifts focus on healing will often get a healing deity. Those whose path is that of the warrior will resonate with warrior deities. We all play many roles in life, and will no doubt be able to cultivate relationships through meditation and ritual with many gods and goddesses.

When we have such a relationship, we can ask questions, get advice, receive healing, and feel guided and loved by the Great Spirit always. Such relationships are life changing and transforming. If I only focused on the scientific aspect of witchcraft and never opened the door to the spiritual, I would not be half the loving, healthy, balanced, guided, confident person that I am today. I know if I don't have any answer or can't solve a problem that the solution will come. I feel myself loved and know it will work out, and have the tools, and divine support team, to help me transform my life for the highest good. That is the perfect trust I have in the divine.

WERE THE GODS EVER REAL?

One of the most frequent questions I get asked is, "Are the gods real? Did they ever walk around with people? Are they just an idea, or are they real?" The answer depends on what you mean by real. I believe the gods are very real and ever present throughout creation. The only thing that changes is our perception of them. The question usually stems from those from a Christian background saying that Jesus was real. He walked the Earth. He was both a person and the divine. Were the pagan gods like Jesus? Did they walk the Earth? And the very simple, truthful answer is, "I don't know."

Such questions are part of the mysteries of the gods and goddesses. As you develop a relationship with each, ask. That is the only way you will find the answer for you, but your truth might not be someone else's truth. The easy answer is to say the gods are beings of pure consciousness, living in the nonphysical realms, and manifesting through nature and through visions. But both Christianity and Eastern religions have a belief in the divine made flesh, as an avatar. Did the pagans have similar experiences, but their knowledge of them was reduced to fable? Did embodiments of the gods walk the world?

In Italian myth, Aradia is said to be the daughter and avatar of the Moon goddess Diana, so the concept does sneak into paganism. Other traditions looks to those who have developed enlightened consciousness through their spiritual paths as a guide and teacher, giving them almost godlike status. The ascended masters, known as the bodhisattvas in the East, were those who broke the cycle of death and rebirth, who were prepared to merge with the divine mind yet chose to remain behind on a spiritual plane, in love and service, to help all others. That would explain the gods' very human and often "unenlightened" aspects, as well as their strong personalities and temperaments. Was there a wise woman named something similar to Athena, and from her life grew the myth of the Greek goddess of wisdom? Did the memory of her actually walking the world die out in favor of the much grander image of the immortal on Mount Olympus?

Our current records of mythology, particularly from those cultures whose stories were recorded by Christians, such as the Celts, make the waters very muddy between who is a god, who is a hero, and who is simply human. The line is blurred and great transformations occur during the story, taking mortal into the divine and the divine to the mortal realm. The two are not as disconnected as modern people often believe.

Fivefold Divinity

Modern paganism draws from the roots of many religions and ideas. Many neopagans don't realize that our modern interpretations of the old faith are just that, modern interpretations. The concepts we will discuss were held by ancient cultures, but perhaps not in the fashion we hold them now. Beliefs in the Triple Goddess, Horned God, Grain God, and Earth Mother are eternal images and truths in the collective realm of the archetypal beings, but each culture probably did not focus on them all at the same time, through the same lens as modern humans. Hunting societies focused on the Horned God. Agrarian societies focused on the Grain God. Modern witches see the validity of both, and assign them different attributes, holidays, and times of the year. In our world, the ancient traditions blend together into something new and beautiful, just as valid and powerful.

As each culture has its specific creation stories, and so many of us were raised with the book of Genesis creation story, neopagans reweave their own creation story, borrowing threads from the ancient and making a modern tapestry. By uncovering the oldest creation tales, we get a greater sense of what the first stories were. When you dig deep enough, stories of the Father God often cover images of a Great Mother, a bisexual, androgynous being, or a race of creator goddesses and gods, like giants. For a more scholarly yet controversial approach to these ancient goddess-focused stories, I suggest reading Merlin Stone's book *When God Was a Woman*. Such books make you rethink the stories you carry in your heart and help create the new, inclusive world mythology.

Here is a general creation myth of the Goddess and God, variations of which can be found in many traditions of witchcraft. The words are not as important as the meaning. This is not scripture, but a mystery to be experienced and lived on every level.

In the beginning, there was the Great Void filling the divine mind of the Great Spirit. The void had nothing and everything in it. The void was the great chaos of all possibilities, churning like a cosmic ocean in its possibilities. And in the void was the Great Goddess, the First Mother. And the void was the Great Goddess. The Goddess separated the light from the dark, giving the first form and shape into being, and the Goddess gave birth to the Great God. The God was her child, her son, and her lover and consort. Like the Goddess, he existed in the light and the dark, for together they were all things.

Through their love, the two who move as one in the Great Spirit birthed the first children. Together they created the stars of the cosmos. They created the planets. So great was their love that light and life teemed within them everywhere, contrasting with their darkness and the void.

The Goddess and God took many forms and many faces through their children, yet all lead back to the Great Mother and Father. They created on all levels, seen and unseen, known and unknown. The Goddess took shape in the Earth, the land, the oceans, and Moon. The Goddess could be found in all women. The God took shape in the sky, the animals, grain, and the Sun. The God could be found in all men. But the Goddess could be found in the heart of all expressions of the God, as the God could be found in the heart of all expressions of the Goddess. They found expression in the forces of nature, and voices in the gods and goddesses of living myth.

As the Goddess and God are found through creation, they, too, were created and re-created in the cycles of life. The Goddess would journey through many cycles, seen in the Moon, the seasons, and the life of woman. She rises as the Maiden, young and full of possibility, as the Great Goddess did in the beginning. The maiden of the forest, the warrior, the daughter of all, brings her strength and light. She moved into the realm of the Mother, creator, provider, sustainer, mother of all. She became the Crone, the dark one, full of power, knower of mysteries.

The God was a god of light and life, growing with the green, growing with the sunlight. He is the baby, the child, the young lover and passionate youth. He is the king of the land, the consort, but he, too, would wane, and become his shadow, the lord of sacrifice, Underworld, and the hunt. He is the horned one, and protector in the winter darkness. From the cycles of life the world is continually created and destroyed in the love of the

Goddess and God. All these forms, all these faces of the divine lead back to the Two Who Move As One in the Love of the Great Spirit, the Great Goddess and God, the First Mother and Father. As it is, as it was, as it ever shall be, from the Beginning.

From the story of creation, we are struck with some powerful images of the divine, as Goddess and God with many forms and faces. In this model, the Goddess is viewed as the source of life, which always made more sense to me, since we are born of our mothers, not our fathers. The God is the seed, the changing pattern, but the Goddess is the manifestation, the center from which all things spring and all things return. Both are needed for creation, as mother and father, egg and seed are needed. But like the Yin-Yang symbol of the Eastern mystic, both contain the other. Each polarity contains the essences of the other. Within all men is a female energy and all women contain a male energy. Through this balance of the divine do we find our magick.

Figure 3: Yin-Yang

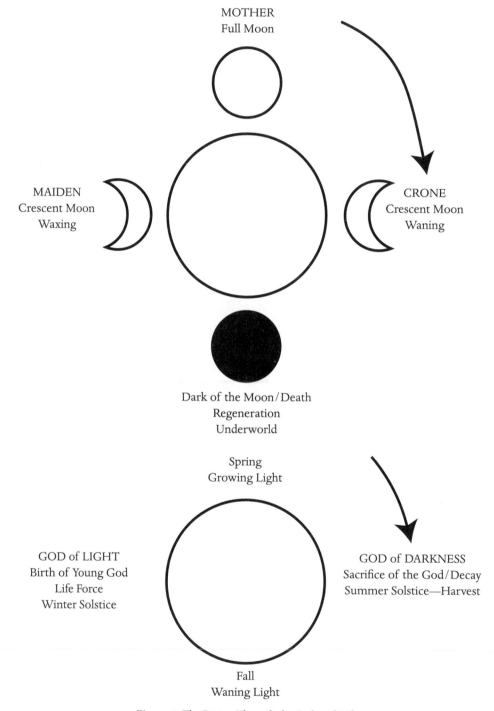

Figure 4: *The Divine Through the Cycles of Life*

Modern witches have recognized these images as a fivefold divinity, in the shape of the five points of the pentagram. The Goddess is represented by three points: as Maiden, Mother, and Crone. The God is the remaining two points, the God of Light and the God of Darkness. From these five images of the archetypal beings come the vast majority of gods and goddesses.

Figure 5: Pentagram of Divinity

The only problem with this model is that it lacks the image of the Magician/Trickster God, the walker between worlds. This traveling god is represented by the change between the God of Light and Life and the God of Darkness and Death, passing from one realm to another, traveling between worlds. These light and dark images are not moral judgment calls of good and evil, as some would have you believe. They are simply aspects of nature. In nature, there is a time of light and a time of dark, literally and symbolically. There is a time of life, and then a passing from life. It's a part of nature. Just as a storm can bring life-giving rain and another storm can flood and kill, a storm is not good or evil. It simply is. Nature is.

With the fivefold divinity and the walker between worlds, the archetypal beings manifest, and from the archetypal beings come the godforms, the deities of pagan mythology. Explore the following energies, and see what resonates with you. What sings to your soul is usually something significant, but also pay attention to the images you have an aversion to. Sometimes what we like least is what we need to see the most.

The Archetypal Beings

Even though the primary forms of divinity are found in the fivefold image, there are many facets to our diamond, each reflecting another archetypal being. There are many faces to each aspect of the Goddess and God.

The similarities between so many of these beings, found in cultures from around the world, really point to me as universal truth. Each culture calls the beings by different names, interpreting their message through their own cultural lens, viewing the beings as various godforms or individual deities from a specific mythology, but the striking similarities are powerful.

The more different the cultures are, the more difficult it can be to see such similarities, but they do exist on a deep, primal level of consciousness. My first exposure to witchcraft was in the Celtic vein, but starting with Celtic mythology was very confusing for me. Celtic myth consists of Irish, Welsh, Scottish, and British tales, in a variety of incarnations and perspectives. Though wonderful and wise, Celtic myth is very confusing to someone not raised with a Celtic perspective.

I often tell students to start with the godforms of the ancient Greco-Roman deities. Western culture is far more based on the Greek/Roman mode of thinking, even though the West has discarded much of their mystical lore. Many people study the Greek themes in school, and they pop up quite a bit in popular entertainment, albeit with historical inaccuracies. Having a more linear based concept, each deity embodies basic principles. One embodies love. Another embodies war. We have a god of storms. We have a goddess of the earth. Everything is much more straightforward. The Romans adopted much of the Greek deity structure, grafting their own gods onto Greek figures, and usually renaming them.

Celtic culture is much less linear. Simply look at a Celtic knot to get a feel for Celtic consciousness—beautiful, balanced, intricate, but difficult to follow or reproduce. Knowledge, wisdom, and talent are prized above all else in Celtic culture, so the more powerful a deity, the more they could do, and you find gods and goddesses who embody a little bit of everything, making the archetypal energy harder to see until you get a feel for it.

True Celtic scholars could make the argument that Greek and Celtic mythology are not even comparable because the cultures are so different, but my understanding of the basic archetypes I learned through Greek mythology personally gave me a firm foundation to see patterns and energies in other cultures, from Egyptian, Sumerian, Celtic, Norse, Hindu, and even South American.

Those pagans in the ancient world often saw their own gods in other cultures. Lists transposing gods between the Egyptian and Greek pantheons exist. Julius Caesar, writing about the Roman invasions of Celtic Gaul, clearly states that the most beloved god among the Celts is Mercury. We are certain the Celts did not worship the Roman Mercury, but Caesar could see the correspondences between their main god and the god he knew as Mercury.

In essence, each archetypal being really contains all the various godforms of the different cultures. A magickal comic book, *The Sandman: Kindly Ones*, stated it so well. In a conversation with the archetypal Triple Goddess and a character, the following primal truth was said. "Are you . . . are you the Furies?" "Are we the Furies? Are you a hand? Or an eye? Or a tooth?" "No, of course not. I am myself. But I have those things within me . . ."[1] To me, this modern bard, author Neil Gaiman, summed up a magickal truth so perfectly; I carry that wisdom with me in my heart.

Earth Mother

The Earth Mother is the most long-standing and powerful image of the Goddess, starting with our earliest Stone Age ancestors. Most ancient mythologies start with the creation of the world as the Mother, from whom all things spring and all things return. She gives of herself, providing her children with all that is needed to live and thrive in balance. In the earliest mythologies, the land itself is considered to be the living Goddess, but such people were only versed in the land. The concept of the Great Mother is that the entire material world is made up of the body of the Goddess, from the stars and planets, to the soil beneath our feet. The Great Mother is all life everywhere. Because of this, some Earth Mother godforms also exist as Heavenly Queens. As mythologies changed, and godforms became more complex, the archetypes were individualized in human perception.

The Greek Gaia is the most well-known expression of the Earth Mother, as her name has been reclaimed in modern mythology, particularly in the scientific Gaia hypothesis. Gaia created herself from the chaos, and then her son and husband, the sky god Uranus. In the Celtic culture, most goddesses embody the concept of divine Mother and sovereign Earth. Danu, the Great Mother of the race of gods known as the Tuatha De Danann, or Children of Danu, is the Great Mother, both in an earthly and cosmic sense. The Danube River is believed to be named after her, along with several other sacred sites. Modron, another vision of the Celtic Earth Mother, is the parent of the young god Mabon. In Norse mythology, Freya, a fertility goddess of land as well as a goddess of magick, healing, and sexuality, is most often viewed as Earth Mother. All these other traits are part and parcel to the Earth Mother. Magick and sexuality is a part of motherhood, not exclusive or in addition to it. She finds similarities with the Norse goddesses Frigga, consort to the father god Odin, and golden-haired Sif, wife to the storm god Thor. The Middle Eastern goddesses Innana, Ishtar and Astarte, Egyptian Isis, and to a certain extent Greek Aphrodite and Roman Venus all have both stellar and earthly associations. Some godforms don't focus on the land itself, but on the grain and harvest, such as the Greek Demeter, Roman Ceres, and Cherokee corn-mother figure Selu.

Sky God

The Sky God image is the power of clarity, intellect, logic, and precision. As cultures turned from the earth to the sky, these attributes came into prominence. The sky gods carry a great potential for love as father figures and protectors, but also contain the potential of cloudiness, stormy conflict, and remoteness. Sky gods are protectors of the Earth. They hold safe the Earth and all her children in their protective canopy, as the Earth Mother gives them a place to hold and gather their energy. Often the Sky God is painted with some fallibility in human myths of the gods, as the sky becomes more smothering than protective.

In Greek myth, Gaia gives birth to Uranus, and he becomes both son and consort. Together they create all things, and their children become the first race of gods. Uranus becomes too forceful in his rule, fearing his children will overthrow him, and locks them in Gaia's womb. His son Chronos castrates him to gain release, and takes his place, but falls into similar pitfalls. His grandson, Zeus, the father of storm and lightning, eventually rules the gods. Some myths portray him as loving and wise, a fine father figure, and others show him chauvinistically unfair. Different points of the culture recorded the male sky principle in different ways. The process of making a personal connection and reconciling these varying images is a part of the mystery.

In the early Celtic culture, Tarranis is a prominent sky and storm god. Llud and Nuada are other sky, storm, and cloud figures in Celtic culture. To the Norse, Thor is the ruler of thunder and lightning. The Sumerian lord Marduk uses lightning as his weapon, but the god Anshar is the god of the sky. To the Hindus, Indra is the lord of storm and lighting. Brahma, the father and creator god, is sometimes associated with the Sky God archetype. Egyptians didn't focus on the sky as much as the Sun. The sky was embodied by the goddess Nuit, or Nut, but the heavenly king archetype was embodied by the pharaoh. Amon-Ra, the early aspect of the solar father god Ra, is the earthly king and embodiment of this divine pharonic power, and Amon-Ra is sometimes correlated with Zeus.

Moon Goddess

In most cultures, the Moon evokes a feminine presence, associated with intuition, magick, menstruation, reflection, and the cycles of a woman's life. The Moon evokes the many faces of the feminine, often embodied by the Triple Goddess—Maiden, Mother, and Crone—though a few cultures see the Moon as the masculine timekeeper. To me, the Moon Goddess has always been the archetype of the witch as keeper of the mysteries. The Moon, like the Goddess, must be felt, and cannot be rationalized or put into words and still convey the full power.

In the Greek world, there are many Moon goddesses. Artemis is the maiden of the hunt, goddess of wild animals. Her silver arrows are shafts of moonlight. She is the protector of mothers and children. Selene is the Moon goddess who pulls the Moon itself in her chariot across the sky. She steals away to visit her eternally sleeping lover Endymion, causing the dark of the Moon. Hecate, a triple goddess in her own right, is the Mother of Witches, goddess of the Underworld and crossroads. She is the crone and guide at the crossroads. In Roman mythology, they are known as Diana, Luna, and Hecate respectively.

In Egypt, the goddesses Isis, the cat-headed Bast and the cow-headed Hathor have Moon associations, along with the gods Thoth and Knoshu. Egyptian mythology can be peculiar because usual gender roles found in the world are often mixed. Instead of having a traditional Earth Mother and Sky God, they have an Earth Father, Geb or Seb, and Sky/Star Mother, Nuit. Ancient Egypt was also one of the few to associate male figures with the Moon. The Sumerian god Sin also has Moon associations, as well as the Hindu gods Chandra and Soma.

To the Celts, most goddesses had an otherworldly and mystical association, tying them to Moon lore in ancient and modern traditions. The Welsh Arianrhod, whose name means "silver wheel," is associated with the Moon and the concepts of resurrections and rebirth. Cerridwen, the archetypal witch mother stirring her cauldron, has Dark Moon associations. The war goddess Morgan, in various incarnations, is associated by some with the Dark Moon mysteries as well.

Sun God

As the Moon evokes the feminine principle, the Sun most often evokes the masculine archetypes. The Sun God embodies concepts of both the sky and vegetation gods, being a principle figure of light and life. The Sun is the source of life, instilling the seed energy to the Earth to create life and sustenance. These gods are most often the gods of light, beauty, inspiration, knowledge, and healing. They embody the eternal fire of life and the human soul.

Apollo in the Greco-Roman traditions is the god of light, pulling the chariot of the Sun across the sky. He replaced the Titan Helios, who also once pulled the chariot of the sky. Among his attributes, Apollo is a god of medicine and grants the gifts of prophecy. Originally the Temple of Delphi was a temple to Gaia, but later became the temple of the priests of Apollo. Ra is the primary Sun God and father figure in the Egyptian world, and in some tales, being the first creator of the universe. Ra's secret name embodies the power of the universe. Shamash is the god of the solar disc for Sumerian practices. With the Norse, the well-loved god Balder is the god of light and beauty, and veiled solar figure. Tricked by the god Loki, his blind brother Hodur, the old god of winter, slays Balder with a piece of mistletoe, starting the end of the world, but symbolically the end of the solar cycle. Their tale is reminiscent of the Oak and Holly Kings of the Celts. The Celtic solar kings are associated with Lugh in Irish myth, and Lleu in Welsh myth, as well as the youths Mabon and Bel, celebrated on the holidays Mabon and Beltane. In the Hindu traditions, both Surya and Vishnu are described with solar attributes.

Triple Goddess

The Triple Goddess figure is the most powerful image found in Wicca, depicting the great creatrix as Maiden, Mother, and Crone. She is three, who is one, who is three, the great mystery of life. Images of triplicity are found throughout all cultures, be it goddesses or other representations. Triple images stand for the energy that starts and creates, the energy that sustains and the energy that destroys, so that something new can be created. In Hinduism, they are represented by the gods Brahma the father principle, Vishnu the Preserver and Shiva the Destroyer (or Dissolver). In astrology, these forces are called cardinal, fixed, and mutable. In Christianity it is the Father, Son, and Holy Spirit, originally personified in early Christianity as the Holy Sophia, a feminine creative force. Some would look to it as Father, Child, and Mother. One of my teachers uses the word "God" as an acronym, G for generating, O for organizing, and D for destroying.

In Wicca, this triple force is the Goddess as Maiden, Mother, and Crone. She is seen in the phases of the Moon: as she waxes, she is the Maiden. Full Moon is the Mother, and the waning Moon is the Crone, entering the dark to be reborn again as the Maiden. The Earth embodies the Triple Goddess. Spring is the reborn flower maiden. Summer is the harvest mother, full in her bounty. Fall brings the withering crone, to enter the darkness of winter, the Underworld, and be reborn again in the spring. The Goddess is also seen in all the spheres of creation. In the celestial sphere, the Goddess is She Who Is Above Us, as the Moon and stars. She is the light that sustains and creates. In the terrestrial sphere, the Goddess is She Who Is With Us, as the planet itself, and all of material creation. In the Underworld sphere, the Goddess is She Who Lies Below Us, as the dark queen, crone, and lady of death and transformation. All things come from the Goddess, and all things return to it.

Modern reconstructionists will point to a lack of archeological evidence to demonstrate an ancient concept of this Triple Goddess in the way modern witches interpret it. There are many goddesses linked together in triplicities, but not necessarily in relationship as maiden, mother, and crone. The war goddesses that collectively comprise the Morgan in Celtic myth, Anu, Babd Catha, and Macha, or some say Babd, Macha, and Nemain, don't hold to this image. Neither does the Hindu triplicity of Paravati, Durga, and Kali Ma. The Greek Moon trio Artemis, Selene, and Hecate are not related as family. And the goddesses Isis and Inanna seems to embody all three spheres in themselves entirely. The Norse concept of triplicity is in the Norns, the three Fates or Wyrd Sisters (Urdhr, Verdhandi, and Skuld), who are beyond the gods, weaving time, but not directly worshiped. They are more like past, present, and future; what was, what is, and what will be, rather than daughter, mother, and grandmother. But what strict reconstructionist fails to see in the evidence is what experience is so clearly evident in the psyche of ancient pagan people living with the land and animals in a way we cannot, living with their own mortality, not avoiding it through age-defying techniques. In such cultures, the passage from maidenhood to motherhood to cronedom is clear, ever present, and celebrated. We lack a lot of archeological evidence of things we know are evident to a culture. The concept of the evolution of the feminine in a spiral cycle is something more evident to the Goddess-reverent cultures than to our own Western civilization.

Horned God

The Horned God or Animal Lord is the most misunderstood of god archetypes. The horns represent wisdom, vision, and power, but have unfortunately been grafted on to the fiction of the Devil as an embodiment of evil. These divine features were linked to a concept of evil to force pagans to convert to Christianity and prevent others from returning to the old ways. The Horned God is one of protection during the winter months, of magic and mystery, or male power and sexuality.

The Greek Pan is a well-known Horned God, depicted as a satyr, half man and half goat. He is the father of wild things and a lord of nature. Faunnus holds similar function in the Roman pantheon. The image of the horned god, from Buffalo to Stag, is ancient, dating back to pre-Vedic society in the Indus Valley. A Buffalo man/god is depicted in ancient caves, a precursor to the more modern image of the Celtic Cernunnos, meaning "horned one." Cernunnos is not even his Celtic name, but the Roman translation of it. His original name is lost, but perhaps closer to Herne, another horned Celtic figure. Cernunnos is the great father, said to be a master of magick and shamanism, and ruler of the spirit world or astral plane.

Vegetation God

The god of grain and growing things is a god of life, often with solar attributes as well. While the Goddess represents the land as eternal and unmoving, the God represents the transitioning grain, dying and being reborn in the love and strength of the Goddess. The Vegetation God is symbolic of the sacrificed king figure in the agrarian society. The king symbolically brings fertile land if he has the appropriate relationship with the goddess of the land. Kings ruling under infertile times represent an unhealthy relationship with the Goddess, and in some cultures were symbolically or literally sacrificed with the harvest to ensure fertility in the next year. Symbolically, the God's sacrifice is the grain and harvest, giving life so others may live from it.

Dionysus is the Greek god of wine, grapes, inspiration, poetry, unconditional love, and madness. He is considered a resurrected god, dying more than once and returning to the world of men to teach the mysteries. Bacchus is his Roman equivalent, though most often portrayed less youthfully than Dionysus. Adonis is a figure that finds his way into both Greek and Middle Eastern mythology, finding a correspondence with the Sumerian Tammuz or Damuzi. In Egypt, Osiris was first a god of vegetation, depicted green in much of his art. In a modern sense, the figure of Jesus is a resurrected vegetation king, borrowing from these sources as a god associated with love, grapes, grains, and resurrection.

Celtic legend is filled with the sacrificed king archetype. The popular image of the Green Man, or Jack of the Green, is the basic form, but he is also found in the myth of the Oak King and Holly King, or the Green Knight and Red Knight. The two represent the forces of the waxing and waning year, fighting on the solstices for dominance. The Oak King/Green Knight is the god of life, green and youth. Mabon is young god lost in the Underworld, often associated with the fall fruit harvest. Lugh, an Irish god of many skills, is sometimes associated with both solar powers and grain god images in modern Celtic witchcraft. The good father of the Celts, the Dagda, can be seen as a god of vegetation, but he embodies life and so much more. The Dagda, a great giant, is a figure of magick, healing, and the mysteries of both the living world and the other world. He is a force of love, life, magick, abundance, and protection.

Underworld Goddess

The Underworld Goddess is the being who rules the shadow lands, sometimes with a consort, and sometimes alone. She can be an aspect of the Crone, the dark queen and the destroyer. The Underworld Goddess represents all that is feared and repressed coming to the surface. She is a goddess of love, but fierce, unforgiving love, forcing you to confront the dark side, your own personal shadow (to use the Jungian term). Those who partner with this aspect of the Goddess receive great gifts in personal development, but it's a hard road to walk.

In the Greek myth, the Underworld queen is Persephone. She, as the maiden Kore, daughter of the grain mother Demeter, was taken into the Underworld by King Hades. Earlier myths say she was seduced, later myths say kidnapped and raped. Through her experience she became queen of the dark mysteries, presiding over life and death. Only if she returned to her mother for half the year did the earth grow, and when she left the waking world, it would wither away. Kore was renamed Persephone, She Who Must Be Feared. Her Roman name is Proserpina. The Norse did not have an Underworld king and queen, but simply a goddess. Her name is Hel, and her land is also called Hel, leading to the Christian corruption to the concept of Hel. Originally it was simply the land of the dead, flanked by a realm of fire and a realm of ice. Hel is a beautiful woman above the waist, but below, she is a rotting corpse, linking, as so many mystical cultures do, the concepts of sexuality, death, and transformation. In Sumer, Ereshkigal, the dark sister to Inanna, ruled the Underworld. Fearsome in her power, with leeches for hair, Ereshkigal had a consort but still held the reins of power when her sister visited the Underworld on her quest.

In Egyptian myth, the consort of the Underworld God, Osiris, is Isis, though she is not usually portrayed as an Underworld figure. Her dark sister, Nepthys, has many Underworld associations as goddess of death and decay, but has no fear or power associations and does not necessarily reside in the Underworld. Likewise, the Hindu destroyer Kali Ma is a goddess of destruction and fire, but does not necessarily reside in the Underworld. Many also associate Kali with Mother Nature, as the force of creation and destruction simultaneously.

In the murky world of the Celts, the concepts of otherworld and Underworld can be difficult to distinguish. Many Celtic myths to not have a linear view of realms above and below exactly, but realms parallel and adjacent to the physical, mortal realm. Many of the dark goddesses, Moon goddesses, and war goddesses mentioned have otherworld associations and can be construed as Underworld queens in their own right, including the goddesses Rhiannon, Epona, Cerridwen, Morgan, and Macha.

Underworld God

The Underworld God is often tied strongly with the Horned God, being a darker expression of the divine male energy. The Underworld God rules the land of the ancestors and power beings. Here, one may undertake a quest for great healing or knowledge, but fear, particularly fear of death, must be faced. Some associate the Underworld God with the riches found beneath the soil, in the form of gems and gold, but the true riches of the Underworld are in spirit, not money. Hades in the Greek pantheon, and Pluto in the Roman, are the kings of the Underworld, ruling with their consort queens. Nergal is the consort of Ereshkigal in the Sumerian pantheon, and in that context, could be seen as an Underworld king. The Norse have no real Underworld king, being ruled by the queen of Hel without any consort. Rudra is the Hindu aspect of the Underworld divinity. The Underworld God of ancient Egyptian faith has more of a heroic quality, also previously having solar and vegetation associations. Osiris is the resurrected king, killed twice by the power of his brother Set and reborn twice in the magick of his wife and sister Isis. In the Celtic legends, the Underworld kings and otherworld kings are often intermixed. Pywll and Arawn, in Welsh myths, are associated with Underworld aspects by some modern pagans. Cernunnos has Underworld associations, too. The Romans called the Celtic Underworld figure Dis Pater and associated him with the horned ones, and many Celts believed they were direct descendents of this figure.

Goddess of Love

The Goddess of Love has evolved out of the archetypes of fertility and the Earth, to embody the concept of true love, be it unconditional spiritual love, family love, and the most often sought-out type of love, romantic love. The myths of these goddesses are embodied of romantic twists and turns, as well as symbolic powers of love. Not only are they associated with the land itself at times, but the Morning Star (Venus), flowers, water, and in particular, the ocean, are their symbols.

The most well-known and beloved of these goddesses is the Greek Aphrodite, known as Venus to the Romans. She rules over all love and relationships, inspiring love in gods and mortals alike. "Aphrodite" means "foam born," as she was created when the genitals of Uranus fell into the ocean. Lakshmi is the Hindu foam-born goddess resonating with Aphrodite. Hathor is the Egyptian goddess most closely associated with Aphrodite, though a goddess of love and pleasure in many ways, she is also symbolic of the nourishing cow, giving love to any and all. In Sumeria and Babylon, Inanna, Astarte, and Ishtar are associated with love and the planet Venus. To the Norse, Freya is a goddess of fertility, sexuality, and the rites of love. In Celtic lore, most goddesses who are not of a dark nature have associations with the land, fertility, and love, chief among them being Gwnhwyfar, transformed into Arthur's queen in the Camelot legends, but chiefly symbolic of the king's relationship with the land itself.

God of War

The God of War is often a misunderstood figure. Many are gods of war and destruction, but many are peaceful warriors originally, much like our figure of the knight or marital arts warrior. A few are more strongly associated with "right action" or justice than war itself. Some are associated with fire, passion, and sexuality. Tyr, the Norse god of war, is the god of justice and self-sacrifice, giving his hand to the wolf monster Fenris so that the creature could be chained. All the Celtic king figures, sacred warriors, including King Arthur to the Welsh Bran and Irish Lugh, are involved in this energy. In Egypt, the God of War had two sides. The destructive powers are embodied by Set, brother of Osiris. Set is the red-headed god of the storm and sand. His nephew, Osiris' son Horus, is the god of justice, retrieving the stolen kingdom of Egypt from Set, and ruling it justly and wisely. Karttikeya is the Hindu war god. Ares, the Greek god of war, survives in myths as an instigator, being arrogant and causing conflict. He is the secret lover of Aphrodite, and often painted a villain by modern reinterpretations, but at one time he was also known as a god for healing and courage.

Goddess of Wisdom/Truth

The Goddess of Wisdom is the embodiment not of knowledge, but of the proper application of that knowledge, using it for a higher good. These deities are the ones with clarity and insight, the ingenuity to transform a problem into a solution, on any level. Athena is the Greek Goddess of Wisdom, credited with many inventions, such as weaving and olive branch grafting. The city of Athens was named for her. Minerva is her Roman equivalent. In Egypt, Maat is the goddess of absolute truth, universal truth, and credited as a great universal power. Maat is often embodied as being beyond form and shape, although sometimes she is depicted like traditional goddesses. Neith is an Egyptian goddess directly corresponding to Athena and Minerva. In ancient Sumer, the wisdom goddess is Tashmetum. In India, Sarasvati is the great inventor and communicator goddess, skilled in writing, music, and medicine.

To the Celts, most goddesses possessed wisdom, though some more than others. Cerridwen gives the wisdom of the poet. Brid, known as Bridget and eventually St. Bridget, is a triple goddess talented in poetry, healing, and smithcraft, a bestower of knowledge and how to use it. The Norse also saw all goddess aspects as wise, but the archetype that strikes me most in this realm are the Valkyries, the handmaidens of Odin, called the Choosers of the Slain. They travel the Norse worlds, choosing those who have died heroically in battle, seeing the slain souls truly for what they are, and taking them to a reward of eternal feasting in Odin's hall of Valhalla.

Messenger God

The Messenger God is one of the most important magickal archetypes to study. The messenger is the image of the magician and shaman, the one who travels between worlds bringing messages and magick, and guiding souls. A psychopomp is one who guides souls, the new souls to the land of the living, and bringing the dead to the Underworld. These are gods of invention, magick, writing, mystery, and higher consciousness. They are the tricksters and healers.

The main archetype of the scribe magician is Thoth of ancient Egypt. Some say he is a cosmic force, others say an ascended man, but he is the god of wisdom, credited with inventing the first forms of writing. He is the inventor of magick and alchemy. In Sumer, Nabu is the scribe god and magician. Thoth was later associated with the Greek Hermes, though some distinguish Hermes, the Greek Messenger God (Mercury to the Romans) from the Greeks' notion of Thoth by using the appellation Hermes Trismagestius, or Thrice Great Hermes. Hermes is the god who is not bound by any one location or task, but does everything and goes everywhere. He is another god credited with the inventions of civilization, including writing, philosophy, medicine, sports, music, and gymnastics, and is even the patron of travelers and thieves. In India, the elephant-headed and many-talented Ganesha is seen as a Mercurial figure, being the remover of obstacles on the path you travel, literally and spiritually.

The Egyptian Anubis can also be considered under this archetypal energy, since he holds the mysteries of traveling to the land of the dead and medicine, and invented the art of mummification. Some would put the Greek centaur scholar, teacher, and physician Chiron in this category as well.

In the European myths, the archetype often takes on more wild man shamanic characteristics. Wotan, the earlier name of the Norse all-father Odin, is the wanderer, a great magician, trickster, and sacrificed god, who hung himself from the World Tree to unlock the secret power of the magickal runes. His blood brother, Loki, is portrayed as a more rebellious and malevolent trickster. Other Norse figures are Heimdall, for his guardianship of the gates of Asgard, the realm of the gods, and the messenger Hermod.

To the Celts, the shaman magician figures, such as Merlin, Math, Gwydion, and Taliesin are a part of this archetypal energy. Oghma is a warrior, but credited with a honey tongue and inventor of the ogham tree alphabet. Manannan Mac Lir is the Irish god of travel, particularly travel by sea, and his magickal skills are very powerful. Lugh, the many-skilled king of the Tuatha De Danann, was considered a Mercury equivalent by Caesar. Diancecht is the physical god of the Tuatha, skilled in healing magick.

Goddess of the Home

The Goddess of the Home is an aspect of the mother goddess as goddess of hearth, home, and children. Many ancients kept shrines in the home to invite the blessings of the Goddess of the home to them. The Greek Hestia, along with her Roman counterpart Vesta, are two of the most well-known. Most mother goddesses have this aspect.

The Celtic Brid is often called upon in home blessings and in the protection of children. In Egypt, Nepthys is the goddess of home.

Forge God

The power of the forge, to smith and shape metals, is the power of magick and creation. How wondrous this invention is, a true gift from the gods. The gods of the forge are the gods of magick, creativity, craftsmanship, and transformation. In Greek myth, the lame, malformed god Hephaestus is the smith god, creating marvelous inventions, including Zeus' lightning bolts. His Roman name is Vulcan. In Egypt, Ptah is the god of the universal forge. In Sumeria, it is Nusku. Middle Eastern myth cites Tubal Cain as a smith god. To the Germanic and Norse, this forge figure is Volund or Weiland. To the Celts, the goddess Brid is a forge goddess, but so is Govannon. Another image has a triple god, Goidniu or Goban, and his brothers Luchtaine and Creidne as forge masters.

Water God

The Water God figure is often in the form of the sea king, though the ocean mother or river goddess image appears in tribal cultures. Many of these figures not only have seawater associations, but freshwater ones as well. Water is a symbol of the love and the fluidity of emotion. Water is the power to flow and change, but also the unconscious, of what lies beneath and is hidden unseen. Water is the great dissolver, breaking down barriers and merging all together.

The archetypal king of the sea is Poseidon, the Greek ocean master, who is also associated with horses as well as fish. Greek myths tell of creatures half horse and half fish. Neptune is a Roman figure, originally of fresh water, grafted on to the image of Poseidon with the Greek cultural invasion into Rome. Khnemu is an Egyptian water god. Osiris is associated with the waters of the Nile. The Nile is said to be his semen, as the land is the fertile earth of Isis. In Sumer, both Apsu and Ea are deities of water. In Norse myth, Aegir and Ran are linked with the sea. With the Celts, Manannan Mac Lir, and his father Lir, are associated with the sea and sea travel. In the Welsh tradition, Dylan is the son of Arianrhod, born to the ocean and swimming with the dolphins. Nuada, as a sky and storm god, often has oceanic associations, too. In some interpretations of Hindu material, Shiva has been associated with the oceans, not the earthly oceans, but the cosmic oceans. As the great dissolver, he returns all to the cosmic ocean.

Archetype	Greek	Roman	Egyptian
Triple Goddess	Artemis, Selene, Hecate	Diana, Luna, Trivia	Isis as the Moon, Earth, and Underworld with her husband Osiris
Vegetation/Resurrection God	Dionysus	Bacchus	Osiris
Horned Animal God	Pan	Faunus	
Moon Goddess	Artemis, Selene, Hecate	Diana, Luna, Hecate	Isis, Bast, Hathor. *Gods Thoth and Knoshu were both linked to the Moon.*
Sun God	Apollo, Helios	Apollo	Ra, Horus
Earth Goddess	Gaia	Tellus	Isis. *God Geb/Seb linked to the Earth.*
Sky God	Uranus	Coelus	*The goddess Nut is linked to the sky.*
Grain Goddess	Demeter, Kore/Persephone	Ceres, Proserpina	Isis
Underworld God	Hades	Pluto	Osiris
Underworld Goddess	Persephone, Hecate	Proserpina, Hecate	*None officially, but Isis, as Osiris' wife, or Nepthys, Isis' dark sister, could be called.*
God of War	Ares	Mars	Horus, Set. *Goddess Sekhemet is associated with fire and violence at times.*
Love/Fertility Goddess	Aphrodite	Venus	Hathor, Isis
Wisdom Goddess	Athena	Minerva	Maat, Neith, Seshat
Sky Goddess	Hera	Juno	Nut, Isis
Storm God	Zeus	Jupiter	Amon-Ra
Water God	Poseidon	Neptune	Khemnu, Osiris
Magician/Messenger/Scribe/Trickster	Hermes	Mercury	Thoth, Anubis
Forge God	Hephaestus	Vulcan	Ptah
Ancient One	Chronos and the Titans	Saturn	Ra, Thoth

Sumerian/Middle Eastern	Norse	Celtic
Innana as Queen of Heaven, Earth, and later Underworld	The Norns—Wyrd Sisters Urdhr, Verdhandi, and Skuld	Morgan as Anu, Babd, and Macha; Brid as healer, poet, and smith
Tammuz, Adonis	Frey	Green Man, Oak King/Holly King, Lugh, Mabon
		Cernunnos, Herne
Inanna, Astarte, Ishtar. *God Sin is linked with to the Moon.*		Arianrhod, Cerridwen, Morgan
Shamash	Balder	Lugh, Mabon
Kishar, Tiamat, who is also linked with water.	Freya, Nerthus, Audumla	Modron, Danu. *Many Goddesses are linked to the land.*
Anshar	Odin and his tribe, the Aesir, are all considered sky gods	Llud, Nuada
Nishaba	Freya, Sif	Danu, Modron, Ostara (Teutonic)
Nergal		Pywll, Arawn
Ereshkigal	Hel	Morgan, Cerridwen, Rhiannon, Epona
Ninurta	Tyr, Thor	Tarranis, Bran, King Arthur
Inanna, Astarte, Ishtar	Freya	Aine, Brawen, Lady Gwenhwyfar
Tashmetum	Freya, Frigga	Brid, Cerridwen, all goddesses
Sarpanitu, Shala		Arianrhod
Marduk	Thor	Tarranis. *Dagda, while not a sky god, is often associated with these archetypes.*
Apsu, Ea Nuada	Aegir, Ran	Lir, Manannan Mac Lir, Dylan,
Nabu	Odin, Loki, Heimdal, Hermod	Ogham, Gwydion, Math, Merlin
	Volund, Weiland	Govannon, Goidniu, Goban, Nusku, Tubal Cain, Luchtaine, Creidne
Anu	Ymir	

Figure 6: Archetype Chart

The notion of multifaceted divinity is a hard one to accept for many aspiring witches coming from either a monotheistic background or an agnostic path. As my student Jim once said, "I just have to get used to the idea." It's not an idea we come across in everyday Western society. I had to get used to the idea myself. It was an easy pitfall to intellectualize the process, and think of each godform, each archetypal being, as an idea, not a living energy with consciousness and personal essence. When we intellectualize, we are often afraid to get close, afraid to experience their power and beauty firsthand. The gods are often described as blinding and frightening for a reason. They are vast, and when our mind is confronted with the vastness of their consciousness, we often recoil.

Building a personal relationship with the divine helps us expand our own consciousness, and move further into our own divinity and vastness, and we realize we are all a part of the divine mind. We are all a part of the diamond. We are all one.

CULTURAL PANTHEONS

The reasons to study mythology are vast. I highly suggest a study of comparative mythology for any serious witch. Through it, you see eternal truths and images everywhere. You see that this wisdom is not held by any one faith or culture, but by all. You might see the cultural changes to each mythology, tracing the story back to more primal, original roots, and understand the culture that made the changes. Often figures are demonized, becoming Devil figures in Christian-era translations. Certain symbols, such as the snake, are completely maligned in these renditions. You see the archetypes of human existence played out in mythic themes, and recognize those themes in your own life, and in our current culture. By learning this universal, symbolic language, you become versed in a new way of communicating with, and interpreting messages from, the divine mind. Here is the true wisdom of the dream interpreter, the counselor, and the witch.

For now, I would pick a culture that resonates with you and your craft. Study the deities of that culture, called a pantheon by most, and learn their names, correspondences, and stories. Students often ask why do we call upon a particular goddess, such as the Roman Venus, if the Norse Freya or Sumerian Inanna are also goddesses of love? Or why don't we simply call on the Goddess of Love? Good questions. And only each individual can answer why they call upon a specific deity for magick. It comes from what resonates with them. Although they are all goddesses of love, Venus, Freya, and Inanna all have different myths and personal energies. Each feels different in ritual. Each comes with other attributes, besides love. Which of them resonates with you most? That is why we pick a particular culture, and more specifically a particular goddess, for a ritual. Calling upon a godform, rather than simply the archetypal being, makes the experience more personal. It's hard to connect to the vast Goddess of Love, but Venus can open the doorway to the full power of that archetype in a very personal, loving, and gentle way if you build a relationship with her.

Now you can call upon the same deities in every ritual, or expand your relationships by working with a variety of gods. There is a lot of fear-based material that says you should not mix pantheons, either in your life or in your rituals. The first means if you picked Egyptian, you are sticking with Egyptian deities and rituals. If you want to call on Celtic gods now, you must give up Egypt, and work exclusively with the Celts. The second interpretation means any one ritual or meditation should only call upon deities from the same culture—no mixing and matching cultures. The original reason is to get familiar with a cultural energy and not get confused. It is a learning rule. But the teachings are laced with horrible and veiled threats about what will happen if you don't follow this rule. Funny, I thought our only rule was "Do what thou will and let it harm none." Within these threats, no one says what will happen to you if you do mix deities, but it's horrible.

So, of course, not doing as I'm told, I've mixed deities and let me tell you, I'm fine. Really. No horrible curses. No demonic possessions. No judgments from the cosmic powers. They were all deities I had a relationship with. They all fit the rituals I was doing. If doing a group ritual, one might be of Celtic flavor, another Greek, and another Norse. Each person wants to call upon his or her favorite goddess or god for the ritual. I think the goddesses and gods get along better than people, so any arguments to be had in such a ritual would be between the practitioners, not the divine. The gods are all on the same page and ready to work with us if the cause harms none. Such rituals, when done with thought, preparation and love, are quite beautiful. We are children of the global mythology. We are mixing and matching ethnicities, languages, and food, so why not images of the divine? They all lead to the same source, the center of the diamond.

Patrons

At times, a particular goddess or god will make themselves known to you in a special way. You might read about them and feel a special resonance in your soul. You might not seek them out, but instead the deity seeks you out. The nature of this god or goddess, whether you know it or not, resonates with your soul's purpose in this life, the nature of the work you are here to do, learn, or share. This diety becomes your patron, and you become the diety's priestess or priest in the world. You build a more intense relationship than you do with most other guides and gods, and the benefits for all are enormous.

Not everyone receives a patron or finds one right away. It's a big responsibility when finally accepted. I know it took me time to accept it. I didn't have a great love for working with the divine as the gods of myth. I was in witchcraft as a science. But one of the rituals I learned called upon the Crow for the element of air, and with it, the Celtic crow/horse goddess Macha. I loved spellwork, but wasn't trained to feel a lot in ritual space, but when I called upon Macha, I felt a breeze. I was only calling her because that is the way I learned the ritual. But there was a higher purpose. I felt the breeze and would sense a shimmer and shape slightly. The energy was strongest from her direction, but honestly, I thought I was making it up.

As I continued my meditation practice, along with my monthly Moon rituals, a woman's face appeared to me, dark haired. She spoke to me softly and lovingly most of the time, but would show up when I was making a jerk out of myself and being immature, to tell me to shape up and set things right. As she pulled back and I saw more of her, she had a long, crow-feathered cloak, and her raven hair was interspersed with braids of red hair. She introduced herself, and our relationship began. I eventually did the research, and learned that Macha was often called Macha of the Red Tresses. I found that very interesting, and it was verification that I was not crazy. As our relationship deepened, she guided me to the life path I'm on, sometimes in a less than gentle manner when I was not listening to the signals. Although she embodies many powers, I initially called on her as a patron of air. We will learn the element air is of the mind, and deals with speaking, communication, writing, teaching, and learning, all things I am dedicated to do in this life. Macha is also a dark goddess, and much of my healing work, personally and in helping others, is about facing the shadow and fear, to move on in life. Her sphere of influence is the area I am most happy and successful working in. She is my patron, and I've become her agent in this world to help others.

As you explore the path, a particular goddess or god might pick you to work with intensely. You could have one in mind, but often what you desire and what is your path can be two different things initially. You often don't pick, but the gods pick for you. Before I "met" Macha, I wanted to be a rock star and entertainer. My college degree is in music. I had no conscious desire to teach, write, or heal, but life prepared me for it anyway.

Don't worry about finding a patron. Your patron will be known to you when the time is right. I simply explain it so you will know it better as it happens. I wish someone had explained it better to me as my process unfolded.

RELIGIOUS WORSHIP

The last topic of the gods that worried me when I started was worship. I had just left a self-sacrificing, bow-your-head-in-shame form of religion, and didn't want to put myself in a subservient position to anyone or anything again. So the idea of worshiping the gods seemed strange to me. Did I even want to? Did I have to worship them to be a witch? Again, this depends on who you ask and how you define worship. I say, ask the gods themselves, but until you feel comfortable doing that, here are my thoughts on the matter.

In modern paganism, I don't think worship comes attached with any sense of shame or self-degradizing. To me, it means acknowledgement and partnership. These archetypal beings exist now, have existed, and will continue to exist. At times they were acknowledged and worshipped in a variety of ways. In other times, they were mostly forgotten by all but the most visionary and artistic of society. They do not need us to survive, but when we partner with them, the gods are able to more effectively make changes in our consciousness and in the world for the better. Through them we are able to acknowledge life, and our own energy, on many levels of existence. Without them, we often see life on just the Earth plane, and do not recognize a higher divinity in any form.

Worship is the act of inviting the gods into your life, acknowledging their life force as the cycles of the Sun, Moon, and Earth change, and celebrating in their love. It's not about sacrifice or martyrdom. Many try to make offerings in some of the same way as the ancients—offering fruit, wine, water, incense, and the like. That is fine and a wonderful sign of respect. I do that, too, but lately I've been more about offering my time, my love, and my service to the world in honor of the goddesses and gods. That is simply where my worship takes me.

EXERCISE 6

Meditation with the Goddess and God

1. Start Exercise 2: The Inner Temple, conjuring the great World Tree and standing before it.

2. Hold the intention to visit with the Goddess and God. We will climb the roots down into the land of the ancestors and power beings, to meet one deity, and then climb the branches up to the sky realm, to meet the second deity. Reach out and touch the tree, feeling the bark, and through your touch, place your intention to visit the Goddess and God below and above.

3. Look for an opening in the roots that will lead to the Underworld. This opening will probably be different than the one you used to find your inner temple.

4. Enter the passageway and spiral down the tunnel into the Underworld, the realm of the divine ones. The land is dark and vast, yet not fearful, perhaps like a primordial ancient forest, seemingly illuminated from within. You feel the great power of this land.

5. Before you is an illuminated path, inviting you deeper into the Underworld. This path will lead you to a goddess or god who is correct for you at this time. Follow it.

6. Stay on the path, but notice all things to your left and right. Notice the plants of the Underworld. Do you recognize any? Notice the trees. They seem to whisper their power. Look for any animals that cross your path, or watch you from afar. An animal could even guide you on the path for a while. Notice and remember everything.

7. The path winds through the Underworld, by rocks and hills, rivers and streams. Look ahead, and follow the path as you are guided. You enter deeply the lands of power.

8. Soon you see the end of the path, and at the end, a divine being is waiting for you. Take notice of this one as best you can. What does the deity look like? What does it wear? What mannerism do you notice?

9. When you reach the end of the path, introduce yourself, as you would to an honored elder. Take this time to build a relationship. Ask the deity its name and culture. Ask any questions you have, about the divine, or about your life and personal issues. Be prepared to answer questions in return. Listen to every word. Watch every action. Everything has significance.

10. Once the exchange is complete, this divine one touches your forehead, giving you a blessing, and possibly a gift of some sort. Accept with love and grace, as a symbol of your new union and relationship. You can ask the deity for a symbol to evoke its power and presence in the world. Say your

farewells and follow your path back, unless the deity gives you another path to walk, a short cut leading back to the World Tree.

11. Make your way back to the roots and the tunnels of the World Tree. Notice if the Underworld has changed, or at least if your perception of it has, now that you have an ally in it. Do any more animals, plants, or trees catch your notice at this time?

12. When you are back at the tunnel, climb your way back to the surface, but instead of coming out at the trunk, continue onward, spiraling up, higher and higher, until you reach the Upperworld. You come upon the heavenly lands, a bright and sunny land, filled with clouds and green fields, a veritable paradise, the land of milk and honey. You are filled with a sense of peace and awareness in this place.

13. Before you is a warm and inviting path, taking you to the heart of the Upperworld. This path will lead you to a god or goddess who is correct for you at this time. Follow it.

14. Stay on the path, noticing all things to your left and right. Notice the land, plants, and animals of the Upperworld. What do you recognize? Feel the breeze. Hear the birds. An animal may cross your path, or even guide you for a while. Notice and remember everything on the path.

15. The path wanders through the Upperworld, through fields and springs, orchards and hills. Look ahead and follow the path as you are guided. Enter the lands of enlightenment.

16. As you reach the end of the path, a divine being is waiting for you. Take notice of this bright and shining one as best you can. What does the deity look like? What does it wear? What do you notice about it?

17. Introduce yourself to the divine one as you would a respected and well-loved member of your family. Take this time to converse and commune.

Ask the deity its name and culture. As before, ask any questions you have and listen carefully to all that is said.

18. When your time is done, the shining one touches your body, giving you a blessing and perhaps a gift or message of some kind. Accept all with love and grace to mark your connection together. You can ask the deity for a symbol to evoke its power and presence in the physical world. Say your goodbyes and follow the path back to the World Tree, unless the divine one shows you another path back.

19. Follow your way back to the branches of the great tree and climb back down, entering the tunnel and into the trunk of the tree, spiraling down to the base of the trunk. Exit the tree and stand before it, thank it for safe passage. Thank the Goddess and God for all blessings.

20. Step back through the screen of your mind's eye and let the World Tree gently fade from view.

21. Return yourself to normal consciousness, counting up, giving yourself clearance and balance. Do any necessary grounding.

Typically one being is a goddess and another is a god. Usually the Underworld figure is darker in imagery, and often a goddess, but not always. Likewise the Upperworld figure is usually a light or sky deity, and often a god. But that is not a rule. There are dark Underworld gods and light Upperworld goddesses. You could even get two gods or two goddesses, depending on your needs at this time. There is no right thing to get. Whatever you get is the most perfect thing for you at this time.

If either gave you a symbol to evoke their power, write it down immediately. The symbols are powerful forms of magick to connect with the divine. In Voodoo, such symbols are handed down as a part of the ritual tradition, and called *vévés*. Other traditions use symbolic evocations to summon spirits, angels, and deity.

THE NEXT STEP

At this point, you might not be sure what to think about the gods and goddesses. That's okay. In fact, it's perfectly normal unless you were raised in a polytheistic culture. I didn't know what to think, but I called upon the Goddess and God, simply and generically, without specific godforms, in my rituals and meditations because that is what I was taught. And there was a reason to it. As I made the evocations, they answered it in ways I could not have dreamed. As my spiritual view grew and widened, the Goddess and God, in their many faces and forms, have become a tremendous source of love, strength, and magick in my life. They reveal me to myself and walk with me, hand in hand, upon the path.

A popular saying in Wicca is "All goddesses lead back to the Goddess. All gods lead to the God." That's not to say all goddesses and gods are the same. They simply lead to the same fundamental divine truth. I hold this wisdom with me whenever working with someone of a different faith, be it another pagan tradition, or any of the mainstream religions. We all discover the mysteries in our own way.

HOMEWORK

- Complete Exercise 6. Record experience in your Book of Shadows. Continue to build a relationship with the many aspects of the Goddess and God.

- Start researching any deities you met in meditation, or any deities or cultural pantheons to which you are intuitively connected. Pick one culture to start with, and by the end of this year, have a strong background in the deities, myths, and images of the culture you resonate with. Research it not only with New Age or neopagan mythology books, but also traditional mythology books and direct translations of the myths. Get a wide perspective in your mythic quest.

- Continue journaling regularly.

1. *The Sandman: Kindly Ones.* Written by Neil Gaiman. DC/Vertigo Comics. New York, NY. 1996.

LESSON TWO
THE ELEMENTS

Everything is made up of the four elements—earth, air, fire, and water. The elements are the building blocks of reality. This is the cornerstone of many worldwide mystical traditions. But science cannot isolate the fire element in a rock. The scientist does not see the earth element in oxygen. The researcher finds no water in dry dust. And neither did I, until I opened my witch eyes.

As a child, I was drawn to the discipline of alchemy. My interest in fantasy and science-fiction books led to an interest in the age-old art of alchemy, the art of transmutation. Most books at my local library said the alchemists were medieval pseudo-scientists searching to transform lead into gold to get rich. The mystical arts of alchemy and astrology, rubbish to the scientific world at the time, led to the creation of logical, factual, linear chemistry and astronomy. The Dark Ages led to rationalism and science.

These historic authors missed the spiritual implications of the operation, and that the transformation to golden light, on a spiritual level, was far more important in the soul of the alchemist than in the laboratory. Most people misunderstood the true alchemist's goal. But in these alchemical works, I first came across the concept of the four elements. Alchemists, like many other mystics, believed that everything is made up of these four sacred elements. Everything. If you seek to transform something, you change the balance of the elements, and you have a new substance. Or, ideally, you have a new, more purified and refined person in a spiritual sense. And like those historians, in the light of logical, rational science, I thought the concept of four elements was rubbish. You couldn't prove it. In fact the evidence pointed that it was wrong. Science had proved the multitude of elements in the periodic chart—hydrogen, helium, carbon, and the like. So I started my pursuit of chemistry, biology, and physics to unravel the mysteries.

I had a yearning to understand the universe, and I thought I would find it in the scientific world. I found knowledge, but not understanding. The image of the old alchemists followed me. I left the rational world of science to pursue the intuitive worlds of art and music. I found expression, but not knowledge. It wasn't until I found myself in witchcraft, calling upon the four elements from the four sacred directions in ritual, did I understand just what they were all about.

The elements are not literal, quantifiable substances contained in all things, even though they are named after substances. The elements are immeasurable archetypal energies of creation. They can be felt and experienced, but not measured by our current scientific methods. Their names are symbolic for their nature. Other cultures have recognized these energies, but named them differently. The elemental energy of water is named water because it has qualities like water—cool and flowing, clearing, soothing, and filling the shape of what surrounds it. Likewise the other elements are named after symbols that correspond to their energy. In a general way, each element corresponds to a sphere of life and a state of existence. Earth is the physical realm. Water is the emotional, or what some call the astral realm. Air is the realm of the mind and thought. Fire is the realm of pure energy, the spark of the soul. Everything extends to these four planes of existence, in some manner, so everything is made from the four elements. The elemental model usually credited to the Greek philosopher Empedocles, who used the word *rhizai*, meaning "roots," to describe them, since collectively the four elements are the roots of our reality.

Each element contains its own blessings and gifts. Each contains its own challenges and fears. Working with the elements is the path of balance, because you balance these gifts and challenges in the way that uniquely suits you. The elements are mysteries to be explored and experienced directly. Only through your relationship with them do you grow. As everything is created on these four planes, as you partner with the four powers, you become more clear, conscious, and powerful in your personal creation. This creation is the heart of true magick!

ELEMENTAL REALMS

The elements exist in everything we connect with in our world, but the elements also exist in a pure state, in what are often called the elemental planes or elemental realms. These realms are not someplace we can physically go, although certain landscapes are dominated by the energy of a particular element. These planes are energetic vibrations, places we cannot point to anymore than we can point to where the inner temple or astral plane is. They exist concurrently with all of reality, intersecting with it, yet in some space remaining centered and pure.

Collectively these planes are known together as the Plane of Forces, because through them, the forces of the universe are harnessed to create anything in the world. They are the forces of magick, and all magick workers use them, regardless of their conscious involvement with the element. The more conscious one becomes with the element, the more powerful and spiritual the magick becomes.

Each elemental realm embodies the energy of that element. Visionaries will experience that realm. Those connecting to the realm of fire could experience heat and smoke, see fire and light, feel energized and vitalized. Those visiting earth can feel solid, stone-like, dry like a rock or soil, and see trees, plants, stones, and crystals. Visitors to air feel the breeze, smell clean air, and are refreshed and awakened. If you work in the water realm, you feel cool, wet, soothed, and fluid. You just might see the ocean, lakes, rivers, or even be underwater. The realms are pure energy, but our senses put the energy in terms we can understand and relate to, and relay that information on a conscious level. We know that water is a symbol for the energy of the water realm, but since we don't process energy directly, feelings, visions, and sensations associated with water are the best way our brains can process and translate the energy.

For the ease of understanding, most traditions place the elements, and the doorway to the elements, in the four sacred directions, corresponding to the cardinal points north, east, south, and west. These points become anchors in our sacred circle. As the realms exist between worlds, so does the circle of the witch.

When meditating, I envision the great World Tree that leads to the realms above and below, and to the inner temple, with four mighty branches, and each branch leads to one of the four realms, aligned with the cardinal direction. I simply climb that branch to find the energy I need to partner with for my journey. The tree trunk exists in the center. I also envision my inner temple at the center of my tree, at the center of my universe, and in the temple are four different doors leading to the four elemental planes of existence.

A great debate exists among traditions as to the "right" or "true" way of laying out the elements with the directions. From my experience, many tribes and traditions put the elements in a variety of ways. Some people get stuck into the idea that only one way is right. I've been to public circles when participants were aghast that an element was called from the "wrong" direction. It was wrong simply because they learned it another way. As we just discussed, they literally are not in a physical direction, so as long as you have all four and put each one in a different direction you are going to be fine. Each tradition has a reason why they place a direction and element together, often relating to the original culture and setting of the tradition, as well as personal style and preferences of the founders. So if the traditional directions I discuss for each element are different from what you learned, feel free to experiment and substitute. Once you have a strong understanding, foundation, and experience, never fear experimentation if you are intuitively called to do something different.

ELEMENTAL BEINGS

So why do these elemental realms exist? They are the "homes" for the elemental beings. These entities consist of pure energy, pure consciousness in the energy of a particular element. They embody the element, and regulate its function in the physical world. Like the Native American story, they are also "little dreamers," in charge of a specialized section of creation.

Most traditions call them elementals, though there is a lot of disagreement to exactly what an elemental is in the New Age world. Some use the word "elementals" synonymously with nature spirits, faeries, and what have been called devas. But in my experience, these are all different things, and energetically more complicated than pure elementals. An elemental embodies one element, while the spirit of a tree, plant, or stone contains more than just one element.

The concept of the elementals is found in many cultures, and the images of them are found in folklore. The most popular in Western magick come from European folktales. Earth elementals are in the form of little men (and sometimes women) called gnomes or dwarves. The air elementals take the form of sylphs, winged, airy, faery-like creatures, but not necessarily the same beings referred to as the faeries or fey folk in myth. The water elementals are called undines, envisioned as mermaids and mermen. Fire elementals are called salamanders, pictured like tiny red lizards. A salamander is said to exist in the heart of every flame.

These common conceptions of the elements are not the only way they appear. Some view them all as faery-like creatures, but consisting of the element itself, creating fire faeries, water faeries, and so on. Others see men and women made of the element and its colors. Earth could be a woman in brown or green robes, with a stony complexion and heavy, sturdy, earthy features. Fire brings a red-haired, fair-skinned man in red or orange. Air brings a thin, lithe, and wispy man in blue or yellow. Water brings a curved woman in sea blue or green. These elemental beings often manifest through animals forms. The animal is usually associated with the element, such as fish for water, or birds for air. Elementals can even take an angelic form. At their purest form, elementals appear as balls of light, or spinning vortexes of energy, with little shape and form. Animals, angels, and other shapes serve as guardians and guides to elemental energy.

Why do the elementals exist? Why do they regulate this energy? What's in it for them? All these questions I have asked myself from time to time. But why do birds fly, or plants photosynthesize? It's their nature. It's what they are made to do. And the same can be said for elementals. Certain mystics say the elements come when called upon by witches and magicians because they are forced to, because we know the magickal words to command them. Others say the elementals are learning just as much as they are giving from the experience. Each consciousness wants to master an element, and then move to another element. Once all the elements are mastered, reports vary as to their "reward" but it could be transformation into a nature spirit, faery, dragon, angel, or human soul, depending on who you ask. Many I've talked to believe elementals are angels or faeries before they get their wings. I think it's a cute idea, but I don't know how true it is, and never got a straight answer from an elemental or faery to know for certain.

ELEMENTAL GUARDIANS

Traditions and mythologies often describe a hierarchy in the elemental realm, suggesting some elementals travel from realm to realm in a linear fashion, while others ascend to greater mastery in the realm itself. At the pinnacle of these realms are beings classified as elemental queens or kings. The Norse named them for the four dwarves who hold up the four corners of the world. The Egyptian viewed them as the four sons of the god Horus. The Greeks had the kings of the four winds. Traditions of modern Celtic Wicca gives us a ruler for each element, although their names sound strikingly Middle Eastern to me.

In ritual, witches and magicians call upon elemental guardians, those with power or dominion in each elemental realm, to open a gateway to that realm and bring in exactly the right amount of energy for the ritual. Sometimes called the guardians, the watchers, the watchtowers, or the guardians of the watchtowers because they maintain the balance between elements, these beings have dominion over the given elemental sphere they maintain.

Imagine the guardians control the doorway, or more appropriately, a lens, and only let the perfect amount of energy into the sacred space, to blend with the others. They prevent too much or too little coming in, as well as moderate the rate so it is not overwhelming for the magick at hand. In the end, the elemental guardians are the partners of the witch. They are our partners of creation. Without them, magick can still work, but it is not as powerful, nor as moving a spiritual experience. Through the elemental guardians and the ritual of the magick circle, we awaken all aspects of ourselves— physical, mental, emotional, and spiritual.

The image and name we invoke for the guardians varies among individual practitioners. Some plainly, but effectively, call to the "Guardian of the Watchtower of . . . ," the given element needed, or simply "I call upon the element of . . . ," not bothering with formal names and titles. Other will call upon a specific elemental form, such as, "I call upon the element of earth and the gnomes," or a specific king/queen from the traditions above.

Quite common is associating four archangels to the four elements. Each is associated with a direction and element, and said to guide the elemental king or queen. I shied away from angels initially, because I found the concept too Christian. As a witch, I feared that something "bad" would happen to me, at least before I knew better, because I wasn't Christian but I was calling on angels. But when you truly study the esoteric lore, the concept of angels, like the elements, are found in many cultures, predate Judeo-Christian mythology, and often look nothing like our cute cherub greeting card angels. These are beings of power and guardianship in the universe, created and charged by the divine mind, the Great Spirit, not necessarily Yahweh or Jehovah exclusively. Angels belong to no one culture or religion, but to the universe and anyone can call on them without fear.

Tribal and shamanically oriented witches typically call upon animal spirits that resonate with a particular element. These animal spirits are not necessarily elementals, just as the angels are not just elementals, but they both resonate with the elemental realms. They act as spiritual guides and guardians to the element, and harness the power of the element in ritual. In meditation, they act as practical, down-to-earth examples of that element in action in both the physical and spiritual worlds. If we can relate to an animal rich in a particular element, we begin to understand and relate to that element on a whole new level. Of all the guardians, I have found animal spirits to be the easiest to connect with since most people, regardless of prior metaphysical education, feel a connection with animals.

My favorite elemental guardians are the gods and goddesses themselves. Some deities resonate with a particular element, either embodying that element, or an animal associated with that element. Earth mothers, corn mothers, sea gods, sun gods, and sky gods have obvious elemental connections, as well as crow goddesses, raven gods, horse goddesses, snake goddesses, stag gods, and goat gods. If there is such a hierarchy in the elemental realms, as suggested by many occultists, and the archangels guide the kings and queen, then to me, the deities of each element, the archetypal beings, have dominion over the angels. Their energy is more broad and all encompassing, where an angelic ritual has a certain specific vibe, a certain energy, just as an animal ritual does.

Calling upon the gods as a way of opening a connection to the elements is very powerful, but some traditionalist witches feel such an evocation is disrespectful. A god is much more vast in scope than an element, and calling upon them to act as elemental guardians is trying to limit them. I understand the argument intellectually, but in my experience, it just doesn't pass. A sea god or goddess obviously has not only a connection, but authority over the realm of water. That's not limiting. It's simply resonating with their individual nature. The divine is limitless, but seeks to partner with us in all ways. Disrespect is only created when one intends disrespect. If you feel this is disrespectful, then don't call upon the gods in this way, or I can suggest another image. Simply because you call upon a deity, it doesn't mean the individual god is solely acting as the elemental guardian. Like a good "boss" they might send an entity, with the god's authority, to do the actual work.

I know one of my favorite calls to the elements involves calling both a deity and an animal energy. There are many types of elemental quarter calls you will learn as part of the magick circle ritual. For now, you simply need to understand the element, and venture into each realm one at a time to make a personal connection.

ELEMENTAL TOOLS

Each of the four elements has an elemental tool or "weapon" to be used in ritual. These tools act as not only the symbol of the element in ritual and on your altar, but as a vessel and conduit for the elemental energy. They are primarily the cup or chalice for water, the blade for air, the wand for fire, and the disc, stone, or shield for earth. Some use the pentacle for earth, but it really represents all four elements, plus spirit.

Starting now, and as you study the elements, you will begin a quest for these tools for your altar. When you start the quest to build your altar, at first it seems like a practical job. You need these tools to perform the ritual. But symbolically, the quest means much more. You will find as you gather your altar, one, two, or even more tools will be a challenge to acquire. In this process, think about what each element represents. Think about your coming lessons and adventures in the elements, and your relationship with those areas of life. The quest reflects your challenges in life.

When you have difficulty getting the right chalice for your altar, it has nothing to do with a cup. It is all about your quest to know, understand, and experience the emotional realm, and the highest emotion, perfect love. The same is true for each element; they contain a quest to know them to truly be your allies in magick.

GATEWAYS TO THE ELEMENTAL REALMS

In ritual, the witch opens the gateways to the elemental realm, calling upon the guardian to bring the energy into the sacred circle. Through the use of several techniques, the witch's intent acts like a key, opening the lock between worlds and opening the gateway to individual realms.

Specific traditions have specific "keys." Eclectic traditions seem to use different "keys" unique to each practitioner and ritual. Those in a very traditional structure compare these gateway opening formulas to chemical formulas. If you do it exactly the right way, with the right words and gesture, the gateway automatically opens. This gives rise to the Hollywood movie idea of magick, where one can stumble across the right words and phrases and cast a powerful spell. Eclectic practitioners see their rituals more like cooking than chemistry. As long as you have the basics, you can feel free to be creative. The most important ingredient is intent. If you have the proper intent and energy behind your action, then it will work. Anyone can say magick words, but if they are not fueled by intent and focus, the magick won't go far. This is the true heart of magick.

Elemental gateways are opened through a combination of evocation, visualization, gesture, and tools. They are four techniques to open the space between this world and the elemental realm. Any combination of the techniques work for the eclectic witch, as long as you have a strong intention.

Evocation

To evoke a spirit simply means to call a spirit. Evocation is a statement or phrase made to call a spirit, in this case an element, to the ritual. There are many types of evocation. Sometimes your intention and saying something out loud or with your inner magickal voice is all that is needed to open a gateway.

Elemental evocations are also named quarter calls, because each element is aligned with one of the four cardinal directions. Through your subsequent work, you will learn to use your evocations to evoke, or re-create, the feeling each element gives you and images you associated with it, aiding you with the other techniques to open gateways. Ultimately the techniques are not individual, but a synthesis to open the way.

Quarter calls have a basic structure consisting of calling to the direction you face, the element, and then the elemental guardian or guardians. In witchcraft, we usually end the quarter call with the phrase "Hail and welcome." In a group setting "Hail and welcome" would be repeated back by the group. It is important to release and close the gateways the same way you called them, to keep the balance of the energy. Here is a basic quarter call pattern, using animal spirits as guardians.

To the north, I call upon the element of earth, and the great Stag. Hail and welcome.

To the east, I call upon the element of fire, and the proud Lion. Hail and welcome.

To the south, I call upon the element of air, and the wise Crow. Hail and welcome.

To the west, I call upon the element of water, and the loving Dolphin. Hail and welcome.

The gateways are closed in a similar manner, following the same pattern established with the quarter calls. Closing is often called banishments, farewells, or devocations.

To the north, I thank and release the element of earth, and the great Stag. Hail and farewell.

To the west, I thank and release the element of water, and the loving Dolphin. Hail and farewell.

To the south, I thank and release the element of air, and the wise Crow. Hail and farewell.

To the east, I call thank and release the element of fire, and the proud Lion. Hail and farewell.

Like the circle of Exercise 3, we start in our power place, usually north, and go around clockwise, or deosil. To release, we begin again in the power place, where we started, and move counterclockwise, or widdershins. This is simply one example of a quarter call. You will have the opportunity to write your own calls, with your own guardians and poetry.

Visualization

Visualization simply means to visualize the gateway opening in your mind's eye. This focus for your intention is very powerful, but some practitioners unfortunately feel it is the only way, and others get discouraged if they feel they don't have strong visualization abilities. See the colors associated with the element. See the element itself. See the guardian you have called, using all your imaginative skills. Co-create the image with your elemental allies. You may have an idea that a particular guardian will look a certain way, but if you are open to partnering with it, it may appear in a new way to open your consciousness to a new aspect of it.

Several traditions use symbols to stand for the elements. You can visualize the symbols in the colors associated with the elements when you open each gateway. The first symbols are alchemical symbols associated with the elements. When you place all the triangles together, they form a six-pointed star. Most often associated with Judaism, the hexagram is a sign of balance of all polarities and elements, and a symbol associated with the heart chakra and perfect, unconditional love. Used in Hinduism to represent the union of Kali and Shiva, Goddess and God.

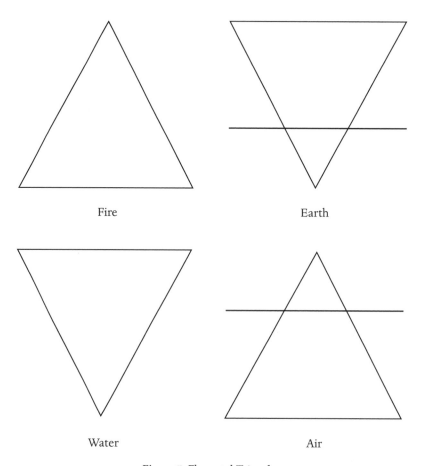

Fire

Earth

Water

Air

Figure 7: Elemental Triangles

The second set of symbols are the Hindu tattvas. Although found in much esoteric lore, they are not a traditional part of Wicca, though many Wiccans use them.

FIRE
red triangle

AIR
blue circle

WATER
silver crescent

EARTH
yellow square

SPIRIT
black egg

Figure 8: Tattvas

Covens will often build group visualizations, so everyone is focusing on the same image, quality, or symbol. This combined focus makes the process more powerful and gives the coven a method to create a stronger sense of group consciousness.

Tools

As each element has a primary tool associated with it, you can hold up that tool when opening the gateways and calling the quarters. Some have a secondary tool, with a ritual action associated with it. When calling earth, you can sprinkle salt or dirt on the ground. When calling fire, you can light a candle. When calling air, light incense, and when calling water, pour a bowl of water on the ground. Formal traditions often have a candle of each element in the four quarters of the circle, which is then lit when the element is called. The wand or blade can be used to draw certain symbols in the next section on gesture. In the traditions I learned, a *peyton*, or ritual pentacle, is held aloft when facing the direction. If you don't have a peyton, you can spread open your fingers as a five-pointed star. Altar tools will be covered in detail in Lesson Five.

Gesture

Gesture is the use of ritual movement, through the hands, arms, and body, to open the gateways. Myth and folklore is filled with magickal hand gestures to cure and curse. Gesturing to open the gateways may be the origin of such ritual tales.

Gestures can be simple, such as holding up your receptive hand to open and holding out your projective hand to close. I often like to hold up both my arms, like a crescent Moon upturned, and invite the element into the space, opening my heart. When I release, I often bow in respect.

More intricate traditions have more intricate keys to open the gateway. And they are powerful techniques, though their technical aspects often scare an aspiring witch. I suggest you learn these techniques, in case you ever need them, or are with a group that uses them, so that you will know them and their power.

The most simple gesture uses spirals. The opening spiral uses the receptive hand, starting in the center and moving out clockwise, about three times. The releasing spiral uses the projective hand, starts at the edge and moves counterclockwise to the center. Some traditions reverse these gestures or directions, but this is the method I find most effective.

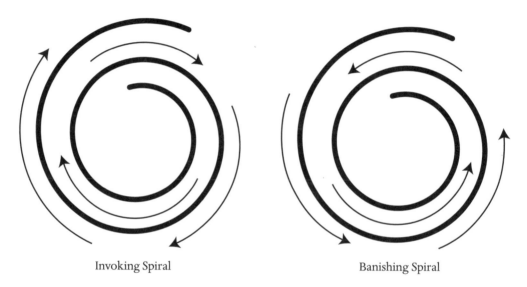

Invoking Spiral   Banishing Spiral

Figure 9: Spirals

The next ritual gesture to open the gateways is through the use of pentagrams, or five-pointed stars. Pentagrams, five-pointed stars, and pentacles (five-pointed stars in a circle) are much maligned symbols by the modern world, usually associated with Satanism. The pentacle is an ancient magickal symbol found in many cultures. This system of ritual is brought into modern Wicca via the ceremonial and Hermetic traditions of

Western magick, but since both systems are so complementary, many witches find this material a basic part of their training.

Found in an apple transversely cut, the five-seed star symbolizes health and knowledge. Apple is the fruit of the otherworld, Avalon. The five-pointed star is associated with the Greeks, as well as Solomon and the three magi who visited Jesus' birth.

Flowers with five petals are sacred to the goddesses of love. When taking a course with flower essence practitioner David Dalton, founder of Delta Gardens, he presented the five-petaled flowers in relationship to this symbol. Both the flowers and the star is a gateway. Some are used to bring energy in, and the corresponding herbs bring in healing life force. Such pentacles would be the opening gestures. Others send energy out, or block it. These pentacles close gateways and protect. Corresponding herbs are hallucinogenic, sending part of our life force out, or poisonous, sending all life force out. Our flowers correspond with our rituals, truly showing as above, so below.

The pentacle is a symbol of the Celtic goddess the Morgan, drawn upon a warrior's shield in blood red to honor her. The pentacle is also called the Druids' foot or witch's cross. In the Middle Ages, witches were said to use the pentagram for protection, much like Christians make the sign of the cross. The self-blessing was from the left breast, brow, right breast, left shoulder, right shoulder, and then again at the left breast, completing the star. The fact the star is drawn continuously, with no breaks, is magickally significant. Magicians believe the unity of the line creates a symbol of protection, to block and confuse harm, much in the same way Celtic knots are used for protection.

The way each star is drawn is the key, the pattern, for opening a particular gateway. Again, the opening, often called invoking pentagram, is usually done with the receptive hand and the closing, or banishing pentagram, uses the projective hand. Many don't care about the hands, and use the dominant hand for all actions.

Figure 10: Basic Invoking (top) and Basic Banishing (bottom) Pentagrams

These two pentagrams are the basic keys, the skeleton keys if you like, to open all the gateways if you have the proper intent. A more complicated system exists, using different pentagrams for each individual element. The pattern is based in the elements associated with each point of the pentagram. Earth and air are paired together on the left, and water and fire on the right. Spirit is the top point. If you memorize this pattern, you will have an easier time remembering all these pentagrams.

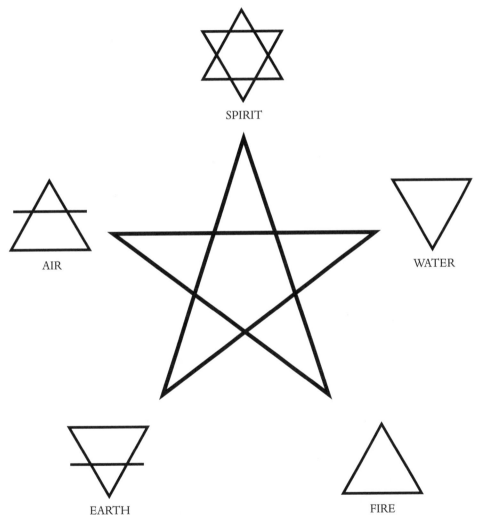

Figure 11: Elemental Pentagrams

To perform an invoking pentagram, pick the point away from the element you seek to invoke, and draw the pentagram with the first stroke moving toward the element. To banish, start at the elemental point, and move backwards from the way you invoked.

Figure 12: Invoking and Banishing Pentagrams

Most traditions use five strokes. Some repeat the first, giving six strokes in all. I've found it doesn't really matter. Both traditions work, as long as your intent is clear. Some even make it a full pentacle, with a clockwise circle to invoke and counterclockwise circle to banish.

Notice how in the first pair, the basic pentagrams, that the basic invoking pentagram is really the fire invoking pentagram. The basic banishing pentagram is actually the earth banishing pentagram. Fire is the highest and most spiritual of the elements, on the top of the ladder, and can be used for all. Earth, on the other hand, is the most dense of the elements, and when you banish it, you banish everything that is as dense or less dense than it. If you are familiar with ITOW, notice how the basic banishing/ earth banishing is also the protection pentagram, used to banish all harm on any level.

Ideally, in ritual, opening and closing the gateways will consist of a combination of these techniques. I always have an evocation, because I feel the spoken word is very important. I usually have a gesture of some sort, and a visualization. Sometimes I use tools, sometimes I just use my hands. But I always have a clear, heartfelt intent, and in the end, that's all you need.

Sometimes simple can be best. In a class of intellectuals, all doing their best to memorize these patterns with fancy evocations and tools, my student Deb knew that was not her way. So she simply faced the direction, put her hands to her heart, spread open her arms, and said the element's name. When she released, she did the same thing, but replaced the element's name with "Thank you" and blew a kiss. We were all awed at the beauty, simplicity, and honesty of her actions.

Often the opener will not feel the gateway in the group setting as much as the other participants. When we experiment with quarter calls and elemental gateways, often the one in front of the class feels nothing at first, when put on the spot in front of the class. But everyone else in the class feels something—a temperature change, a breeze, a vibration, or sound or vision. But the opener does not. So don't be discouraged if you don't feel anything initially. It will come.

Opening elemental gateways is surprisingly easy. The elements are a part of us, and hear our call already. They want to work with us. Sometimes we simply don't notice their presence. As you learn each element on its own, and build a relationship with them, the process will be stronger and more powerful for you. At first, you could feel slight sensations of temperature, energy, or vibration. Some perceive full visions. As your relationship grows, your awareness of these sacred energies grows as well.

Exercise 7

Opening Elemental Gateways

1. Start Exercise 3, creating a sacred circle space around you. Feel yourself in the center of this sacred space.

2. Face the north (or your power starting point) and simply say out loud or in your silent magickal voice: "To the north, I call upon the element of earth to be present. Hail and welcome." (Use whatever techniques you desire.) Take notice of any qualities, sensations, feelings, sounds, or images you perceive. How do they make you feel? (You can physically turn with each call, or if doing this all in your mind, simply mentally turn and bring your attention to each direction.)

3. Turn clockwise, to the east, and say: "To the east, I call upon the element of fire to be present. Hail and welcome." Again take notice of any changes you feel.

4. Turn clockwise again, to the south, and say: "To the south, I call upon the element of air to be present. Hail and welcome." Continue to take notice of any changes you feel.

5. Turn clockwise, to the west, and say: "To the west, I call upon the element of water to be present. Hail and welcome." Notice any changes.

6. Be in the center of the circle and notice how it feels differently from Exercise 3. Feel the power of the four elements in your space.

7. Release the circle, starting in the north and say: "To the north, I thank and release the element of earth. Hail and farewell."

8. Turn counterclockwise to the west and say: "To the west, I thank and release the element of water. Hail and farewell."

9. Turn counterclockwise to the south and say: "To the south, I thank and release the element of air. Hail and farewell."

10. Turn again counterclockwise to the east and say: "To the east, I thank and release the element of fire. Hail and farewell."

11. Complete Exercise 3, releasing the sacred circle.

12. Return yourself to normal consciousness, counting up and doing any necessary grounding.

If you already place the elements in different quarters, feel free to use your own placement. As we complete the four elements, we will discuss the ideas and merits behind the elemental directions. If you are already familiar with quarter calls, and have more intricate calls with which you are comfortable, you can substitute your own calls for these basic elemental calls.

€LEMENTAL HEALING

Once you recognize the balance of the elements within you, you begin to notice that when one element is out of alignment with the others, in your unique, personal relationship with them, you begin to have problems. Balancing the elements is a key component of all holistic forms of medicine, such as herbalism, Chinese medicine, and aryuveda, though they have different names and principles associated with the elements from the individual cultures where the holistic tradition derives.

Through intention and energy, you can use your relationship to bring balance to yourself. Try this balancing and healing meditation. It is very powerful and cleansing, not only healing us on the physical, emotional, mental, and spiritual realms, but also healing the connections each element has to the other three. I often use it to purify myself before rituals and healing work when I cannot do a traditional ritual bathing. It works just as effectively.

EXERCISE 8

Elemental Cleansing Meditation

1. Start Exercise 1: Entering an Altered State to get into your meditative mind-state.

2. Call upon the element of fire to heal and balance your soul. Feel yourself engulfed in flame, surrounding your body. The flame does not cause pain, but consumes your self-image, leaving you as pure light and energy. Thank the energy of fire.

3. Call upon the element of air to clear and heal your mind. Feel a breeze move through your energy, sweeping away any smoke or ash, transforming you into a clear, crystalline, hollow body, filling with the air energy. You are clear, open, and free. Thank the energy of air.

4. Call upon the element of water to heal your heart and astral body. Feel the tides come in slowly, building into waves that start to wash over your body, filling you with water. Feel the tide peak and quickly wash away. Thank the energy of water.

5. Call upon the element of earth to heal your body and bring balance. Feel the ground beneath you, and feel as if a giant quartz crystal point grows up out of the ground, around you, engulfing you, as its point forms at the top of your crown and its vertical axis is parallel with your spine. Feel the energy of the earth rise up through your body, from the crystal, starting at the base of your spine and moving up your body, coming out like a bolt of lightning from the point of the crystal, into the sky. Thank the energy of earth.

6. Feel yourself perfectly balanced and healed as the crystal melts away, leaving you centered.

7. Return yourself to normal consciousness, counting up and doing any necessary grounding.

When another is in need of healing, call upon your healing spirit guides for aid and protection and then try guiding them through this meditation, or visualize them going through it as you evoke each element to bring cleansing, balance, and healing to the recipient, for the highest good, harming none.

ASTROLOGY AND THE ELEMENTS

You already contain and embody all the elements within you. You have a body, earth; a mind, air; emotions, water; and a soul, fire. You exist within these four realms already, but one may prove more of a challenge, or offer a strength. One way of determining what element is offering both challenge and strength is through astrology.

Astrology is the study of the planets and zodiac, and how their movement corresponds with energy on Earth. Astrology works through the Principle of Correspondence: "As above, so below." Patterns repeat themselves endlessly, and by studying the pattern of the sky when you were born, you gain insight to the patterns and energies imprinted upon you and influencing you for your entire life.

Witches often study astrology. The movement of the Sun, Moon, and even other planets affects our celebration and ritual as much as the change of seasons. In fact, the change of seasons corresponds with astrology. Everything does. Spellcraft, crystals, herbs, and all forms of magick relate to astrology. Through understanding it, you can better understand your world, the craft, and yourself.

In our modern-day, pop psychology version of astrology, everyone is concerned with the Sun sign. The Sun sign is the zodiac sign the Sun occupied when you were born, and is the easiest information to look up since it takes about a month for the Sun to occupy a sign before moving to the next. Most people know their Sun sign, a few personality traits associated with it, but none of the deeper spiritual and magickal implications that go with it.

Each sign is assigned to an element. If you are born with the Sun in that sign, you are both working on the challenges of that element, and have gifts that element can offer. Out of the twelve zodiac signs, three signs are assigned to each of the four elements. But each one expressed that element differently.

Each one embodies one of the three forces discussed under the archetype of the Triple Goddess. The energy, also explained using "God" as an acronym, G = Generating, O = Organizing, and D = Destroying/Dissolving, is called cardinal, fixed, and mutable, respectively, in astrology. These three give the quality of the elemental expression.

Cardinal signs begin things and initiate. Fixed signs learn to sustain and organize. Mutable signs adapt and change. When the Sun is in a cardinal sign, a new season begins. When in a fixed sign, it is the middle of the season. When the Sun is found in a mutable sign, the season is ending, changing to the next.

Each sign can be described as a quality and element.

Aries:	Fire	Cardinal
Taurus:	Earth	Fixed
Gemini:	Air	Mutable
Cancer:	Water	Cardinal
Leo:	Fire	Fixed
Virgo:	Earth	Mutable
Libra:	Air	Cardinal
Scorpio:	Water	Fixed
Sagittarius:	Fire	Mutable
Capricorn:	Earth	Cardinal
Aquarius:	Air	Fixed
Pisces:	Water	Mutable

What element and quality are assigned to your Sun sign? You are spiritually working in those realms and can also have some of those gifts. If you accept the challenges in your life, they become transformed into assets. My Sun sign is Taurus, so I am working strongly with the earth element—the physical realm, as well as learning to sustain, to be dependable, solid, reliable, and practical. I've worked on those lessons hard, and although they still present challenges, I have gained traits of the fixed earth sign.

Reflect on your element by Sun sign, and what challenges and gifts it presents to you. Remember that this is simply the first stone in a deeper study of astrology. Sun sign astrology is powerful, but it is not everything. We all have all twelve signs and ten planets. What makes us different is not only the different placement, but how we personally choose to express these energies. Astrology corresponds with our life, but we always have a choice as to how to handle it.

The Fifth Element: Spirit

Plane: Divine

Direction: Center, above, and below

Colors: White, all colors

Sense: Hearing and knowing (the sixth psychic sense)

Gender: Androgynous

Nature: All natures—warm, cold, wet, dry

Season: All seasons

Zodiac Signs: All signs

Witch's Pyramid: Apex

Tarot Suit: Major arcana

Tools: Cauldron, pentacle

Elemental: All angelic and divine archetypal beings

Animals: Phoenix, Dragon, Sphinx

Ruler: None

Archangel: Metatron

Greek Wind: None

Norse Dwarf: None

Egyptian Son: None

Key Words: Unity, harmony, creation, unconditional love, centering, sacredness

Deities: The Great Spirit, Dryghten, the Creator/Creatrix, the divine mind, the One, the All, Godhead, Primal Spirit, Source, God/dess

Although we focus on the traditional four elements, most mystics recognize a fifth element along with the traditional four. The fifth element is unlike the other four. It is the primary force of creation, without the same polarities and dualities as the other elements. The traditional four spring from this fifth element. The four combine to create this element. It balances, rejuvenates, and galvanizes the other elements. The fifth element is the center of the four-quartered circle. It is the top point of the pentagram. The fifth element is spirit.

Witches call this element spirit, but as we use the word "spirit" for so many things, it has lost its meaning. Most sacred languages are precise. In English, we have one word for "love," but there are many types of love—romantic, family, parent/child, friendship, sexual, spiritual. Sacred languages have a different word for each nuance. English lacks that subtlety with the word "love," and with the word "spirit," among many others.

When we talk about spirit, we often think of our individual spirits. The element of spirit goes beyond our individual spirit. I think of the fire element as the spark of individual spirit, sometimes called the soul. The element of spirit is more than our individual souls. It is the sum of all souls, past, present, and future.

We associate the word "spirit" with the Creator, the divine mind, or Great Spirit, whatever name we choose. I was taught the word "Dryghten," said to be a Saxon word for "lord" but without the same gender associations. The Creator is the totality of all expressions of life, on every level, and in every element, so the element of spirit is something less than the Creative Spirit. So what is it?

Other traditions give it a specific name. Some call it akasha. The word "akasha" is most commonly used to refer to the Akashic Records, the great cosmic "library" or storehouse of information and wisdom from the past, present, and future, recorded in the spiritual element of akasha. It is the underlying patterns behind all of creation, and all the elements. Another word for the fifth element is ether. Ether is the subtle life force permeating and sustaining all levels of creation. The word "prana" is often used, along with other words to denote life force, such as "mana," "ki," "chi," and "numen." Prana is often associated with the element of air in Hindu traditions, since prana is often absorbed through breath and enhanced by *pranayama*, or breathing techniques. The Chinese cycle of the elements is a bit different from our Western magick, substituting the name metal for the energy we call air, and using the word "wood" for the fifth element. Out of earth, fire, water, metal, and wood, wood is the only living, cellular, growing element. Celtic Wiccans might refer to the fifth element as *nyu*. Alchemists call it the first matter, the creative chaos from which all things are manifested through the elements. If you removed all qualities from an object, yet left its essence, you would be left with only the spirit element. Another alchemical term is quintessence, coming from the root word of "five." The fifth element is said to be greater than the sum of its parts, and many use the formula $1 + 1 + 1 + 1 = 5$ to show its power. You could possibly use any of these words for the fifth element. I think of it as pure life force, before manifesting in the masculine, feminine, or other polarities.

Spirit is associated with the center, the core of any ritual. In witchcraft, we use many symbols, the center of the circle and the top of the pentagram being only two. Ideally, the entire pentacle, a symbol of all the elements combined, is an excellent symbol for spirit. The eight-spoke wheel is another symbol of spirit, representative of no one season or time, but all seasons and all times.

I also use the cauldron, both because I place it in the center, and because it is symbolic of the Goddess' womb of life, the center of life and creation, from where all things spring and all things return. Although traditionally thought of as a symbol of water, many myths and rituals use the cauldron with all four elements, so I place it in the center. Cerridwen's cauldron brews magickal potions. The Dagda's cauldron gives abundance. We burn spells, wood, and incense in our ritual cauldrons. The Celtic Gundestrup cauldron, a holy relic, depicts resurrection of warriors through the cauldron's power. The cauldron is all elements.

In the tarot, the twenty-two cards of the major arcana, the Fool's path of spiritual initiation, is the suit associated with spirit. Only through spirit do we reach enlightenment and awakening. The sense of spirit is hearing. Hearing not only the audible, but hearing with the inner ear, and opening to all the inner, psychic senses. It is the power of listening to ourselves and listening to our highest guidance. The gifts and challenges of the fifth element are the same—unconditional love. Only though this perfect love and perfect trust, through living it and embodying it, do we really live from the center, unified in balance with all the elements. Trials of spirit are the most difficult, but give the greatest rewards.

The animals associated with the fifth element are the mythic animals. Sometimes they are called upon in ritual, but often they are not unless they come of their own accord. The dragon is a mythological mix of all the elements. Living in the spiritual realms, it represents a balance of the elemental energies of the Earth. Wings for air, fire for breath, and serpentine, living in the earth or water, the dragon is the power of all elements. The Egyptian phoenix, the bird of resurrection is another symbol of spirit. Although called a bird of flame, it is a bird of spirit, resurrected from its own ashes and associated with the highest spiritual powers. Another Egyptian symbol, the sphinx, an amalgam of the four elemental "animals" found in many symbol systems—bull, lion, eagle, and man, is a powerful image of the fifth element, the wisdom of the mysteries.

The archangel Metatron, leader of all angels and archangels, is the archangel of spirit, though traditionally is not often called upon in the witch's circle. All the gods and goddesses manifest through spirit. Spirit radiates from the center of the diamond.

EXERCISE 9

Spirit Attunement

To attune to the element of spirit, take some time to sit and center yourself. You can be anywhere—inside, outside, in nature, in the city—anywhere. Spirit is everywhere. Just sit and be aware. Feel your body. Feel whatever you are sitting on. Feel your clothes up against your skin. Feel the temperature around you. Take in any smells around you as you breathe deeply. Some smells are so strong, it's as if you can almost taste them. Look around. Don't focus on any one thing, but let the light and color come into focus. Soak up the panorama of color. Listen. Take in all the sounds, near and far. You don't have to identify them, just take them in. Let your thoughts and feelings flow you through you. Don't focus on any one, or obsess on feeling the right thing. Just like a breeze or gentle wave, let it come and go. Notice that "you" are someone who has these senses, has a body, has thoughts, has feelings, but you are not these things. You are something more. You are spirit manifest through these elements. You are a part of them, and at the same time, beyond them, encompassing them. Feel spirit.

The spirit attunement can be long or short. It's up to you. Practice it every so often when you need to get in touch with your true self.

EXERCISE 10

Spirit Meditation

1. Start Exercise 7, casting a circle, and invite all four elements into the circle space. Initially count yourself into a deeper meditative state before casting the circle, and create the sacred space mentally, while sitting down. You can call the quarters in your silent, inner, magickal voice. Feeling the energies is more important than moving for this meditation.

2. Bring your attention to the center. Invoke the element of spirit with your inner voice, and feel a beam of crystal-white light descend down from the stars and through your circle, filling it. With the other four elements, it is as if you are in the center of a giant X or equal-armed cross. The beam of light descends down into the heart of the Earth.

3. Feel the element of spirit. Be aware of any sensations, images, or experiences you have.

4. When done, release the space by first releasing the element of spirit, grounding the beam of light into the Earth. Then release the space as you normally would, starting in the north, and moving counterclockwise and releasing the circle, just as you did in Exercise 7.

5. Return yourself to normal consciousness, counting up and doing any necessary grounding.

Use this exercise to start your relationship with the elements, starting with the element of spirit.

HOMEWORK

- Complete Exercises 7–10. Record experiences in your Book of Shadows.

- Research your astrological Sun sign. Although most astrology books write Sun sign descriptions as your personality type, think of it more as who you are learning to be in this lifetime. Think of your Sun sign as your teacher. What is the highest expression of this Sun sign energy? Meditate on its gifts and challenges to you.

- Continue journaling regularly.

Lesson Three
Fire and Water

Fire and water. Hot and cold. Dry and wet. Sun and Moon. Together, they are the primal polarity, the action of energy, movement, and creation. Both create the spark of life needed to manifest change, to make magick. All things need that initial charge of life force and all things take shape and form. They are partners of creation; intense, volatile, and mystical. Through the creative powers of these elements, we begin our journey.

Fire

Plane: Spiritual
Direction: East or south
Colors: Red, orange
Sense: Sight
Gender: Male
Nature: Hot and dry

Season: Summer or spring

Zodiac Signs: Aries, Leo, Sagittarius

Witch's Pyramid: To will

Tarot Suit: Wands

Tools: Wand, candle (some say athame, blade, or sword)

Elemental: Salamander, fire drake

Animals: Lion, Red Fox, Ram, Horse

Ruler: Djin

Archangel: Michael (when in the south)

Greek Wind: Notus (when in the south)

Norse Dwarf: Austri (when in the east)

Egyptian Son: Akeset, Horus' human-headed son (when in the south)

Key Words: Will, passion, power, light, intuition, desire, sexuality, spark, intensity, movement, drive, soul

Deities: Ares/Mars, Apollo, Helios, Hephaestus/Vulcan, Hestia/Vesta, Bel, Lugh, Lleu, Mabon, Brid/Bridget, Govannon, Goidniu, Goban, Luchtaine, Creidne, Oak King, Balder, Loki, Freya, Tyr, Volund/Weidland, Ra, Horus, Sekhemet, Set, Ptah, Shammash, Nusku, Tubal Cain

Fire is the least dense energy of the elemental realms. Its symbol, the burning flame, is not even a physical symbol, but a transitional state between matter and energy. Elemental fire represents just that, the transition between our resources and talent to action. Fire is the ability to apply our power in the world. Without it, we just have fuel. With the spark of fire, we can do something with that fuel. With the fire element, we apply our abilities to make a mark in the world.

Fire is our passion, where we put our energy, and as such, can be the most difficult to explain because everyone puts their energy in different places. When teaching or reading tarot cards, the fire suit, wands, are the hardest to explain because each person values different things, and places different amounts of energy into these arenas. This is why most books and teachers all have different explanations regarding fire. They are biased by their own personal fire tendencies.

Fire is often described as sexuality and sexual relationships. It is romantic passion and intensity. And it can be, but that is not its only expression. Fire can be your career, your ability to create in the world through business, finance, and opportunity. Most dynamic business people are strong with the fire element. Athletics, being active in the body, and the personal fire, the metabolism, are aspects of the fire element. Quite literally, our physical activities take the food we have as fuel and transform it into energy for action, like an internal furnace. Fire requires our movement, and our movement is provided by the chemical reactions of our body, releasing our inner metabolic fire. Fire is also creativity, the spark and drive not only to imagine, but also to manifest the inner images through image, word, song, or sculpture.

WILL AND WANDS

To the witch, fire is the power of will, the ability to direct your energy and attention to the universe to make magick. If you don't have control over your willpower, your magick will be ineffective. The tool of will is the wand. A wand is a long, slender tool, usually made of wood, metal, glass, or stone, used to focus our will. It magnifies the will of the user, catalyzing their intentions into reality, like a chemical reaction catalyzes food into energy, into action. Wands help magnify the energy needed to manifest something into a reality. You need the fire element to start the process.

In ritual, wands are used to cast the boundary of a circle, and to direct energy in general. I use wands for healing, and have several different wands depending on the situation. You can have more than one wand. Most witches have at least two. One of the two is the internal wand. Although tools are very magickal, and their substances help us partner with the spirits of the world and add to the energy of the ritual, we all carry a wand with us every day—our finger, hand, and arm. Traditional wands are the length of the middle finger to the elbow. We always have that length with us, and our hands are used to direct energy in all magickal traditions. The tool will help, but don't feel you can't do magick because you don't have your magick wand with you. Your will is the most important tool you need, and a good witch always has that.

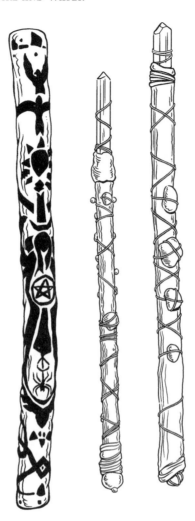

Figure 13: Wands

The material used to create a wand will "flavor" the energy. Think of the substance as a lens through which the will is magnified. Traditional wands are often made from the trees sacred to the Celts, found in the lore of the tree alphabet ogham. In particular, oak, ash, and hawthorne are favored, but I like willow a lot myself. Apple, birch, and pine are also favorites of my friends and covenmates. My first wand was bamboo, so you don't have to follow tradition. Wooden wands are often decorated with wire and crystals. Although gold and silver are ideal, most witches I know are on a budget, and make their wand of copper tubing, filled with crystals, stones, herbs, feathers or animal hair. Or, they can be kept hollow, and plugged with a cork, to store special magickal items and oils.

My mother's wand is a piece of driftwood decorated to look like a bird, one of her totems. The point is the beak, and she has two rubies for eyes. I have also used a quartz point as my wand that I find particularly powerful for healing spells. Wands can be commercially bought, or disguised as everyday tools. I've known witches who use their wooden kitchen spoon and mechanics who use their screwdriver. Wands can be as fancy or simple, durable or delicate as the owner. Use your imagination when questing for your own wand. And you can always have another as you grow and develop in your magick.

EXERCISE 11

Wand Quest

Begin a quest to find your wand. If you already have a wand, reflect on its meaning in your life, and how you have used it. If you don't, seek out your wand. If you intend to find it, and thereby exercise your will, you most assuredly will find it. You can buy, find, or make your wand. While on this quest, a branch might fall near you, or cross your path. The perfect materials can come your way. If you harvest the wood from a tree, or find it in nature, and even if you don't and buy it commercially, be sure to thank the spirit of the wood, metal, or stone for giving itself to be your teacher and tool. If you decide to make it, or further embellish it, research what materials you find. A good place to start with woods, metals, and stones is the correspondence section of this book in chapter 12, but look elsewhere, and see what other witches have to say on the subject. Keep in mind a wand does not necessarily have to be the traditional length. They can be bigger or smaller. I've used a small crystal point, and I have a large five-foot oak staff. Be open. Let it come, but apply your will and seek it out as well. Follow your intuition and you will find the right wand for you. Don't lose sight of the fact that it isn't just a quest for a wand, but a quest to express your divine will.

ATTUNING WITH FIRE

To truly work with the fire element, you not only have to find your will, but integrate the qualities of fire into your consciousness. Hermetic magicians describe fire as having the qualities of warm and dry. The warming principle is about bringing action. As things take on warmth, the energy gets moving. Molecules that are warmed, meaning energy is added to them, are stimulated. Ice molecules warmed become water. Water molecules become vapor. If you continue the warming process you get plasma, moving closer to the state of elemental fire. The drying principle is removing moisture, the liquid, nebulous quality of water. Moisture softens and slows. Fire removes it to be direct, clear, and dynamic. Summer, the season strongly associated with both warmth and dryness, is the season of fire. It is also the pinnacle of growing action in the green world, just prior to the harvest. This action is nature's will manifesting.

Sight is the sense associated with fire, since fire is the power of light and our ability to perceive visually is based on physical light. But fire is also the internal, spiritual fire. The fire of enlightenment and divinity, purifying us to higher states of consciousness.

EXERCISE 12

Fire Attunement

Before continuing on with the fire exercises, take time to attune yourself with the energy of physical fire, and explore the mysteries of the element through its representative. Light a fire and sit quietly in front of it. This exercise can take under ten minutes or as much as two hours, and done as often as you want. There are no rules for when and how to do it. The fire itself can be a campfire outdoors, or in a fireplace. Simply light a candle, or several of them. I like to make a large circle of candles and sit in the center.

Once you are in the presence of fire, truly feel its energy. Feel the heat. Feel the warmth and watch the light. Let your gaze go in and out of focus with the light. Watch the space around the flame. Feel the dryness, or if the fire is strong enough, how it draws the moisture out of you, its drying principle. Reach out and connect with the fire, and feel yourself become a part of it. Feel the fire in you. Make friends with the fire energy and honor it. You may notice the flames flicker with your thoughts and feeling. You might even be able to control the flame's intensity and direction with your will. Try it. Experiment. Play with this new friend and partner. When you are done, thank the fire before you extinguish it.

Now reflect on your own fire, your own awakened will. Where do you put your fire, your energy, your passion and enthusiasm? What part of your life is the fuel that keeps your inner fire burning? Do you have an inner fire? Is it a blaze or a flicker? Is it moderated and refined, or out of control? Ponder the fire within you. Gaze within your own embers and flames as you did in the exercise above. Then write about both experiences in your journal or BOS. How were they the same? How were they different?

Fire Guardians

The fire guardians are those who hold the keys to the gateway of fire. They open and close the gate in our circle, and regulate just the proper amount of fiery energy needed for any spellwork, meditation, or ritual. The medieval form of fire elementals are referred to as salamanders. Magickally, they can appear as red lizard-like creatures living inside a flame, as the source and center of the flame. To the medieval magicians, each flame has a salamander in it, and when the flame is extinguished, the salamander returns to the plane of fire. Sometimes larger images of salamanders are called drakes or fire drakes, with an almost dragon-like appearance. A tarot student of mine describes fire elementals as fire faeries, living in each flame. They are beyond form, and take shape according to our human ideas and expectations. They can be a human form entirely made of fire. According to legend, the king of the fire elementals is Djin, a term also used for certain Middle Eastern spirits, and where we get the popular reference to the wish-fulfilling genie.

Power animals of the fire element embody the aspects of will and drive. The animals associated with the fire signs of astrology—the ram of Aries, the lion of Leo, and the horse of Sagittarius—all exhibit their own fiery power in the world. I first learned to call the Red Fox for fire in my rituals. In some traditions, fire animals are all warm-blooded creatures who make their living on land (rather than flying, warm-blooded creatures).

The archangel attributed to fire is the angel of the south, Michael, most often depicted as a warrior with a flaming sword or spear. Some lore says he stands at the southern gates of Eden. He is the angel of protection and light, considered one of the most powerful of the archangels. His color is fire red.

The gods of the fire elements are those who naturally relate to the element of fire. Archetypal forms include the solar gods, such as Apollo, Helios, Ra, and Balder; war and destruction gods such as Ares and Set; smiths like Hephaestus, Volund, and Brid; and the gods of light and life. All the gods of fire are those who spark the will and inner light.

Through this work, you will journey to each of the four realms, starting with fire. In each, you will learn more about your connection to each element, and find guides and partners in the realm. Some may visit just for these meditations. Others will become your allies in later ritual and spellwork.

EXERCISE 13

Journey to the Realm of Fire

1. Start Exercise 2: The Inner Temple, conjuring the great World Tree, entering it and going to the inner temple.

2. Orient yourself in the center of your sacred space. You will notice four doorways around you. You may have never noticed them before, but they will be very clear to you now. Each of the doorways leads to a different elemental plane. Each one will be in a different color and have a different symbol on it for the element, such as the elemental triangles or tattvas. By its markings, find the doorway that leads to the realm of fire, and stand before it. Usually the fire doorway is oriented to your eastern or southern direction in the temple, but your inner temple is beyond direction in the physical world, so go to whatever door calls to you as fire.

3. Hold the intention to enter the realm of fire and in your silent, magickal voice, ask permission to open the door. You are asking permission of the highest aspects of yourself, and the realm of fire. (If you are familiar with your spirit guides from the work in ITOW, ask them to be present and guide you if you are unsure.)

4. If you get a yes response, open the door of fire. It can open normally or melt away. If you know the invoking pentagram of fire, you can use it as your key. Before you is a great swirling ball of fire, filling the doorway and beyond. Feel the heat rush over you. Hear the crackling flame. The ball of light swirls into a tube, a tunnel of pure flame. You know you can enter it safely with your own fiery essence, and you begin to walk into the tunnel of fire.

5. Your skin begins to tingle with the warmth, and you may feel a sweat break. Move slowly, one step at a time, truly attuning with elemental fire. The heat and light refine you, burning away all fear and tension. The fire brings you back to your essence, your passion and vitality, burning away all that does not serve your will.

6. As you move deeper and deeper into the tunnel, you lose sight of the inner temple and find yourself entering the light and the end of the tunnel, leading you to the realm of fire. Take a look around this fiery landscape, with burning trees and bushes, mountains of volcanic glass and ash. You are completely safe and in tune with the fire element. This is the land of fire salamanders, drakes, djin, and fabled cities of brass.

7. Before you is a path, taking you deeper into the realm of fire. Follow the path. Take notice of any animals you see along the way, and any plants on the path. Fiery, sharp, and spicy plants are the herbs of fire.

8. At the end of the path is a figure, your personal guide to the element of fire. It could be an elemental being, animal, deity, or perhaps angel, there to guide you on the path of fire. Introduce yourself, and ask the guide its name and function. Follow this guide, and receive what your guide has to offer. Since sight is the sense of fire, your guide may not speak much, but

show you things in pictures. Take this wisdom in, and ask any questions you have.

9. Ask your guide upon whom shall you call as your guardian of fire in ritual. Sometimes it is the guide itself, but often the guide will point you to a deity or other being of power.

10. Your guide will lead you back to the tunnel of fire and bid you farewell. Thank your guide for this time and knowledge. Know that you now have a link in the realm of fire. The guide may give you a gift to inspire your will and passion, or give you a spark of flame to carry within you.

11. Return through the tunnel of fire, spiraling through the heat and flame. Come back to the inner temple, and close the gateway of fire as you opened it. Orient yourself in the temple. If you have a gift from the land of fire, you can put it in your temple space if you desire.

12. Return back through the World Tree tunnel, and stand at the base of the tree. Thank the World Tree. Step back through the screen of your mind's eye and let the World Tree gently fade from view.

13. Return yourself to normal consciousness, counting up, giving yourself clearance and balance. Do any necessary grounding.

Exercise 14

Invoking/Banishing Fire

Although anyone can call the quarters and elements at any time, there is a special relationship that develops with each element if you build a bridge to it internally first. Many people go "knocking" on the doors of the elements, asking and expecting help, but few actually take the time to seek allies in the elemental realms and work on using the element in their inner consciousness in a healthy manner first, before directing it toward spellwork. Once you have friends, allies, or at least "contacts" in these elemental realms, you can knock on their metaphysical door, and receive much more conscious and loving aid in your craft. So now that you have taken the time to introduce yourself to the fire realm, and enter it, you can more effectively open a gateway to the fire realm in our world.

Start by creating a quarter call to fire. Decide how you would like to learn to invoke and banish the elements. It is very similar to Exercise 7, but we are going to focus on one element at a time.

First decide what you want to say. Here you can express your own voice. My first quarter calls started out very simple, but became more elaborate and poetic as time went on, needing to be memorized. Now I just speak from the heart and don't have a lot of things preplanned other than deciding on the direction, element, and guardian to call. The poetry flows spontaneously. It's often good to state why you call them—to protect, guide, to aid in magick. Here are some examples for you to use, or use as inspiration for your own calls:

> **To the east, I call the element of fire. I call the mighty Ram to join me in the circle and aid in this magick. Hail and welcome.**

> **To the south, I call upon the element of fire, warm and dry. I call upon archangel Michael, keeper of the flaming sword. Michael, bring your guidance and protection. Hail and welcome.**

> **To the south, I call upon the element of fire and the salamanders, the heart of the flame. I call upon the king of fire and the warm southern wind, Notus. Bring your sparks of spirit and flames of passion to this place that is not a place and this time that is not a time. Hail and welcome.**

> **To the east, I call upon the element of fire. I call upon the great Red Fox. I call upon Lord Lugh of the Long Arm. Please bring your warm blessings upon this work. Guide and guard us in this circle. Hail and welcome.**

The releases would echo a similar style.

> **To the east, I thank and release the element of fire. I thank the mighty Ram for this aid. Hail and farewell.**

> **To the south, I thank and release the element of fire. I thank the archangel Michael, and his flaming sword. Hail and farewell.**

To the south, I release the element of fire and the salamanders. I thank the good king Notus for his aid. Hail and farewell.

To the east, I thank and release the element of fire. I thank the great Red Fox and the good god Lugh for their aid and blessings. Hail and farewell.

My student Victoria punctuates her quarter calls with "Hail, honor, and welcome" and "Hail, honor, and farewell" instead of the traditional closings. She feels the aspect of honoring is important, though it does tend to surprise people when she leads group rituals if they are not familiar with her style. Just because a format is traditional doesn't mean it is for you. Change it to suit your own beliefs and creativity.

Once you complete your evocation, decide if you will be using any specific visualizations for the call. You can visualize the element itself, its symbol, or the guardian. If you met the guardian in your journey, you will have a more vivid image to call upon.

Do you plan on using tools? If so, what? For fire, you can use a wand, candle, or hold a peyton for all four elements. If you are not using a tool, are you going to use a more elaborate ritual gestures, such as the basic invoking/banishing pentagrams, specific elemental pentagrams, or spirals? You don't have to use all these techniques, but find the ones that resonate with you. Then put them together. Write it out if needed, and practice both invoking the element, feeling the energy, and then releasing and banishing it. Notice the shift in your energy, and the room. Build your relationship with the fire element and your ability to easily open and close the gateway. Record your experiences and experiments in your BOS.

WATER

Plane: Emotional (upper astral), astral, psychic
Direction: Usually west
Colors: Blue, aqua, sea green, black
Sense: Taste
Gender: Female
Nature: Cold and wet
Season: Fall

Zodiac Signs: Cancer, Scorpio, Pisces

Witch's Pyramid: To keep silent (some say "To dare")

Tarot Suit: Cups

Tools: Chalice, bowl, cauldron, shell

Elemental: Undines, sea nymphs, mer-people

Animals: All fish, in particular Trout and Salmon; Dolphin, Whale, Crab, Snake, and Eagle

Ruler: Niksa

Archangel: Gabriel

Greek Wind: Zephyrus

Norse Dwarf: Vestri

Egyptian Son: Qebhsennuf, Horus' hawk-headed son

Key Words: Emotion, love, empathy, feeling, healing, dream, unconscious, ending, death, ancestors

Deities: Poseidon/Neptune, Amphritite, Aphrodite/Venus, Lir, Manannan Mac Lir, Dylan, Cerridwen, Nuada, Danu, Freya, Aegir, Ran, Osiris, Khnemu, Ea, Apsu, Tiamat, Ereshkigal

Elemental water is the energy of shape and form. Just like the physical representation, water will conform to its container. It is easily shaped by the intentions of the stronger elements, such as fire and air, will and thought. Water is the astral plane, the psychic energy shaped and formed by others, forming the energetic foundation for our reality. The astral is also the place of some dreams, since the energy takes on the shapes and images of our consciousness as we return from our dream swims in the water astral, bringing back our emotionally charged imagery.

But just like physical water, its power flows everywhere, into everything, connecting all. Given the tiniest space, it will flow and fill it. Elemental water is the power to flow, to move, to change shape and be fluid, but it is also the power that connects all. All living things are connected by our need for water, physically and psychically.

Water is the power of emotion. Emotion flows, forcing us to shift, bend, and adapt, like the stream, yet is fierce and powerful, like the raging river or mighty ocean. Emotions are life sustaining, but can also be destructive. The cups represent water in the tarot suits, and the cups, like emotions, are passed between people and shared. The water flows from cup to cup, as emotions flow from person to person.

Water in its highest form is love. Starting as personal love, the love of family and friends. Water is the love of romance, the deep connection between partners. The power of water deepens to its most powerful form, the love of the divine, unconditional love, what witches call perfect love. It is in this love we find the heart of the water element.

Love is the component of all true, deep, lasting healing, be it a realization of self-love convalescing in a hospital bed, or the magickal healing love of the most perfect ritual. Love is the true force of healing, and much of our healing must be done on the emotional level, where we lose our connection to love. The element of water is the element of the healer. Water holds the power of compassion and emotional sustenance.

This deep, unconditional, compassionate love is never ending, never depleted, and lasts beyond this lifetime. Because of this, water is most often associated with the west. The west is the land of endings, ancestors, death, mystery, paradise, and karma, because the Sun ends, or sets, in the west. The realm of the dead is often beyond or under the oceans of the west, wherever you are. Water is associated with the mysteries beyond the veil, with the spirit worlds, and most importantly how those mysteries can bring healing and divine love to those here. Psychic ability, spirit work, mediumship, and magick are all aspects of western water. Water, and emotion, must be experienced to be known. No book can do more than describe another's experience.

LOVE AND THE CHALICE

The vessel of water comes in many forms. Most popular is the chalice, known as the grail or Holy Grail from Christian myth mixed with pagan themes. The original form of the Celtic grail is most likely the Goddess' cauldron. The goddess Cerridwen brews a magickal potion of inspiration called *greal,* and some modern pagans speculate it led to the name "grail" and the association with Jesus' cup. Ultimately the cup, cauldron, or grail is a vessel for unending water, unending love and healing. It is the container that cannot be emptied. It is the well that never runs dry. The love of the chalice is the love of the Goddess, sustaining the land and sustaining the heart on all levels. It is the principle of giving, nourishing, and living, but like the old grail myths, it must be respected. Those who don't respect and honor it must quest for it. And in that quest, the true seeker finds the holy vessel of love within, as the good knight or the holy mystic will never find it outside.

In Wiccan rituals, the chalice symbolizes the Goddess, as the vessel of love and womb of creation. Traditional chalices are often made of silver, to symbolize the silvery Moon Goddess energy, but in reality, they can be made of anything. I've seen and used chalices of wood, clay, stone, metal, glass, crystal, and various combinations of materials. Some are very ritualistic and fancy, specifically crafted for ritual use. Others are antiques, collectibles, or simple housewares. Any meaningful vessel can be your chalice as long as it can contain liquid and you can drink from it. Although you could use a hollowed horn from cattle, many would associate the horn with the God. But if you want to use it, then go ahead and follow your intuition. Many goddesses are associated with cows and horns.

Tradition says crafting your own tools is best, and I agree, but sometimes it is not practical. If you are not a woodcarver or silversmith, your only option for chalice creation is clay. Clay is a great medium, but some of us have difficulty working in it. I think a chalice that calls you but might be crafted by someone else is just as powerful.

EXERCISE 15

Grail Quest

As you begin your grail quest, your search for your own chalice, follow your feelings. Your psychic perceptions are such a strong part of the water element. Feelings are a great part of witchcraft. Emotions are powerful, but through our process of water attunement, we discern which feelings are serving us, and which feelings must be healed and transformed. Such feelings are very valid, and lead us on the spiritual path of the witch. They are great teachers. Without them, you will not be able to fulfill your quest. And as you search, remember you are not just seeking a cup, but you are searching for the inner love you will bring to the craft. The experiences below will help you in your search for inner love as you look in the outer world for the tool to embody it on your altar. Reflect on your beliefs, feelings, and experiences in the watery world of emotion, and, on its deepest point, unconditional love.

ATTUNING WITH WATER

When diving into the magick of water, you have to open your heart to it. You have to not only feel it, but embody it. In many ways, the heart is truly the grail, the cup that cannot be emptied, the well that never runs dry, but you have to open it and look inside to find such healing waters inside yourself.

Water is described as cool and wet in ceremonial magick. The wet, or moist, aspect is apparent in the fluid, flowing, and filling nature of water. The nature of elemental water is also cooling. To find the healing waters, we must be still, calm, peaceful, and reflective. Unlike the energy, excitement, and passion of creation, the coolness of the water slows and steadies, so one can look within. In Norse magick, cold temperatures, via shaking and shivering, are methods to enter trances and commune with spirits. Coolness brings your energy within, rather than externalizing and projecting it.

EXERCISE 16

Water Attunement

Use this experience to truly tune into the power of water before going on with the next section. Find a means to spend time in cool water. It can be natural water, such as a lake or pond, smooth and steady. Your source can be a gentle stream or steady river, or the steady pulse of the ocean and its tides. You can use a pool, bath, or even shower. Anything where you can get in comfortable, yet somewhat cool water. Feel the water on your skin. Submerge yourself. Feel the flow around you and with you. Feel its cleansing, soothing, healing power. Feel the power of love flowing all around you. Open your heart and feel. How are you feeling? Who do you feel strongly for, and what kind of feelings are conjured? What comes up for you? What needs to be cleansed and healed? Really contemplate the power of water.

Think about the fact that you have so much water inside you, as well as the water around you. Feel yourself become one with the water, your consciousness gently expanding in the liquid, no boundary between you and the water. Make friends with the element of water. When you are done, thank the water spirit, and conclude your attunement by writing about your experiences in your BOS.

WATER GUARDIANS

Water guardians hold many keys, or rather, one key that leads in many nebulous directions. Water guardians open the way to the astral plane, dreams, the collective consciousness, and the realm of the ancestors. They hold the key to the mysteries that must be experienced, and ultimately they hold the key to the heart opening fully, like a beautiful flower.

The elemental beings of the water realm are called undines, and they are basically pictured as mer-people, half human, half fish, like the traditional mermaid sirens of mythology. They are also called sea nymphs, sea elves, and mer-folk. Niksa is the ruler of the plane of water.

All sea creatures are the totems of the west. Traditionally, cold-blooded sea creatures are most common, but I like to include Dolphin and Whale. In Celtic myth, the Salmon holds particular power as a magickal symbol. In the zodiac, the water signs give us unusual totems. Pisces' symbol is two fish. Cancer is the crab. But with Scorpio we have the unusual totems. Although a fixed water sign, Scorpio is related to the Scorpion, definitely not a water totem. Some traditions view fixed water as the stagnant swamp, and look to the Snake, the Serpent, as the totem. Snakes are about change, death, and rebirth, shedding their skin, along with mysticism, befitting Scorpio. Magickally, Scorpio is about transformations, and the Snake is said to transform, and rise above the swamp, becoming a bird of spirit, usually an Eagle, so in the context of spirit, the Eagle can be a totem for the western water realms.

The angel associated with water is the archangel Gabriel, ruler of the west, carrying the golden trumpet. I always found this correspondence strange. Gabriel is the messenger angel in most of the myths, relating news, and an angel of water, ancestors, or healing. But upon meditation with Gabriel, I learned that these messages are messages from the other side, from the deepest mysteries. The messages are ultimately of love, and listening to the heart, and for that reason, Gabriel is the ruler of water.

The gods of water are the sea kings and ocean mothers, as well as the patrons of rivers and lakes. Underworld deities and goddesses of love are rulers of this realm. Most popular among my students is Poseidon, or King Neptune, the archetypal sea father. His wife Amphritite is a sea goddess. Aphrodite, goddess of love, was born out of the ocean sea water, and one of her symbols is the shell, even though she could be considered a fertility goddess. The Celtic Lir, and his son Manannan Mac Lir, are patrons of the sea and sea travelers. Danu, a great mother figure of the Earth and all reality, is a patron of rivers, such as the Danube. Dylan is a Welsh god of dolphins. Cerridwen stirs her cauldron of transformation. The Norse Aegir and Ran are associated with the seas, and Freya, a great goddess of love, sex, and magick, cries tears transforming to amber in the Nordic seas. Osiris is the god of the Egyptian underworld, but his semen is the water of the Nile. Khnemu is also a god of the Nile. Ea, Apsu, and Tiamat are primal creator gods of Sumerian myth, all associated with water, while Ereshkigal, the goddess with leeches for hair, is the ruler of the Sumerian Underworld.

EXERCISE 17

Journeying to the Realm of Water

1. Start Exercise 2: The Inner Temple, conjuring the great World Tree, entering it and going to the inner temple.

2. Orient yourself in the center of your sacred space. You will notice four doorways around you. You may have never noticed them before, but they will be very clear to you now. Each of the doorways leads to a different elemental plane. Each one will be in a different color and have a different symbol on it for the element, such as the elemental triangles or tattvas. By its markings, find the doorway that leads to the realm of water, and stand be

fore it. Usually the water doorway is oriented to your western direction in the temple, but your inner temple is beyond direction in the physical world, so go to whatever door calls to you as water.

3. Hold the intention to enter the realm of water and in your silent, magickal voice, ask permission to open the door. You are asking permission of the highest aspects of yourself, and the realm of water.

4. If you get a yes response, open the door of water. It can open normally or dissolve like salt in water. If you know the invoking pentagram of water, you can use it as your key. In the doorway is a swirling vortex of water, as if a water spouts funnel is covering the gateway, creating a tunnel of water for you to travel. Enter the realm of water.

5. Feel the cool mist all around you with the spinning waters drawing you deeper. Feel the chill in the air as you attune with this elemental energy. The splash and spray clean away all hurts and pains from the past, opening your heart to the love of water.

6. As you move deeper into the tunnel of water, you lose sight of your inner temple and immerse yourself in the element. Ahead you find a light, leading you out of the tunnel and into the realm of water. You find yourself immersed in water, in a vast ocean, yet you can breathe and move with safety and comfort. Take notice of all things around you, the fish, the plants, the sea floor. Feel the currents and temperature shifts. This is the land of undines, mer-folk, undersea kingdoms, and the fabled Niksa.

7. You feel a current pull you, like a beckoning pathway, taking you deeper into the realm of water. You might cross the path of fish, dolphins, or whales. You could find healing sea plants.

8. At the end of the path is a figure, your personal guide to the element of water. It could be an elemental being, animal, deity, or perhaps an angel, there to guide you on the path of water. Introduce yourself, and ask the guide its name and function. Follow this guide, and receive what your

guide has to offer. Since taste is the sense of water, not sight or hearing, your guide may not talk a lot or show you things, but impart a sense of feeling, memory, and empathic communication. Here, feeling is more important than knowing. Take this wisdom in, and ask any questions you have.

9. Ask your guide upon whom shall you call as your guardian of water in ritual. Sometimes it is the guide itself, but often the guide will point you to a deity or other being of power.

10. Your guide will lead you back to the tunnel of water and bid you farewell. Thank your guide for this time and knowledge. Know that you know have a link in the realm of water. The guide may give you a gift to inspire your emotion and love, or give you a drop of compassion to carry within you.

11. Return through the tunnel of water, moving through the mist and water. Come back to the inner temple, and close the gateway of water as you opened it. Orient yourself in the temple. If you have a gift from the realm of water, you can put it in your temple space if you desire.

12. Return back through the World Tree tunnel, and stand at the base of the tree. Thank the World Tree. Step back through the screen of your mind's eye and let the World Tree gently fade from view.

13. Return yourself to normal consciousness, counting up, giving yourself clearance and balance. Do any necessary grounding.

EXERCISE 18

Invoking/Banishing Water

Now you have started to build your relationship with the water realm, you can more effectively open its gateway into this world and your sacred space. To do this, we craft a quarter call to the plane of water.

Like fire, begin with the evocation. What will you say? Here are some examples in the same styles as above.

> **To the west, I call the element of water. I call the protective Crab to join me in the circle and aid in this magick. Hail and welcome.**

> **To the west, I call upon the element of water, cool and moist. I call upon archangel Gabriel, messenger of the heart. Gabriel, bring your loving wisdom. Hail and welcome.**

> **To the west, I call upon the element of water and the undines, the mer-folk. I call upon the king of water and the wet western wind, Zephyrus. Bring your waters of love and healing to this place that is not a place and this time that is not a time. Hail and welcome.**

> **To the west, I call upon the element of water. I call upon the loving Dolphin. I call upon Cerridwen of the Cauldron. Please bring your powerful magick to this work. Guide and guard us in this circle. Hail and welcome.**

The releases would echo a similar style.

> **To the west, I thank and release the element of water. I thank the protective Crab for this aid. Hail and farewell.**

> **To the west, I thank and release the element of water. I thank the archangel Gabriel, and her loving words. Hail and farewell.**

> **To the west, I release the element of water and the undines. I thank the good king Zephyrus for his aid. Hail and welcome.**

> **To the west, I thank and release the element of water. I thank the loving Dolphin and the crone mother Cerridwen for their aid and blessings. Hail and farewell.**

Now think about what visualizations, tools, and gestures can aid you. Match the style of the fire quarter call. Be consistent. If you used invoking/banishing pentagrams for the other element, continue to do so. Write your quarter call and practice opening and closing the gateway. Feel the energy. Notice the shifts in the room as the water element rises to meet your intention. Record your experiences in your BOS.

HOMEWORK

- Complete Exercises 11–18. Record experiences in your BOS. If you can't complete your tool quests, simply continue the search for the right wands and chalice.

- Continue journaling regularly.

TIPS

- To put fire into your daily life, try to do something spontaneous or passionate every day. Offer your fire element to another, or to society. Be of service to a greater light, a greater good, sharing your flame. Reflect on your use of energy, of fuel—from personal energy to the resources of this world, such as wood, oil, gasoline, and even candles. Are you using these things with respect? Are you conserving them? Think about the many ways fire manifests in your life.

- To put water into your daily life, reflect on water as you drink any fluids during your day. Notice flowing water, fountains, and even plumbing. Think about the life-sustaining qualities of water. Make all your drinking and bathing experiences magickal rituals to attune with water. Think about what you put into water, how much water you use and why you use it. Do you respect it and honor it? Do you conserve it as the precious resource it is? Think about all the uses of water in your life.

Lesson Four
Air and Earth

Air and earth. Sky and land. Partners eternally linked as images of the God and Goddess in pagan mythology. Both forces sustaining and protecting each other. Each force exchanging with the other, as the mountains rise to meet the sky, and the winds descend upon the land. While fire and water are the primal sparks of life in the elemental world, air and earth are the expression of sustained life. Both are denser expressions of the primal powers in the universe. And with their stability, we shall continue our journey.

Air

Plane: Mental
Direction: South or east
Colors: Sky blue, yellow
Sense: Smell (some say hearing)
Gender: Male

Nature: Hot and wet

Season: Spring or summer

Zodiac Signs: Gemini, Libra, Aquarius

Witch's Pyramid: To dare (some say "To know")

Tarot Suit: Swords

Tools: Athame, blade, sword, incense (some say wand)

Elemental: Sylph, faery

Animals: All birds, but in particular Crow, Raven, Eagle, Hawk, Wren

Ruler: Paralda

Archangel: Raphael (when in the east)

Greek Wind: Eurius (when in the east)

Norse Dwarf: Sudhri (when in the south)

Egyptian Son: Tuametef, Horus' jackal-headed son (when in the east)

Key Words: Mind, thought, intellect, logic, communication, truth, life, expression, language, abstract, symbolic

Deities: Uranus, Zeus/Jupiter, Hera/Juno, Hermes/Mercury, Macha, Nuada, Llud, Arianrhod, Tarranis, Thor, Odin, Nut, Isis, Thoth, Anubis, Anshar, Inanna, Marduk, Sarpanitu, Shala

Air is the element of the mind. Like our minds, the sky can be clear and sunny, full of peace and serenity. At times the wind blows and agitates. Clouds can fill the sky, obscuring vision and clarity. Water can mix with sky, as emotions mix with mind, darkening it still with storm and rain.

Through our breath, we speak and communicate. One breath must be exchanged for another. As air comes in, words come out. Likewise, to exchange ideas, we must listen, letting the voice, vibration, come into our consciousness, and then we can send out our own vibration, our own idea. Without air, nothing would carry the vibration of sound. Without breath, we would have no mechanism to carry our words. Air is associated with the sense of breath, the sense of smell as air comes in. Still others associate it with hearing, the vibration that comes riding on the air.

Breath is also associated with life force. Through breath, we receive vital energy, called prana by some. Yogic breath work is often called pranayama. Through this energetic exchange with the universe, we revitalize and transform our bodies and our consciousness.

Through breath the mind is revitalized. Many conceive of the mental body and air element as simply cold, hard logic, facts, figures, and raw memory, much like a computer program, but the mind is much more complex than that, and rules many other functions. Expressing your fire element, your passion and creativity, is an air lesson. Fire needs air to burn. Social interaction, wit, storytelling, creative writing, and innovation are all aspects of the air element. Bursts of insight, like Einstein's eureka experience of $E = MC^2$, are still ruled by air. Insight is ruled by the highest forms of air, directly knowing the divine mind.

Truth and the Blade

The tool of air is traditionally the blade. The highest expression of air is the truth. Truth can be subjective, but the blade symbolizes the eternal truth, the divine truth, not necessarily about personal, social, or political matters, but inherent truths found in all things. Even when we express our own personal views with clarity, conviction, honesty, and peace, we are speaking our own personal truth, which is personally important to each of us. We need to acknowledge and recognize our own personal truths while simultaneously realizing our truth is not everyone's truth.

Such blade symbols seemed odd to me. The sword is mightier than the pen, and I originally thought the pen would be more appropriate, but our language holds the keys to our air associations, even if our collective memory has forgotten. When we talk about the mind, we describe it in terms of being sharp or dull like a blade. We tell speakers to get to the "point," the culmination of their truth. When people misuse the power of the word, twisting words and messages, betraying truth, we say they "stabbed" us, "cut" us, or "ripped" us. The power of words cutting is not only symbolic, but energetic. Those who see auras often find energetic rips, tears, and holes in the aura of someone who is verbally abused or under constant verbal assault. The truth is energetic. It resonates with us or rips us.

Ritual blades come in many forms. The most well-known is the sword of truth, the hero's weapon. In our Western traditions, this is most popularly known in the myth of

Excalibur and King Arthur. Many versions have Christianized the tale; but remember, the sword comes from the Lady of the Lake, a water goddess figure. The sword is found in the stone, a symbol of the Earth Goddess. The sword gives the king a partnership with the land and the Lady, all in truth and peace, like earth and sky are partners in all. The sword has little to do with war, and everything to do with protection and honor, a form of defending the sovereign truth.

Ritually, the blade is found in the athame, a double-edged ritual knife. There are many ways to pronounce "athame," and seems to vary from different locations in the US and Europe. I was taught "a-THA-may"; stress on the middle syllable with a short "a," the last syllable rhyming with "day."

Traditionally, it has a black handle, to draw in the power of the light and to resonate with the Goddess, even though it symbolizes the male element of air. Many traditions have specific symbols, or the owner's name, crafted in runic or Theban symbols on the handle or hilt. The knife is double edged to show how the power of the witch can cut both ways if not careful, although most traditions are adamant that the athame is never used to cut anything physical, but only cut things energetically. It can cut doorways in sacred space, cut energetic bindings, and some use it to cast the circle, like a wand. I come from a more kitchen witch background, and find it acceptable to use it to cut items while in the ritual circle, such as carving a name into a candle or cutting a string to represent releasing a binding. During the Burning Times, the kitchen knife also served as the ritual knife. In stricter traditions, such cutting and the ritual harvesting of herbs is reserved to the boline, a white handled knife used for magickal cutting.

EXERCISE 19

Blade Quest

Start a search for your ritual blade, your athame. And as you do, reflect upon the truth of yourself, your craft, and your life. Where are you living in the truth and where are you not? Only you can answer. The blade is the single most-forgotten tool in Wicca. I know so many witches, both self-taught and formally trained, that refrain from getting a blade. The wand will be used as a substitute, and incense symbolizes air in the circle. For some, the idea of a ritual blade is reminiscent of sacrifices or Satanic misconceptions. The blade is a hard concept to deal with, even if it's not sharp enough to cut, as many are not. But what is harder is the concept of truth and your responsibility to the truth. In essence, when many people reject the athame, consciously or unconsciously, they are rejecting the truth and the power of personal truth. The excuse can be made that it is difficult to obtain. Some states have laws against double-edged blades of certain lengths. (So make sure to check with your local witch shop as to state regulations.) It can be hard to find something you feel is special enough. You can't easily handcraft it without knowing metalworking. None of these excuses are acceptable. Own your truth, and use the air element to be creative. The tool is important, but symbolic. Use a nice letter opener. Many are shaped like swords. Carve a wooden knife. Use a butter knife if you have to, but use something. Don't wait for the perfect athame and find yourself waiting years. When you claim your truth, it won't be perfect and will continue to evolve, so as you search for your truth, allow your blade to manifest in the way most perfect, and if it, like your truth, doesn't come to you, go seek it out.

ATTUNING WITH AIR

Although it may seem self-evident, to work in the realm of air you must have an open mind. One with a strong air element is not only working in the realm of reason, but must be creative and adaptable to other information and viewpoints. Strong air folk learn to think and listen as well as speak. Balancing each of these three dynamics can be the difficult part.

The element of air holds the qualities of warmth and moisture. The warmth indicates its dynamic, active nature. Warmth is symbolic of its relationship to fire, feeding it and being warmed by it. Being a male element, it activates and initiates. The sword must be plunged into the stone. The stone receives, but the sword must penetrate. The wetness is the principle of fluidity, of being able to adapt and shift form. It is also symbolic of the relationship with water. Air can contain water, as clouds and later precipitation. And water can contain air, in the form of bubbles and effervescence.

Exercise 20

Air Attunement

To attune physically with the element of air, get outside and get some fresh air. Breathe deeply and let it fill your lungs. Practice your breathing, watching your breath. Try fast breaths, slow breaths, deep breaths, and shallow breaths. Notice how many ways you can breathe it in. Ideally, if you can go to a place and time with strong wind, you will become more attuned. If you can, go to breezy hill or mountain top, or simply go outside on a windy day. Feel the air.

Another air attunement exercise is to play with your sense of smell throughout the day. Play with different scents, oils, foods, plants, etc. Try to smell them and notice how the scents alter your mood, mind, and body.

Reflect on how your mind is like the wind and air, how it changes suddenly, how it is influenced by outside stimuli, be it wind, cloud, or scent. Reflect on your own relationship with the mind. Do you struggle with it, and try to force the "clouds" of illusion back, or do you let them pass out as easily as they came in, without attachment, to resume your peaceful blue skies? Build your relationship with the element of air and your own mind. When you are done, thank the spirits of air, and conclude your attunement by writing about your experiences in your BOS.

Air Guardians

Air spirits are the keepers of the truth, granting insight and vision into your own mind, and ultimately the higher mind. The air guardians are often the tricksters and pranksters, playing with our mind so we can stop identifying with the middle self, or ego mind, as our sole identity, and start finding a sense of self with the true, higher mind.

The medieval image of air elementals are called sylphs and look much like our Victorian image of the faery folk, tiny humans with gossamer or butterfly wings. While most think of this image of the faeries to be attuned to the earth and nature spirits, sylphs are said to live in wispy clouds and near mountain tops. They ride the winds, traveling with the speed of thought. I have pictured air elementals as small human shapes with no features, just "hard" air, swirling around in a vortex, giving shape and form. Others see air elementals take the form of twisting tornadoes or other winged creatures. The mythic king of air elementals is a being known as Paralda.

The animal spirits of the air realm are the intermediaries between the earth and the heavens, the divine emissaries and messengers. Being an element of warm and moist principles, warm-blooded flying creatures and the bird families are assigned to air, though one could make a case for flying insects I suppose. The most popular air totems in witchcraft are the Crow and Raven, two dark birds associated with the Goddess in her many forms, although a few gods are also associated with them. Other favorites are the Hawk, Falcon, Eagle, and Wren.

The angel attributed to the element of air and the east is Raphael, the healer and physician. Again I had another correspondence I found strange, since I learned to associate healing with the element of water. And the corresponding angel of water, Gabriel the messenger, I would associate with air, for messages and information. But upon meditation, Raphael told me that healing is about communication—communicating between the thoughts, mind, and body, and he healed communications breakdowns that prevented the parts of the self from aligning to true health.

The godforms aligned with the air element are primarily the sky gods and goddesses. First are the sky and storm fathers, such as Uranus, Zeus/Jupiter and his wife Hera/Juno, Thor, Nuada, Llud, Tarranis, Nut, Isis, Anshar, Marduk, and Inanna. I've also associated the Welsh Arianrhod, goddess of the Moon and the aurora borealis, with the air and sky elements. My favorite air goddess is Macha, an Irish crow goddess, who is also associated with death, the otherworld, and horses. Another archetype of the air element is the messenger and magician figures. They are the gods of writing, communication, and magick, the highest form of communication. They are the soul guides and shamans, traveling from world to world. Such figures include Hermes/Mercury, Thoth, Anubis, and Odin/Wotan.

EXERCISE 21

Journeying to the Realm of Air

1. Start Exercise 2: The Inner Temple, conjuring the great World Tree, entering it and going to the inner temple.

2. Orient yourself in the center of your sacred space. You will notice four doorways around you. You may have never noticed them before, but they will be very clear to you now. Each of the doorways leads to a different elemental plane. Each one will be in a different color and have a different symbol on it for the element, such as the elemental triangles or tattvas. By its markings, find the doorway that leads to the realm of air, and stand before it. Usually the air doorway is oriented to your eastern or southern direction in the temple, but your inner temple is beyond direction in the physical world, so go to whatever door calls to you as air.

3. Hold the intention to enter the realm of air and in your silent, magical voice, ask permission to open the door. You are asking permission of the highest aspects of yourself, and the realm of air.

4. If you get a yes response, open the door of air. If you know the invoking pentagram of air, you can use it as your key. Before is a great swirling vortex of air, filling the doorway and beyond. Feel the air swoosh and swirl around you, dancing upon your skin. Hear the roar of the wind. It is like stepping into the mouth of a tornado. You know you can enter it safely with your own mental air essence, and you begin to walk into the tunnel of wind.

5. Although the wind cycles around you, there is a strange calm in the center of the wind tunnel, an unearthly peace that stabilizes your path. Move slowly, one step at a time, truly attuning with elemental air. Feel yourself fill with this peace, like the center of the eye of the storm.

6. As you move deeper and deeper into the tunnel, you lose sight of the inner temple and find yourself entering the light and the end of the tunnel, lead-

ing you to the realm of air. Take a look at this world, as you are deposited by the edge of a misty mountain. The wind blows strong through the fog and mist. This is the land of sylphs and bird spirits, and the ruler Paralda.

7. Instead of a path to lead you up this daunting mountain, a strong wind picks you up, responding to your thoughts, and flies you up the mountain, soaring over all paths. Below you can see trees, plants, fragrant flowers, and animals of the air realm.

8. The wind carries you to the peak of a mountaintop, shrouded in mist. You penetrate the mist and before you is your personal guide to the element of air. It could be an elemental being, animal, deity, or perhaps angel, there to guide you on the path of air. Introduce yourself, and ask the guide its name and function. Follow this guide, and receive what your guide has to offer. Since smell is the sense of air, your guide triggers feelings and memories with scent, as well as speaks to you in detail through words. Take this wisdom in, and ask any questions you have.

9. Ask your guide upon whom shall you call as your guardian of air in ritual. Sometimes it is the guide itself, but often the guide will point you to a deity or other being of power.

10. Your guide will lead you back to the tunnel of air and bid you farewell. Thank your guide for this time and knowledge. Know that you now have a link in the realm of air. The guide may give you a gift to inspire your ability communicate your truth, or give you a fragrant flower or magick word to take back with you.

11. Return through the tunnel of air, spiraling through the vortex of wind. Come back to the inner temple, and close the gateway of air as you opened it. Orient yourself in the temple. If you have a gift from the land of air, you can put it in your temple space if you desire.

12. Return back through the World Tree tunnel, and stand at the base of the tree. Thank the World Tree. Step back through the screen of your mind's eye and let the World Tree gently fade from view.

13. Return yourself to normal consciousness, counting up, giving yourself clearance and balance. Do any necessary grounding.

Exercise 22

Invoking/Banishing Air

Like the previous two elements, you have a connection with this realm and must now craft your quarter call to open and close the gateway of element of air. Start with your evocation. Here are some further examples to match the previous styles above. Be sure as you craft your quarter calls that your style on all four matches.

> **To the south, I call the element of air. I call the heavenly Eagle to join me in the circle and aid in this magick. Hail and welcome.**

> **To the east, I call upon the element of air, warm and moist. I call upon archangel Raphael, the healer and physician. Raphael, bring your guidance and knowledge. Hail and welcome.**

> **To the east, I call upon the element of air and the sylphs, the creatures of thought. I call upon the king of air and the warm eastern wind, Eurius. Bring your winds of change and clear thoughts to this place that is not a place and this time that is not a time. Hail and welcome.**

> **To the south, I call upon the element of air. I call upon the dark Crow. I call upon Mother Macha of the Feathered Cloak. Please bring your wisdom upon this work. Guide and guard us in this circle. Hail and welcome.**

The releases:

> **To the south, I thank and release the element of air. I thank the heavenly Eagle for this aid. Hail and farewell.**

To the east, I thank and release the element of air. I thank the archangel Raphael, and his wise knowledge. Hail and farewell.

To the east, I release the element of air and the sylphs. I thank the good king Eurius for his aid. Hail and farewell.

To the south, I thank and release the element of air. I thank the dark Crow and the dark Mother Macha for their aid and blessings. Hail and farewell.

Contemplate the rest of the call, including visualizations, tools, and gestures, keeping your own personal calls consistent with each other. Write your quarter call and practice opening and closing the gateway. Record your experiences in your BOS.

EARTH

Plane: Physical, etheric
Direction: Usually north
Colors: Green, brown, black, tan
Sense: Touch
Gender: Feminine
Nature: Cold and dry
Season: Winter
Zodiac Signs: Taurus, Virgo, Capricorn
Witch's Pyramid: To know (some say "To keep silent")
Tarot Suit: Pentacles/discs/coins
Tools: Stone, crystal, salt, soil, pentacle/peyton, mirror, shield, coin
Elemental: Gnomes, dwarves
Animals: Bull, Stag, Goat, Bear, Snake, Beetle
Ruler: Ghob/Ghom
Archangel: Uriel
Greek Wind: Boreas
Norse Dwarf: Nordhir
Egyptian Son: Mestha (Hapi), Horus' ape-headed son

Key Words: Body, home, fertility, material, manifestation, law, healing, money, art, comfort

Deities: Gaia, Demeter/Ceres, Kore-Persephone/Proserpina, Pan, Danu, Dagda, Cernunnos, Modron, Audhumla, Freya, Frey, Geb, Osiris, Isis, Tammuz, Kishar

Earth is the most easily understood of the elements, for the elemental energy of earth is the energy animating the physical plane. Earth is the result, the manifestation of the elemental energy. Earth energy is the physical result and forms all that which the physical senses can perceive.

Our body is made of the earth element. Although symbolically all elements are found in the body—blood for water, breath for air, metabolism for fire, and earth for bone and tissue—they are all physical symbols of the elements, and are all under the domain of earth energy. The body is the physical vessel, the receptacle and vehicle for the other elements while on the physical plane. The body is our first home and our first possession.

As the element ruling our first home, earth energy is about being present, grounded, and centered in the moment. People who are flighty and spacy, what others accuse as typical New Age behavior, lack earth elemental energies. Our overall physical health is part of this element. Caring for the body, through diet, movement, and being centered are earth lessons. Touch, the ability to feel the earth element, is the sense of this realm. Earth magick is also the magick of the home, domestic life, food, shelter, and creature comforts. Such gifts, in particular our food, come from the planet Earth and the physical elements. These physical aspects sustain our physical body, while their energetic, spiritual components nourish our energy bodies.

All our possessions, money, goods, and luxuries, all things of a physical nature, are ruled by the earth element. Our practical actions that sustain our day-to-day existence are also part of the earth element, such as eating, drinking, daily chores, exercise, and other routines. They provide a solid, steady framework for us to function in the world. Too much of the earth element leaves us locked in place, stuck, stagnant, and heavy. As with all the elements, balance is the key.

SOVEREIGNTY AND THE STONE

The ritual tools and symbols of the earth element are many. In tarot, the suit of pentacles is used to represent earth, though the pentacle, with its five points, is often ritually symbolic of all five elements, not just one. This tarot suit is often called coins, and since the element of earth deals with practical, material, and financial concerns, a ritualistic coin is a proper tool. Other traditions view this suit as the shields, and likewise, the tool that protects is the most practical in the long run, keeping with the earth theme for a tool.

I learned to use an actual stone, a rock, or crystal for the element of earth, or a bowl of soil, sand, or salt. The symbolic tool is actually the literal substance as well. Although earth is the most easily understood element because of its literalness compared to the other elements, the magical power inherent in the element of earth is often forgotten, making its use and tool choice more difficult.

Earth, both element and planet, are intimately tied to the execution of our personal power in partnership with nature. On the earth plane we learn to deal with life manifest, but we learn to manifest our own lives. The sword of truth is buried first in the lake, and then later in the stone. Only with the blessing of the earth can the new king claim the sword. Only with the sovereign blessing of the Goddess does the world flourish.

The first thing we "rule," that we have sovereignty over, is our body; but again, we cannot rule it harshly. We must rule with it, not over it, in partnership. It is a temple, a treasured resource housing the other elements. It must be honored. The same law can be said about any other physical resource, from food and clothing to land and buildings. Only when we work with, rather than force, do we claim divine sovereignty. The hardest lessons are saved for the "easiest" element. Here, in the physical, we work with the physical representations of all the elements. That is why the pentacle often symbolizes the earth element. Here we must find our mastery of the five elements through sovereignty by being in the world. So many religions seek to bring us out of the body, but witches know the key is to be spiritual while in the body, to meld and merge all elements into a harmonious whole.

EXERCISE 23

Stone Quest

As you contemplate the concepts and lessons of the earth element, seek out a symbol for your altar. Any of the symbols discussed before can be perfect, if they resonate with you. Are you the protector, seeking the symbolic shield? Are you working with the earth itself, and desire rock, soil, or crystal? Do you seek the ritual pentacle, a larger pentacle carved on a disk of wood or metal, or cut out? Such tools are called peytons, and act as both ceremonial shields, keys, and plates. Find the most-suited earth tool for yourself at this time. Know that it is not just an object you seek, but a sense of partnership and mastery with the physical world.

ATTUNING WITH EARTH

As earth is the element of personal sovereignty, the energy of attunement is finding your power, finding your home, in the world. We find our home in the sacredness of nature all around us, and through the sacredness of the body. Acts of pleasure, of touching, are intimately linked to the earth element. Through these joys we can find the spiritual ecstasies of the mystic.

Earth energy as an element is cool and dry. The heat of creation is no longer needed. It is manifest in the physical. The wetness, the fluidity of ever-changing shape is no longer present, being solid, stable, fixed in form and shape. Earth is the power of being present in manifestation, creating and dealing with creation.

EXERCISE 24

Earth Attunement

Any physical activity will attune you to this primal element. Be present in your body. Run, dance, jump, and play like a child. Children are naturally attuned to earth energies. All physical acts, from exercise to eating, are acts of earth. One of the best ways to attune to such energy is to spend time outside, in contact with the land itself. Meditate under a tree. Sit on the ground. Lay down in a field. Feel the earth energy around you. Garden. Plant seeds and saplings. Dig in the dirt and feel it between your fingers. The minerals in the soil are the same minerals that make up your body.

Feel the earth, and notice how it makes you feel. Feel your body, all the things that touch and create sensation in your body. How do they feel? What sensations and textures do you enjoy, and what are more difficult for you? What parts of you don't like touch, or are overly or underly sensitive? Listen to your body's messages. Can you tell when you are hungry, full, warm, cold, tired, relaxed, and tense? Or do you just assume these things under certain conditions, without taking a moment to listen to your body?

Make friends with the earth element around you, and in you. Feel the presence of the physical. Be conscious in the body and practice being present. Don't let your mind and feelings disconnect you from your body. Most importantly, don't let intense feelings and thoughts and sensations push your awareness out of your body. Be present for them, all of them, and notice how the body reacts to them. When you are done, thank the earth element around you and in your body, and record your experiences in your BOS.

€ARTH GUARDIANS

Earth guardians are the keepers of the deepest riches. Literally they are interpreted as the keepers of wealth and fortune, but they hold the deepest spiritual riches, which are far more important. They hold the lessons of how to be present in the body, yet open to the universe. They hold the ability to root in deep wisdom, yet reach for the heavens. They help us listen to the world around us.

Earth elementals are typically called gnomes. When I think of gnomes, I think of that rather modern image of the garden gnome, a little man, bearded, with a red hat. And that is a typical image of the gnome folk, but they are often given other names and pictured less human-like, as dwarves, goblins, or imps of folklore. Ghob (some say Ghom) is their king. Certain modern lore mixes earth elementals with nature spirits, devas, elves, sprites, faeries, and the sidhe, which are not all necessarily the same. Earth elementals work strictly in one element, while these other faery folk and nature spirits are working in more than one element. I tend to see earth elementals as little people made of soil, sand, and dirt, with small sprouts coming out of them. At times, earth elementals can appear as great stone giants and rock creatures.

All animals that walk the earth are the power totems of this element, but certain animals are favorite guardians. The Bull, for the zodiac sign Taurus, is popular, along with the Goat for the sign of Capricorn. Celtic traditions love the Stag figure, as well as the more gentle Doe. The introspective Bear makes a great earth guardian. Snake, crawling close to the earth, is a totem here, as well as Beetle, digging its nest in the ground and resurrecting each day, reborn in Egyptian myth.

The angel of the north and earth is Uriel, though many spell it "Ariel." Uriel is the angel of the physical realm, and, as such, is sometimes depicted as an angel of death with dark wings, easing those into the grave. Because of the earth associations, Uriel is often the most feminine of the angels depicted, even though technically all the angels are considered beyond gender and form.

The gods of earth element are also associated with the planet, as the earth mothers and grain goddesses, as well as the good gods of the land and wild things. Gaia, the Greek image of the Earth mother is the primal archetype of the first goddess. Her granddaughter Demeter/Ceres, and her daughter, Persephone/Proserpina, also have sway over the earth element, though Persephone/Proserpina is more known in her aspect as Underworld queen. Pan, the horned satyr god, is a primal earth father figure. The Celtic mother Danu is associated with all life, including the land. Modron is another name of the primal mother. The Dagda, the arch-druid and all-father, is linked with the magick and abundance of the land. Cernunnos, the horned father and stag lord, is a strong guardian of the earth element. In Norse myth, the land deities are from the Vanir tribe, and foremost are the goddess Freya and her brother Frey. In Egypt, the sky is feminine and the earth is masculine. The earth god Geb (or Seb) embodied the land. Isis is the goddess with strong links to the fertility of the Nile Valley and is both a sky and earth goddess. For those in the ancient Middle East, Kishar is the Earth goddess. Tammuz is the resurrected god of the grain.

EXERCISE 25

Journeying to the Realm of Earth

1. Start Exercise 2: The Inner Temple, conjuring the great World Tree, entering it and going to the inner temple.

2. Orient yourself in the center of your sacred space. You will notice four doorways around you. You may have never noticed them before, but they will be very clear to you now. Each of the doorways leads to a different elemental plane. Each one will be in a different color and have a different symbol on it for the element, such as the elemental triangles or tattvas. By its markings, find the doorway that leads to the realm of earth, and stand before it. Usually the earth doorway is oriented to your northern direction in the temple, but your inner temple is beyond direction in the physical world, so go to whatever door calls to you as earth.

3. Hold the intention to enter the realm of earth and in your silent, magical voice, ask permission to open the door. You are asking permission of the highest aspects of yourself, and the realm of earth.

4. If you get a yes response, open the door of earth. If you know the invoking pentagram of earth, you can use it as your key. Feel the heavy earthen door slowly sway open. In the doorway is a dark tunnel, digging deep to the earth plane. Enter the realm of elemental earth.

5. Feel each step as you walk deeper into the darkness without fear. Feel your body move into the unknown, growing quiet, immobile, and solid. Smell the fresh earth. Feel the sacredness of the land around you.

6. As you move deeper into the tunnel, you lose sight of your inner temple and immerse yourself in the earth sensations. Ahead you find a light, leading you out of the tunnel and into the realm of earth. You find yourself at the edge of a primordial forest, a place of power. This is the edge of the realm of earth, the realm of gnomes and dwarves and their ruler Ghob.

7. Before you there is a path into the heart of the forest. The path pulls you deeper. Take notice of the plants and animals you see in the forest. Walk deeper into the place of earth power. At the end of the path you arrive in a clearing with a mound and an opening. You enter the mound and find yourself in another deep tunnel. The tunnel has minerals and crystals shining in it as you descend into the land.

8. At the end of the tunnel is a cavern, and in the center of the cavern, a figure, your personal guide to the element of earth. It could be an elemental being, animal, deity, or angel, there to guide you on the path of earth. Introduce yourself, and ask the guide its name and function. Follow this guide, and receive what your guide has to offer. Since touch is the sense of earth, this experience could be very tactile. Follow your feelings and impressions. Take this wisdom in, and ask any questions you have.

9. Ask your guide upon whom shall you call as your guardian of earth in ritual. Sometimes it is the guide itself, but often the guide will point you to a deity or other being of power.

10. Your guide will lead you back through the mound tunnel, back through the forest, and to the tunnel of earth leading you to the inner temple. Your guide will bid you farewell. Thank your guide for this time and knowledge. Know that you now have a link in the realm of earth. The guide may give you a gift to inspire your own grounding and mastery.

11. Return through the tunnel of earth, feeling each step as you return. Come back to the inner temple, and close the gateway of earth as you opened it. Orient yourself in the temple. If you have a gift from the earth realm, you can put it in your temple space if you desire.

12. Return back through the World Tree tunnel, and stand at the base of the tree. Thank the World Tree. Step back through the screen of your mind's eye and let the World Tree gently fade from view.

13. Return yourself to normal consciousness, counting up, giving yourself clearance and balance. Do any necessary grounding.

EXERCISE 26

Invoking/Banishing Earth

Complete your quarter call cycle. Continue in the tradition and style you have begun with the first three elements. Use these evocations to inspire your own magical quarter calls.

> To the north, I call the element of earth. I call the steady Bull to join me in the circle and aid in this magick. Hail and welcome.

> To the north, I call upon the element of earth, cool and dry. I call upon archangel Uriel, angel of change. Uriel, bring your dark wings. Hail and welcome.

> To the north, I call upon the element of earth and the gnomes. I call upon the king of earth and the cool, dry, northern wind, Boreas. Bring your strong foundation to this place that is not a place and this time that is not a time. Hail and welcome.

> To the north, I call upon the element of earth. I call upon the great Stag. I call upon horned father Cernunnos. Please bring your powerful magick to this work. Guide and guard us in this circle. Hail and welcome.

The releases would echo a similar style.

> To the north, I thank and release the element of earth. I thank the steady Bull for this aid. Hail and farewell.

> To the north, I thank and release the element of earth. I thank the archangel Uriel, and her gifts of change. Hail and farewell.

> To the north, I release the element of earth and the gnomes. I thank the good king Boreas for his aid. Hail and farewell.

> To the north, I thank and release the element of earth. I thank the great Stag and the horned father Cernunnos for their aid and blessings. Hail and farewell.

Complete your call with visualizations, tools, and gestures. Practice it and record your experience in your BOS.

HOMEWORK

- Complete Exercises 19–26. Record experiences in your BOS. If you can't complete your tool quests, simply continue the search for the right blade and earth tool.

- Continue journaling regularly.

TIPS

- To put air into your daily life, pay close attention to your words and thoughts. Do you speak what you are thinking? Do you think one thing, but say another? Are you true to your word? Do you effectively express your thoughts and ideas, and do others understand them? Most importantly, do you listen when others speak to you? Pay attention to your breath. Notice how the breath changes as your mind changes. Do you hold your breath when tense? Does it speed up when excited? Can you calm down your thoughts by taking a few deep breaths? My yoga teacher Stephanie says, "Breath goes where the mind goes. The mind goes where the breath goes." If you can control one, you have a better chance of mastering the other. Watch your words, mind, and breath for greater understanding of the air element.

- To put earth into your daily life, pay attention to your body. Truly pay attention to all sensations of your body that we normally ignore, from our clothes' texture to the sensation of a breeze, to the touch of another person. Listen to your body's messages about hunger, temperature and health, and partner with it. Bless your meal before eating it, giving thanks to the Goddess and God, and all plant, animal, and mineral spirits that gave themselves to you for you to eat. It will also energize and purify it. Do this with all food, not just your nutritious, whole foods. Bless your snacks, medicines, vitamins, and desserts: anything you put into your body. Feel your body movements, and exercise your body in a manner correct for your health and lifestyle. Take care of your body as a temple in the world.

Lesson Five
Tools of the Craft

Witchcraft is a path of many tools. You won't find all of them on the altar. Witches have as many internal, personal tools for making magick as we do external, ritual devices. The four tools of the elements symbolize the most important internal ingredients—will, truth, love, and sovereignty.

The internal technology led a great debate as to the need and purpose of outer tools. A common teaching you will hear in some pagan circles is that you need no tools. They are just props. They are just a focus for your power and have no inherent power of their own. I understand the sentiment, but such statements are not entirely truthful.

It is true that you don't "need" any other tools to do magick. You have all the tools you need within you. The sentiment is to empower beginning students to know they are a part of the magick, and powerful magick is not based on the age, expense, or purity of your tools. I agree wholeheartedly and feel that this is a powerful message to send. You are the integral part in your magick.

Tools do, however, have power. Their power is beyond the symbolic power of what they represent, but that's important. The power is beyond their functional abilities, based on their nature and shape. These abilities do give us focus in ritual. If we want to directly experience physical water, we need a vessel to hold it. We can still experience the element of water, or any of the elements, as you did in the previous chapters without a physical representation. Still, their power goes beyond symbol and function.

The first power of magickal tools comes from their vibration. Each tool consists of different substances, each with a different energy, a different vibration. The metals, woods, stones, and clays, along with the colors, symbols, designs, and intention of the artisan, give each tool a particular vibration. These vibrations add to magick. The time-honored traditions of natural magick have witches partnering with the energy, the vibration, the spiritual essence, of a plant, mineral, or metal to do magick. Part of the art of nature magick is to choose partners that are in harmony with our own energy and the task at hand. Our tools are our first natural partners. Certain traditions will specify the materials and construction of ritual tools for this reason. If a book or teacher says you must have a silver chalice, then the tradition chose silver because this metal resonates with the Moon. Both the Moon and the chalice are associated with the energy of the Goddess. When you use them, you can more easily connect with her vibration. But you don't have to use silver. Other traditions have just as much success with clay or glass chalices. Again, it is finding what resonates with you as well as honoring past traditions.

The second power of ritual tools is their ability to store and release energy. Anything used in sacred space resonates with sacred space, particularly if it is consecrated in that space. The lingering vibrations of that sacred space in the tool make re-creating sacred space much easier next time. When you partner this sacred energy with a specific intention and blessing to enhance the function of the ritual device, then that tool becomes an anchor for that intention and energy. Using the energy and intention you have conjured and placed into the tool, the tools will help you create sacred space again. It is particularly helpful if for whatever reason you are not feeling at peak performance. The stored energy and intentions of the tools will help you create sacred space. It is particularly a great asset if you are doing a ritual with others and are nervous about it. You can still create sacred space without tools, and I highly suggest you try it sometime, but for now, they are great helpers.

In one sense, the tools would not have any of this power without you, but they do act as partners and aids in our magick, and shouldn't be relegated to being props to be casually discarded. They are sacred, as are all things, because everything is a manifestation of the divine.

BUILDING THE ALTAR

The altar is the witch's magickal workplace. Altars reflect the style and craft of the individual witch. They can be in any part of the home. Some are temple-like, while others have a kitchen witch, down-home hospitality. Some altars are permanent places of worship, while others are temporary for a specific ritual or gathering. You can have more than one altar. I have a home altar I share with my partner, office altar, and traveling work altar for my classes and public rituals that generously borrows tools from my other two. I also have "mini altars" all around my home and office, which do not function for ritual, but represent something sacred to me and my life. They are another aspect of working with sacred space.

I highly suggest creating a permanent altar where you do your meditation and magickal work. If that is not feasible, you are not any less of a witch for lack of a permanent shrine, but come up with a creative solution. I have a friend who disguised her altar with other household items, so no one would know that it isn't a funky coffee table, until someone tries to put a cup on it and she kindly asks them not to. Another uses a trunk and gingerly places all her tools inside the trunk when others come to visit. Cabinets with doors make excellent altars, too, because they can be closed and locked when needed.

The purpose of keeping an altar is not only functional, as a place to keep your tools and do magick, but an act of magick in itself. The altar is a microcosm of the sacred space of the magick circle. All the energies called in the magick circle are represented on the altar. As the altar is a magickal microcosm, a reminder for the sacred circle, the circle is a microcosm for the divine universe, for all of creation. By constructing an altar, you are remembering the divine in all things and creating a focus in your life, a touchstone to remind you of the sacred. It may not seem important now, but when you have difficult times in life, the altar can be a wonderful constant, a foundation to help you open your gateway to the divine.

Most importantly, the altar holds the symbols of the four elements, the four elemental tools of wand, athame, chalice, and stone. They are the fundamental forces of creation, and your magickal partners.

Also of great importance are the symbols used for the energy of the Goddess and God. You can use statues. Other symbols would be a shell and horn respectively, stone/crystal sphere and point, or anything else embodying the essence of the divine couple. You can also have something for the Great Spirit, a ritual tool for union.

I learned to use a black candle for the Goddess, on the left of the altar, and a white candle for the God, for the right of the altar, as I face it. If you have ever seen the traditional images of the Priestess card in tarot, it is like you are looking between her pillars, her gateway of consciousness. The imagery is from the Tree of Life. The black candle also draws in energy for magick, since black absorbs light and color, while the white candle sends out magickal energy, since white reflects all light. I often put another, larger candle in the center, for the Great Spirit. The color of the candle usually represents the season (see Lesson Ten) or whatever my intuition feels is appropriate at the time. From the light of the Great Spirit, I light the black candle, and then from black to white, from Goddess to God.

Other items are placed on the altar. Some are functional, like matches. Others are indicative of what you are currently working on at this time. You can have a tarot card, an herb or stone, spell components, photos, or anything else that is important to you.

Here is a list of rituals tools used both on and off the altar.

Altar Cloth

A variety of cloths to cover the altar are used. Most stick with traditional black, but you can vary the colors to match the seasons, or fit a particular spell you are doing. Although I like plain wood, having at least partial covering protects your altar from stray wax and embers that can fly during a ritual. A throw rug beneath or next to the altar can serve the same practical purpose.

Ash Pot

A small vessel or urn used to collect ashes from burned spell paper, offerings, and incense and the remnants of other spell components. Traditionally ashes are buried on Samhain, or released in other rituals. I prefer to bring my ashes to the beach each year with my mother, and release them into the ocean.

Asperger

A tool used to evenly spread blessed water or potion, usually to cleanse and bless a space. I use a pine branch dipped in consecrated mixture of sea salt and water. Quickly flicking the branch releases drops of water into the area.

Basket

Witches often use a basket to carry their tools when doing ritual outside of their home, or when gathering in groups.

Bell

Ritual bells are usually made from silver, pewter, or brass, and used in a variety of ways. They can punctuate parts of the ceremony, welcome the quarters or deities, or be used in meditation or trance-inducing music.

Besom

A besom is a witch's broom. The broom is a symbol of purification, and traditionally made with an ash or birch pole, with broom or birch "bristles" wrapped in willow. Ritually, it is used to cleanse the circle space before ritual, cleansing out psychic debris. It can be placed in the "doorway" of the circle, between north and east, and is used in certain initiation and handfasting (marriage) ceremonies to be jumped over, symbolizing the crossing of a threshold and into a new life. A coven can line their brooms end to end, creating a physical boundary of the circle.

Boline

A blade differentiated from the athame because it can be used to cut material things, both in ritual and out of ritual. Usually used for the ceremonial gathering of herbs.

Not necessarily double edged, but sometimes shaped as a crescent sickle. Traditionally created with a white handle.

Bottles

Witches keep various bottles on their altar for potions and oils.

Bowl

Vessel used to hold liquids, including water or oil. The bowl can be another symbol of the element of water.

Candles

Candles can be used as a symbol of the element of fire, as well as specific intention as the Goddess and God, as mentioned above.

Cauldron

Flame-proof metal container used to burn, brew, and mix things. Cauldrons have represented all the various elements from time to time: used to burn offerings, fire; used to brew potions of healing, water; used for incense, air; and, mythically, a cauldron of abundance, like a cornucopia, earth. Also, the three support prongs symbolize the triple Goddess and the two points for the handle symbolize the dual God. I use the cauldron as a symbol for spirit, in the center of the altar.

Censer

A flame-proof vessel used to burn incense. It is usually filled with sand at the bottom, to absorb the heat. I use a brass bowl filled with sand a friend brought me from the pyramids in Egypt. Some are cauldron like vessels hung on chains or suspended in tripods. The censer is a tool of air. Other names used for ceremonial incense burners are thurible and brazier.

Crown

Some traditions use a crown, often a silver crescent crown for the priestess and a horned crown for the priest. In covens such tools are reserved for the High Priestess and High Priest.

Crystals

Many witches use a variety of stones on the altar, from beach rocks to fine mineral specimens. They can represent the element of earth, and metaphysical crystals also have other elemental associations. Points are phallic and can represent the God.

Crystal Ball

A traditional device of the witch, used to divine answers to question. Due to their curved nature, they represent the Goddess.

Drum

For those using ritual music, the drum's beat can be used to achieve ritual consciousness, punctuate a ritual, and achieve a state of shamanic journey.

Horn

Ritual horns are usually from either stag or cattle and used as a symbol of God or Goddess. Some bull horns are hollowed out and used to hold herbs, scents, or liquids. A symbol of power and awareness.

Incense

Sacred herbs burned to clear a space, create sacred space, or add energy to a ritual. Tool of the element of air.

Jewelry

Some witches wear certain pieces of jewelry specifically for ritual, and no other time. Each has a different meaning, use, or symbolic power depending on its design and materials. Certain stones are considered particularly magickal and silver is the usual metal of choice among witches seeking to enhance psychic ability. For more on magickal materials, read Lesson Nine. Pentacle necklaces are often a symbol of first-degree initiation, while rings are a symbol of second-degree initiation. Necklaces of alternating amber and jet beads are popular among traditionalists, as a symbol of a High Priestess or High Priest, but are gaining popularity among eclectic and solitary witches not using ranks. One way of interweaving magick into your everyday life is to wear one piece of ritual jewelry in your everyday outfits.

Libation Bowl

A vessel used for offerings. Traditional libations of water, wine, or ale are poured on the ground to give thanks. While doing rituals inside, the bowl holds the libations until they can be brought outside after the rituals are done.

Matches

Tool of fire used to light candles and incense. Some traditions insist on matches, while others insist on lighters. Those against lighters don't like to use petroleum products, or mechanical devices in the circle, particularly if the lighter is plastic. Those against matches feel the power of sulfur is destructive and will harm your magick. I've learned to use matches, and had wonderful spells. I've also used a lighter, and that worked, too.

Mask

Ceremonial tool used in some covens by the High Priestess and High Priest. Also used in shamanic rituals, healings, initiations, and rites of passage.

Mirror

Magick mirrors are used for scrying much like crystal balls. They can also be used in beauty magick and in creating magickal portals and gates. Mirrors can reflect the light of the Moon or Sun onto the priestess or ritual tools for empowerment. Mirrors are symbols of the Goddess and the element of water.

Mortar & Pestle

Traditional tool used to grind herbs and powders. Favored by most witches over electric grinders because the act of sitting with the herb and grinding it by hand helps you build a relationship with the plant and trigger its powers.

Musical Instruments

Instruments beyond those listed here can be used to create sound and tone to alter consciousness, heal, and carry energy.

Parchment

Parchment paper, or its modern-day facsimile that is manufactured rather than made from animal hide, is used to write spells. If using recycled paper, you must cleanse it of all previous energies and intentions before using it. See "Cleansing and Consecration" section later in this lesson.

Peyton

A ritual pentacle, symbolizing either the earth element or spirit. Used to open elemental gateways, evoke the divine, and protect and bless ritual tools and food.

Protection Potion/Oil

A special potion used for anointing during ritual, and sometimes for consecration of ritual tools. See Lessons Seven and Eight.

Rattle

Ceremonial rattles are used much like the drum, but also have a function of cleansing and clearing unwanted energies from a space or person.

Robes & Cloaks

Special ritual attire, usually consisting of a black robe and/or black cloak, is the traditional witch's outfit. During the Burning Times, such dress concealed practitioners in the night forest, as well as being the color of the Goddess and drawing in energy. They serve another purpose, much like ritual jewelry, to help prepare the psyche for ritual consciousness. If you wear something only when doing magick and entering sacred space, you condition your mind to use it as a trigger, to aid you in achieving that state of consciousness more quickly and completely. For some, it's analogous to putting on your "Sunday best" to go to church. It creates a different mindset. Many traditions are insistent that the robe be sewn by the witch's own hand, but I personally believe we all have skills to contribute to the community. Sewing is not one of mine.

Salt

Certain traditions use a bowl of sea or kosher salt for the element of earth. Others mix it with water for the element of water, or between the points of water and earth, in the northwest part of the altar. Other traditions substitute salt with pieces of black coral, since both are items of protection, but salt is far easier to procure.

Scourge

A ritual whip similar to a cat o' nine tails, used to induce ritual consciousness by drawing blood to the affected part of the body and away from the brain. Some relate it to the Egyptian flail. Because of the sadomasochistic overtones, most traditions do not use the scourge.

Scythe/Sickle

A crescent blade used similarly to the boline. Symbol of the Moon.

Staff

A long wand used in the same way as a traditional wand, to direct energy and cast the circle. Staves are often the height of the practitioners, or slightly shorter. Some use walking sticks and canes as staves. If the staff is forked at the top, it is called a stang, a symbol of the horned God. A stang is often decorated like an altar itself.

Sword

Extended double-edged blade used much like both an athame and wand. Often used to cast a circle. Foremost in initiation ceremonies of traditional covens, one is asked by sword point to only enter the circle in perfect love and perfect trust.

SETTING UP THE ALTAR

Various books and traditions will give you the definitive way to set up your altar. Once you are armed with that information, it is hard to believe there is another way to do it, until you read another book or speak with a teacher who does it differently. In truth, there is no one right way to set up an altar. Each altar is as unique as the individual creating and using it. Each altar will have a different purpose, and will be as unique as any moment in space and time is unique. An altar will change to reflect the change going on in the witch who uses it.

Then why do we have so many "rules" about the proper way to set up an altar? The rules come about as a teaching tool. The altar is a reflection of the magick circle. Its set-up reflects the organization of a tradition's particular ritual. As different traditions associate the elements with different directions and tools, or have more simple or complex rites, the altar reflects the items of both symbolic and practical importance to the ritual. The "rules" become rules to prevent the student from misunderstanding the energetic realities that match the ritual and to prevent forgetting any of the needed tools to actually perform the ritual.

I believe there are no hard-and-fast rules about altar set-up. It has to suit you and fit your surroundings. The altar doesn't have to be any particular shape or size, color, or wood type. Take all the rules as suggestions. As you learn more about the rituals you do, the patterns and set-up will become more apparent.

With that in mind, there are some pretty standard suggestions found in most traditions of witchcraft, with some variations. Your altar should face the direction where you start your circle casting, usually north or east. I use north myself. But it must also fit your home. I had a tall bureau as an altar and at one place I lived, there was a window on the north and east walls. The altar would have blocked them, so I put it on the south wall but still started my ritual facing north.

Usually items associated with the feminine energies of the Goddess are placed more on the left side of the altar, and objects associated with the God and male energy are on the right. So rounded and dark objects are more Goddess oriented, and light, pointed, sharp, and long objects are more God oriented. I like to remember that there are also light and fire goddesses and dark gods by placing one light object on the Goddess side and a dark object on the God side, but that is my personal use, not a traditional rule.

Each of the four sides of the altar is associated with an element, and typically the tools associated with each element are placed in that area. Some tools seem to be a combination of two elements, and can be placed in the midpoints. Salt water is usually seen as a water tool, but fits both earth and water, which are usually next to each other in most traditions. Incense is traditionally an air tool, but really suits both air and fire. Air and fire have a strong overlap between the witchcraft and ceremonial traditions, and are usually placed next to each other as well.

Figure 14: Altar

For any other items, use your intuition and creativity. Nothing "bad" will happen if you don't have it perfect. There is no perfection in the circle other than the perfect love and perfect trust you hold. All other things are free and flexible. Do what thou will and let it harm none.

PROBLEMS WITH ELEMENTAL CORRESPONDENCES, TOOLS, AND ALTAR SET-UP

Each tradition has its own way of doing things. None are absolutely right or absolutely wrong. In fact, for a witch, a matter of "right" could simply be the one you learned first. If you don't understand the concepts behind your symbols and actions, all others seem "wrong." I lead many public rituals, and I can't tell you how many times someone has come up to me afterward and said something like, "You know that part at the quarters, it was wrong." I would ask why, but usually the answer boiled down to "That's not the way I learned it" or "That's not how I do it."

If you understand the concepts behind not only your tradition, but also the symbolic thinking behind many traditions, you have a greater appreciation for all aspects of craft, even if one way is not your way. Even if you are a solitary, eclectic witch, you never know when you will be in a situation where you are faced with a different style and tradition. You can also take this philosophy out into the world beyond witchcraft and magick. You can see the original symbolic beauty of other religions and ceremonies, even if they come from faiths and institutions with which you don't feel a kinship. Even though we are witches, we often attend weddings, funerals, and celebrations in other religions. See the symbolic beauty in all.

When really starting my studies, one of the most confusing things about the elements and quarters was fire and air. Everybody uses them differently. It continues to be a source of frustration for many people in my classes. Some creation stories start with light and fire, others start with air. Some put fire in the south and others put it in the east. Is the wand the tool of air, or of fire? Depends on whom you ask.

Fire and air are the masculine elements, and each has some similar qualities. Their symbolism is different. Fire is the will, passion, and energy. Air is the mind and intellect. I put fire at the top "rung" of the elemental ladder, because it is the more ephemeral. I think of it as the light of spirit creating the first sparks of fire, then air is created to sustain the fire. But others would argue the air is needed first so the fire can spark. It's symbolic, not literal, so use what image works best for you. But I feel the soul comes before the mind.

When using the wand, do you think of it as the focus for will? Then it is a fire tool. Many tarot decks depict the wand as the torch, leading the way with light, warming and protecting. I see the magick wand illuminated by the light of willpower, the light of the soul. Others depict it as a spear, to reach forward, making the will manifest.

But perhaps you think of the wand as the magician's tool, a focus for the mind. Wave your magick wand, and your thoughts come to life. Wooden branches sway in the wind. With that view, an air correspondence is more appropriate.

When working with the blade, the air symbolism is about the mind. We use terms like "the mind is sharp," "keen like a razor's edge." If someone is less than sharp of mind, they are like "a dull knife." When we speak, we must "get to the point." When we argue, our words are "sharp" and "cutting." When someone's words betray us, they "stab us in the back." The blade, as athame or sword, is the symbol of the precision of truth. It cuts away all falsehood, lies, and illusions. It cuts the cords of ignorance. Like the double-edged blade, our words can cut both ways.

All blades have a second side. Many witches view the blade as the tool of the fiery warrior. Such strong actions, literal or symbolic, are of the fire element because they direct the will. The dark side of fire is uncontrolled anger and aggression, which fuels the conflicts of the blade. The metal of the blade is forged in fire.

As you probably guessed, my personal favorites are fire for the wand and air for the blade, and that is how I will use them in my practice. My prejudice comes from learning it this way first, and even after more understanding and research, I still like it best. Feel free to adapt this material to suit your own tastes, but always understand the concept behind it.

Another great debate among witches is the elements and their directional correspondences. Bottom line—if you have all four traditional elements, and put them in a quarter, it works. Really. I've tried them all and had others experiment. The elemental kingdoms are not in specific directions. That is symbolic of the culture the tradition comes from and personal symbolism, along with literally geographic symbolism as well.

In most traditions of witchcraft, earth is in the north because we are in the Northern Hemisphere and the closest earth energy magnetic pole is the North Pole. Also by default, it fits best in that direction when we consider the other three elements.

Likewise, in most traditions, water is the west. The reason being European witchcraft sees the western sea, the Atlantic, as the great mystery, since most travelers knew the Eastern lands, but did not have conscious knowledge (that we factually know about) of the Americas until Columbus. Symbolically, water is the element of endings, mystery, and the ancestors. The Sun sets in the west, "dying" to be reborn in the east. But if you now live on the East Coast of America, should you put water in the east, since that is the closest body to you? It's up to you. I still put it in the west, because for me, the symbolic importance is stronger than the literal.

Again, our problem elements are fire and air. Most traditions of witchcraft that I've seen put fire in the south. In the Northern Hemisphere, the further south you go, the warmer it gets. Also, the noonday Sun is hanging in the southern sky. The southern direction, fire, and the season of summer all correspond well together. So if fire was in the south, air would be in the east, for the fluxuation of spring with the cool air of the new day.

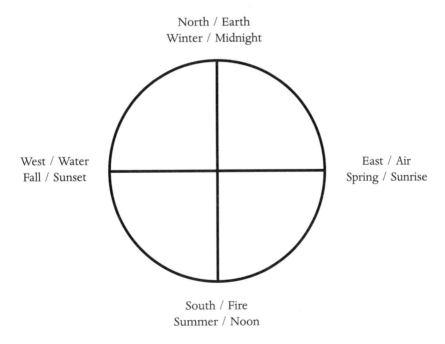

North / Earth
Winter / Midnight

West / Water
Fall / Sunset

East / Air
Spring / Sunrise

South / Fire
Summer / Noon

Figure 15: Wheel, Seasons, and Times of Day

When I started my training in witchcraft, I learned to put fire in the east for the rising Sun, the first place where fire touches the day. Although fire literally corresponds well with summer, the spring starts in the fire sign of Aries, and fire is the first, starting element. So in turn, I put air in the south. With this configuration, you have earth and air opposing each other, like Mother Earth and Father Sky. You have the primal powers of fire and water on the second axis. For some, this pattern is too dynamic. Personally, I find it very powerful and prefer it to most other alignments, including the more traditional fire in the south and air in the east. I also associate fire and water with cleansing, and positioning them with spring and fall makes sense to me, because I do my own herbal body cleansings and fasts in the spring and fall.

This quarter design also gives us an interesting alignment into the dry/wet and hot/cold schemes of the elements. Many traditions give these correspondences, but never explain their purpose, because they do not see the pattern inherent in this quarter design. Any element can transform itself into any other, by giving up certain qualities. This is the true act of transmutation for the witch and alchemist, and these qualities unconsciously play a great role in natural magick with the elements, herbs, and stones.

For example, fire is hot and dry. If you take away the heat, by letting the fire burn out and become cold, you have ash, the earth element, which is cold and dry. One element can transform into another, even if they have no quality shared between them. The transformation will simply have to take a secondary step. If you add enough moisture, or wetness to the ash, you create a solution, which is of the water elemental quality. If you heat the solution, trading the cold for warm, you get a vapor, of the air element, which is moist and warm. If you remove the moisture from the air, breaking it down to the components of hydrogen and oxygen, you get combustive combination, creating fire.

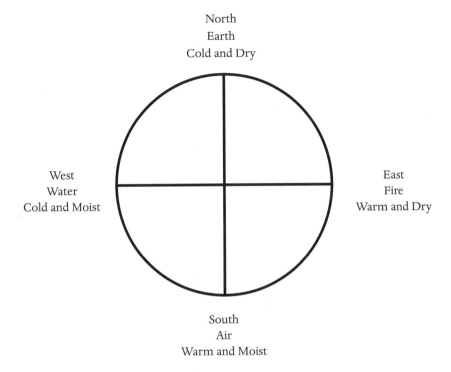

North
Earth
Cold and Dry

West
Water
Cold and Moist

East
Fire
Warm and Dry

South
Air
Warm and Moist

Figure 16: Wheel and Qualities

Traditionally, the same gender elements do not often oppose each other. You don't often see something like earth and water on the north/south axis or fire/air on the east/west axis. They can be found in experiments in astrological magick, but it is unusual in traditional forms of witchcraft.

CLEANSING AND CONSECRATION

Consecration is the act of catalyzing the inherent properties of a tool, and imbuing it with your energetic intention, to hold a specific energy for your rituals. Consecration is also called charging, blessing, or hallowing.

To start, you must cleanse each object, purifying it of any past vibrations and energies. If all thoughts and emotions are energies, then the object will imprint the thoughts and feelings of everyone who handled it before you. You don't want those unknown vibrations in your circle with you. You want to be clear and focused, undistracted. To do that, you must cleanse. Learning proper cleansing techniques will serve you in all other areas of your magick and life.

Cleansing has nothing to do with soap and water by itself, though they can be considered a technique in cleansing. Spiritual cleansing is changing the vibration, the energy of an object, place or person. You raise the energy to a higher vibration, and any vibrations that are not as pure are forced to rise with it, or remove themselves from the space. Cleansing is like the movement of clocks. If you put many mechanical clocks in a room together, all at slightly different paces, they will eventually entrain to the same pattern. If one clock is larger or louder, its pace will dominate. Cleansing vibrations is the same as entraining them, but choosing the highest vibration to be the dominant pattern, clearing out all the distractions and harmful, mundane, day-to-day energies that do not serve the highest purpose of the ritual. Energy cannot be destroyed; it is simply transformed, or removed and replaced.

Magickal cleansing is done through the use of the five elements. Each technique is powerful by itself, and only one is needed. Powerful cleansing rituals will use many techniques combined together.

Air

Incense is the first tool of air cleansing. By using a purifying incense as previously discussed, you raise the vibration of the tool by passing it through the smoke of the incense. The purifying incense, when burned, releases a higher vibration used to remove unwanted energies. The incense itself can be consecrated before using it. Students in my classes have remarked that consecrated incense smells different from non-consecrated incense, and some can tell me when I've forgotten to bless my incense before using it by the smell of it.

Another air technique is blowing or breathing on the tool, but you must be very clear and centered yourself when doing it.

The last technique of air cleansing is placing the tools outside—hanging them, if possible, on a windy day and letting the actual wind clear them. Think how you feel walking outside on a cool, crisp, windy day. It refreshes and cleanses our energy field, so it will naturally refresh a tool's energy.

Fire

Fire is very purifying tool, but difficult to use by itself. The ritualistic way of cleansing with fire, yet not destroying the tool, is to cleanse and consecrate a candle for purification, preferably red. Then hold your object a few inches above the flame, making sure not to burn yourself. Then imagine the heat and light of the flame, the energy, not the actual flame, getting larger, and surrounding your object. Pass all sides of the object over the flame, through this light. Feel the light of fire cleanse the unwanted energies.

Another flame method of cleansing is to leave the object out in the Sun for a few hours, letting the Sun raise its vibration. This is a favored method among Central American shamans, to raise the vibration of their sacred elixirs for shamanic journey. (Moonlight is amplifiying and empowering, but lacks the cleansing qualities of the Sun.)

Water

Water is used ritually to cleanse and wash away. Pure water or sea salt (or kosher salt) and water is used. Protection potion or oil, straight or a few drops in water, could also be used (see Lesson Twelve). You don't need any cleaning agents, though some will put a few drops of rose water hydrosol, orange water hydrosol, or witch hazel extract. Traditionalists will use a magickal wash, a dilute tea, of monkshood (aconite). Monkshood is very poisonous, so at this point in your training, I don't recommend it. Other more modern witches, myself included, use a safer yet wonderfully magickal wash of vervain. In fact, I use this formula:

    1 tablespoon vervain
    1 tablespoon rose petals
    1 tablespoon yarrow
    1 tablespoon mugwort

Place into two cups of boiling water, along with a stone from a sacred place. It can be from an ancient sacred site, or more likely, a special place to you, like a mountain or beach. I used a stone a friend retrieved from the pyramids of Giza. Let it sit for at least twelve hours in a sealed glass container, like a Mason jar, and then strain, add one to two tablespoons of a high-quality alcohol to preserve (such as vodka or brandy), and bottle it. Use to cleanse and consecrate your objects with magickal power. When you learn more about potions, you can create this wash in a magick circle ritual, just like other types of potions.

You don't have to submerge the object, and if it is water soluble or a rust hazard, this wouldn't be advised. Simply rub a few drops on the object, and imagine it washing away the harmful energies of the tool. For metallic objects, make sure you dry them completely.

Most traditional ways of water cleansing are bringing the objects to a running spring, or to the ocean or similar body of water. Moving bodies of water and the ocean are preferred because of their cleansing properties, rather than still bodies. Water cleansing is not practical if you don't live near such a source of water. Some substitute the running water of the faucet, which works, but it is not quite the same.

Earth

Earth techniques of cleansing take the longest, since earth is the most dense element. Such cleansing require either burying the object in a bowl of salt, or in the land itself, for a few hours to a few days. The salt or soils absorbs and transforms the energy like a decaying leaf or body, making the old energies into something new and useful somewhere else. If you do bury your tools to connect with and cleanse them, be sure to place a sturdy marker, so later you know where they are.

Spirit

Spirit is the easiest way to cleanse, but the way students are least sure of initially. Cleansing with spirit means cleansing with clear intention. Hold the object for a few moments in your hand and focus your will. Call upon the Goddess, God, and Great Spirit for aid. Then imagine the object filling with crystal-white cleansing light. The light burns away all unwanted vibrations. You can either "wipe" the discarded energies away with your hands or your mind, or blow on the object, combining an air technique with spirit into a powerful cleansing ritual.

This is not the only technique of cleansing with spirit. Meditate on it, and find a way that speaks to you.

Cleanse all your tools right before you charge them, particularly for the first time. If you are not confident about your cleansing techniques, you can use a pendulum (see

ITOW, chapter 13, for more on pendulum use) to determine if the object is clear before going to the next step.

Once the object is cleansed, hold it with your hands. Feel your pulse mingle with its pulse. The object may feel magickally alive in your hands. Feel your energy connect with it and start your partnership with it. Call upon the Goddess and God for aid. Call upon whatever energy, element, or quality the tool is used for, and, out loud or silently, say a blessing. They can be as poetic or simple as you desire. Feel the blessing and impart the blessing to the tool.

For instance, I might hold the black candle, and think about the Goddess, asking for her aid. I will feel the power of black, of the Goddess, the divine mother. A blessing I learned is: "I charge this black candle in honor of the Goddess, the Moon and the Night. I charge this candle to draw in energy for my magick. So mote it be." I would send this energy, this feeling, into the candle. If I was charging a candle in the fire corner, I would think about fire, passion, will, and an intensity. I would send those intentions into the candle and say, "I charge this candle for the element of fire," or more poetically, "I charge this candle for the element of fire, may it bring guidance and protection. So mote it be." All the objects on the altar should be charged, from candle holders, to matches, bottles, and statues.

Your four-element objects are particularly important, and often require special blessings in certain traditions.

Athame

One of the favorite ways of cleansing the athame is with incense and breath. Traditionalists will acquire a lodestone, a naturally magnetic rock, and rub the stone across the edge of the blade in one direction several times to consecrate it, combining the magnetic energies of the Goddess with the airy power of the mind. Traditional witches often stab the blade into the ground and leave it in the earth for one moon cycle.

Wand

Wand is usually cleansed with fire and incense. Tantric traditions might anoint it with sexual fluids. Others could use a drop of blood from a pinprick, but neither are found frequently in modern Wicca.

Chalice

Both the cleansing and the blessing of the chalice can be done with particularly special water taken from a sacred site. Now before you think you have to dash off to the UK and get water from the Glastonbury Well, sacred sites are all about. It can be from a particularly special spring, river, or lake near you. Or, you can simply bless regular water if you have no site in mind. If you take water (or anything from a sacred site), it is first important to meditate a moment at the site, and check in with your higher guidance, and the spirit of the site, to make sure you have permission. If you do, it is customary to leave something in return. Traditional offerings are coins, incense, cakes, wine, honey, or today, even chocolate. You can leave healing energy and a loving intention. Then use the water to anoint the chalice as a part of your consecration ritual for it.

Stone

Your earth tool should be left on or in the earth for a few days to harmonize it with the power of the land. You can also take it to a sacred site. I cleanse my stone in the earth for a few days, dig it up, and then place it in a special herb garden as my sacred site. I don't cleanse it in the garden because I don't want the unwanted energies to seep into the plants and herbal medicines I make from them.

EXERCISE 27

Consecrate Altar Tools

For the next exercise, there are no step-by-step instructions. Let your heart, mind, and intuition lead you through a cleansing and blessing process of all your altar tools. Create and set up your altar as a spiritual exercise to get in touch with all the tools you have and the power they embody.

If you don't have all your tools, have no fear. You don't have to do them all at once. Charge the ones you have, and continue your quest for the additional tools. Charge each as you get them and place them on your altar. You don't need everything listed above, but the basic tools outlined are customary.

I prefer to charge objects in the magick circle when possible. Anything done in the circle is more powerful and purposeful. For now, simply cleanse and consecrate your tools before you begin your ritual work. Once you are familiar with the magick circle ritual, you can do it again in circle.

I also cleanse and consecrate the entire altar. I learned to take salt water, and trace the edges of the altar top and smudge the entire structure with incense before using it.

One the tools are charged, some practitioners are adamant about letting no one touch their tools, for fear of contamination. I can understand that perfectly, but I think the "threat" is exaggerated. I think if someone holds a tool with respect and genuine interest, then nothing too detrimental happens. But if someone is handling it haphazardly or playing with it, then the tool does pick up on such energies and needs cleansing again.

I believe the entire altar should be cleansed and rededicated at least once a year. You might think that is not often enough, or too often. Some witches do it once a month. Do it when you feel the need, but I've recleansed objects as needed, and done a greater cleansing about once a year. The more you use the object and feel that energy, the less likely the tool will "lose" its purpose and energy.

My tools are touched by many people as a part of my teaching work, and although I cleanse them often, I don't feel they are overly contaminated. Part of their purpose is to help people with the craft. Again, the intent of the holder is the determining factor.

ALTAR DEVOTIONALS

Altar devotionals are a form of tuning into the forces of the universe daily, via the altar. Everyday, I redevote myself to this path, to the Goddess, God, and Great Spirit, and to my purpose in this world. I do that by standing before my altar and taking the time to speak with the divine. I take this time to center myself in sacredness and create my day, inviting in the highest guidance and help for what is before me. Sometimes it is a casual conversation. Other times, it is a more structured verse.

Although witches shy away from the word "prayer," seeking to distance themselves from Judeo-Christian dominance, a devotional is very much like a prayer. The difference is that it is in my own words, in my own space, in my own way, rather than something done by rote with little understanding or energy.

Altar devotionals can include short meditations, particularly the daily upkeep meditations, cleansings, and chakra-balancing exercises from ITOW. You can light a candle and incense, but I usually don't if I'm going off to work. I keep things simple and put my energy into the devotional. That way I don't have to worry if I left a candle or incense burning as I leave the house. You can also include any meaningful poetry, readings, or sayings that move you. For a while, I used the reiki principles, statements of how to live your life, used in the reiki tradition of healing. I've used quotations from Celtic poetry and inspirational sayings from world religions. Some recite the Wiccan Rede or "The Charge of the Goddess." When intensely studying the tarot or runes, I made them a part of my devotional. Such oracles are a great way to let the divine speak back to you when not in a place to hear messages directly. You can call upon specific deities or spirits you wish to build a relationship with as a part of your daily experience. I often include my affirmations, sending light to myself and others, and most importantly, a sense of thankfulness for all that I have.

The thankfulness is more important to me than the requests to create and affirm. As you think thankfulness, joy, and abundance on all levels, you create more joy and abundance that will return to you on all levels. In essence, the devotional is the most powerful form of life-changing magick, even though it seems so simple. The very act of it will transform your worldview.

A usual devotional for me would include:

I would start with a quick Earth and Sky Meditation (from Lesson Four in ITOW).

I, Christopher John, thank the Goddess, God, and Great Spirit for
This body, heart, mind, and soul,
For this place and time and all opportunities given to love and learn
I thank you for the people in my life

I then list and envision the people who are on my mind, including myself, and send multicolored light to them all, for the highest good.

I thank you for my talents and path and ask to continue to serve you for the highest good.

I would then include any affirmations of things I want to create in my life. As of this writing, I was working on:

I thank you for my eyesight, and my eyesight continues to grow stronger and clearer on all levels, without the aid of corrective lens or surgery.

I thank you for my body, and continue to build a strong, healthy body in my ideal image.

I thank you for my partner Steve, and continue to build a healthy marriage and home with him.

I thank the Goddess, God, and Great Spirit for all gifts and ask that all come with ease, grace, and gentleness.

I end with viewing my protection shield, affirming it will protect me. See Lesson Five in ITOW.

The previous altar devotional has morphed into a form based on the four elements, and when I do it, I do "miniature" versions of the elemental attunements, doing earth, water, air, fire, and spirit.

I, Christopher John, thank the Goddess, God, and Great Spirit for my body, health, and home. I continue to build a relationship with my body and the world.

I thank you for my heart, for my partner, my family, coven, friends, students, and teachers. I ask to send all these loved ones the light they need for this day.

I thank you for my mind, and my ability to write, speak, teach, and heal. I ask to continue my path of service for the highest good.

I thank you for my soul, for my inner light and protection. I thank you for my spirit guides and the goddesses and gods. I thank you for the path of the witch. I thank you for all things. Blessed be.

Another devotional I do when I am in my office, before teaching or seeing clients, is to light a white candle, and say:

I ask the Goddess, God, and Great Spirit to guide my every thought, word, and deed. By your divine will, so mote it be.

Devotionals can be longer or shorter, based on your own style or need. They will change over time, as you change. Mine have changed greatly, but if I had to say that any one technique from witchcraft helped me the most, it is the daily devotionals, combined with short meditations, daily, before starting my work. Regular meditation would be a close second, but the daily commitment, showing up and devoting myself to this path, was the one things that really brought witchcraft to me as a way of life rather than only a science or art. Even if I didn't do any other ritual, magick, meditation, or psychic talent, I was living as a witch every day.

Annie Laurie, a witch with a strong Native American leaning, uses these words as her daily devotional, commenting that when she doesn't do it, or doesn't do it with feeling, something is missing in her day and she feels off center.

Today, Mother Earth, Father Sky, Brother Sun, Sister Moon,
I honor you
Today, guardians and winds of the north, east, south, and west
I honor you.
Today, elements and allies of
Earth, on which I stand and which grounds me;
Fire, which ignites my inner spark and which heats me;
Air, which I breathe and which moves me;
And water, which I drink and which flows through me;
I honor you.
Guide me as I serve the Greater Good, harming none. To those with me on my path of perfect love and perfect trust, stay me with me if you will, go only if you must.
So mote it be.
Blessed be and thank you.

In the evening, Annie does this devotional to close her day.

I surrender the events, the remains of the day,
To the Goddess and God, to do with what you may.
Grant me my rest, as I sleep this night,
O Goddess and God, of this earth's delight.
Teach me, speak to me, or grant me pleasant dreams.
Send what you will, on Luna's moonbeams.
Goodnight. Thank you. Blessed be.

The commitment to do a devotional can take from two to ten minutes a day, and its not much to ask of one who wants to commit to the way of the witch as a life path. I have heard similar stories from friends and students who have shown me that altar devotionals are truly important and life changing.

Even though they are called altar devotionals, and traditionally done at the altar, they can be done anywhere and at anytime. You can do them before longer meditation sessions. I usually start my meditations with a quick devotional, asking for guidance and protection. I meditate at night, so I do a more normal form of devotional in the morning before work. If you are traveling, don't let the lack of altar stop you; create a small traveling altar in your quarters. The altar is just a touchstone for the sacred forces, and a place to remember and gather power, but remember you have them within you, wherever you go.

EXERCISE 28

Altar Devotionals

Create your own altar devotional and practice it daily. Let it flow, grow, and change as you change, until you start to find a pattern and style that works consistently for you. Use the examples above for inspiration, but make it your own. Make daily use of your devotional if possible. If not, try to do it at least three to five times a week.

HOMEWORK

- Start gathering all your altar tools as needed and create a space for them.

- Do Exercises 27 and 28, and record your first experiences in your BOS.

- Practice your altar devotional.

- Continue journaling regularly.

- Continue a regular meditation practice, using the meditative tools from this book, ITOW, and any other techniques you find helpful.

TIPS

- Don't get upset if you lack the discipline to do your altar devotional consistently. You are learning discipline. If you get angry at yourself or feel guilty about it, you will never want to do it. Devotionals are a blessing and a joy. This path is not about guilt or shame. For now, do it as often as you can. Strive to do it regularly and watch your discipline grow.

LESSON SIX
DIVINATION OF TRUE WILL

Before getting personally involved in Wicca, my image of the witch was the little old Gypsy fortuneteller gazing into the crystal ball, reading palms or shuffling the deck of tarot cards. She was the fortuneteller of the Old World. I thought the idea of fortune-telling was pure superstition. As I continued on my path and discovered witchcraft, and discovered the validity of psychic abilities and magick, how could I so quickly dismiss the possibility of fortunetelling? At first, such tools didn't appeal to me, but like so many techniques in the craft, until I had a personal experience, I completely misunderstood the ancient wisdom behind it.

As a spiritual experience, fortunetelling is better known as divination. Divination is the act of divining. "Divination" loosely translated is "to read the future," but in the structure of the word we learn the profound sacredness that is inherent in the act. To do any divination, one must connect with the divine, and enter a divine viewpoint. The very act of making this connection, regardless of the tool used, is a sacred act. The tools seem silly to some—cards, crystals, and stones—and have come to draw attention away from the very important connection that is being made to the divine mind, through our psychic senses. With our psychic mind we hear the voice of our soul. Through the soul, we hear the soul of the Goddess, God, and Great Spirit, the souls of the universe. From this perspective, many truths are revealed for the highest good. Then, through this divine connection, wisdom is shared with others. Nothing could be more sacred.

Divination is learned for many reasons. We often make the connection to the sacred to receive. We ask for spells. We ask for results, from prosperity to healing and love. We ask and many do not learn to listen. Divination, like meditation, is a form of learning to listen. In divination, we are primarily asking the divine, "What do I need to know? What am I not seeing? Does this course of action conform with the highest good, or am I blinded by my own ego?"

Learning the art of divination is like learning the art of listening. It is about seeking heartfelt advice before diving into a new situation. Many traditions believe you cannot divine for yourself. You must seek an intermediary. The thought behind such rules is that you are too attached to your personal outcome in a given situation and will not see the signs clearly and in an unbiased way.

Other traditions recommend you divine for yourself often, before every spell cast, and before any major decision. The purpose is to be open to advice from the gods for this juncture, and to practice separating your ego view from your divine, higher self view. By identifying with the divine self even when you personally want something, by learning to be open to the answers even your ego doesn't want to hear, you are becoming a master of consciousness. Only through practice do we discern our personal will from our divine will, and ultimately learn our personal will is a tool, a vehicle to manifest our soul's desire, rather than our personality's. The process is not done overnight, but with much practice, patience, and love. Many witches feel the real heart of the Wiccan Rede, "Do what thou will," refers not to your personal ego will, but your divine true will, and the will of the Goddess, God, and Great Spirit. When you do divination before taking action or doing magick, you are asking, "Is this work part of my soul's truest desires, for my highest good? Is this work in harmony with the Goddess and God's highest aspects?" Then you are truly listening for the answer and acting upon it.

NONLINEAR TIME

We are all thoughts in the divine mind. We are all connected. All places are one place. All times are one time. We know this from our study of mysticism and Hermetics, but the reality of it can be hard to face. Even though we know these truths intellectually, our experience gives us past, present, and future. Although there is no past or future, only the present moment, containing all memories and possibilities, we, as human beings, perceive ourselves going in a line so to speak. Behind us is what has happened and before us is the potential future. We stand in the present moment. Even the Triple Goddess embodies this truth in the form of She Who Was, She Who Is, and She Who Will Be.

I imagine all events united and together, like beads in a large bowl. Each event is a bead, and all the beads are in the bowl of the divine mind. But our experience is like a thread stringing many beads together, giving them order and precision. While we are on the string, we only see the beads that are on the string. We don't see all the possibilities and potentials all around us. That is our experience of human, linear time.

When we do divination, we step out of the string, and watch above the bowl. We see where we are in the present, and have a whole new perspective of the past, and its unrealized potentials, as well as the future, and new possibilities. Suddenly our perception is no longer linear, but multidimensional. When in this altered state of awareness, receiving psychic information through our divination tool, we get a viewpoint, a higher viewpoint, that is not normally available to us. Through this more godlike view, we can receive information from the divine, from our spirits, guides, and patrons, and make wiser, more complete decisions based on a broader knowledge rather than our limited linear view.

TOOLS OF DIVINATION

A variety of divination tools exist. They come from different cultures, time periods, and magickal traditions. Some are seen as more acceptable by mainstream culture, such as I-Ching, while others are often surrounded with some fear, such as tarot. All of these tools have one thing in common. They act as a key for our psychic ability. Through the complex system of symbols encoded in the tool, a witch can use these symbols as a springboard to new information via their natural psychic abilities. Often basic answers are strongly imbedded in the cards themselves, and once you know the system, little psychic interpretation is needed. The more detached you are from the situation or question, the more psychic information is available. Because of this, many psychic readers feel you cannot effectively read for yourself because you won't get a lot of new psychic information that you are unaware of. Although this is true, if you understand the messages and symbols of your divination tool, you can get a great amount of direction and guidance without getting startling new psychic information. Divination really comes in two basic forms. The first is a defined system of symbols, with basic fundamental meanings, such as tarot, runes, ogham sticks, I-Ching, and a variety of other modern card and symbol systems available. The second is symbolic interpretation of random shapes and images suggested to the reader's mind through a changing medium, such as crystal gazing and tea leaf reading.

ORACLE SYSTEMS

Oracle systems comprise a set number of symbols with basic archetypal meanings, but can be open to intuitive interpretation based on the technique used to read them and the reader. In some systems, meanings are changed depending on the symbols next to it, the type of layout used, and the position of the symbol.

Such systems are often referred to as oracles. They are devices that serve many functions. An oracle historically refers to a person who acts as a diviner, a intermediary between humanity and the divine will, giving omens and advice. The most famous of oracles was the Oracle of Delphi, originally dedicated to the goddess Gaia, but later the temple was run by the followers of Apollo. Both deities are seen as givers of the gift of prophecy. The system an oracle used was also called an oracle device, though many ancients divined the future through the patterns in animal entrails, which is a system modern witches do not use. One tradition found worldwide is "throwing the bones" or "throwing stones," a group of bones or stones each with a symbolic meaning, used much like runes or tarot cards. These devices are a form of primal technology, a device to communicate with the realms of the gods and get definitive answers. They also serve to stimulate the reader's own natural, intuitive, and psychic ability, yet have a foundation of meanings and symbols to draw from, rather than simply using psychic ability alone.

The advantage of this type of divination is that the reader is inspired by archetypal images. Although there is room for symbolic interpretation, the basic meanings and lessons of the symbols are somewhat standard. This prevents the reader from either always interpreting the symbols with rose-colored glasses, or from a perspective of gloom and doom. Without a set system of symbols, it is easy to see only your preconceived notions.

With this type of system, it is possible to do a reading for yourself. You would probably not get a lot of brand-new psychic information, since you know your life well. Other readers who are less involved and less attached to your life are more likely to have new psychic information come through during the reading. If you are not focusing on future events, but asking for sincere advice about your life, you can pick symbols from your oracle system that will guide and inspire answers.

Tarot

Tarot is a complex system of divination favored by many witches. Although many imply the ancient origins of the tarot, no one is absolutely certain from where it originates. The concepts and mystical lore involved in the tarot is eternal, but the practice of using cards for divination is up for debate. Many believe it is Egyptian or Indian in origin. It is named after the royal road, the road of life that we all walk.

The tarot itself is a pack of seventy-eight cards divided into twenty-two major arcana, symbolizing the major experiences of life, and fifty-six minor arcana, detailing more day-to-day situations and experiences. Through picking cards, the archetype of each card, its energy and essence, synchronistically matches the energies of our life. You can pull one or several cards out to get advice about a current situation, for yourself or others. Dabblers have noticed that even if you don't know what the cards mean, and simply look up the meanings in a book, the cards have relevance. Therefore, they believe the cards themselves are the source of this magick, but it is your interaction with the cards and your willingness to listen to the universe that catalyzes the magick of tarot.

If you are drawn to use the tarot as your divination tool, but have never formally used it, try this basic primer to start. Then expand your studies as you work within the craft.

The major arcana, also known as the trumps, consists of twenty-two cards numbered zero to twenty one. Each one is associated with different astrological signs, planets, or elements, and symbolizes a range of spiritual experiences and events. Below is a very basic overview of these powerful symbols, with a basic archetypal meaning and its challenge, warning, or "reversed" meaning.

0—Fool: The Fool represents the birth into the world as an innocent, with endless possibility, eternal optimism, and divine grace. The Fool can also be a warning for those who are acting foolishly or too optimistically without any proper planning.

I—Magician: The Magician is the card of magickal power, where one learn to express willpower into the world to create change. The Magician also indicates travel, communication, and writing. He warns us of abuses of power from not thinking things through, or a lack of clear intention and communication.

II—Priestess: The Priestess is the guardian of the gates of consciousness. She is the Moon goddess who tells us to listen to our intuition, emotions, and magick. She helps us prepare for the future. She can also warn us when secrets are revealed.

III—Empress: The Empress is the earth mother, and shows up whenever there are issues of motherhood, family, or fertility. She is the provider, but also tells us when others are taking advantage of our good nature.

IV—Emperor: The Emperor represents power and authority, both our own power and ability to handle responsibility, and those who have power over us. The Emperor appears with issues of father or employers, and asks us to reflect on the qualities of leadership in our life. Are we kind rulers, or under wise rulership? Or are we dictators, or under the sway of the power-hungry?

V—Hierophant: The Hierophant is the spiritual teacher. In the best situations, this is the mentor or wise guru, guiding one through life, but allowing you to find your own answers. He is kind and loving. In the worse situations, this is the institution of dogma and religions, where only one way is shown and all others discouraged. The Hierophant calls us to find our teachers or our inner teachers, and often to become teachers ourselves by sharing what we know with those who seek it.

VI—Lovers: In the earthly level, the Lovers indicates a loving, often romantic relationship. On the spiritual plane, it is the path of self-love, where the inner male and inner female come together in divine love. The Lovers asks us to look at our personal and inner relationships for true love.

VII—Chariot: The Chariot is the start of a new journey. On a mundane level it is travel and transportation. On a higher level, it is the process of choosing your next path at the crossroads of life after some previous success by going within and using your intuition.

VIII—Strength: This card indicates finding and using your personal power. The highest personal power is spiritual love. The woman tames the lion not through weapons, but with her bare hands, showing her understanding of the lion. Strength asks us to tame our inner animal and harness its power.

IX—Hermit: The Hermit urges us to take time to be alone and go within. On a mundane level it can be loneliness, but simultaneously the chance to get to know yourself and follow your inner light through reflection.

X—Fortune: Through the wheel, we see the cycles and seasons of our life, and how all patterns repeat. The Fortune card often indicates a favorable turn of events, including prosperity or spiritual guidance. Fortune asks us to remained centered in the wheel as it turns.

XI—Justice: Justice is about taking action to bring balance. Balance can be in your life and relationships. Many associate it with legal issues. Others assign karma to it. Both systems, human law and karmic law, are about bringing balance to a situation.

XII—Hanged Man: When upside down, the Hanged Man offers a new perspective. This archetype initially feels like being stuck in life, but if you surrender to the "hanging," you see that you are being granted a new view and a different opportunity to solve the issue at hand.

XIII—Death: Death signifies an ending. It can be the death of a situation, relationship, or even a sense of identity or ego. Through this death we find transformation and rebirth.

XIV—Temperance: Temperance is to temper, to forge or create, like a blacksmith, alchemist or even artist. Through Temperance, we explore through creation, unifying extremes and bringing new ideas into material form.

XV—Devil: The Devil has two strong meanings. First is enslavement of your own making, a bondage to something you could escape if you only took action to do so, but your material needs and fears out weigh your spiritual calling. Second is the archetype of the outcast, one who is a rebel, and marches to the beat of his or her drum.

XVI—Tower: The flash of enlightenment strikes the tower, knocking down all that doesn't serve your highest good. This card is drawn when situations are brought back down to their foundation for re-evaluations and rebuilding, but the process can be traumatic.

XVII—Star: The Star appears to signify finding situations where you can be yourself and understand your role. You can truly shine like a star and attract the resources you need. It also warns us when we become too detached from earthly concerns.

XVIII—Moon: The Moon is the gateway of initiation, symbolizing deep emotions that bring us to new depth. It asks us to follow our emotions and intuitions, but at the same time warns us about seeing through our personal illusions and desires.

XIX—Sun: Feeling like a bright and sunny day, the Sun card appears to indicate health, happiness, prosperity, romance, and many blessings. The clouds have lifted, and you are joyous on the new day. You may feel your work is complete, but as the nineteenth card, the Sun warns us the journey is not over yet.

XX—Judgment: The Judgment card represents the New Age. Often it appears to show you have found where you need to be and now is a time of rejoicing. Other times it appears when we are judgmental of self or others, or near a great calamity that forces us to see things clearly.

XI—World: The world is the dance of the universal Goddess, all matter and space. It indicates the study of nature and personal mastery in the world. It indicates your home or roots, and often moving your roots to a more harmonious space, both physically and spiritually.

The minor arcana can be divided into four suits, each based on an element and a fundamental area of life.

Discs/Pentacles: Earth—money, investments, health, body, home

Wands: Fire—will, identity, passion, career, sexuality, energy

Swords: Air—mind, communication, thought, memory, travel

Cups: Water—emotion, love, family, romance, healing

These cards are numbered ace through ten, and each number has a potent power to it, reflected in the element of the suit. The path of one through ten is a journey, a journey through the elemental realm. All aces have something in common, regardless of the suit. All twos have something in common, and so on throughout the series. This is a simple method of getting an overview of each of the cards.

Ace: Signifies new beginnings. Brings unity, harmony, inspiration and confidence.

Two: Signifies polarity. Energetic movement to create something new. Often indicates balance or partnership.

Three: Signifies the trinity and change. Growth and expansion, often dealing with communication.

Four: Signifies solidity. Brings stability and foundation, like the four legs of a table. Indicates security or stagnation.

Five: Signifies the cycle of life, bringing change from the balance of four. Often appears to be imbalance, upset, discord, or loss.

Six: Signifies synthesis and unity with higher forces. Often manifests as an achievement or victory.

Seven: Signifies mysticism and emotion. A time to withdraw and reflect, but often appears as a temporary setback or stepping stone.

Eight: Signifies mental preparation and focus. Eight can manifest as a need for balance and taking action or inaction to create balance.

Nine: Signifies the climax of the cycle, and the opportunity to master the lessons of the suit.

Ten: Signifies the completion or manifestation of the cycle. The result or outcome, and the true lessons of the suit.

So in practice, the Ace of Discs can signify new beginnings in money or finance, such as a new job. The Ace of Wands brings new energy to a passionate project or relationship. The Ace of Swords clears out past confusion and brings new mental clarity and communication. The Ace of Cups washes away old wounds and brings a new sense of love and healing to the individual or family.

The minor arcana suits also contain court or royalty cards. Most readers interpret court cards to signify different people who interact with the one receiving the reading, or aspects of the recipient's personality. Each type of court card is modified by an element, creating a blend of elements. Different decks name the court cards differently. Some say king, queen, knight, and page, while others use knight, queen, prince, and princess. In essence there is an adult male, an adult female, a young male, and a young female/child/androgynous in each suit.

King/Knight: Father, adult male—fiery aspect of the suit

Queen: Mother, matriarch, woman—watery aspect of the suit

Knight/Prince: Son, young man—airy aspect of the suit

Page/Princess: Daughter, young woman—earthy aspect of the suit

So if you choose the Queen of Pentacles, you have chosen the watery aspect of earth. It denotes a person who is emotional or reflective on life, the home, health, or finances. Each court card can be similarly interpreted based on the combination of elements. The suit denotes the main element at hand, while the court card shows its approach to those issues.

When interpreting the card, one would also intuitively go by the scene depicted by the artist on the card. Your feelings and first reactions to the cards are as important as any book meaning. Some read the cards differently upside down and right side up, but I don't prefer this method. Generally the reversed card is the "negative" or unwanted meaning, or warning, while the upright is the original meaning of the card. I think tarot is a complex system beyond positive and negative, since life falls in the many shades of gray. I use intuition and the other cards chosen to decide how "positive" or "negative" to read a card.

There are many ways to choose the cards. Each reader has a ritual for it. I simply hold the cards, think about my life, situation, or question, then shuffle the cards, fan them out, and choose enough for my layout.

To ask for guidance about spellwork, I may pick one to three cards. For other situations, you might want to do a formal spread. Most tarot decks come with booklets detailing the author's intended meaning and potential spreads to use with the deck. Favorite is the Celtic cross spread among many, but personally I don't like it. I prefer my own spread.

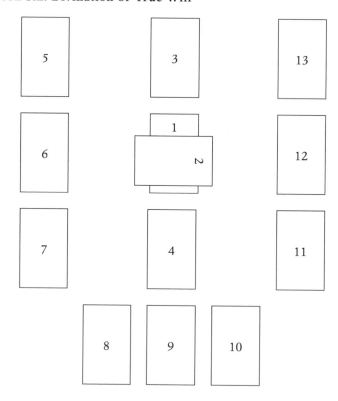

Figure 17: Tarot Layout

Card one indicates who you are reading for, and their state of being. Card two indicates the problem crossing the person. Card three indicates the conscious thought of the person, and card four indicates the subconscious thoughts of the person.

The remaining cards are like a U arching in time, from past to future, left to right. Cards five, six, and seven are the past events influencing the situation, with five being the furthest past and seven being the most recent. Cards eight, nine, and ten are the present. Cards eleven, twelve, and thirteen are the future if the current course of action is followed, with eleven being the immediate future and thirteen being the furthest future. I use this spread for general life-readings and detailed situations.

For myself, I use simpler spreads, and pick one to three cards most mornings before I begin my day. If I planned on doing a relationship spell and picked the Hanged

Man, Knight (young male) of Cups, and Ten of Wands, I would determine it was not the best time for this spell. The Hanged Man urges me to surrender and see things in a new way; the Knight of Cups, the air aspect of water, also asks me to think or intellectualize things, or indicates a partner who is too intellectual and not emotional enough; and in my deck, the Thoth deck, the Ten of Wands is called the Oppression card.

If I picked the Two of Cups, Fool, and Sun cards, I would say that the spell was a fortunate thing to do for my higher good. The Two of Cups is called Love in my deck, the Fool indicates unlimited opportunity, and the Sun card is blessings and success.

Often the answer will not be as clear-cut as these examples, so really strive to learn your cards.

Runes

The runes are a system of magick and divination from the Teutonic tribes, and is primarily associated with Norse traditions. Each rune is simultaneously a pictoral symbol, a word of power, and an archetypal mystery. Runes can be used for divination and for creating change through talismans and amulets.

Many systems of the runes exist, but the most well-known among modern pagans is the Elder Futhark. Below is each rune and its various interpretations upright and reversed. This is a very basic list of meanings. Just as each tarot has a multitude of lessons, so does each rune, and each is open to interpretation by different scholars and practitioners.

To truly be understood, each rune is a mystery of power, and must be delved into through meditation and serious study of runic lore. Use this as a basic springboard to further a deeper understanding of the system.

Symbol	Old English	Germanic	Image	English Letter
ᚠ	Feoh	Fehu	Cattle	F

To these pagan people, cattle is the symbol of wealth. Through it you have food, materials, and something to trade. When Feoh is chosen, it symbolizes prosperity, success, and fulfillment of your needs. Reversed, Feoh is a loss of prosperity or status. Feoh can accompany delays and frustrations to your needs and desires.

Symbol	Old English	Germanic	Image	English Letter
ᚢ	Ur	Uruz	Wild Ox	U, V

The wild ox, rather than the tamed, is a symbol of strong will, health, vitality, and un-broken spirit. Ur denotes all these qualities when chosen. Reversed, Ur is a failure, often in the body, denoting weakness or illness. Ur reversed can also be a lost opportunity due to lack of will or daring.

ᚦ	Thorn	Thuriaz	Vexing Thorn	Th

Thorn is associated with protection and luck. Some link it with protection from frost giants, mythic enemies of the gods of the Norse. Reversed, it denotes an unfortunate turn of events, and a feeling of powerlessness, particularly to the forces of chaos.

ᚩ	Os	Ansuz	Mouth	A

Os is not only the mouth, but the words spoken from the mouth, including advice and wisdom given by another. Reversed, it is the poison of the mouth, lies, deception, or simply lack of clear communication.

ᚱ	Rad	Raido	Wagon	R

Rad is the rotating wagon wheel, showing travel and movement, be it spiritual travel or physical journey. Reversed, it shows an unexpected or unwanted journey, again either physically or a journey of the soul.

ᚲ	Cen	Kenaz	Fire	C, K, Q, X

Cen is the blessing of fire, quite a powerful force in any culture, but doubly so for a tribe so far north. It brings the blessings of energy, power and general good fortune. Reversed Cen indicates an ending, loss, unwanted change or time of darkness.

ᚷ	Gyfu (Gifu)	Gebo	Gift	G

Gyfu indicates good luck, unexpected resources, and a healthy partnership. It has no reverse meaning.

ᚹ	Wyn	Wunjo	Joy	W, V

Wyn is the rune of success and happiness. It is joy and pleasure from life. Drawn when things are going your way. Reversed, Wyn is the rune of failure and unhappiness, when forces seem to work against you.

Symbol	Old English	Germanic	Image	English Letter
ᚺ	Hagal	Hagalaz	Hail	H

Hagal appears when we are faced with things beyond our control. Its archetypal image is hail, frozen water raining down upon the world. In practical terms, it shows delay and restrictions. No reverse meaning.

	Nyd (Neid)	Nauthiz	Patience	N

Nyd indicates a period of testing, where one is faced with difficult trials. The only advice Nyd gives is to have patience, as all things will pass. No reverse meaning.

ᛁ	Is	Isa	Ice	I

Is means ice, or frozen water. Ice is an archetypal creative force in Norse myth. Here it indicates a situation being frozen or stuck, or filled with coldness. While water can be clear, ice is usually opaque, and, reflecting sunlight, can blind. But like ice, this energy will eventually melt and flow bringing change. This rune has no reverse meaning.

	Ger	Jera	Harvest	J, Y

Ger is the harvest, the reward of a season of hard work and planning. Symbolically it is what you deserve based on your efforts, and some would equate it with justice or karma. Since it is about reaping what you have sown, there is no reversed meaning, but it could be considered good or bad, depending on your own actions.

ᛇ	Eoh	Eihwaz	Yew	I

Yew is the tree of protection. Ash and yew are associated with the Norse World Tree. This rune comes up when one is in need of protection, or already is under protection.

ᛈ	Peord	Perth	Mystery	P

Peord is the lot cup, the vessel in which runes or other oracles are held. Peord holds the mystery of what was, is, and will be. Drawn it indicates hidden things, secrets, and the mystic. Reversed, it shows unpleasant surprises coming to light.

ᛉ	Eohl-Secg	Algiz	Elk	Z

Eohl-Secg is the elk. Elks, like most horned creatures, have a powerful sense of instinct and perception, often from picking up vibration and energy from the horns, like spiritual antenna. The elk is a symbol of trusting your instinct, good fortune, friendship, and protection. Reversed, it is vulnerability from not following instincts, or sacrifice for a greater good.

Symbol	Old English	Germanic	Image	English Letter
⚡	Sigel	Sowelu	Sun	S, Z

Sigel is the ray of the Sun. Two rays together look like the Sun wheel. It symbolizes power, victory, and success in any endeavor, and has no reversed meaning.

Symbol	Old English	Germanic	Image	English Letter
↑	Tir	Teiwaz	the god Tyr	T

Tir is named for Tyr, the god of justice. He lost his hand to subdue the Fenris wolf. This rune is about order, justice, self-sacrifice, and overcoming obstacles. Reversed, it is failure, injustice, or a waste of your sacrifice.

Symbol	Old English	Germanic	Image	English Letter
ᛒ	Beorc	Berkana	Birth	B

Beorc is both literal and symbolic. It can mean family issues and new things in the family, such as children, but most often means symbolic birth and creation in your home and life. Reversed, Beorc indicates family problems or creative blocks.

Symbol	Old English	Germanic	Image	English Letter
ᛖ	Eoh	Ehwaz	Horse	E

Eoh, the horse, symbolizes change, movement, and shifts. Sometimes it indicates a new home or new mindset. Horses often work in teams to pull larger sleds, so teamwork is also included in its meaning. Reversed, it indicates difficult or far journeys, or the planned changes are not fortuitous at this time.

Symbol	Old English	Germanic	Image	English Letter
ᛗ	Man	Mannaz	Man	M

Man literally means "man," but in the sense of humanity, communication, and cooperation. Reversed, Man indicates no help from others, or open enemies.

Symbol	Old English	Germanic	Image	English Letter
ᛚ	Lagu	Laguz	Lake	L

Lagu is the lake, and in the reflection of the lake, we can scry (see "Scrying" below) and be open to psychic abilities and intuition. When drawn, Lagu tells us to listen to our intuition. When reversed, it says we are deceiving ourselves with illusions to see what we want, rather than what is.

Symbol	Old English	Germanic	Image	English Letter
ᛜ	Ing	Ingwaz	the god Ing	NG

Ing is named after the god Ing, but very little is known about him. The rune is said to indicate a period of rest after a success, much like rest after a good harvest. It shows endings, relief, and a period of internal, unseen growth. No reverse meaning.

Symbol	Old English	Germanic	Image	English Letter
ᛗ	Daeg	Dagaz	Day	D

Daeg is the daylight in its increasing form. It is the growing season, where light and awareness grow. It has no reverse meaning.

Symbol	Old English	Germanic	Image	English Letter
ᛟ	Ethel	Othila	Ancestral Land	O

Ethel is the ancestral lands, and in modern times has come to mean inheritance, possessions, and even inheriting gifts and talents as well and money and land. Reversed, it indicates financial problems with no help from family members.

Some systems use a blank rune, Wyrd, to signify fate, but most traditional rune users dislike this modern addition to the twenty-four classic symbols. I use the Wyrd rune and find it helpful. Runes can be bought or handcrafted. Any basic introduction book to the topic should include information on how to craft a set. I use runes much like cards. I ask a question or think of a situation, and pick one, two, or three runes out of my rune bag. You can also do layouts like tarot, but I prefer a simple method of three runes.

OTHER ORACLE SYSTEMS

Here are some other oracle systems worth investigating.

I-Ching

A Chinese form of divination based on sixty-four hexagram shapes, each with a different symbolic meaning. Based on the ancient Chinese text known as the Book of Changes.

Lithomancy

A system of divination using stones, precious or semiprecious, each with a symbolic meaning.

Numerology

Using a system of numbers, primarily for birth dates, names, and addresses, to see the archetypal influence of the number on a person, place or situation.

Ogham

A Celtic system based on tree symbolism. Though many modern writers cite it as an ancient calendar and zodiac, it was most likely a symbol system for memorization, divination, and magick.

SCRYING

Scrying is the second type of divination. This system does not use a standard set of symbols. Scrying speaks more to the creative mind, and uses a seemingly fluid and adaptable medium that allows a variety of symbols and interpretation. The reader gazes into the divination medium, allows symbols to be suggested from the psychic mind, which allows the conscious mind to interpret these symbols creatively and apply their meaning to life. Scrying works best when your ego is not involved, so scrying for others, or when you feel detached from the question, is the most effective time to use this technique.

Such free interpretation seems esoteric, but the process is quite simple. If you have ever been a cloud gazer, then you already understand perfectly, and simply have to take it to the next step. When you gaze into the clouds, the winds change the shape of the fluffy, white mist, and suggest symbols to your mind. We see animals, ships, and symbols. I've seen dragons, whales, arrows, and stars. The next step is to allow those shapes to have meaning. The ship could mean travel, and the direction of the ship's movement could tell you where you are going. A turtle could symbolize slow movement or a need for a protective shell.

Although scrying is most often thought of as psychically gazing into a reflective surface, not all gazing mediums are reflective. This type of divination is extended into the shapes of tea leaves, wax, oil, smoke, or sand in a variety of mediums. Most commonly used is quartz crystal. I even knew of a Guatemalan shaman who gazed into the intricate patterns of his colorful, woven headdress.

The ultimate extension of this free-form symbolic divination is to project the screen of your mind into your medium to truly see visions to answer the questions posed to you. Skilled practitioners don't even need a medium. They simply project their vision onto a wall, corner of the room, floor, or even the cloudless sky.

The following are the most common mediums for scrying. You may find one or more becomes a favorite. And don't be surprised in your experimentations that several mediums just don't work for you. Everyone has their own preferences and tools that work best.

Crystal

The classic scrying device is the crystal ball. A sphere of polished quartz crystal makes an excellent object. You can scry on the surface, using the play of candlelight to suggest shapes and images to you, or you can gaze into the ball itself for your information. Crystal scrying is also known as *crystallomancy*. Great debate rages over the need for an absolutely clear piece of quartz versus those with inner inclusions or other murkiness. Traditionally, the ball should be clear, but honestly, I prefer ones with an inner landscape of inclusions. I use the lines within it to suggest shapes. When I use a clear ball, I get very few psychic impressions.

Crystal balls traditionally are covered with a black or white cloth to keep their psychic energy contained after consecration in a magick circle ritual; but again, I challenge that and like to have my crystal ball out in the open on my altar. Balls are often held on a stand, and a favorite stand is a psychic "pillow," one filled with various herbs to help promote psychic ability and cleansing the stone itself. Such pillows are usually white, black, purple, or blue. The recipe I use is:

2 parts sea salt

2 parts anise seed

3 parts vervain

1 part yarrow

1 part oak moss

½ part frankincense

½ part myrrh

A part can be any measurement, but the total of these ten parts should fill your pillow, depending on the size of the crystal ball. Each ingredient is consecrated ritually for psychic power. Make such pillows like a charm bag, but sew them shut (see chapter 13).

Crystal gazing doesn't have to be in a clear quartz sphere. Other crystals work, too. Large points are wonderful scrying devices that are often neglected. Other stones that are transparent, semitransparent, or highly reflective can be used, such as smoky quartz, obsidian, amethyst, citrine, hematite, rainbow moonstone, and a few forms of calcite. Some practitioners, my mother included, have wonderful results with lead crystal balls.

Scrying Mirror

Scrying mirrors, or witch's mirrors, are reflective surfaces used for psychic gazing. The technical term for mirror gazing is *catoptromancy*. Although a traditional silvered mirror can be used by not looking directly into it but catching the light at an angle, most witches have for more success using a black mirror. The oldest forms of black mirrors used for this purpose were most likely pieces of polished obsidian, but now it is simple to make or buy such a mirror. I learned this technique from *Dark Moon Mysteries* by Timothy Roderick, as shared with me from my student Lisa. I've changed the herbal formula and timing to suit my tastes, but the concept is the same.

You can make a magick mirror with a glass picture frame, black paint, and a few herbs. Mix this formula on the dark of the Moon (see chapter 12), and grind it to a fine powder. Traditionalist will use a mortar and pestle, but many herbal witches use the "sacred" coffee grinder. Consecrate each, and add to the mix.

    1 part star anise
    1 part oak moss
    1 bay leaf
    1 pinch of dragon's blood

Place a cleansed and charged moonstone in the mixture, cap it, and leave until the Full Moon. Take the stone out, and mix the finely ground herbs with your black paint. Consecrate the paint. Cleanse the glass and frame physically and psychically. Paint one side of the mirror evenly. Paint while in a meditative state, focusing on your intention to create a powerful scrying device. Let it dry, and place the glass, unpainted side facing out, back in the frame. Leave it under the Full Moon's light and take it back inside before the Sun rises. You now have an excellent scrying tool. Bless it in a magick circle when you have the chance, and like a crystal ball, traditionalists will tell you to cover it to retain its power.

Periodically I will ritually wash my mirror and crystal ball with a dilute infusion of psychic herbs. Try a teaspoon of vervain and teaspoon of lavender with one tablespoon of sea salt and two cups of boiling water. Let it cool and wet a cloth in the solution. Wipe over your tools and then use a cloth wet with only water to wipe away the residue.

To use, uncover the mirror and light a candle. When you delve into candle magick, charge the candle for psychic ability (see chapter 12). Hold the mirror at an angle and gently move it, catching the flickering candle flame in different ways, allowing the patterns of light to suggest shapes to you, and then gaze deeper into the mirror, allowing it to become like a view screen to bring you images, or become a gateway, to take your vision elsewhere.

Tea Leaves

Tea leaf reading is a wonderful tool for those who resonate with it. One of the first readings I ever received was from a woman who used tea leaves and her reading was amazing. Ideally, the tea is blessed and brewed in a magickal way. The one receiving the reading drinks a little more than half of a full cup with many loose leaves at the bottom. The reader will take back the cup, and either swirl it around, looking for the moving leaves to make symbols and using the reflective water as a scrying device, or will dump the leaves and tea out into the saucer, and gaze at a wider surface. The technical name of this technique is *tasseography*.

Wax

Wax divination, also known as *carromancy* and *ceremancy*, finds shapes and meaning in melting wax. My preferred method of wax divination is to prepare a special candle, and meditate with the candle, silently asking my questions. If this is for others, they hold the candle and meditate upon their questions. Then the candle is lit, and after it burns for a few minutes I ask for guidances from the Goddess and God. I then drip wax into a large bowl of cool water, allowing shapes to take form. Sometimes I take the wax out after it hardens, and gaze at the pattern that was submerged. I continue this process, emptying the bowl of wax as needed until the questions have been answered.

Hydromancy

Hydromancy is also called water scrying. You can use the reflective surface of still water as a scrying mirror. In fact, this is often the witch's favorite medium. The still water can be in the ritual chalice, under the Full Moon, or in any still body of water. Dropping stones into the water of sacred springs, ponds, or wells and reading the resulting ripples is called *pegomancy*.

Pyromancy

Pyromancy is the act of divination through fire. Gaze deeply into the fire for your images, though many see nothing, but say the fire speaks to them of the future. The flame can be from a candle or a larger flame. Most witches prefer a fire of sacred woods and herbs, often burning in a cauldron. Woods would include oak, pine, ash, willow, and hawthorne, but I prefer to use whatever is most available, and then throw some vervain or other psychic herbs into the pyre. You can also divine from the smoke of a sacred fire or incense. Certain forms of divination also use various objects melted in the fire, or the ash and embers from the end of the fire, as their medium.

Use this beginner's collection of symbols as your foundation for interpretation. They are culled from many sources and cultures, along with my own experience. Look for these symbols in your scrying medium. Let them suggest and speak to you. Use the list, but add to it. Adapt it. Make it your own, based on your experiences, and, as ever, record your experiences. You will find your own symbolic wisdom.

Angel: Divine aid, receiving messages. Pay attention to the help others offer to you.

Arrows: Movement, changing directions. Arrows to the left mean going backward; to the right, going forward.

Arrow, Down: Defeat, loss, need of a break, grounding.

Arrow, Up: Success, ascension, assuming power, or higher vision.

Baby: Conception, childbirth.

Bird: Message, spirituality.

Bull: Stubbornness, planning for the future, being rooted.

Bumblebee: Hard work, group work, sweetness of life.

Coin: Money, job, pay increase, financial concerns.

Crab: Retreating in your shell, motherhood, listening to your intuition

Crow: Message, wisdom, times are changing, listening to sacred law and the inner voice, inability to do things for yourself.

Crown: Success, promotion, new job, assuming a position of power, responsibility.

Cup: Family, love between family.

Dagger: Communication issues, argument, betrayal.

Diamond: Money, possessions, valuables, clear sight or being blinded.

Dollar Sign: Money, investment, financial concerns.

Dolphin: Aid, kindness, hearing, breath, benevolence.

Egg: New things to come, incubation, rebirth.

Feathers: Wisdom, writing, change.

Fish: Religion, spiritual journey, inner talents.

Flag: Honor, pride.

Flower: Love, spirituality, awakening.

Goat: Stubbornness, nagging, social climber.

Heart: Love, relationship, romance.

Horse: Travel, freedom, need to escape.

Infinity Loop: Never ending, power, magick.

Lightning: Inspiration, illumination, reflection, destruction.

Lion: Father, pride, humility, arrogance, sensitivity.

Moon: Womanhood, intuition, emotions.

N: No, negative.

Mountain: Climbing ahead, journey, far to go.

Pen: Communications, creativity.

Pyramid: Spiritual focus, protection.

Ram: Leadership, headstrong.

Ring: Marriage, fidelity, cycles.

Rose: Love, spirituality.

Scales: Justice, balance, legal issues.

Snake: Change, new beginnings, shedding old identity.

Star: Guidance, balance, humanity.

Square: Building a foundation, balance of the four elements.

Sun: Manhood, success, good marriage, good health, going forward.

Sword: Argument, fights, communication issues.

Torch: Light, new way, passion, vitality.

Twins: Balance, two sides to the story, something hidden.

Y: Yes, affirmative.

So, for an example, I gaze into the crystal ball thinking about my female friend, and ask if there is anything I need to know about her. I might see a mountain in the images, and feel like my friend is at its bottom. She has a long climb to go up. I think she is starting a new phase in her life, and she has just begun. As I turn the crystal, I see flowers, and think this journey is one of a spiritual nature, not just physical. Perhaps it is not a physical journey at all, but the journey of the soul. Turning the ball further, I see daggers or swords, something pointed. I'm not sure what, and feel like she will be in conflict with others, and then I see a crab, showing me that my friend will want to retreat or enter her shell. Then I see an upwards arrow and a pentacle. I see this to mean she moves beyond the arguments and ascends, protected. She is also a witch, so I assume the pentacle is a symbol of her spiritual journey as well. I feel that after a period of verbal conflict, she will reach a plateau of peace.

That was just a generalized sample of a reading I had done in the past for someone. They can be much longer or shorter, depending on the situation. Sometimes someone will ask a yes or no question, and you get either an up or down arrow, or a *Y* or *N* response. If I did scrying work before doing a spell, and simply asked if I should do this spell now, and I saw a lightning bolt followed by an egg, I might interpret that as a time to reflect on the light I am shown, and wait for an incubation period before taking action. If I saw a Sun or torch, I would do the spell.

Play with scrying and see what comes to you.

PSYCHOMETRY

Psychometry is a technique to receive information by reading the "vibrations" of an object. The reader holds an object and tunes into it to receive psychic impressions. This information can come visually, and use any of the symbols above, or it can be a simple sense of knowing.

Psychometry takes two major forms. Some practitioners focus on the object's history. They can tell where it is from and who has held it, often with great accuracy and detail. They will have impressions of the owner's physical health, mental state, and emotional well-being at the time of ownership, and can often pinpoint the country or state where the object was created.

The second form of psychometry uses the object as a link to the owner, and the psychometrist reads the owner's past, present, and future, not the object's. The object can be present, or at another location. The object itself is just a medium to connect with the owner's energy, his or her own "thread" of linear time in the eternal bowl of event beads. From that link, the reading takes off and has nothing to do with the object itself.

For this second form, ideally the object must be in the owner's aura for an extended period of time, and few others should ever touch it. Objects that are metal or stone imprint the vibrations better than wood or cloth.

The technique for tuning into an object is similar in feeling to consecrating your objects (see chapter 9) or merging your mind with an object (ITOW, chapter 8). You do not want to cleanse an object before you attempt psychometry, since you would be clearing away the very vibrations you try to read. Simply feel its pulse in your hands, and allow information to come through your intuition. Go with the first thing that comes to you.

In class I have students bring objects in without telling to whom they belong or what their history is. Participants pair off, and read each other's object, often surprising themselves and each other with the accuracy of the information. Each reader will have a specialty. Some focus on history. Others focus on health or emotions. Each reader brings information through in different ways. Honor the way your psychic voice comes through.

ᴏᴛʜᴇʀ ꜰᴏʀᴍꜱ ᴏꜰ ꜰʟᴜɪᴅ ᴅɪᴠɪɴᴀᴛɪᴏɴ

The study of divination in itself is a lifelong art. Use the information above as your foundation, but then find the tools and techniques that work best in your life. Here are some other forms of divination you can explore.

Astrology

Divination based on the movement of the planets and signs. Astrology can be used in many ways, and is considered both an oracle system and a fluid form of divination. Using astrology for divining the answers to specific questions, rather than birth chart analysis, is usually called horary astrology. Divination is simply one expression of astrology, and for a witch, the full art of astrology plays a key role in astrological timing and ritual planning.

Aeromancy

A style of future prediction based on the atmospheric conditions, cloud patterns, and the weather.

Augury

Divination based on the behavior and movement of animals.

Dowsing

Divination using a pendulum or diving rods. (Dowsing is covered comprehensively in ITOW, chapter 13.)

Geomancy

Using shapes on the earth or an earthlike substance to gain divination answers.

Muscle Testing

Also known as kiniesology, muscle testing finds wisdom in the strength or weakness of the physical body. (You can find detailed instruction on it in ITOW, chapter 13.)

Palmistry

A method of divination using the lines and shapes on the palm of the hand.

Oneiromancy

A form of divination where answers come through dreams and dream interpretation.

Ornithomancy

Receiving psychic information from the flight, sound, and appearance of birds. A form of augury.

EXERCISE 29

Divination

Start practicing a divination technique. I would experiment with a few forms, both from oracle symbol systems and the more fluid techniques, to find what works for you. If you choose a symbol system such as the tarot, study it deeply, using resources outside of this book.

The goal is to become proficient in divination before going on to deeper spellwork, so you may divine if the spell is for your best interest. Sometimes intuitively performing a spell will just feel right or wrong, but other times we need council through divination. For such personal work, I suggest working more with an oracle system rather than scrying. You can get a more objective answer this way.

A great way to practice this work is to use divination often, if not daily. I have made it a part of my daily altar devotional, choosing a tarot card as I do my devotional, asking for the gods and my highest divine self to give me the guidance of the day to manifest my true will. Other times, you will ask specific questions, or have intentions to get information on specific situations in your life. The more you work with your system, the more its innate spirit, and your own guidance, will lead you to the perfect methods for you.

Homework

- Study and experiment with a divination technique of your choice. Do Exercise 29 regularly. Work with this technique to build your experience and confidence. Record your experiences in your BOS.

- Regular altar devotional and any other regular meditative practice.

- Continue journaling regularly.

Tips

- Practice. Divination can be hard, particularly when it's your own questions. If you can practice with others to get some perspective in your divination process, do so. The detached feeling you have when divining for another should also be present when divining for yourself.

Lesson Seven
The Witch's Circle

Enter the witch's circle, a sacred space beyond space, a time beyond time. When you cast your circle, you create a temple between the worlds, with one foot in the physical and one foot in the spiritual. You create a holy place of power, where the creative forces of the universe gather and partner with you.

The circle is known by many names. Witch's circle, magick circle, magician's circle, and moon circle are only a few. One great hoop honoring the four directions. Echoes of its magick are found in traditions across the world, from the medicine wheel to Eastern meditation mandalas.

The magick circle is universal because the circle is the symbol of oneness. It is the egg of creation that brings the universe into manifestation. It is the cosmic egg of the great mother, hatching all the worlds. It is the circle of protection, a higher vibration of spiritual energies, creating a refuge and sanctuary. The circle is the outline of the Sun, eternal in its power, and of the ever-changing Moon, reminding us of our cycles. It is the shape of the Earth, solid and stable, yet passing through seasons.

The circle is the microcosm of the universe. "As above, so below," the Hermetic masters tell us. When we create a model of the universe in our sacred space, through the circle, the four elements, and the divine polarity of Goddess and God, we create a miniature universe. Whatever we create in this miniature universe, in our sacred space, in the below, is destined to manifest in the outer world, the above. When you create the energy, intention, or image of something in the magick circle, from prosperity to love or healing, you are creating a large reflection of it in the waking, physical world.

Being between the worlds, anything done in the sacred circle is magnified. Think of it as a cosmic magnifying glass. It is a mystical lens, through which you magnify your intention. Like a laser beam, it focuses your will into a sharp, powerful beam of light, communicating your intention to the universe.

Another image of the circle that dazzles me is the cauldron. The magick circle is the witch's cauldron. It is a container, a boundary, much more like a bubble or bowl than a ring. We invite the powers of the universe into the cauldron. We invite our co-chefs to add their special ingredients to the stew. The powers of earth, air, fire, water, Goddess, God, Great Spirit, and all our guides are added to the mix. We invite them to add their special magick for the highest good. Together, we create a unique stew between the worlds. The cauldron is like the womb of life, like our egg of creation. Whatever we create with this magical "stew" we create in the world. Without the powers of nature and the forces of the elements, we could not create as effectively, and in harmony, with the divine.

Witches learn to make sacred space and partner with magick in all the worlds, through folk magick, instant magick, meditation, and psychic ability, but creating a sacred space between the worlds is a very special and powerful experience. All other experiences are magnified, from folk magick and spirit work to consecrating talismans, when done in the circle. Circle casting is a major component to most traditions of modern witchcraft. The ability to cast a true circle and make magick is like an initiation unto itself. Until you do it, you can never really understand the abilities and energies involved. You can participate or observe and feel things, but once you create it, all other experiences pale.

SELF-PURIFICATION

If the magick circle magnifies energy, a good witch makes sure that only the most perfect energies for the ritual are allowed into it. When we take the stress and tension from our daily lives into the circle, we muddy the purity of the energies. In fact, we magnify our problems. Energy is neither good nor bad, and the circle has no moral judgment; it just does as it is programmed to do. Although there are ways to "program" the circle to block out unwanted influences, it basically acts as both container and magnifying glass, particularly for spellwork. Whatever is put into the circle will be distilled, magnified, and released. It is up to you to have the good judgment to make sure it harms none, including yourself.

If we take the time to purify ourselves on all levels before entering the sacred circle, our will and emotions are much more clear, and more easily manifest our heart's desire and will. We can receive the psychic information we need, and project a clear intention to the universe to make magick.

Ritual Bathing

Ritual bathing is the most traditional of the purification rites. A witch takes a magickal, ritual bath, with the intention of psychically cleansing along with physically cleansing. Many witches make ritual bath salts to cleanse and clear the aura. If you can't take an actual bath, simply showering or washing up before a ritual refreshes you mentally, physically, and spiritually. Water is a very cleansing, purifying power.

Smudging

Passing yourself through the smoke of a cleansing, purifying incense is a powerful way of removing unwanted energies and vibrations. It works through both scent and vibration. Such substances release purifying energy when burned. Sage, frankincense, myrrh, cedar, juniper, lavender, copal, and cinnamon are all powerful cleansing smokes. Pass the burning leaves, stick, cone, or powder all around your body. You can smudge yourself, or in a group ritual, participants would smudge each other. Shamanic traditions would use a feather to waft the smoke to purify others.

Meditation

Quieting your mind of unwanted distractions is another method of purification. The other techniques really help prepare the mind, which is one of your most important tools. Take some time to breathe deeply, center yourself, and do any meditations that help align your energy. Many basic meditation exercises perfect for this work can be found in ITOW, such as Exercise 16: Polarity of the Earth and Sky, Exercise 21: Showers of Light, and Exercise 25: Chakra Opening and Balancing. I also love Exercise 8: Elemental Cleansing Meditation, from this book.

RITUAL CLOTHING

One of the reasons witches and magicians wear ceremonial cloaks, robes, scarves, and jewelry is to maintain a magical state of consciousness. Part of the purification process is to shed the mundane concerns of the outer world, and mundane identities, by shedding our everyday clothes. We purify our energy, and then don our magickal attire. When we wear ritual clothing, we more easily enter a magickal state of mind, making ritual, magick, and psychic work easier than when we are stuck in our daily issues. Ritual clothing creates a boundary to step through, like passing from one side of the veil to the next, from the physical world to the spiritual world. Some witches go skyclad, or naked, to create this change, but if you are comfortable with nudity in your daily life, then skyclad rituals will not have the same change on your consciousness for ritual work. The purpose is to do something different from the ordinary for you.

I highly recommend new witches obtain magickal garments. I prefer the traditional robe, and when outside, a cloak, but your ritual attire can be anything. It can be a special outfit, dress, sweater, or blanket. My student Melissa uses a set of special silk pajamas when doing magick at home. Usually they are black, to absorb and attract energy, as well as to honor the Goddess. Black is the color of receptivity. But many witches will wear white because they prefer its effect. You can even coordinate your ritual garb to the type of magick you are doing, based on the elements, planets, or zodiac signs. The simple act of changing clothes brings purification, like shedding your skin.

Once you have obtained your ritual garb, you can bless it, on or off, in a ritual circle, to consecrate it like a ritual tool. This blessing helps you remain in a purified state of being before and during the ritual.

Although I talk about the division between the magickal and the mundane, this is only an arbitrary division, and most evident in the beginning of your life as a witch. When you start out, there is a greater sense of division between the two, and your daily life can drag you down and out of a magickal experience.

As you progress in the craft, you begin to inject your magickal viewpoint into your daily life, completely transforming it. All things are magickal. It can just take a while to truly recognize it and live from this point of view. As you begin this transformation, you can't help but see the magick in all things and to live the magick. Suddenly you no longer have mundane jewelry and ritual jewelry. You have sacred jewelry, for all occasions. You no longer have mundane clothes and ritual clothes. Some may be more appropriate for certain occasions and environments, but all things are sacred.

Until that point, however, and even after it, ritual dress is a powerful technique to remain in a purified state for magickal working.

PURIFYING THE SPACE

Not only must the witch be purified, but the space where the circle is cast must be cleansed before any work is done. You don't want the vibrations of the day to become a part of your circle, particularly if there has been stress, tension, or illness in the space. You want the energy of the space to be as pure and clear as possible.

Usually this cleansing is necessary for all indoor spaces. I like to do it outdoors as well, but some feel the energy of nature is the most powerful cleansing agent there is. I still like to feel centered in the space, and make this process a part of my cleansing meditation for myself as well as the land. I guess it depends on where you are, who else has been there, and what has been done in the area.

Home Cleaning

All the techniques for cleansing tools and cleansing yourself can be used in cleansing a space. Actual cleaning (with soap and water), dusting, and vacuuming is an often forgotten cleansing technique, akin to a home's own ritual bathing. You can make environmentally friendly cleaning agents with biodegradable soaps and a magickal mix of essential oils, to make housecleaning a ritual.

Smudging

When smudging a room, I start in the center, and bring the incense to the north, then center, east, center, south, center, west, center, and then move in a circle. I prefer clockwise, but some will use a counterclockwise circle to clear a space.

Salt Water

Though salt can be sprinkled for the earth element and then vacuumed up, salt water cleansing is more common indoors. The salt absorbs and grounds any unwanted energies. Use an asperger to sprinkle water in the four directions.

Candle

You can bless a white or black candle for purification and let it burn in the room for a while before doing your ritual. The heat, light, and magickal intention is a powerful purifying force.

Ritual Sweeping

A besom, or ritual broom, can be used to cleanse the room of unwanted vibrations by sweeping them away. You can use intention and ritual movements such as circles, both small sweeping circles and moving in the ritual area with a circular direction. Again, clockwise or counterclockwise is acceptable, based on your own intuition.

Psychic Cleansing

Psychic cleansing is using your intention and will to clear a space, with or without other tools. Get into a light meditative state, and visualize the space clearing. Unwanted energy and psychic debris can be visualized as murk, smoke, sludge, or dark mist. You can imagine mentally gathering up all this unwanted energy and bringing it outside, either into the ground or into the Sun, for purification. You can fill the space with light, visualizing crystal-white light or violet flame in the room, burning away the murk. You can use other elemental images to cleanse, such as fire, ocean waves, showers of light, psychic winds, or crystals of light, all cleansing and removing unwanted energy.

Warding

Warding actually refers to protection spells, to seal a space from unwanted influence. Wards can be simple or complex. Many involve rituals, tools, and chants, but you can do a simple sealing of the space through intention. Do this once you have cleansed a space. Like the protection shield meditation in ITOW (Exercise 20), visualize a shield of crystal-white light around the space you are protecting. It can be egg or sphere shape. I often use the image of a pyramid or castle. The intention is to create a barrier that will prevent harmful energies from entering, but still allow any needed energies to pass freely, like a gatekeeper. Like cleansing, wards have to be periodically maintained, or they lose their effectiveness over time.

EXERCISE 30

Home Cleansing & Protection

These techniques work well for cleansing all ritual spaces, but I like to use them in my home, office, car, and anyplace else where I experience strong energies, both of my own making and magickally. It "resets" the space to a neutral charge, and leaves me feeling more centered and even. Occasional home cleansing and blessings are a big part of witchcraft, both for yourself, and when you are called upon by others to clear their home of unwanted vibes or spirits, or bless a new home for joy and happiness. Many witches I know magickally cleanse their own regularly, on certain Moon days, such as the New Moon, or on the eight seasonal Sabbats.

For this exercise, pick the techniques that call to you, and clear your entire home of any unwanted energies. Be as creative as you would like. Then create a protection shield, a ward, to block out harmful outside influences. Once you have completed it, notice how both you feel and, in the days to come, how all those in the home feel and act. The difference will surprise you.

Casting the Circle

If you have been keeping up with the earlier exercises, you will find that you have all the spiritual inner tools necessary for creating a sacred circle. Our relationship with the circle, the four elements, and the divine are a fundamental part of circle casting. Some traditions teach circle casting before building a relationship with these powers, and, as a credit to the power of the ritual itself, it will still work. But those with a relationship to the divine powers will have a much deeper experience.

The witch's circle consists of the following parts:

Cleansing self and space

Circle casting

Quarter calls

Evocation

Naming the work

Anointing

Great Rite

Raising energy

The work

Raising the cone of power

Grounding

Final blessing

Devocation

Release the quarters (after this, some traditions then perform the devocation)

Release the circle

Different traditions divide the steps in other ways, adding or omitting parts depending on the nature of the circle, but these are the fundamentals. Use this list as a checklist and outline for your own ritual creation.

Cleansing Self and Space

Though traditional techniques of cleansing are handled above, I start any circle work by entering a light meditative state, what I call ritual consciousness, before casting the circle. This allows greater awareness and access to magickal ability. Use Exercise 1 to enter this state. You don't necessarily have to count out of it at the end of the ritual, since the grounding techniques should return your awareness back to the physical world.

Circle Casting

The first step in creating a sacred space is marking the boundary of that sacred space. Usually this is done with a magically consecrated wand, but it can also be done with a staff, athame, or sword. In a pinch, you can use your finger.

The circle is usually cast three times in a clockwise direction, from the north or east, visualized in light, as you did in Exercise 3. This time, make sure the circle is big enough to accommodate your space. Fill the room. If you are in a group of people, make sure it is big enough for all, even if it goes through the walls of the room.

I usually accompany the circle casting with the following words, with each ring created:

We cast this circle to protect us from all forces that come to do us harm.

We charge this circle to allow only the most perfect energies for this work, and block out all other energies.

We charge this circle to create a space beyond space, a time beyond time, a temple of perfect love and perfect trust, where the highest will is sovereign. So mote it be.

I say "we" because I am identifying with my many divine selves—my higher self, personal self, and psychic self— and acknowledging all the great spiritual helpers, guides, and gods who are drawn to my circle. We are doing this in partnership.

Though most circles are cast with pure energy and intent, some traditions cast circle by pouring or asperging water in a circle, or with salt, incense smoke, candle flame, twigs, or grain. Best done outdoors, these circles can replace or be in addition to the traditional wand/blade circle casting.

Quarter Calls

To stabilize your circle, you anchor it between the worlds by calling upon the four quarters and elements. Use the quarter calls you previously created, as you call clockwise around the circle.

Many traditions keep elemental candles, one in each quadrant, on the altar or actually on the perimeter of the circle, and light them as the quarters are called. In certain cases, traditions hold up their elemental tool, or move it clockwise around the circle, sometimes sprinkling it, if applicable. Salt, candle flame, incense, and water can be brought around to strengthen the circle and the elemental connection.

Evocation

Evocation is the inviting of spirits to manifest in your space. In witchcraft, this aspect of the ritual formally acknowledges and invites the Goddess, God, and Great Spirit, along with any other guides, angels, or spirits that are appropriate to your magick. When you learn more of spellcraft in subsequent chapters, you will learn how to research the appropriate spirits and energies for evocation. I usually say:

> **I call upon the Two Who Move As One in the love of the Great Spirit, the Goddess, and God, to aid me in this magick. I call upon my highest spirits guides and guardians to be present. Hail and welcome.**

Although the Goddess, God, and Great Spirit are ever present in everything, this evocation is a true call and invitation by the witch to partner with them in magick.

At this point, I personally visualize the ring of light forming a sphere around the sacred space, like a big bubble of light. I don't put any intent into it. The process simply happens on the edge of my awareness if I am relaxed enough to notice.

Naming the Work

"Naming the work" simply means to state the intention of your circle, be it celebration, rite, or magick. If you are only doing one type of magick, you would state that intention, such as "healing magick" or "love magick" at this point. Naming the work focuses the energy and gets all your spiritual partners on the same track, working for the same goal. If your magick is diverse, then you can omit naming the work specifically, and say something like:

I call this circle to partner with the power of the Moon and the Moon Goddess.

or,

I ask for divine aid in my magick tonight.

You can also use this time to block out and neutralize any specific forces you feel are contrary to your magick. If the planets are in a particular placement that is inauspicious, you can nullify them with such words as "I neutralize the power of Mercury in retrograde." Visualize the symbols for Mercury in retrograde, ☿℞, and imagine a white X across them, blocking them from your circle. You can emphasize things that are supporting your magick at this time as well, such as, "I call upon the power of the Moon in Taurus," or, "I call upon the power of the goddess Bridget on Imbolc, this her sacred day." You will learn more about the specifics of astrological timing in a later lesson.

Anointing

Anointing is done with protection potion (see chapter 13) in my tradition, but others use a solution of sea salt and water for blessing and protection. One of my favorite questions ever asked in class was, "Why do we need so much protection? What can harm us?" We cast the circle for protection. We use potions of protection. Why? Medieval magick will say the circle blocks out evil spirits, and in truth, it does protect us from all harmful energy while we do our work, but ultimately, we use things like protection potions in the circle to protect us from all harmful energy, most importantly our own. Even with cleansing, it is easy to bring in unbalanced energy to the circle space. If you do a spell, and have a fleeting thought, "Oh, this will never work," then you have harmed your own magick. The circle magnifies and manifests all intentions, including unwanted ones, unless you use this technique to block them out. The potion protects us from outside influences and our inner unwanted influence. With these ritual actions, our magick is not spoiled. Our spells will manifest what they are truly intended to do.

I anoint the wrists with a banishing pentagram, and say:

I use this potion to protect me from all harm, on any level. Blessed be.

Great Rite

The Great Rite is the union of Goddess and God ritually in the circle. Usually done through the symbolic enactment of the blade into the chalice, though in some forms of high magick it is the wand into the cup.

Some traditions are known to use actual sexual intercourse between the High Priestess and High Priest, usually done in the bounds of a relationship. The practice isn't as common anymore, particularly in coven settings, but it is a wonderful and valid form of the Great Rite that many practitioners unfortunately shy away from completely. Witchcraft is a religion recognizing the honor and magick of sexuality and pleasure. With the same wisdom, we shouldn't be forced into situations that are beyond our boundaries just because a priest or priestess in authority demands it. Finding a personal code and the right partner or group is the most important thing. Do what thou will and let it harm none.

The union of the Goddess and God is reenacted to manifest the energies of creation, of spiritual fertility, in the sacred circle. The magick circle is a microcosm of the universe, and the primary force of manifestation and creation is the constant love and interaction between the Goddess and God, as they continually unite, create, sustain and destroy, to create again. Their energies are simultaneously polar and complementary, a fundamental force in creation, and necessary in any magick to manifest on the Earth plane. This honors both love and sexual energy in the process of creation.

Traditionally the priest holds the athame, embodying the God, and the priestess holds the chalice, embodying the Goddess, but solitary practitioners take on both roles simultaneously. We all have Goddess and God energy in us, regardless of gender. Certain traditions invoke the energy of the Goddess and God as primal powers, or specific godforms, into the bodies of the priestess and priest. At certain times, the priestess and priest speak with the authority and insight of the Goddess and God, channeling their wisdom for a short time during the ritual. Although this can happen intuitively and intimately, the complete instruction of such invocations is beyond the scope of this ritual work, and will be covered in the next book of this series.

I hold the blade up and then recite the following blessing, adapted from the first teachings I learned from Laurie Cabot, as I plunge the blade into the water three times, draw a pentacle, and tap the blade three times on the rim of the chalice before drinking it.

As the sword is to the grail, the blade is to the chalice, truth is to love, I draw together the power of the Goddess and God, and drink it in.

You can pour a libation, or offering, of water to the Earth, either before or after you drink. Ideally you should offer it before, but most traditions do it after everyone has drunk from the chalice. If performed inside, you can use a libation bowl.

A practice intimately linked with the Great Rite is drawing down the Moon. This rite can be viewed as an extension of the Great Rite, and in reality, is not limited to the Moon, but can be done with the Sun or stars. Traditionally done in a Moon circle, or Esbat, the male energy of the athame is used to attract the feminine energy of the Moon, visualized as a beam of light entering the blade and/or witch. Other variations include reaching up to the Moon and grabbing it with your hands, but I prefer attracting the energy with the blade as a silver beam of light. Once filled with the Moon energy, it is transferred to the water in the chalice during the Great Rite. Often the reflection of the Moon is "caught" in the waters of the chalice right before the plunging of the blade. The waters are then seen as a mix of male and female energy, a primal soup of creation and sacrament for witches. Witches who drink from it embody the Goddess and God, as a form of invocation.

Raising Energy

Our circle is the container, but now we need to add our all ingredients and heat things up before we serve our intentions out into the universe. Raising the energy is primarily for spellwork, and can be done in a variety of ways. Many are quite subtle, while others are extroverted. Some visualize strongly when doing spells. Others have a force of will and recite spells dramatically. You can light incense to release energy, chant, sing, dance, drum, read poetry, have sex, or raise the energy quite literally, using energy exercises to call the energy of the Earth, sky, and elements. This prepares your circle for its peak power.

To raise energy, or as part of the Great Rite, "The Charge of the Goddess" is often recited.

The Charge of the Goddess

Listen to the words of the Great Mother, Who of old was called Artemis, Astarte, Dione, Melusine, Aphrodite, Ceridwen, Diana, Arianrhod, Brigid, and by many other names:

"Whenever you have need of anything, once in the month and better it be when the Moon is full, you shall assemble in some secret place and adore the spirit of Me, Who is Queen of all the Wise.

"You shall be free from slavery, and as a sign that you be free you shall be naked in your rites. Sing, feast, dance, make music and love, all in My presence, for Mine is the ecstasy of the spirit and Mine also is joy on Earth. For My law is love unto all beings. Mine is the secret that opens upon the door of youth and Mine is the cup of wine of life that is the cauldron of Cerridwen that is the holy grail of immortality.

"I give the knowledge of the spirit eternal and beyond death I give peace and freedom and reunion with those that have gone on before. Nor do I demand aught of sacrifice, for behold, I am the mother of all things and My love is poured out upon the Earth."

Hear also the words of the Star Goddess, the dust of Whose feet are the hosts of heaven, Whose body encircles the universe:

"I Who am the beauty of the green Earth and the white Moon among the stars and the mysteries of the waters, I call upon your soul to arise and come unto Me. For I am the soul of nature that gives life to the universe. From Me all things proceed and unto Me they must return.

"Let My worship be in the heart that rejoices, for behold—all acts of love and pleasure are My rituals. Let there be beauty and strength, power and compassion, honor and humility, mirth and reverence within you.

"And you who seek to know Me, know that your seeking and yearning will avail you not, unless you know the Mystery: for if that which you seek, you find not within yourself, you will never find it without. For behold, I have been with you from the beginning, and I am that which is attained at the end of desire."

Figure 18: "The Charge of the Goddess"

"The Witch's Rune" is also a favorite traditional chant to be done.

The Witch's Rune
Darksome night and shining Moon
East then south then west then north
Harken to the Witch's Rune
Here we come to call thee forth

Earth and water, air and fire
Wand and pentacle and sword
Work ye into our desire
And harken ye unto our world

Cords and censer, scourge and knife
Powers of the witches' blade
Waken all ye unto life
And come ye as the charm is made

Queen of Heaven, Queen of Hell
Horned Hunter of the night
Lend your power unto our spell
And work our will by magic rite

By all the powers of the land and sea
By all the might of the Moon and Sun
As we do will, so mote it be
Chant the spell and be it done

> Eko, eko Azarak
>
> Eko, eko Zamilak
>
> Eko, eko Cernunnos
>
> Eko, eko Aradia

Figure 19: "The Witch's Rune"

For a general energy-raising chant, which also aligns a practitioner or group to the circle, I like this simple chant my coven uses:

> We are the Earth
>
> We are the Green
>
> We are the Love
>
> We are the Dream

Figure 20: Chant

A favorite method of energy raising for my circles, but often unseen in modern paganism, is an exchange of energy through an offering. Some consider it a sacrifice, and are turned off the word "sacrifice," but basically it consists of offering energy to the divine as part of your interaction to make magick. It is not a tit-for-tat, "if I do this, you'll do that" arrangement. Nor does it have anything to do with animal sacrifice. Modern pagans will often offer grain, fruit, incense, or perfume. All are wonderful, but in our society, they don't mean as much, since they are not as personal or precious as they were in ancient societies. I prefer offering my time, teaching, commitment, creativity, and financial charity to my community. I am giving back to the world that is supporting me through my magick. It's the law of return in action. How can you hope the universe will aid you magickally, if you don't aid others selflessly? Ultimately witchcraft is the path of community service. I hope such personal offerings will become a greater part of the reciprocity of magick. When you make such an offering, you set in motion the energetic wheels of reciprocity. As you send out good, good returns to you, fulfilling your magick even more strongly.

The Work

The work is the purpose of the circle, and includes spellcraft, healing, psychic work, and spirit work. You can charge and consecrate other tools, jewelry, and talismans, or send healing prayers to the world. Whatever you choose to do in the circle is the work and it consists of the primary act of the ritual.

Raising the Cone of Power

When doing magick, if you plan on manifesting an intention, you must release that energy into the universe to do its work. Some traditions raise only one cone of power per circle with all intentions, but I learned to raise the cone of power for each spell done in the circle.

After the spell is performed, usually ended with an emphatic "So mote it be" at the conclusion, witches raise their arms up, sending the energy out like a burst from the top of the magick circle "bubble." This is known as the Goddess position, reminiscent of Stone Age goddess images that have survived into modern day. Then the arms are crossed over the heart, in the God position, reminiscent of Osiris and the pharaohs of Egypt. It is a time of reflection, receiving psychic impressions as to how the spell will manifest, and for focusing on all power coming from the heart space, and that the spell is done in perfect love and perfect trust.

Grounding

After the last cone of power is released, practitioners ground themselves, releasing any excess energy absorbed from the circle back into the ground, with the intention of healing Mother Earth as it is returned. You might be tempted to keep the energy and not ground, giving you a spacy, "high" feeling for a time. Such energy addicts often experience nausea or intense emotional upheaval after the circle, and can suffer with health problems later in life. The high level of energy is meant for circle work, for a short period of time, but is too unstable to remain in the human body outside of the circle.

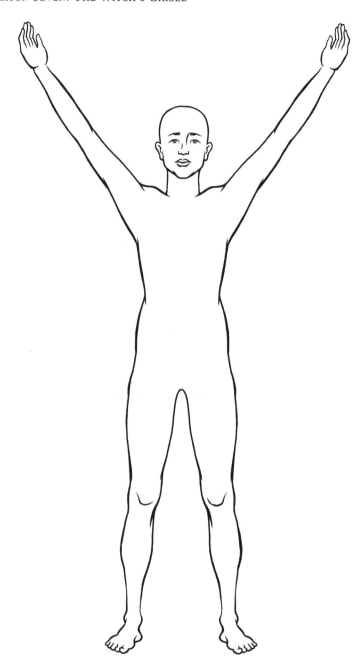

Figure 21: Goddess Position

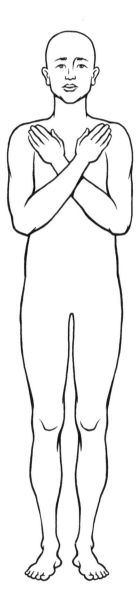

Figure 22: *God Position*

You can ground by getting on hands and knees and pressing into the ground or floor. If you are inside, imagine it traveling through the building and into the earth. Some bow forward in an Eastern prayer-like position. If getting on the floor is difficult, you can place your hands on the altar and channel the excess energy through the altar and into the ground, or use a wand, staff, or sword to channel the energy into the ground.

Grounding releases only the excess energy, and helps bring you back to the physical world and keep you functional here and now. If you still feel lightheaded after the ritual, you can do additional grounding techniques. One that is very powerful is to eat something. Many in the craft pass cakes, usually of corn or oat, blessed in the circle as a symbol of the God, but also for practical purposes, to ground. When you start your digestion, you put your energy back into your physical body. Cakes are typically found at the Wheel of the Year holidays, but can be used at Moon circles, too. Some use ale, mead, or wine instead of water in the chalice.

Final Blessing

Final blessing is a time of doing any last work or consecrating. My tradition ends with a circle of light and healing. Everyone places the names of those people, places, and situations they wish to send healing light. Then we raise a "mini" cone of power, without the God position or serious grounding, just sending the excess remaining energy of the circle with the intention of healing out into the universe.

In the name of the Goddess, God, and Great Spirit, we ask that all those in this circle receive the light and healing they need, for the highest good, harming none. So mote it be.

Devocation

Devocation is the release of all spirits gathered, including the Goddess, God, and Great Spirit. They are present in everything, and cannot be released as a traditional spirit, but it is a matter of respect, to bring the space and your intense, intimate contact to a close. Remember, it is a release and farewell, not a dismissal of a servant. They are our partners and allies, and must be treated with respect if we wish to receive the same.

I thank and release the Goddess, God, and Great Spirit, any and all spirits who came in perfect love and perfect trust. Stay if you will. Go if you must. Hail and farewell.

Release the Quarters

Release the quarters, starting where you began, and moving counterclockwise.

Release the Circle

Release the circle, tracing it counterclockwise, as you did in Exercise 3.

I cast this circle out into the cosmos as a sign of our magick. The circle is undone, but never broken. So mote it be.

TYPES OF CIRCLES

The magick circle comes in many different forms. Each one is a unique moment in time, even if it follows a previous ritual word for word. You cannot completely recapture a unique moment in time, and the energy of those present. Nor should you try. Let each circle be alive and unique.

Circles are created for a variety of reasons. Each may have a different theme and energetic base, depending on those who create it. Here are some examples.

Spellcraft

Most witches create a circle to do magick, since the circle amplifies all magick. This is the primary form of circle casting, with many variations to it. Spell casting can be the only purpose, or combined with any other type of circle.

Meditation

Circle can be created to protect the witch while doing meditation, shamanic journey, and astral travel. It provides a safe "home base." Energy does not have to be charged and released.

Protection

The circle is not only a container but an additional protective shield, and can block out unwanted forces or spirits from your life, giving you a safe space to plan and resolve difficulties. Protection is one of the reason why a witch might cast a circle before doing spirit work or psychic journey.

Worship & Celebration

Rituals are created not only to do work, but to celebrate, enjoy, and honor the many manifestations of the divine. Most Wiccan rituals resonate with either the Sun or Moon, and the deities and magick of solar and lunar spheres. Some circles are holiday rituals, for the solstices, equinoxes, and agricultural days known as the Wheel of the Year.

Spirit Circles

Other circles partner and celebrate with the spirits of those called, particularly those spirits called to anchor the quarters. Each type of quarter call flavors the circle with a different energy, and different partners. You can cast a circle to partner and know the energy of the angels, elementals, faeries, animal totems, dragons, and cultural deities. The most specific your circle, the more specific the energy will be. If you call upon Celtic gods, you can flavor your ritual with appropriate Celtic elements. If you use Greek gods, you would use corresponding Greek elements. Others could be eclectic, sharing the wisdom and flavors the world.

No Reason

If you feel called to cast a circle, but you aren't sure why, there is nothing wrong with creating a sacred space and enjoying it. You can cast a circle to commune with nature, laugh, breathe deeply, and share with others. Creating sacred space can be a daily part of your life if you choose. Circle casting is just one way of bringing the sacred alive in your life.

PRACTICAL ADVICE FOR THE MAGICK CIRCLE

Often we discover things through trial and error. No one tells us practical, common-sense points that can be so elementary to the seasoned practitioner, but never even thought of or questioned by the new witch. Here are some things I've found out from my own work and conversing with others. I hope it will keep you from "rediscovering" the wisdom through trial and error.

Deosil vs. Widdershins

Deosil, or sunwise/clockwise, movement is universal to most witches. Circles are cast deosil. Quarters are called deosil. In general, one should always move deosil in the circle, to keep the energy flow consistent. This is particularly important in spellwork, to build the energy to the cone of power. If you need to move around the circle, always move clockwise, even if the path is longer for you. If the altar is at the center, keep it to the right of you as you move and you will never go wrong.

Usually the circle is released widdershins, but some traditions do not follow this. They will determine the circle casting direction based on the type of magick. Banishing or Dark Moon rituals, to release and diminish something, will be done widdershins, or anti-sunwise, to lessen its power. The circle would then be released deosil. Gaining rituals would still be done deosil and released widdershins. I don't happen to follow this particular path, since all my circles, banishing or gaining, are cast deosil, but if your intention is clear, the metaphysical reason behind it makes sense to you, then try it. Experiment and find what works for you.

Clothing

Make sure your ritual clothing is comfortable for you and suits your work. Watch out for long sleeves around candle flames. They catch fire easier than you would think!

Comfort

Ensure that you are comfortable. If you are doing a particularly long ritual, or plan a meditation and you would usually use a chair, then use a chair for the meditation. Although not traditional, there is nothing wrong with that. If you are attending a group ritual, and it is particularly long and you have issues standing for any length of time, do not suffer. Make sure you have appropriate seating before the ritual starts in case you need it. If your body can't do something that is called for in the ritual, such as standing, dancing, or running, don't force yourself because it is magick. Honor your body first and foremost.

Watches

The circle is a time beyond time and as such, many traditions feel it is inappropriate to wear a watch in the sacred space. Some circles are adamant about it, and take out all clocks. Sometimes I think the Goddess and God are adamant about it, too, since watches break down in circles all the time, freezing at the time the circle began. The real "reason" behind it is the energy overloads the tiny quartz crystals in most watches. Witches who do energy work and hands on healing like myself often cannot wear a watch for that reason. But that doesn't account for the tradition colorfully known as Pagan Standard Time, meaning if you are a pagan you can be as late as you would like since you are beyond time. Oh, no; pagans should be responsible, honorable people. Our word is our bond. So for me, I wear a pocket watch when doing healing, and keep it out of the circle. So far, so good.

Boundaries

If your room cannot accommodate a comfortable circle, visualize the boundaries of the circle passing through the walls. The circle is still perfectly round, but comfortable enough to fit you. If you are doing this, make sure you cleanse the adjoining rooms and, with intention, cleanse the space between the walls.

Electrical Wires

Ideally, do not have electrical wires cross the boundary of the circle. This can disrupt the flow of energy. Sometimes it cannot be helped, but if it can, avoid electrical wires. I like to turn out electrical lights in general. If I use a tape player, I try to run it on batteries so a wire is not crossing the boundary of the circle. If it can't be avoided, then I deal with it, but I prefer to have everything self-contained.

Cutting a Door

What do you do if you have cast a circle, and for some reason, you or someone else needs to get out or get in? You cut a doorway. Yes, you can create a gateway to open and close the circle. Ideally it is done before energy is raised for spellwork. You might have established the circle and realized an important tool was left out. Someone might show up late for a public circle. Someone could have a medical emergency. A friend of mine burned herself in the circle, but suffered through until the end without speaking, because she didn't know she could be let out if an emergency arose.

Different traditions cut doorways differently. I learned two very effective methods. Both require the athame and are usually done in the northeast section of the circle, though no one is really sure why. Some traditions have you enter from the northeast and lay a broom at the threshold, to symbolize the doorway space.

The first entails you visualizing the circle like a curtain around the ritual area. You imagine the athame is pulling back the curtain as you face out and move from right to left. When the door needs to be sealed, you again move the "curtain" but now from left to right, retracing that portion of the circle with a partial clockwise direction.

The second method requires you to "cut" an upside-down V shape in the northeast. You bring your athame to the bottom right of the V, by the floor, and move up to the left and then down to the ground to complete the motion. Anyone passing in or out steps through this triangular door. Then retrace it from left to right to seal the door.

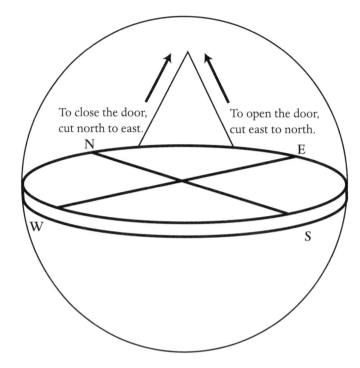

Figure 23: Cutting a Door

In the end, intention is the most important aspect of opening and closing doorways, not tools, motions, or directions. I've had situations where I've opened and closed a doorway mentally, without tools or motions, when someone decided to leave a circle abruptly.

Animals

Some witches are adamant that no one and nothing should cross the bounds of the circle once cast. All pets are locked out of the room. Other witches feel that animals, particularly cats, move beyond the bounds of space and time, and are always in a sacred space, so they can enter and leave the circle with grace. Often pets in the circle won't leave until the circle is done anyway, but some will and this is a point of great concern. I know of a handfasting magick circle, a pagan wedding, where a bird flew into the circle and landed on the High Priestess. I can't believe that disrupted the circle. It was a gift from the Goddess and God. So I tend to think animals can pass in and out with harm to the energy or spells.

Notes

Contrary to popular belief, it is okay to have notes in the circle, and read from them when needed. You don't have to have everything memorized. It is great to do a circle when you are comfortable with all parts and don't need to look at anything, and know that it is the intention, not the words, that make it perfect, but until that point, use notes. My mother, quite a great witch but someone who is not comfortable remembering all the parts to long circle rituals, still refers to an outline when she needs to. The intention makes the magick, not memorization. Covens may require memorization, but if you are eclectic and/or solitary, do what works for you.

Laughter and Mistakes

Such seriousness surrounds the circle. And I must admit, I am one to be very dramatic and serious in ritual, but it is okay to play, laugh, cry, and make mistakes. Though I strive for a perfect ritual, I strive for perfect intent of love and trust. If I make a technical mistake and get mad at myself, or someone else, then I am not in perfect love and perfect trust. If I can laugh it off, I am. Mistakes are how we learn. Sometimes the gods do something funny so we won't take our ego so seriously. Try casting out the ashes of your sacred spell and have the wind blow them back in your face. You have to laugh.

Asking Questions

You should be comfortable with what you are doing. Ideally, ask questions about the ritual before you start. Make sure you are in harmony with other people's intentions for the ritual, and if a part of it doesn't make sense to you, particularly if you are working with others who are unfamiliar to you magickally, make sure you are clear. It never hurts to ask, and can save on future difficulties.

WHEN TO ENTER AND NOT ENTER THE CIRCLE

Witches strive to enter the space with the consciousness of perfect love and perfect trust. Some traditions have you swear to this by sword point. "Better to fall upon this sword then to enter the circle without perfect love and perfect trust in your heart." I understand the sentiment, but such admonishments can cause problems.

The basic idea is that your thoughts are magnified, so if you intend to enter the circle with harmful thoughts, you should not. You should enter in a state of purification and clarity. Conflicts between coven mates should be resolved before entering any ritual space. You don't want to create from conflict or harm, because such things will be magnified and eventually return to you, as well as harm others.

If you are entering the circle with the intention of hurting someone else or yourself, or the first thoughts in your mind are anger, violence, hate, rage, or jealousy, then you should not enter the circle for spellwork. If thoughts, worries, and problems of your day are foremost on your mind, and you cannot be rid of them after meditation for a time, then do not enter the circle for spellwork. If you can move through these things, and purify yourself, even if it is only temporarily, but you feel you are really clear and calm, and can feel divine love, even if you cannot muster personal love, then you may enter the circle.

Unfortunately, at times, this vow prevents people from doing any magick when in a difficult place in life. During phases of depression, anger, and other issues that need to be worked out, practitioners will avoid the sacred space of the circle. They feel if they cannot lighten their mood and reach clarity, they should not enter a sacred space. I disagree. They should not do spellwork for changing others or the world, but sacred space is exactly what they need.

Sacred space uplifts, enlightens, and transforms. Even in the midst of difficulty, if you come with the intention of creating perfect love and perfect trust, the circle space, through the ritual and intention, can heal you. You can do spellwork for guidance, for healing, for releasing things that hold you back. Despite feeling stuck in an unhealthy emotion, you can hold the intention of healing. You can say, "Yes, I know I'm very angry now, but I ask the Goddess and God to help me work through this anger in the best and most healing way, so I may move on and continue my path." That's all it takes. Nothing fancy is needed.

You can talk to the gods, meditate, celebrate, or simply be in a safe space. You don't have to raise energy or create a traditional spell circle. You can simply enjoy the balanced energy of the circle and the four quarters, without "filling" the cauldron and releasing it to the universe. Not all circles need a purpose, other than simply doing ritual.

I had a friend who avoided circle casting, ritual, and celebration, alone and with us, while she was going through a serious break-up in her life and was filled with anger and depression. She held fast to the rule of never entering the circle without perfect love and perfect trust, and I think she lost some opportunities to heal and feel loved by us, the Goddess and God, and the world because of it. She was not in a fit of rage before a circle; she just had a general feeling of unresolved anger toward a former partner. With such feelings lurking, she would not enter the circle.

I understand her reasons, but no one really told us that it was okay to do ritual and not necessarily do spellwork. No one said it is okay to simply feel the love of the circle for a time, and ask for help by the gods. I tell you this now, so you will know, and have these tools in your time of need.

EXERCISE 31

Magick Circle

Write and perform a simple magick circle ritual. You don't have to do any working. Don't worry about astrological influences or Moon phases. Simply cleanse and create a sacred space without raising energy or doing a work. Feel it. You could meditate in the circle if you desire, or bless tools and jewelry. Then move to a final blessing if you want, and release the space. Make circle casting a part of your regular spiritual practice.

HOMEWORK

- Do Exercises 30 & 31. Record your experiences in your Book of Shadows.

- Practice regular altar devotional and any other regular meditative practice.

- Practice divination techniques.

- Continue journaling regularly.

Lesson Eight
The Science of Spellcraft

Spellcraft is a science. Just like witchcraft, there are basic principles, foundation stones, upon which magick and spells operate. As long as you are on the basic foundation, you have a wide range of creative possibility when executing your spells and you will be successful. If you are ignorant of the science of spells, and your creativity takes you off this foundation, your spells will not work.

The science of spell casting is not based in superstition or religion. Every religion has used these principles at one time or another. They are universal, and found in the most primal tribal cultures to the most sophisticated magickal lodges. Even those in mainstream monotheistic religions who really know the secret power of prayer are doing spellwork. They just don't know it as such.

Many witches, myself included, have described spells as the pagan equivalent to prayer. That is only half true. While the sentiment and the concept is similar, most people who pray do not understand these universal laws, while most people who do magick as a spiritual path do, even if it is only an intuitive understanding.

Spell work is a partnership with the divine, and a clear intention to create something and take responsibility for that creation. Witches partner not only with the divine creator, as we see it as Goddess and God, but also with all levels of nature to create change and balance.

Many who use traditional forms of prayer lack the basic understanding of energy. They ignore all their potential helpers in nature. They pray with uncertainty, with a sense of lack, guilt, shame, or punishment. Many feel they have to give up something they like, or make a deal with God, to receive what they want. This sounds much more like Dark Ages demonic pacts than anything a modern witch does. When you pray with these feelings and send them out, you only receive them back. That is why many people tell me they pray and have never had their prayers answered. They didn't know how to ask in the right way.

When you expect results, your energy returns results. When you focus on and expect failure, you get it. Energetically you get what you send out. The universe is ever abundant, but if you expect you will suffer for your wish, then you will suffer for it. The fundamental law of magick is you create your own reality. When you pray from a position of love, trust, confidence, and clarity, you are making magick. You are casting a spell. Many Native American traditions do prayer work, with plant, animal, and nature spirits, but to the witch, they are doing spells.

A spell is any specific act of magick that creates change in accord with your will. If you do a ritual with the intention of getting a new job, that was a spell. If you are just "lucky" and get a new job without creating the intention, you did not consciously execute a spell. You have been divinely guided, or unknowingly influenced the situation, but you did not perform a spell. In spellwork, we must take conscious action and responsibility for our magick.

As we progress in our spellcraft, every thought, word, and action becomes both ritual of worship for the forces of life, and powerful acts of magick to transform ourselves and all that is around us, with perfect love and perfect trust.

THE THREE KEYS

There are three keys, three basic components to all successful spellwork. When any one of these is missing, you run the risk of failure with your magick. If you do not have all three aspects accounted for in your spell, they seriously reflect on your magick before going any further.

To successfully cast a spell, one must have a strong will. Strong will refers to both your personal will, your desire for the spell's outcome, and an alignment with divine will. You must feel a connection to the source. Witches embody that source as Goddess and God. When your personal will is in alignment with divine will, your higher purpose, your magick is very powerful.

Not only must you have strong will, but you must have a clear intention to direct that will. Many people have strong wills, but become frustrated because they don't know what they want to create. Most people don't know what they want. They send out vague intentions to the universe, and get vague results. Witches must be focused! You must know your intention. Be very clear in your end result. You can be very open to the means through which it manifests, since magick is often seemingly coincidental, but the outcome must be clearly set. Always do spells for the outcome, not the means to the end. If you do a spell for money, do you really want money? Or do you need the money for something else? Then do the spell for what you want, rather than the money.

Spells usually come in the form of words. We make petitions to the universe for what we want to create. Since the nature of the universe is mental, as discussed in the Principle of Mentalism (ITOW, chapter 8), it responds strongly to our own creative thoughts and words. We have the word "spell" and the word "spelling" because both deal with alphabets. Both use symbols to communicate. In ancient days, the magickal languages were the only languages, and they were used to write, record, and perform spells as well as common, everyday information. Many creation stories start with the word—relating the power of the word, to the power of the divine creator. In India, the key creation word is OM or AUM, signifying the resonant sound of the universe. Even in the Bible, God is related to the word. To the universe, there is not a lot of difference between the words you speak in your daily life, and the words you use for your magick. Both create change, but a witch realizes this and is careful with the power of words. Spell casting is the power of language, in its many symbolic forms.

The last piece is a method to direct energy. Your will and intention are energy, but they do you little good if they can't work for you. You must have a method to send them out into the universe to manifest. Rituals, spells, charms, visualization, herbs, chants, stones, and symbols are all ways to generate, gather, and direct energy.

So many people have the first two keys, but lack a method of direction because we are not taught how to direct our energy. Often, people who pray hold the intention of unworthiness, lack, or fear. If they send out that energy, they only get it back. If you don't think you are worthy enough to get what you want, you usually won't. If you are afraid of your power and your fear contracts you, you will not release your intention. Your own awareness and willingness to partner with the divine is the most important component.

Ritual is the technology we have to align our intention, will, emotions, and body with our spirit; to raise and release the energy and manifest magick. Spells and ritual let us talk to the divine. Ritual is so powerful, so universally recognized the world over because it is hardwired into our make-up. Everyone can do spells, not just special people. In fact, everyone does spellwork, but is unconscious of the fact. We need to become more conscious of our will, intention, and energy. To the witch, the material and the spiritual are not separate, but part of a harmonious whole, and all needs are to be met. In tribal cultures, everyone is involved in ritual, not just the medicine person. Ritual serves us on so many levels, and as a culture, we have been stripped of our magickal rituals and need to reclaim them. We are made for magick. It is our birthright.

THOUGHTFORMS

The energy generated and programmed with your intention is called a thoughtform in traditional magickal training. Although the name implies only mental energy, it contains many forms of subtle energy. Thought is just the most easily recognized.

Many wince at the idea of thoughtforms, since they are only familiar with unwanted thoughtforms, which are self-created or projected on to us by others. In the

ITOW, we learned to cleanse the aura of unwanted thoughtforms and unhealthy connections. In reality, thoughtforms are just like any tool, neither good or bad. The intention behind their creation is the key in determining their function. Every spell, prayer, or healing uses a thoughtform.

Thoughtforms are constructs of energy, like spiritual robots programmed with our will and intention. They go out into the universe with our specific instructions, gathering momentum to return our desires to reality.

THE BOUNCE-BACK EFFECT

Spells work on all levels of reality. When we send out a spell into the universe, we use physical gestures, words, thoughts, images, symbols, and pure will to manifest it. Each act corresponds to an element and a subtle level of reality. Through our actions, we engage these realities to manifest our desire.

I think of these realities like a ladder. You can group the rungs on the ladder by the four elements, or the seven levels of reality corresponding to the seven chakras.

Level of Reality	Element	Concept	Action to Manifest
Divine	Fire	Will	Connect to divine will by calling on the gods in ritual
Psychic	Fire	Image	Outcome is imagined or visualized and attached to thoughtform
Mental	Air	Idea	Clear idea is formed and attached to thoughtform
Emotional	Water	Heart & Mind Unite	True power of magick by uniting thought with Perfect Love
Astral	Water	Astral Double	Thoughtform takes shape on astral level, coming to life
Etheric	Water/Earth	Formation	Thoughtform takes on elemental energy to manifest
Physical	Earth	Manifest	Thoughtform becomes a physical reality

Figure 24: Levels of Reality

When you do spellwork, a ritual on the physical plane, you engage these other parts of yourself and send your thoughtform up the ladder, as high as it goes. Like sending a bouncing rubber ball, you toss it out with all your might. If you are in alignment on those levels, and acting in partnership with the beings and forces of each reality, the ball will reach the edge of known reality, like hitting the ceiling. Due to the law of return, the ball will bounce back to you with greater momentum, calculated at three times as strong. As it returns down through the levels of reality, it gains the power it needs to take shape and form to manifest. Some think of it as water trickling back down to its source, as all things return to their source, energetically. Results manifesting on the more subtle planes—the mental, emotional, or astral, such as dream work—are easier and quicker to manifest than the physical, since they have a shorter "distance" to go until they manifest. Things from the higher levels can take a while to precipitate down on the physical realm.

VISUALIZATION

Visualization, or imagining the result of your spell, is a powerful component to magick. I do it. I know many others who do it, too. Unfortunately, some books on magick will say that you have to, that visualization is the only way to do magick, or is the only thing you really have to do to make magick work and all the rest is superstition. That leaves quite a few people who do not feel comfortable about their visualization skills out in the cold.

I know many witches who do wonderful work, who do not have strong visualization skills. Will, intent, and a method of energy direction are needed. Visualization is just one way to make clear intent and direct energy, but it is not the only way.

I like to the look at the pentacle as my teacher, and its five points to give me ways of doing magick.

Figure 25: *Pentacle*

Fire	Visualization of your intention manifested
Air	Spoken or written words about your intention
Water	Strong emotion or symbolic actions to represent what you desire
Earth	Ritual movement—physically doing the ritual makes magick
Spirit	Faith—just believe in your magick and divine power

Ultimately all these components together make the best spell, but go with your strengths. If you work well with one or two aspects, but not the others, focus on what you do best and you will have great success.

PETITION SPELLS

Petitions spells are the first form of magick I learned. They are easy and very effective. Basically you are making a statement of intention while in the magick circle. No special tools are needed, though many prefer a particular paper and ink, using special parchment paper, colored to match the intentions of the spell, or ink with magickal colors, herbs, or stones mixed in it. They are fun and enhance the magick, but are not mandatory.

After reading your petition in the circle as the work, burn the spell and raise the cone of power. As it burns, I visualize my intention, bring up my strong emotion to back it up and repeat the key words in my mind.

When you have done all your spells, ground the energy. You can raise energy before the working through dance or chant, or simply through your petition. I often read the petition three times when working alone, for three levels of consciousness to align—conscious, psychic, and superconsciousness (ITOW, chapter 5). That usually raises enough energy for me if my intention is clear and my will is strong.

Proper witch "etiquette" suggests that you do only three spells per circle, and only one circle per day, at least for spellwork. Although I see a point in not being greedy, I think it has more to do with not spreading your energy too thin, and allowing the things you want to manifest. If you do ten spells in one circle, each spell might not get enough energy to manifest. Besides, you can always do them later. I write a complete and separate petition for each one.

Although I prefer to release them via fire, if that is not practical in your living situation, you can bury your spell papers, toss them in a river, or rip them into pieces and scatter them to the wind. The releasing through the elements is the most important aspect. Some witches hold on to their petitions. I have found that never works for me.

Petition spells can be divided into five basic parts. They can be done in any order, but have this basic natural flow.

Announcement

The announcement simply tells those gathered in the circle who you are. You are announcing yourself, and your intention to do magick, to the universe.

Evocation

The evocation is asking the divine powers—Goddess, God, and Great Spirit, as well as specific deities, angels, spirits, etc.—to be present. I usually focus just on the Goddess and God, and ask for other beings at the beginning of the magick circle.

Intent

Here is the basis of the work. This is the actual spell. You are stating what you want to manifest as clearly and succinctly as possible. This is the meat of the petition.

Conditions

With the conditions, you put in any parameters or limits you want to the spell. Usually conditions include some request that it be in balance with divine will, so your own ego doesn't supersede the spell. Phrases such as "I ask this be in accord with divine will," "I ask this be for the highest good, harming none," and "I ask this be for the good of all involved, harming none" are all possible conditions. My student Melissa ends her spells with, "In perfect love and perfect trust, past, present, and future, forever, always and eternity, for the higher good, for the greater good, harming none, so mote it be."

You can also put time locks on the spell, asking that it occur by a specific time. You can denote a specific date, or a particular moon or sun cycle. What you want now might not be what you want later in life. I often just add "immediately" in my spells.

Conditions are where you can spare yourself a lot of grief. Better for a spell not to work than to work in a way you do not want. The trick is that you must really mean it when you say it. If you really put your energy into the intent, and half-heartedly say something that you don't really mean about the conditions, sometimes they will not protect you.

Gratitude

Gratitude acknowledges the divine help and gives thanks. Often entwined with the conditions, it ends with an affirmation that puts all requests into a positive tense. "So mote it be" means "so be it" or "it is so." The gratitude assumes that since the magick circle is beyond space and time, that the event requested has already occurred on some level and we are giving thanks, even though we haven't physically realized the result.

Petitions spells often look like this:

I (*state your name or magickal name*), ask in the name of the Goddess and the God to grant me/remove from me (*state your intent*). I thank the Goddess and the God and ask this be correct and for the good of all involved, harming none. So mote it be.

You will determine spells using the words "grant" or "remove" by the phases of the Moon. Basic petition spells can be done more personally or poetically, such as:

> **I *(state your name or magickal name)*, ask in the name of the Two Who Move As One in the love of the Great Spirit, the Goddess, and the God, to grant me/remove from me *(state your intent)*. I thank the Goddess and the God for all favors and ask this be in a spirit correct and for the good of all involved, harming none. So mote it be.**

Petition spells can be combined with the other arts of the craft, including charms, potions, and symbols. I'll often take the ashes of the petition and add it to my magickal concoctions.

ASTROLOGICAL TIMING

Astrological timing is an important aspect of the science and art of spell casting. The heavens correspond to the cycles of energy on Earth, and magickal cultures have used these patterns when planning rituals, doing trade, planting, harvesting, constructing, and making treaties. The energy of the moment influences the success of whatever you do. The Principle of Correspondence (ITOW, chapter 8) tells us, "As above, so below." Patterns repeat themselves endlessly and you can gain great wisdom if you know where to look.

Think of the skies as reflecting invisible currents, vast waves of energy most people don't see. Sometimes you are flowing with the tides. Other times you are swimming against them, like swimming upstream. At rare moments, it is like you are caught in a stagnant pool or rippling whirlpool.

If you can feel these tides, or better yet, predict their movements from the patterns of the sky, you will know when to act and when to wait. Why exhaust yourself fighting the natural pattern when you could wait a short time and have the forces of the universe back your will?

Although astrology is a lifelong study of universal wisdom when done with a spiritual approach, you can learn the basics of astrological timing relatively quickly. The universal mysteries encoded in astrology are also encoded in the craft of the witch.

You are already familiar with concepts such as polarity, gender, the four elements, and the triplicy. You have already been introduced to the twelve zodiac signs. Now we broaden that knowledge to understand how to work with the tides. Although it can seem complicated at first, a strong foundation of astrological studies makes the art of spell casting, as well as the higher mysteries of the craft much more accessible to the conscious mind.

THE MOON

For witches, the cycle of the Moon is the most important determining factor of magick. In fact, many witches look to nothing but the Moon. If the astrological arts do not call to you for further study, simply use the Moon magick contained in this section. It is the most powerful of all astrological helpers.

The Moon embodies the Goddess as Maiden, Mother, and Crone. Each aspect of the Goddess brings different gifts and challenges. Some are appropriate for certain magick and not for others. You must be in alignment with the Goddess to have true blessings upon your magick.

The general rule of Moon magick is to divide the cycle into two basic parts. The Moon is waxing when it is gaining light, leading toward the Full Moon. At this time, do magick to gain things in your life. Symbolically, the tide is coming in, and will bring in whatever you want. Your spell done in the waxing Moon will be permeated with the energy of the waxing moon and will continue to bring things toward you, even if it takes a few months to fully manifest. Whatever is begun at the waxing Moon will have waxing Moon energy. The closer you are to the Full Moon's peak, without going over, the stronger and more immediate its effects in your life.

When the Moon has peaked at full and begins to grow in darkness, it is waning. Waning Moon magick is for banishing and removing. The tides are going out of your life, and will take whatever you cast upon them. Most books focus on waxing Moon magick, since most beginners in witchcraft focus on getting "stuff." Satisfying desires is good, but I have found that as I continued to practice, I do more waning Moon magick now, to make space in my life. This energy can be used for protection, to banish all harm. It is used to banish illness and injury. It can be used to be banish unwanted influences and personality traits. It doesn't make them go away without any effort, it simply supports the personal transformation process. If you banish your anger, it doesn't disappear, but the energy supports the process of working out your anger, with ease, grace, and love, often going much more quickly if you did not call upon this support.

When you do a petition spell, ask to be granted a boon with waxing energy. Ask to banish or remove something with waning energy. Although it is not the highest wisdom, if you really need to do a certain type of spell and the cycle of Moon is against you, you can reword your spell to get the support you need. If the Moon is waning and you need to manifest, ask to banish all obstacles that prevent you from manifesting your desire. If it doesn't occur quickly enough for you, follow that spell up with a waxing Moon spell. If you need to do waning magick, such as protection, during a waxing Moon, ask to be granted protection, a safe journey, a clear path, or however else you wish to phrase it. Again, follow it up when the Moon changes its cycle.

Although we see the Goddess as triple in the Moon, astronomy and astrology divide the moon cycle into four quarters, and in these four divisions, we still see the Maiden, Mother, and Crone. These four quarters can then be subdivided into eight sections, but such divisions are not all that different than the simpler four categories in practice.

First Quarter

The first quarter of the Moon is when the Moon starts waxing, but might still be dark to our eyes. This phase continues until the Moon reaches half full. The first quarter is a time for long-term magick, when we plant seeds for the future and begin new projects. The start of the first quarter can be referred to as the New Moon, and can act like a mini "new year" to begin again with a fresh start. The first quarter Moon is associated with the Maiden. The silver crescent symbolizes the silver bow of the huntress/ lunar goddess Artemis, who is often depicted as the maiden or virgin. Anything done in the first quarter will grow strongly over time. So spells that require a lot of real-world groundwork and preparation are best performed at this time.

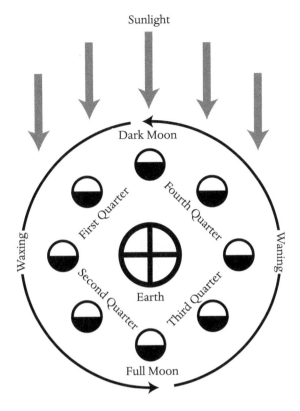

Figure 26: *Moon Quarters*

Second Quarter

The second quarter starts when the Moon is half full with light and continues until the Moon reaches its peak light reflection at the Full Moon. At this time spells will manifest more quickly, particularly if they are direct and simple. The Full Moon embodies the Mother goddess, pregnant and giving birth to life. The closer you are to the peak of the Full Moon, before it enters the third quarter, the more powerful the energy will be. The Full Moon hangs at the top of the sky at midnight, the witching hour, which is the most powerful time to do Full Moon magick. Although some traditions believe you have three days before and three days after the Full Moon to do this magick, I have found it preferable to do Full Moon magick before it enters the third quarter. It's like catching a wave. You want to jump onboard before it crests. The wave might still get you there if you miss it, but you lose the initial power you could have caught.

Third Quarter

The third quarter starts when the Moon peaks at full and immediately begins to wane. Contrary to popular opinion, the Moon does not hang in its full state for a time, even though it appears to. It is either waxing or waning, and when it peaks, it begins to wane. The third quarter lasts until the Moon becomes half dark. Do magick to banish and remove things that need to disappear gently. It is a time for gradual loss and healing. Don't expect immediate results by this Moon's light. The third quarter is sacred to the Crone, who is waning in physical strength, but is growing in spiritual wisdom and power.

Fourth Quarter

The fourth quarter begins when the Moon is half dark, and continues until the Moon goes fully dark and begins to wax again. Though popularly called the New Moon, the end of the fourth quarter should be referred to as the Dark Moon, since new energy doesn't begin until it starts waxing again. Like the opposite of the Full Moon, the closer you are to the Dark Moon, the more powerful and immediate your waning Moon magick. Some traditions call this the witch's holiday, and say no magick should be done the days the Moon is dark, but historically this has not been the case. I think that rule was created by modern people who are more concerned with waxing magick than honoring the full cycle of the Moon. The transition of the fourth quarter to the first is the death and rebirth of the Moon Goddess, from Crone to Maiden once again.

Although the cycle continues on, it doesn't match our solar calendar year. There are twelve parts of the solar cycles in our calendar year, each being approximately a month's time for each sign of the zodiac. The lunar year takes thirteen whole lunations, and will only match the solar year every nineteen years, or what is called the Great Year or Meton's cycle. In our modern day of timekeeping, a Moon is called blue, giving us the phrase "once in a blue Moon" when two Full Moons fall in the same calendar month, since our calendar months have variable days. Although there is no ancient lore to this practice, some witches find the blue Moon to be very powerful and special.

PLANETS

The Moon is not the only heavenly force influencing your magick, but being the closest body to the Earth, its effect seems the strongest in our daily life, particularly to witches who are both naturally aware of and learn to be attuned to its mystical power.

Although technically called luminaries, since they generate or reflect light and are not traditional planets, the Sun and Moon are considered to be planetary energies by mystical scholars. The ancient civilizations used seven planets including the luminaries, since these are the planets most easily visible without magnification. Since the discovery of the three outer planets, witches and mages now have ten planetary energies to call and many speculate that two others will be discovered at some point, making twelve in all, to match the zodiac.

Each planet has a specific energy and sphere of influence in earthly life. When you are doing a spell that falls under that sphere of influence, you are aided by timing your ritual to a beneficial alignment of that planet.

Each planet is named after a god in the Roman myth, and the name gives us clues to the planet's sphere of influence, energetic personality, and the archetype and god-forms associated with it. Most cultures associated the planets with various deities in their pantheon. By calling on those gods or goddesses, you invite the presence of that planet's energy. Each planet's energy also corresponds with specific colors, symbols, tools, animals, metals, minerals, and plants. By using these corresponding tools, you will draw in additional energy from this planet. Ritual design using these correspondences is part of the art of spell casting.

☽ Moon

Archetypes: Triple Goddess, Moon Goddesses

The Moon's sphere of influence is all magick, and specifically the astral, emotional, and psychic realms. Luna influences all intuition and psychic ability and rules our power to manifest or banish by its waxing and waning. The Moon is the gateway to other realms, and aids in any astral travel or shamanic journey work. It holds the key to past-life memories and the talents we bring with us into this lifetime. The power of the Moon helps us listen to our intuition and see reality from illusion. The Moon is particularly attuned to the feminine, aiding in magick regarding feminine cycles, relationships, fertility, motherhood, family, childbirth, and wisdom that comes with age.

☉ Sun

Archetypes: Solar King, Divine Youth

The Sun's energy is the power of life. It is the seed that bears fruit and the nourishment of the land. The Moon's light is the Sun reflected to us, through her sphere. Magickally, the Sun is associated with health and vitality and the powers that go along with such strengths: prosperity, creativity, and the power to manifest. Think about how the Sun holds the entire solar system together. That is power. When you want your presence to be known in the world, use the Sun's energy in ritual.

☿ Mercury

Archetypes: Messenger, Magician, Scribe

Mercury is the power of the mind. Spells involving intellect, memorization, and knowledge fall under its domain. I used Mercury magick often while in college to assimilate information and pass tests. More importantly, Mercury is the power of communication, and all magick is communication, so the magician deities are Mercury patrons. Mercury in Roman mythology is the messenger, but more accurately the psychopomp or shaman, the guide to souls between all worlds. Travel, spiritual or physical, is a form of communication. Mercury is used for guidance and protection with all forms of travel and communication, including cars, planes, and electronic devices.

♀ Venus

Archetypes: Love Goddess, Fertility Goddess, Ocean Goddess

Venus is the power of love and attraction. Venus is the goddess of love and fertility, birthed from the foaming ocean, and her planet governs all aspects of love and relationship. Romance, pleasure, sensuality, beauty, erotica, and attraction are all under this domain. Venus is the magnetic power, and it attracts all things of value. Anything you value can be drawn to you with Venus, from love and sex, to money, art, and luxury.

♂ *Mars*

Archetypes: Warrior, Protector

Mars is the god of war, and the flipside to Venus. While Venus receives and attracts, Mars projects outward and manifests. Mars energy is active and aggressive. Like the masculine Sun energy it, too, can be used to manifest your will, your fire in the world. This power is great when you are feeling stuck and needing a boost of vitality and passion. Mars is also very protective and guarding.

♃ *Jupiter*

Archetypes: Sky God, Storm God, Wise King, Teacher

Jupiter is the energy of expansion. Traditionally it is called the planet of good luck and prosperity, because when applied to those areas of life, it expands them. More accurately, Jupiter is the power of the highest self or superconsciousness, and when you are in touch with it, you have an expanded view. Your prosperity expands because you are doing what serves your soul. Your good luck expands, because you are naturally at the right place and at the right time, and your spirituality expands. When your physical needs are met, you can focus on the higher purpose of life. Jupiter is embodied by the storm and sky kings. When the sky is clear and peaceful, all can be seen. When it is clouded by anger, fear, or sadness, we cannot see our path.

♄ *Saturn*

Archetypes: Grain God, Death God, Old Man/Grim Reaper/New Child, Crone, Underworld Goddess, Destroyer Goddess

As Jupiter is the power of expansion, Saturn is the power of contraction. Its energy is restrictive, disciplined, and orderly. Saturn energy is the energy of karma, forcing you to see things you would rather not see. The name "Saturn" comes from the elder Roman grain god, with his sickle, the symbol of Saturn, who ruled over the golden age. Later the image was transformed in the Grim Reaper, or the old man and newborn child, both sides of the same coin, like the popular image of Father Time and Baby New Year. Kabalistically, Saturn is feminine: Jupiter is King, Saturn is the dark Queen who teaches through fear. Magickally, the rings of Saturn represent restriction, binding, and crystallization. Use Saturn for protection magick, including binding spells and shields, for understanding karma, and for manifesting things in your life you need to move to the next learning, which may be manifestations that your ego-self doesn't want.

♅ *Uranus*

Archetypes: Sky God, Divine Rebel, Trickster

Uranus is the first "new" planet, which breaks the limits of Saturn. Magickally, Uranus is the planet of breaking new ground, unusual thinking, eccentricities, new thought, and inventions. Uranus is higher communication, directly with the divine mind, and represents our intuition, our sense of divine knowing. Uranus can trick us into seeing things in a new way. Call on Uranus to stimulate your mind into seeing, doing, and communicating things differently.

♆ *Neptune*

Archetypes: Sea King, Sacrificed God

Neptune is named after the Roman sea god, and astrologically represents the highest form of love: unconditional love. As Uranus is the higher mind, Neptune is the higher heart. Neptune rules the creativity and expression that flows from that love, including art, music, dance, and the spiritual visions of the healer, shaman, or witch. Neptune influences psychic ability and dream magick. Its dark side is the power of addiction, disillusionment, escapism, and disenchantment with the world, though its power can be used to heal these things as well.

♇ *Pluto*

Archetypes: Underworld King, Horned God

Pluto is the god of the Underworld, and the last of the outer planets. Though small in size, it packs a strong punch astrologically. Discovered when humanity was discovering the power of nuclear energy (hence the name "plutonium"), Pluto is the power of death and resurrection. Magickally, it destroys what doesn't serve to create something new. Pluto is the higher will, the divine will, and not the will of your personality. It is the will of the gods, the will of your soul. The gods of death, the Underworld, and the horned animal lords are all part of Pluto. Call upon Pluto when you want to add sheer power, power to transform, to your spell, but always be mindful of the consequences.

Remember this information is a generalization of the most commonly accepted themes in modern magick. Other cultures and time periods would associate different types of deities and qualities to each planet.

The Earth is not included on this list because every act of witchcraft calls upon the power of the Earth. It is a planet, and some systems of astrology and magick use it as such, along with asteroids, comets, planetoids, and stars, but in the spirit of keeping things more basic, we will stick with the ten planets of astrology. With these ten planets, you have a working palette of magickal "colors" to call on.

PLANETARY DAYS AND HOURS

Planetary days and hours are a system of magickal timing based in the ancient world, before the discovery of the outer planets. You find them both in witchcraft and in modern ceremonial magick, with a variety of interpretations and systems for their use.

The concept of planetary timing basically states that all cycles of time flow in a pattern. Each day and each hour is influenced by a particular planet. Things done on a specific day or hour are helped or hindered by the energy of that moment. The pattern of planetary influence is regular and predictable and, once known, can be used to your advantage, magickally or otherwise.

The pattern of influences starts with the Sun and continues through the Moon, Mars, Mercury, Jupiter, Venus, and Saturn. This pattern rules the seven days of the week, giving us our days' names from Roman and Norse mythology. The Sun's day is Sunday. The Moon's day is Monday. Tyr's day, the Norse war and justice god, is Tuesday. Wotan's day, the Norse wandering magician and all-father is Wednesday. Thor's day, the Norse thunder god, is Thursday. Freya's day, the Norse goddess of love, fertility, and magick, is Friday, and Saturn's day is Saturday.

If you want to do Sun magick, you are aided if you do it on Sunday. If you want to do a love spell with Venus, you are helped if you perform it on Friday. You should still check with the phases of the Moon, but working in these influences is quite easy to do.

Not only are the days are influenced, but every hour is influenced, too. Every day, the first hour is influenced by the day's planet, and then an hourly pattern continues through twelve hours of the day and twelve hours of the night. This pattern is Sun, Venus, Mercury, Moon, Saturn, Jupiter, and Mars. If followed through twenty-four hours, the first hour of the next day will complete the pattern. The last hour of Sunday is Mercury, followed by the first hour of Monday, the Moon.

	Sun	Mon	Tues	Wed	Thurs	Fri	Sat
DAY							
Hour 1	☉	☽	♂	☿	♃	♀	♄
Hour 2	♀	♄	☉	☽	♂	☿	♃
Hour 3	☿	♃	♀	♄	☉	☽	♂
Hour 4	☽	♂	☿	♃	♀	♄	☉
Hour 5	♄	☉	☽	♂	☿	♃	♀
Hour 6	♃	♀	♄	☉	☽	♂	☿
Hour 7	♂	☿	♃	♀	♄	☉	☽
Hour 8	☉	☽	♂	☿	♃	♀	♄
Hour 9	♀	♄	☉	☽	♂	☿	♃
Hour 10	☿	♃	♀	♄	☉	☽	♂
Hour 11	☽	♂	☿	♃	♀	♄	☉
Hour 12	♄	☉	☽	♂	☿	♃	♀
NIGHT							
Hour 1	♃	♀	♄	☉	☽	♂	☿
Hour 2	♂	☿	♃	♀	♄	☉	☽
Hour 3	☉	☽	♂	☿	♃	♀	♄
Hour 4	♀	♄	☉	☽	♂	☿	♃
Hour 5	☿	♃	♀	♄	☉	☽	♂
Hour 6	☽	♂	☿	♃	♀	♄	☉
Hour 7	♄	☉	☽	♂	☿	♃	♀
Hour 8	♃	♀	♄	☉	☽	♂	☿
Hour 9	♂	☿	♃	♀	♄	☉	☽
Hour 10	☉	☽	♂	☿	♃	♀	♄
Hour 11	♀	♄	☉	☽	♂	☿	♃
Hour 12	☿	♃	♀	♄	☉	☽	♂

Figure 27: Planetary Hours Chart

You would use this to modify your spells with two planetary energies. If you are doing a love spell, but want to create a relationship with good communication, you can do it on Friday, in the hour of Mercury. If you are doing psychic work, but feel you need extra protection, you can do it on Monday, but in the hour of Mars or Saturn.

The outer planets are not represented by this system, since they are newly discovered bodies. Modern mages often work the outer planets in by describing them as upper octaves of other planets, and using the second hour of the day or night as the upper octave of that planet for that day. One system says the Uranus, Neptune, and Pluto are the upper octaves of the Sun, Moon, and Mars, using the planetary day pattern of Sunday, Monday, and Tuesday. Another system, the one I prefer, says that Uranus is the upper octave of Mercury, both related to the mind. Neptune is the upper octave of Venus, both related to love, and Pluto is the upper octave of Mars, both related to will. So use the system you prefer, if you want to incorporate outer planet energy into the planetary days and hours.

The only problem in this system comes from calculating when the hours begin and end. There are several systems and each has its advantages, drawbacks, and proponents. There is not one right way to do this, but there may be one way that works best for you, so I suggest experimenting with all of them until you find out. Record your experiences in your Book of Shadows, so you can thoroughly compare.

Modern Clock Hours

Modern clock hours are the easiest method, but the least traditional. They do require considerably less math, however! Basically, the first hour of the day starts at midnight, and lasts for sixty minutes, just like our modern clock. The first night hour starts at noon. Simple. Easy. Fast.

Day and Night Hours

Unfortunately, most ancient cultures did not measure time by midnight and noon, rather by sunrise or sunset. Lore on planetary hours with these day and evening divisions suggests that for calculating day hours, you take the amount of daylight from sunrise to sunset, and divide by twelve, giving you a planetary hour "unit." You can then calculate from sunrise twelve periods. Likewise, the same can be done for the hours of darkness, by calculating the time from sunset to the next sunrise and divide by twelve. Such information is available for your area in the newspaper, almanacs, and even online. They will only be close to sixty minutes near the equinoxes. During the summer, day hours will be longer and night will be shorter, with the opposite occurring in the winter.

Here is a hypothetical example, simply to show you the mechanics of the calculation.

Sunset: 5 PM
Sunrise: 7 AM

5 PM to 7 AM is 14 hours of night.
14 hours equals 840 minutes of night ($14 \times 60 = 840$).
Divide 840 minutes by the 12 planetary hours of darkness, giving you a unit of 70 minutes.

Hour 1—5:00 PM
Hour 2—6:10 PM
Hour 3—7:20 PM
Hour 4—8:30 PM
Hour 5—9:40 PM
Hour 6—10:50 PM
Hour 7—12:00 AM
Hour 8—1:10 AM
Hour 9—2:20 AM
Hour 10—3:30 AM
Hour 11—4:40 AM
Hour 12—5:50 AM

Though it requires more work, it seems much more effective in my experience. I tend to save these calculations for when I really need to boost my magick with the planetary hour. Some magickal and astrological software programs will calculate these hours for you. If you like planetary hours, but don't like math, look into such resources.

SIGNS

As the planets move through their orbits, they seem to occupy the various signs of the zodiac. Each sign colors that planet's energy. Your Sun sign is the sign that Sun was in when you are born, but you also have a Moon sign. Moon sign lore is less popularly known by the public, but just as important. Every planet occupied a sign when you were born, just as every planet is in a sign now. The sign it occupies influences its energy, as if the planet is a light, and the sign is a colored plastic gel the light shines through. It's the same light, but each sign tints it a little differently.

Each planet has a different orbital cycle to move through the signs. Some move quickly, like the Moon, going through all twelve signs in twenty-eight days. The Sun takes approximately a year. Mars takes about two years, while planets beyond Mars can take many years to complete a cycle. For practical magick, we tend to be most concerned with the Moon sign. Moon sign magick really helps amplify the phases of the Moon. We can also look to the Sun sign for additional information. The Full Moon will always be in the opposite sign from the Sun, giving us a powerful, dynamic, yet balanced polarity for our magick.

Each sign represents an archetype of life, a mode of operating. There are no good or bad signs. Each is a unique and necessary part of our journey. Each has gifts and challenges to offer, both in life and in magick. The signs correspond with different images and qualities, as well as a relationship with a "ruling planet," meaning they have much in common in form and energy. Each sign is also associated with a body part. If working to heal a particular part of the body, it is helpful to have key planets, such as the Moon, in the sign influencing that part of the body.

Here is a brief description of each sign, its energy, and sphere of influence.

♈ Aries

Symbol: Ram
Statement: I AM
Ruling Planet: Mars
Gender: Male
Triplicy: Cardinal
Element: Fire

Anatomy: Head

Qualities: Aries is the archetype of the leader, charging forward and facing fears like the charging ram. Ruled by the warrior planet Mars, Aries energy is used for drive and power. As cardinal fire, it initiates and begins. Call upon it when you need courage, passion, leadership, aggression, and aid in discovering your identity.

♉ *Taurus*

Symbol: Bull/Cow

Statement: I HAVE

Ruling Planet: Venus

Gender: Female

Triplicy: Fixed

Element: Earth

Anatomy: Throat

Qualities: Taurus is the sign of the bull, and, as a fixed earth sign, is symbolized by the Earth itself. Ruled by the planet of love and luxury, Taurean energy is the power of material wealth, comfort, home, fine food, art, music, and sensuality. Use it for spells exploring materialism and the finer things of the world. This sign brings grounding and stability, but like the bull can also bring stubbornness.

♊ *Gemini*

Symbol: Twins

Statement: I THINK

Ruling Planet: Mercury

Gender: Male

Triplicy: Mutable

Element: Air

Anatomy: Shoulders, arms, hands

Qualities: Gemini is the sign of communication, and its energy enhances our ability to speak with others, learn new information, be social, and adapt to different situations. As the sign of the twins, and mutable, the energy has two currents and can multitask with the powers of the mind. The drawback of this Mercury-ruled planet is focus. Accustomed to do many things at once, it has a hard time focusing on a specific task.

♋ Cancer

Symbol: Crab

Statement: I FEEL

Ruling Planet: Moon

Gender: Female

Triplicy: Cardinal

Element: Water

Anatomy: Chest, breasts, stomach

Qualities: Cancer is the sign of the crab, but also of mother ocean and the Moon. The archetype is the nourishing mother who creates life. Cancer magick is used for family issues, motherhood, children, and birth, but also any caretaking situation. Cancer is a very healing sign. Cancer is a sign of protection, like the crab's shell, but also teaches lessons about emotional boundaries.

♌ Leo

Symbol: Lion

Statement: I CREATE, I WILL

Ruling Planet: Sun

Gender: Male

Triplicy: Fixed

Element: Fire

Anatomy: Heart, upper back

Qualities: Leo is the sign of the lion, but its archetype is both performer and king. Leo is the sign of attention and ego, and using it in magick can develop a healthy sense of ego, including the qualities of leadership, confidence, charisma, and creativity. As a fixed fire sign, Leo energy shines like the Sun that rules it, but such attention can also bring great sensitivity when involving criticism.

♍ Virgo

Symbol: Corn Maiden

Statement: I DISCRIMINATE, I ANALYZE

Ruling Planet: Mercury

Gender: Female

Triplicy: Mutable

Element: Earth

Anatomy: Intestines, lower digestive system

Qualities: Often called the Virgin, but more accurately the Corn Maiden, Virgo's image is really the harvest. Mutable earth is the temporary gifts of the Earth, such as the crops that sustain us. Virgo magick involves service to others, particularly in social charity and the healing arts. This sign rules our day-to-day work. Virgo energy, ruled by Mercury, is a grounded mental energy involved in analysis and discrimination of details (separating the wheat from the chaff), and craftsmanship.

♎ *Libra*

Symbol: Scales

Statement: I BALANCE

Ruling Planet: Venus

Gender: Male

Triplicy: Cardinal

Element: Air

Anatomy: Kidneys, lower back, hindquarters

Qualities: Libra is the sign of balance, teaching us to find balance in both our life and our relationships, since it is ruled by Venus. Librian magick involves partnerships of all kinds, from business to romance, marriage, and cooperation. As a Venusian air sign, Libra has an intellectual love of art, as well as a love of justice and fairness.

♏ *Scorpio*

Symbol: Scorpion / Snake / Eagle / Phoenix

Statement: I DESIRE, I TRANSFORM

Ruling Planet: Pluto

Gender: Female

Triplicy: Fixed

Element: Water

Anatomy: Reproductive and eliminative organs

Qualities: Scorpio is the most misunderstood and maligned sign. Scorpio is the sign of power, and teaches the lessons both of having power and desiring power. Its greatest gift is the power of self-transformation, and is symbolized by its changing image, from the lower scorpion or snake to the rising eagle or phoenix, even though it is a fixed sign. Because of this transformation, Scorpio is associated with sex and death, two of our most transformative energies. Both are associated with psychic ability. Scorpio magick can be used to create and transform, deal with obsessions, power struggles, investigations, surgery, and personal rebirth.

♐ *Sagittarius*

Symbol: Archer / Centaur / Horse

Statement: I UNDERSTAND

Ruling Planet: Jupiter

Gender: Male

Triplicy: Mutable

Element: Fire

Anatomy: Thighs

Qualities: Sagittarius is the power of freedom. Two archetypes are the teacher, who desires intellectual, philosophical, and spiritual freedom, and the horse that seeks personal and physical freedom. Sagittarian images range from scholar, athlete to business person, but each are seeking to push their limits. Sagittarius magick is used for business, administration, prosperity, exploration, physical competitions, and good "luck." It is also for philosophical and spiritual learning.

♑ *Capricorn*

Symbol: Goat

Statement: I USE

Ruling Planet: Saturn

Gender: Female

Triplicy: Cardinal

Element: Earth

Anatomy: Knees, shins, skeletal system

Qualities: Capricorn is the climbing mountain goat, seeking stability in its disciplined climb to the top. Capricorn energy involves responsibility, particularly to the community, and its key word is honor. This is the sign of truth, ruled by Saturn, the planet of what you need to hear, not necessarily what you want to hear. Capricorn energy is used magickally for spells involving career, public honor, vocation, achievement, respect, confidence, and tradition. It helps you with whatever responsibilities you hold.

♒ *Aquarius*

Symbol: Water Bearer

Gender: Male

Statement: I KNOW

Ruling Planet: Uranus

Triplicy: Fixed

Element: Air

Anatomy: Ankles, nervous system

Qualities: Despite the name, Aquarius is not a water sign, but the water bearer, the person who carries the waves. In this case, they are waves of communication, more like radio waves than water. Aquarius is communication involving friends, but also involving the greater world community. Ruled by the planet of revolution, Uranus, Aquarius brings sudden and swift change, unorthodox thinking, and innovation. Use Aquarian energy to foster the unexpected, including technology and new paradigms. Aquarius can create a sense of universal fellowship, of brotherhood and sisterhood beyond borders, races, and economics.

♓ *Pisces*

Symbol: Two Fish

Statement: I BELIEVE, I TRANSCEND, I MERGE

Ruling Planet: Neptune

Gender: Female

Triplicy: Mutable

Element: Water

Anatomy: Feet

Qualities: Pisces is the last sign, the sign of surrender to the divine and transcending all limits. In one form it is the institution of religions. Disillusionment with such structures and ideals can lead to addictions and loss of faith. Higher expressions are acts of imagination and mysticism. Pisces is the struggle between the spiritual and material. Use Piscean energy to stimulate your creativity, spirituality, to reveal the hidden, generate empathy, and dive into the deep spiritual waters to return with the treasure of self-knowledge.

ASPECTS

Aspects are special angles formed between two planets and the Earth. Each angle allows the energy of the two planets to flow and connect. Each different angle creates a different relationship. Although in astrology there are no good or bad aspects, since each offers its own rewards and challenges, in magick, certain aspects are favorable and others unfavorable.

Certain aspects are helpful, harmonious, and supportive in magick. When planets enter beneficial aspects, their energy is in partnership. There is flow and communication between the planets. Your ritual can call upon both planets and will have powerful energy and support.

Other aspects are not as harmonious. They create a relationship between the two planets that is blocked, struggling, or otherwise disharmonious. The energy grounded through the Earth does not flow freely to support other intentions. If you call upon a planet in such a relationship, its energy will be strained and unsupportive in your magick.

Beneficial Aspects for Spell Casting

☌	0°	Conjunction	Direct support and communication, intensity	Same sign
⊻	30°	Semisextile	Minor support, neutral, reactive	Adjacent signs
✳	60°	Sextile	Complement, understanding, minor support	2 signs apart, same gender, opposing elements
△	120°	Trine	Support, strong understanding	4 signs apart, same element

When two planets share any of the four aspects above, the energy will support your spellwork, particularly if both planets can play a role in your ritual. Since the Moon moves quickest, it is always makes the most aspects and will most likely be involved in your planning. If you are doing a love spell, and if the Moon is making a beneficial aspect with Venus, then the timing of your spell is very auspicious.

Detrimental Aspects for Spell Casting

∠	45°	Semisquare	Friction, irritation	Adjacent signs
□	90°	Square	Tension, obstacles, block	3 signs apart, same quality
⚼	135°	Sesquiquadrate	Abrasive, difficult communication	5 signs apart
⚻	150°	Inconjunct	Misdirection, misalignment	5 signs apart
☍	180°	Opposition	Conflict, no support, cross-purposes	6 signs apart, opposite sign, same quality

If two planets are making any of the five detrimental aspects, avoid using them in spellwork. For our above example, if you are doing a love spell and Venus is making a detrimental aspect with another planet, you probably want to avoid it. Venus doesn't necessarily have to be making a beneficial aspect, but you should try to avoid detrimental ones for that spell.

The exception to detrimental aspects are alignments of the Sun and Moon. The Moon is in opposition to the Sun at the Full Moon, but it is the most powerful time of spellcasting. In fact, the various phases of the Moon correspond to aspects. When the two luminaries are conjunct, it is New Moon. Then the Moon is half light, from first to second quarter, or half dark, when moving from third to fourth, the Moon and Sun are square. When avoiding detrimental aspects, I tend to omit ones between the Sun and Moon.

In general it is best to "catch" aspects as they are building. Each aspect gives us a specific angle, but aspects are like waves that are cresting. Each aspects relates to the planets involved by the distance measured by signs. When the planets enter the appropriate signs to make the aspect, they begin to crest. Astrologers give each aspect an orb, a number of degrees plus or minus that is the variable for the aspects to be considered into a true alignment. Orbs vary from different astrologers, but remain within a few degrees. As the planets enter the orb, the wave is really building in power. When it reaches the exact degree of the aspect, it peaks, and, when it enters the orb again, begins winding down. While in the orb, it is still powerful but the wave has peaked. It loses power when it moves out of the orb, and then eventually moves out of the appropriate signs.

Astrological calendars will give the exact moment the aspects align. The closer you do your ritual to the alignment, the better. Ideally, if you can begin the ritual right before the alignment, perhaps by thirty minutes to an hour, you will have the peak of the aspects energy permeating you. You can even be early. If the aspect involves slower-moving outer planets, then you have more time. If it is quicker-moving inner planets, then you have less time. If you have to wait until just after the peak, you can still do your spell, but it is not the optimum.

The same rules apply for avoiding detrimental aspects. If you want to miss it, wait until after the peak. The longer you wait, the weaker the aspect energy will be, as if the link is breaking apart. The quicker the planets, the shorter the wait. The slower the planets, the longer the wait. Use your intuition to guide your process, or check the planets positions via an ephemeris or astrological software program.

Things to Beware

Most of the techniques we have covered focus on things that add to your power, but we haven't talked about alignments that will take away from your magick. Some are obvious, such as working against the Moon phase. Others are less so, but become more obvious as you start thinking with astrology.

If you are doing a passionate love spell, you might want to make sure the Moon is not in an air sign, since that will foster intellectualism or detachment. Better to wait for a fire or water sign. If you are doing money spells, you should look for an earth sign, but perhaps beware water, since the intuitive and formless energy of water signs would not support this work.

Besides watching out for inappropriate planetary alignments, there are two phenomena to beware. First is something called the Moon void-of-course. The second is retrograde motion.

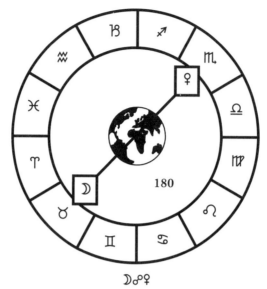

☽ ☍ ♀
The Moon is in opposition with Venus,
180° and six signs apart.
This is a poor time for Venusian magick.

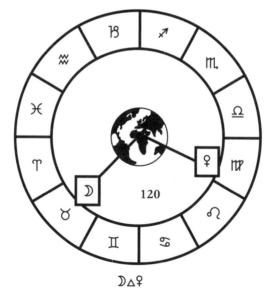

☽ △ ♀
The Moon is trine with Venus,
120° and four signs apart.
This is a great aspect for all Venusian magick.

Figure 28: Aspects

Void-of-course occurs when the Moon is not making any other major aspects before it changes astrological signs. The Moon's energy is not grounded to the Earth by an aspect, creating a spacy, ungrounded feeling in many people. More importantly, anything begun during the void-of-course will not manifest as planned. The energy is simply not present to make magick or anything else. Astrologers suggest not starting any projects, making deals, or initiating anything, magickal or not. The void-of-course is like a astrological time-out. Use this time to continue routines and preplanned events, and to rest and reflect. Luckily it doesn't last long. The rate is variable, but the effect is broken as soon as the Moon changes signs. Personally, I've found spells done during the void-of-course Moon don't manifest. When they do, they manifest in unwanted or partial ways.

Retrograde motion is when a planet appears to be moving backwards in its orbit from our view on Earth. The planet is not really going backwards. The effect is an optical illusion, much like being on a train and passing another train. Both are going forward, but when you are on the faster train, it appears the other train is going backwards. Astrologically, the effect is the planet's energy is directed to your inner consciousness, to reflect on your past, and to work toward inner transformation, rather than outer manifestation. If you try to use the planet's energy to manifest in the world, particularly through spellwork, you might get frustrated since the energy is not naturally directed that way.

All the planets except the Sun and the Moon can go retrograde. Each retrograde is different, depending on the planet and its position in relationship with the Earth's position. Usually the faster the planet's orbit, the shorter the retrograde, and the more frequently it occurs. The longer the orbit, the longer the retrograde, and the less frequently it occurs.

Many people dread retrogrades, but they are times for spiritual exploration and inner work. They are just difficult for outer manifestations. If the planet is in retrograde, and your intention is inner work, then you have no problem. You can manifest inner changes with that planetary energy. Pluto retrogrades are very long, but if you seek inner transformative work, then Pluto retrograde is no problem.

The retrograde that those with just a little astrological knowledge fear is Mercury retrograde. Since Mercury rules communication and travel, when Mercury is in retrograde, it seems like communication breaks down, travel is difficult, misunderstandings occur, and equipment malfunctions. If you have continued an introspective practice, Mercury retrograde isn't that bad. It is simply the universe's way of asking you to communicate with yourself rather than the outer world. Venus retrograde asks you to direct your love inwardly. Mars retrograde asks us to direct our will to our inner life. All retrogrades are teachers when viewed properly.

READING AN ASTROLOGICAL CALENDAR

All of this information can be found in an astrological calendar, such as the annual Llewellyn's *Astrological Calendar*. Each calendar has its own key code explained in its introduction, but most use very similar notation and layout.

Below is a particularly busy day, astrologically speaking. If we go through it point by point, we can understand how an astrological calendar works, and how you can get all this information easily.

21 Sunday			*3rd* ♒	
☽☍♂	3:15 AM	**12:15 AM**	4th Quarter 6:36 AM	**3:36 AM**
☽□♆	5:15 AM	**2:15 AM**	☽ v/c 6:36 AM	**3:36 AM**
☽□☉	6:36 AM	**3:36 AM**	☽ enters ♓ 6:40 AM	**3:40 AM**
☽⊻♅	7:20 AM	**4:20 AM**	☉ enters ♊ 7:43 AM	**4:34 AM**
☉△♅	4:37 PM	**1:37 PM**		
☽✶♀	5:32 PM	**2:32 PM**		
☽∠♆		**10:31 PM**		

Figure 29: Astrological Calendar

On the right side:

- Top right corner says the Moon is in its third quarter, so it is waning, and in the sign of Aquarius. This is a time of banishing, and the magick will be colored by the fixed air qualities of Aquarius. You could banish intellectual blocks, prejudices, or disruptions from your circle of friends.

- The Moon enters the fourth quarter at 6:36 AM Eastern, or 3:36 AM Pacific. (Check your own calendar to see what time zone is being used.) Magick for banishing is even stronger now.

- The Moon goes void-of-course (v/c) at 6:36 AM Eastern or 3:36 AM Pacific. It then enters the sign of Pisces at 6:40 AM Eastern/3:40 AM Pacific, so it was only void for four minutes. During these four minutes, do not start any magick. Once it enters Pisces, banishing magick will be colored by the mutable qualities of Pisces. This could be a strong time to banish and heal addictions, depression, or creative blocks.

- The Sun enters Gemini at 7:43 AM Eastern/4:43 AM Pacific. Now the basic life energy of the Sun has moved from Taurus into Gemini, granting it energy of communication and learning.

On the left side:

- The Moon goes into opposition with Mars at 3:15 AM Eastern/12:15 AM Pacific. This is a detrimental time to use Mars energy.

- The Moon squares Pluto at 5:15 AM Eastern/2:15 AM Pacific. This is a detrimental time to use Pluto in magick.

- The Moon squares the Sun at 6:36 AM Eastern/3:36 AM Pacific. This alignment indicates the Moon is entering the fourth quarter phase, and is a time for waning. If you are doing magick to balance the solar and lunar energies, this may not be the best time, since square is a detrimental aspect.

- The Moon is semisextile with Uranus at 7:20 AM Eastern/4:20 AM Pacific. This alignment allows minor support for magick involving Uranus issues.

- The Moon trines Uranus at 4:37 PM Eastern/1:37 PM Pacific. This aspect gives even greater support to Uranian issues.

- The Moon is sextant with Venus at 5:32 PM Eastern/2:32 PM Pacific. Venusian love magick is supported at this time.

- The Moon is semisquare with Neptune at 10:31 PM Pacific, or the next day for those on the East Coast of the US. Neptune magick is not supported at this time.

Although I chose this day because it gives us many examples to work with when learning to read the calendar, as a magickal day, it has its weaknesses. Many of the aspects seem conflicting. I would avoid power magick on this day, with detrimental aspects to both Mars and Pluto. Uranian magick is powerful. The Moon starts in the sign of Aquarius, the sign ruled by Uranus, but the Moon changes signs before the aspects peak. If I was to do Uranian magick on this day, I would do it while the Moon was in Aquarius, before it goes void-of-course. Since Uranus is a slow-moving planet, you can still take advantage of the other aspects that are building slowly. Creative, artistic magick is also powerful, with the Moon in Pisces, the beneficial aspect with Venus building later in the day. You could argue that the Sun in Taurus before 7:43 AM Eastern would be more beneficial, or you can call on Gemini's communicative abilities in your magick. Neptune's later unwanted aspect is building, but I would be tempted to disregard if it I really wanted to do magick. Everything can't be perfect, so you have to pick the days that have some benefit and take your chances with detrimental aspects.

How Do I Use Astrological Timing?

By now you are probably thinking this is way too complicated to be practical. I agree. How do you get the Moon, Sun, day, hour, aspects, and signs to all work out? You can't. If you tried to match your spells to every factor we have covered in this chapter, you would never do any magick. It would never be the "perfect" time for magick.

Well, in my experience, every time is the perfect time for magick. These are tools; no more, no less. Find which tools are important to you, including sheer intuition, and use them. You will never match the day, hour, signs, and aspects of all the planets. But what ones are important to you? Use them. Some never use days and hours. Some never use signs. Some never use aspects. Some witches use nothing but the Moon and a sense of intuition.

Pick and choose the tools that work for you. Use the tools that are perfect for you and make magick! If your magick is successful, you have chosen the right tools. If you are lacking the success you want, try working with a different set of tools.

Tips on Spell Casting

Though we have covered the basics of making magick, some practical points from those who have gone before definitely help our spellcraft improve.

Be Careful What You Ask For

You just might get it. In fact, you probably will, so make sure you really want it.

You Get What You Ask For

You get what you ask for, not what you think you asked for, or what you meant to ask for. Spells will always take the easiest route to manifest. If you ask for a million dollars, and have no other stipulation, you can get run over by a truck, and then, as a result of your crippling injuries, sue the driver and get a million dollars. But you can't enjoy it. If you ask it "Harm none," then you have a better chance at enjoying it.

Results

Focus on the results, not the manner in which the spell manifests. What is your ultimate goal. Focus on it.

Let Go

Let your intention go. If you do not release it, it will not return. Usually when we do not release, we are lingering in fear and doubt. If you can back up your thoughts with continual reinforcement of your intent, then you can continue to think about it, like an affirmation. But for most of us, it is easier to let it go and know the spell is working, rather than let our doubts sap our magickal strength.

Remember the Witch's Pyramid

From the ITOW, the message of the pyramid, to Know, to Will, to Dare, and to Keep Silent. The one witches forget about the most is keeping silent. Don't share your spellwork with others unless they are of a like mind. And even then, be sure. When you are silent, you allow the energy to remain focused. When you talk, you can scatter it. If you tell it to others who are not supportive, their feelings can sap the spell. If you talk about it, and people ask you why it hasn't occurred yet, it can sow seeds of doubt within you, weakening that spell and future spells.

Real-World Actions

Back up all your spells with real-world actions. If you do a spell for a job, send out résumés, check the newspaper, apply, and network. Open the door in your life to let the results come in. Many people think a job spell means the perfect employer will contact you out of the blue, without any effort from you. Untrue. You must open the door. If you are doing magick for love, meet new people. Get out into the world. Date. If you are doing magick for health, start taking care of yourself. Allow the magick to work with you. Don't fight it. Partner with it. If you need a guide, again, use the pentacle. Before doing the spell, think of five things you have to do to make this intent a reality. When the spell is cast, go out and do those five things to make it happen. You will be divinely supported in your efforts.

Make Space

All things in your life represent energy. If you ask for things and nothing new comes into your life through spells, ask yourself if you have too much clutter in your life. New energy cannot come in if you don't get rid of old energy. Clear your home, work, relationships, and life of all unnecessary elements. This will free up space for new blessings. The old will no longer be tied to you, and both you and your stuff will be able to move on to the next phase.

Was It Magick?

Many witches have amazingly visionary ritual experiences. They see the elements and the gods. They get messages and visions as to how the spell will manifest. Then some of us get no special effects and lighting. We have a peaceful or fun ritual, but wonder if it was really working, since we didn't see anything. Sometimes I do, sometimes I don't, but my magick is always strong. Melissa, who works wonderful spells, tells me that she doesn't really experience anything in circle that would be considered visionary, but her spells work. It is important for everyone to know that. It's not about the special effects. It is about the magickal life you lead.

Neutralizing Spells You No Longer Want

People often ask me how to "break" a spell they have cast as soon as they realize they no longer want its results and fear that if it does manifest, it would disrupt their life. Simply cast a counterspell. Write a petition asking to neutralize the previous spell. As you learn astrological timing, you might want to do it in the opposing phase or sign of the Moon from when you cast the first spell.

Recognize Your Magick

Whenever your magick works, honor it. Recognize it. Thank the gods and goddesses. Thank the universe. The more you acknowledge it and recognize it, the more it will grow. Make saying "Thank you" a part of your daily spiritual practice.

Record Spells in Your Book of Shadows

Keep track of all your spells in your journal or Book of Shadows. Write down all the things you used, who was there, astrological information, and anything else you feel is important. As you keep track of your spells, you begin to find what things work for you and what things don't. Certain times, tools, or intentions may be powerful for you, while others are not. You'll never find your strengths and weaknesses, or pass on your wisdom and repeat a spell, if you do not record it.

Date: _____   Planetary Day: _____

Time: _____   Planetary Hour: _____

Location: _____   Moon Phase: _____

Work: _____   Moon Sign: _____

_____   Aspects: _____

_____   _____

Divination Omens: _____   _____

_____   _____

_____   _____

Offering: _____   _____

Those Present: _____   _____

_____   _____

State of Mind: _____   _____

Dress/Jewelry: _____   Other Astrological Info: _____

_____   _____

Special Tools: _____   _____

_____   _____

Divinities and Spirits Called: _____   _____

_____   _____

_____   _____

Spells: _____

_____

_____

_____

_____

_____

_____

_____

_____

_____

_____

Notes: _____

_____

_____

Figure 30: Ritual Record Sheet

Ritual Checklist

Ask yourself these questions before beginning any spellwork or casting your circle.

Where do I plan on doing this work?

When do I plan on doing this work? Is the timing right?

What type of spell am I doing?

Why am I doing this spell? Do I really want it?

Is anyone helping me, or am I doing this solitary? Do I need help?

What tools or ingredients will I need?

What divine powers do I call on and why?

Am I presenting an offering? If so, what?

Does all this feel right to my intuition?

WHY SPELLS WORK

I have found spells to be more effective and empowering than any other form of manifestation. Other forms are wonderful and bring their own gifts. I use affirmations, creative visualization, mantras, and forms of prayer, but spells have an inherent beauty to them.

Through ritual, we stimulate all five elements needed for creation, and do so through all five senses as well. The more you stimulate these forces and partner with them, the more effective your magick will be. Many people think the use of tools, ritual, and traditional forms of movement are silly or superstitious, but there is a power in these tools and acts that goes beyond our normal consciousness. It stimulates something deep within us.

Sight

You stimulate the sense of sight through candlelight, ritual colors, mystical symbols, and the inner sight of visualization.

Hearing

Hearing is stimulated through the actual spoken words of the ritual, as well as any chants, magickal words, songs, bells, or music.

Touch

Through the anointing with potions, handholding, and hands-on healing, witches stimulate the sense of touch. Often we work barefoot, feet on the ground, to really feel the energy and temperature of the Earth.

Smell

The power of smell is conjured through the exotic scents of herbs, oils, and incense. The smell of burning wood or paper adds to the stimulation.

Taste

Taste is a powerful trigger for memory and power. Witches use pure water, wine, and herbal drinks in the chalice of the Goddess as our sacrament. We share cakes, break bread, and use food and fruit offerings to connect with this deep power.

Spells and rituals also have the opportunity to simultaneously use several techniques from the Eightfold Path (ITOW, chapter 5) to raise power. One enters a meditative state through the ritual, often with relaxation and deep breath. A witch uses words and movements to create the space. Chant or dance can be used to raise more power for a spell. The use of incense, oil, or wine acts as the herbal intoxicant to open the gates. Sex is enacted through the Great Rite, ritualistically or literally. We usually partake in the circle only amongst other witches, creating a type of isolation, or the circle is done solitary. A short fast before the circle, usually from abstaining from food before the ritual, and breaking the fast with cakes and ale or feasting after the ritual. The only path not often partaken as part of the magick circle is pain, though scourging was part of certain ritual initiations.

When designing your own spells and rituals, keep these points in mind to make your work even more magickal.

WHY SPELLS DON'T WORK

Teaching witchcraft, I invariably get the question "Why didn't my spell work? I did it the way you taught." It's a fair question, but one I dread since it comes across so accusatory. People often don't like to hear the answer. Sometimes it's best for a spell not to work. I've been happy a few didn't manifest. I did spells to be a rock star, but now

I'm glad I'm not. I was lucky enough to be in the music business long enough to see how rock stars live, and I would have been miserable. And I never would have found my true calling.

So here are some ideas to ponder when your spell is not working.

Duration

Your spell could be working, but hasn't manifested yet. How long are you waiting before getting nervous? Some spells happen overnight. Some spells take nine months. Be patient.

Mistakes

You were not clear in your intention and received what you asked for, but not what you wanted. If you do a spell for a new relationship, for example, but did not specify a romantic one, you could have got a new friend or acquaintance.

Poor Timing

You were working against the tides of energy that correspond with the Moon, Sun, seasons, planets, or signs. Although your spell was good, you were swimming upstream and didn't have sufficient will to overcome.

Not For You

You asked for something that was not for your highest good and your divine self has overruled it, because you asked it to do so with the spell being for your highest good, harming none. This spell would have harmed you or distracted you from your true purpose. You might have been creating from your ego and not in partnership with the divine. This is the most common reason for a failed spell. It didn't fail. In fact, the conditions worked, so it was a success after all, but it doesn't feel like it.

Not in Alignment

You did the spell, but did not get into a sufficient magickal state to access your abilities. You could not connect to the psychic and divine selves sufficiently. You might have been nervous, tired, angry, or simply sloppy in your spellcraft. Try again later.

No Release

You did not release your intention, and now you are nervously dwelling on it. Each time you focus on it, it's like taking back a chunk of the energy you sent out, leaving less and less to do the job. Soon there will be nothing left to your thoughtform.

No Real-World Back-Up

You didn't follow up the spell with any real-world action. You didn't leave yourself available to receive this blessing. You did not open a channel to it or open the door when opportunity came knocking.

EXERCISE 32

Create and Cast Your Own Petition Spell

Meditate on an intention you have. If you would like, do a divination (chapter 10) asking if this is appropriate at this time. Then formulate a petition spell, using the words and phrases that work for you. If you have a study partner or teacher, discuss the spell wording and make sure you are really asking for what you want. Then choose the appropriate time to do this spell. Cast your magick circle and perform the spell. Release it to the universe and allow it to come back to you manifested. Record all your experiences in your Book of Shadows.

HOMEWORK

- Do Exercise 32.

- Continue your journaling, but now note the Moon phase and sign. Learn your own personal cycles with the Moon. Certain signs may be powerful for you, while others are more difficult emotionally or magickally. Through an astrology book or program, learn your own Moon sign. You may find when the Moon is in the same sign as your own Sun or Moon sign, or the opposite sign of your Sun and Moon is a noteworthy time for you. Learn your own cycles and patterns.

- Regular altar devotional and any other regular meditative practice.

- Practice divination techniques.

Lesson Nine
The Art of Spellcraft

As there is a science to spells, with a basic formula for the foundation of magickal manifestation, there is also an art. Within the foundation is a great amount of space to creatively build and express yourself. A wise witch works magick like life, an endless opportunity to creatively express herself while partnered with the universe. Witches use the tools and helpers found all around them, from exotic ingredients and symbols to weeds in the back yard.

The art of spellcraft has few rules, but does have a legacy of traditional knowledge reclaimed and passed down from older times. We use this tradition to build our own spells and charms, to pay homage to the past, while forging the future of witchcraft.

Use this section to educate yourself on the possibilities of spellcraft. Then use your knowledge of the science to create your own rituals, spells, and charms. Breathe your own life into the magick of the witch.

TYPES OF MAGICK

Magick is divided into many different categories by esoteric scholars. These divisions are arbitrary and are only used to explain different techniques. Ultimately, magick is magick. We are all harnessing the same forces regardless of our background or tradition. Magick is working with the divine powers of life, on every level, to create change. Magick is like electricity. The systems of magick are the various devices, the hardware and software humans use to tap into the vast power of electricity. Through our devices and intentions, we determine what the electricity, or magick, is used for, but the power itself is inherent, and available to anyone with the knowledge and resources to tap into it.

The most basic division of magick is referred to as high magick and low magick. I don't like these terms and find them very biased, but they do have a historical use. High magick refers to ceremonial magick, usually drawing on complex rituals, languages, and symbols. High magick is systematic, and requires a great amount of study. Scholars speculate that it is called high magick both for the high amount of knowledge and formal education one needs, as well as it historically being practiced by those of the upper classes, the royal courts, and those in institutions of power, who resided on the high lands and hills. They avoided much disease that was spread through the waters and vermin of the lower lands, where low magick thrived. Low magick is folk magick, intuitive and simple, using the tools of the land and the cycle of growing and harvest. Low magick is symbolic and primal, changing and adapting with the tools on hand. Most consider witchcraft to be a form of low magick, because of the historical image of the folk healer and hedge witch, but I believe modern witchcraft encompasses both low and high aspects.

Magick is categorized by tradition and culture. People speak of Celtic magick, Egyptian magick, Norse magick, or African magick. The culture will influence the rituals, deities, symbols, tools, and types of spells you will do. Each culture, although magickal, has a unique viewpoint on the world, and that view will influence their rituals and spells. These cultures can be blends of both high and low magick. I know witches practicing "low" Celtic magick speaking in Gaelic. Such knowledge tells me it is a form of high magick as well. Modern witchcraft draws upon all these cultures and more. Whenever you have a people honoring divinity through nature, and partnering with these forces to create change, you have a form of witchcraft. I see all of the world as my ancestors collectively, and their myths and cultures as my global spell book. As long as you have respect, knowledge, and love of the culture you draw upon, you can work with these cultural magicks.

Another division is the mechanism of the magick. Divided into three basic categories—divination, sorcery, and invocation—the modern witch could call them information magick, intention magick, and spirit magick. We have started our path of divination, and can use this psychic magick to gain information about the past, present, or future. Many people who do psychic readings would insist they are not doing magick, but magick is causing change, and sometimes the greatest change you can make is to get information about the situation.

Sorcery has gotten a bad rap. In some cultures, a sorcerer denotes an "evil doer" or one involved solely in the gain of power, not enlightenment. Some equate any magick for personal gain or life improvement to be evil, but modern witches recognize it as practical. You can't focus on enlightenment if you can't put a roof over your head. Once your needs are met, you begin to contemplate higher forces. In other cultures, sorcerers are wise ones, like the witch, spiritual warriors, healers, and shamans. Depends on where you are and who you are with when using the word "sorcerer." In this division, sorcery is spellcraft, making a change in the material world. Most spells books fall under this category.

"Invocation" in this case refers to spirit work. Technically we use this word to denote bringing a spirit into your body, and "evocation" for summoning a spirit, but spirit work is any type of magick involving the use of spirits. They can be called upon to heal, guide, and make changes in the world. In a circle, we call upon the gods and elements. Under this three-tier system, witchcraft encompasses all of these categories.

Magick is also divided by the vessel or technique used to propel your intention. We have herbal magick, candle magick, cord magick, color magick, stone magick, dream magick, rune magick, tree magick, sympathetic magick, instant magick, and petition spells. You may excel in one craft and feel no connection to another. Although I love both plants and crystals, I have found that many people who love one dislike the other and never learn its gifts. That's perfectly fine. We all can excel at certain disciplines, and find others not to our liking. We leave those magicks to other witches.

We divide magick by outcome. People talk about love magick and prosperity magick. We all learn protection magick. Witchcraft has historically focused on healing magick. Each represents aspects of the tradition, and we can excel at some and dislike others.

Lastly, among the uneducated, witchcraft and magick are often divided into white and black, or good and evil. Most witches don't use these terms since they are over-simplifications of life. It's like saying black and white electricity. The power is neutral. It is the user's intent that matters most.

VESSELS FOR MAGICK

Many forms of magick, particularly simple folk magick, use a vessel to hold the intention of the spell. Not only is the vessel a tool, but often the spirit of it, particularly if it is a plant or stone, becomes your magickal partner just like the elementals. When you do these simple folk rituals inside a magick circle, you really amplify their power. They work alone, but in the sacred space of a magick circle, they become a spiritual experience as well as an act of manifestation.

The colors, shapes, and energies of these vessels have magickal resonance to them, corresponding to the energies of deities, elements, planets, and signs. By choosing the right tools and partners for your magick, you increase the type of energy you need to cast a successful spell. When you pick appropriate items to create your spells and find a helpful astrological time, you greatly increase the flow of these universal energies to manifest your will.

Candle Magick

Candle magick is a powerful yet simple form of magick. I have walked many non-witches though simple candle spells and had spectacular results. Candle magick incorporates all the important aspects of other spellcraft into one single, simple vessel. Candles incorporate colors, which are important symbols of intention. Use the astrological color correspondences below, or use your experiences from the showers of light meditation (ITOW, chapter 10). Candles naturally embody the four elements. Earth is the wax of the candle. Most witches prefer beeswax, but it is not a requirement, since beeswax can be expensive. Water is the melting action, as well as the moisture that accumulates on many candles. Air is the oxygen needed to burn, and fire is obviously the candle flame. With one tool, you have all four elements and color.

Candles can be simple, with one candle for one intention, or more complex. You can use many candles of different colors. I have created candle spells with rings of candles, particularly for healing, placing the recipient's picture in the center of the ring. I also mixed this candle healing spell with stones and herbs, by placing them on top of the photo.

You can carve magickal symbols, runes, the name and/or Sun sign symbol of the recipient of the spell, or anything else on it. I use either the tip of my boline or a warmed pin.

Anoint your candles with potions, oils, and powders. This is called dressing your candle. Different traditions are sticklers about how to anoint the candle. The most traditional way is to anoint in the middle, and rub the liquid out to both ends. Some say if you want to attract something, anoint from the top to the base, while if you want to banish, anoint from the base to the top. I've found it doesn't matter as long as your intention is strong. My friend Tim suggested anointing a candle in oil, and then rolling it in a matching herb, to let the herbs burn to release additional magickal energy. It works well, just make sure it is on a flame-proof surface if sparks fly. Some hollow out the candle's bottom and fill the hole with herbs. I also cleanse my candles before using them, by either smudging in incense or rubbing in sea salt. This prevents unwanted energy from affecting your spell. Only use new, unlit candles for your spells.

Once you have your candle prepared, hold it with both hands in the magick circle and create your spell. Speak your intention. Visualize it. Imagine how it would feel when your spell is true. If you want, you can do a petition spell with the candle. Imagine filling the candle with your energy and intent, like filling a glass of water. Once you reach the brim, light the candle. You can then complete the circle and go about your business. Also remember to use sturdy candle holders. Glass ones often shatter from the flame's heat. I prefer to use metal candle holders.

Let the candle burn, but don't leave it completely unattended. If you have to leave, snuff the candle out and relight it later when you are around. Old superstitions say if you blow it out, you offend the element of fire, cursing you with a twisted outcome or no outcome at all. In reality, you are not offending fire if you did not have a mean intent. You are simply unbalancing the elements present in the candle, adding more air, and causing the spell to either fail or manifest in an unwanted way. Snuffing prevents this by keeping the elemental balance inside the candle the same.

Charm Magick

Anything can be made into a vessel for magick. All objects contain energy and can be used to carry intention. All objects' natural abilities can be catalyzed by a witch. Jewelry is a favorite charm. Witches make magick with rings, necklaces, and bracelets. Charms can be handcrafted using paper, wood, cloth, leather, wax, clay, herbs, and stones. Some are containers for other objects of powers. Others are engraved with symbols. Clothing can be infused with a magickal intention. Household objects can be your magickal tool. With a little creativity, you can create magick with anything. A variety of traditional charm procedures are described in this chapter, but use what works for you.

In certain forms of magick, a charm is differentiated into a talisman or amulet. I learned that an amulet is a charm that banishes unwanted influences, neutralizes energies, and protects you. A talisman is something that draws to you fortunate influences or generates the energy you seek. They sound like the division of waning and waxing Moon magick, and are usually created during those respective times.

Each ingredient of the charm must be cleansed and consecrated as you make it, and then the entire thing should be specifically programmed with your intention while in the magick circle. There is no need to raise the cone of power, since the energy raised is going into the charm.

Herbal Magick

Herbal magick is the heart of traditional witchcraft. The Western herbal tradition was almost lost due to the witchcraft persecutions of Europe. The more I practice herbalism, the more I find that so much of the inherent wisdom of witchcraft comes from the plant spirits. Some of my most moving spiritual experiences have been meditating with a plant or making a potion. Charging herbs helps create a magickal partnership.

Herbcraft comes in many forms, and each tradition uses its own terms to describe its herbal products. The terms I use are the ones I've learned, but others use different terms. As long as you know what is meant by each teacher, any term can be used.

"Potions" are a catch-all word, but when I use the term, I refer to a water-based infusion of herbs, as well as oils, crystals, metals, or animal hair, that is preserved with sea salt and only used externally. I use a base of two to four cups of spring water with two to four tablespoons of sea salt or kosher salt. Heat the water to help the salt dissolve and add your herb material to the brew. If you are using many herbs, go heavy on the salt. The proportions are not an exact science, but a guide.

Many witches cook over the kitchen stove. Most prefer gas to electric, to keep the energy flow of the circle. I have an electric stove, so I use a large potpourri simmerer. I love to use it, since it is heated by a tea light candle and can fit on my altar, where I do most of my magickal and meditative work. If you use other cooking vessels, be sure to know what they made from. Iron and steel pots should only be used for protection or Mars magick, copper ones for love or Venus magick, and aluminum is only for Mercury magick and often avoided by most herbalist. Glass and enamel are great all-purpose substances. Charge each ingredient, asking its spirit to help with your intention. Then charge the entire mixture with your intent. Direct the energy of the circle into the liquid. Complete the circle.

When you are done, let the potion cool, strain the herbs out, and bottle the liquid. If you leave the herbs in, it might go rancid. You can strain out the mold and add more salt to save it. If it gets rancid more than once, throw it out and start over. If you put in enough salt and keep the potion out of heat and light, it can last for several years, though its potency will diminish with age. I had a wonderful psychic potion that lasted for about ten years before it stopped working.

If you really like your potion and want to re-create it exactly, use a crystal when you make it, and charge the crystal with the intention to record the pattern of the potion. When you want to remake the potion, use the same crystal, so it will have the same energy even if it is made at a different time with different aspects and energies. Sometimes, however, it is fun to make new recipes and try new things.

Use potions to anoint yourself, your tools, and charms. Potions work on the principle of vibration, and alter the energy of anyone or anything that uses it. Traditionally, the effects are said to last three to four days. They are an excellent way of "storing" power to be used later. If the timing is right for a good money spell, you can make a money potion, and then use it later when you need to attract money, either by anointing yourself or using it as part of a larger spell with other tools. I also like to decorate my potion bottles with other talismans, and make them into ceremonial objects. The more pleasing to the eye a tool is, the more evocative it will be of a magickal state of mind.

Figure 31: *Potions*

A brew is an herbal tea that can be used internally. Usually a light brew made by steep-ing one tablespoon of herb in one cup of hot water for five to twenty minutes is re-ferred to as a tea, while a brew allowed to steep overnight is called an infusion, and used more for medical ailments. I use brews in the chalice during ritual, picking herbs that fit the Moon or Sun sign for the ritual. Herbal teas can also be infused via the Sun (or the Moon) to impart more magick into your spellwork. A common practice is to infuse herbs in a jar during the summer, making a summer tea, or to infuse a small amount of herb in a chalice, perhaps with a crystal, to drink upon sunrise. Teas can also be used as a wash, potion, or asperger fluid, but will not keep long without sea salt, alcohol, or vinegar as a preservative. I prefer to make things fresh anyway, to guarantee a strong level of power in the herb, rather than use something that has been sitting around too long.

Drinking herbal tea from the chalice in ritual is a powerful way to connect with plant spirits and their healing magick. They enrich any spell or ceremony. Make sure to consult a reputable medicinal herbal to determine if a plant is toxic before imbibing any plant. If you find a plant in the wild, make absolutely sure you know its identity before consuming. Many wonderful, magickal plants are highly toxic. Their potent chemicals are what gives them their power. Although things like nightshade, hemlock, mandrake, and monkshood can be found in many medieval witch's brews, they are all poisonous and I do not recommend working with them except as a charm to be carried.

Herbal extracts made in room-temperature alcohol, rather than water and steeped for four to six weeks, are called tinctures. Tinctures are used primarily medicinally, but a few drops can be placed in water for the magickal essence of the plant. Some resins, like frankincense, myrrh, or dragon's blood, are tinctured in a high-proof alcohol, but are not to be consumed, only used magickally for anointing. Herbal juices, such as pokeberry juice, can be preserved with a bit of vodka and if needed, thickened with gum arabic and made into magickal inks. Pokeberries are poisonous, so don't consume it.

Magickal oils come in two forms: infused oils and essential oils. Infused oils are when plant material, usually fresh (unless it is a resin) is placed in a jar and covered in a good base oil, such as virgin olive oil, and left for four to six weeks, often in the sunlight in the garden. Use an airtight container and make sure there is no water or air left in the infusing jar, just oil and herb. Then the herb is strained out and the oil stored, empowered with the herbs' magickal powers. These are used to anoint people and tools, as well as make medicines. Such infused oils can be used as the base for ointments and balms.

Essential oils are commercially distilled volatile oils from plant material, and are used in both medicinal and magickal aromatherapy. It requires large amounts of laboratory equipment and plant material to distill essential oils, so most are available commercially. Essential oils are mixed with a base oil to thin out their concentrated scents and make them last longer, since they are expensive. I learned a ratio of one-quarter to one-half essential oil to base oil, but that creates a pretty strong oil. Oil recipes are often written out by the drop, and use the archaic term "dram" to denote twenty drops. This is witchcraft, not chemistry, so our drops will not be scientifically consistent, but depend on the size of our dropper. I have used one dram of base oil to one total dram of essential oils. Scott Cunningham suggests, in *The Complete Book of Incense, Oils & Brews*, to use five to seven drops of an essential oil to one-eighth cup of a base oil to create a fine magickal oil without an overpowering scent. I prefer jojoba, grapeseed, almond, or apricot kernel oil for a base. Jojoba is my favorite since it is least likely to spoil over extended periods of time. Always make small amounts to make sure you like a formula.

The oils can be empowered with magickal intentions as you add them together in a mix. Stones can be soaked in them, but certain porous stones are damaged when soaked in oil. Use magickal oils as anointing oils, burn them on charcoal as incense, diffuse them in water with a scent diffuser, or mix them into misting bottles to bless a room with your magick. Both infused and essential oil mixes can be used in candle magick, incense, ritual anointing, and other charms.

"Philters" refer to dry potions, a mixture of herbs, resins, powdered gems, and other materials crushed to powder. They can be sprinkled in an area, buried, cast to the winds, carried in a magickal charm bag, or used like potpourri, opened when their energy is needed. You can even burn philters like incense. Most magickal incense is a mixture of gummy resins, herbs, and oils. The combination mixes together quite well and when burned releases powerful vibrations. Homemade incense can be burned on charcoal blocks, available at most New Age and metaphysical shops. This gives the best burn and aroma. You can quickly burn incense by tossing it into a fire, or, if you are want to go through the trouble, you can learn to mix in the appropriate chemicals to make igniting cones, pellets, or sticks.

Herbal charms are often called charm bags, magick bags, spell bags, gris gris bags, or mojo bags. They are simply herbs carried in a bag with a magickal intention infused into them. I often burn a petition spell and add its ashes to the mix, to fuse my specific intention with those herbs. You can use dry herbs, fresh herbs, resins, philters, and incense in your charm bag, along with other items, such as crystals, rocks, hair, beads, fossils, or anything else. It doesn't have to be exclusively herbal.

Herbal magick can be made right into your meals. Kitchen magick is powerful. Using not only herbs and spices, but the very magickal ingredients of your food itself, when cooked ritually and with love, can be amazing. Chicken soup becomes a healing potion. Pasta becomes a ritual of love. You can incorporate magickal herbs and oils into cleaning your home organically, and make housekeeping an act of magick. Simply consecrate all that you are using in your home. It might be impractical to cook inside a magick circle, but empower a few spices and ingredients if you can, but intend mag ick as you mix, blend and bake. Your magick will be there. Cooking and cleaning in themselves are rituals.

Lastly, I do something called cauldron magick. I fill my cauldron with water and sprinkle the herbs that fit my intention into it, calling on the spirit of the herbs while meditating and visualizing my intention. I'm not trying to create a product for later use. I'm not going to consume this mix. I simply let the herbs magickally mingle. I'll often make my intention spell a poem and chant it. When I'm done, I thank the herbs and then pour them out in the earth or a river to carry my magick to the world and beyond.

Stone Magick

Every rock, mineral, crystal, and metal has its own magickal energy and vibration. Knowledge of stone magick is almost as extensive as herbal magick, found all over the world in every tradition. The use of birthstones is an often misunderstood remnant of ancient stone magick. Stones embody certain forces, and by carrying them you harness those forces. You can harness the energy even more consciously by making them a part of your spellcraft. Most witches work with crystals from around the world, with different colors and properties, but the stones at your local field, hill, or river have magick in them as well. You will have to discover their power on your own, rather than looking up an exotic mineral in a book. Each stone must be cleansed and empowered, preferably in a magick circle. Carry a stone with you in jewelry, loose in your pocket, in a special colored bag, with a painted symbol, or with a more complex charm or potion to make your magick.

Symbol Magick

Symbol magick is another powerful technique, but less messy and less involved than herbal craft. It often appeals to the intellectual or scholarly witch. The purpose of symbol magick is to create a symbol that stands for our magickal intention. For some, petition spells don't work. They are too attached to the intention in written form, and never detach enough from the energy to let it manifest. Symbol magick creates an additional step of dissociation. The intent is distilled into a symbol, helping the witch detach the ego from the final outcome. Your psychic mind knows what the spell is about, but your conscious mind is circumvented with this technique. Symbols can be crafted into an item and carried with you or burned like a petition spell. The materials should be cleansed before use, and then the entire symbolic charm should be empowered with your intention while in a magick circle. If you have a long-term intention, such as protection, you can keep the symbol charm near you or place it in your home or office. If you want to release the energy for a specific act of manifestation, burn, bury, or destroy the symbol to release the energy.

My favorite form of symbol magick is rune magick. You can choose runes that are appropriate for your intention. You can draw the runes on wood, clay, or even paper, and carry them with you. I use wooden disks from a craft store, and paint them the appropriate colors and make them fancy enough to be worn as jewelry, gluing wire or string to wear it.

A simple rune charm is just one single rune. You are calling on its power to aid you. A rune tinne is several runes, written in a line, left to right, each one for your intention. I've done this type of charm on Popsicle sticks, tongue depressors, or, more traditionally, on fallen branches I have stripped of bark. Your rune tinne can be a modern "translation" of your intention. Boil your magick down to one word or phrase, and then use the runic equivalent of the English letters. The last type of rune charm takes several runes, and creatively binds them together into one harmonious whole. Runes can be in any direction, upside down, or even reversed, to fit into a pleasing geometric design. Bindrunes are a great avenue for creativity.

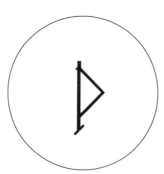

Figure 32: Rune of Protection

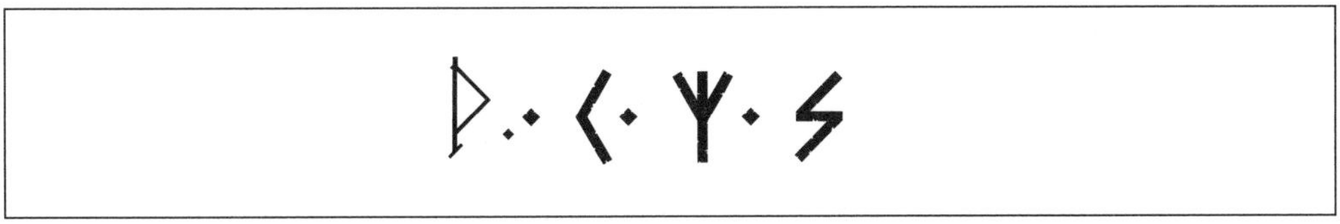

Figure 33: Rune Tinne of Protection

Figure 34: PROTECTION Translated into Runes

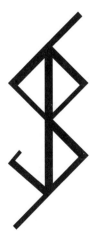

Figure 35: Bindrune

Runes are not the only system of symbols. There are many others, from Celtic ogham, to Sanskrit and Egyptian hieroglyphics. Even combinations of tarot cards on your altar can be used to make magickal change. Each system takes some study to learn the proper use of the symbols for magick. I like to use a free-form system of symbols called sigils.

Sigils are way of translating your intentions from the written alphabet to a free-form magickal symbol. You start by creating your intention. Make it a simple, but clear as you possibly can. It doesn't have to be as long or as formal as a petition spell. You could use something like:

NEW PROSPEROUS JOB

Figure 36: Sigil 1

The next step is to cross out all the repeated letters in the phrase, reducing it to its minimal components.

N E̶W ~~P R O S P E R O U~~ S J O̶ B

N   W   U   J   B

Figure 37: Sigil 2

Then you can arrange the letters creativity into a stylized symbol. The Latin alphabet can be quite magickal on its own.

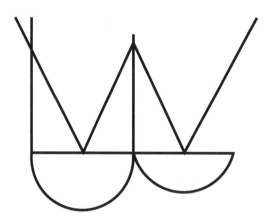

Figure 38: Sigil 3

Or, you can translate your remaining letters on to the witch's wheel. Although called the witch's wheel, it is really an adaptation of a ceremonial magick symbol system. Connect each letter to the next with straight lines. Traditionally you put a circle where you start, and a perpendicular line when you end. Then "lift" that symbol off the wheel and use it as your magickal charm.

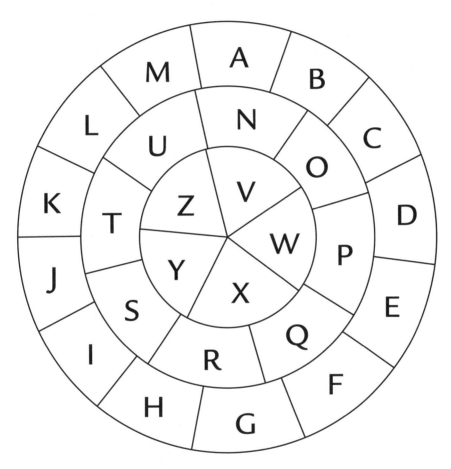

Figure 39: *Witch's Wheel*

Figure 40: *Sigil on Witch's Wheel*

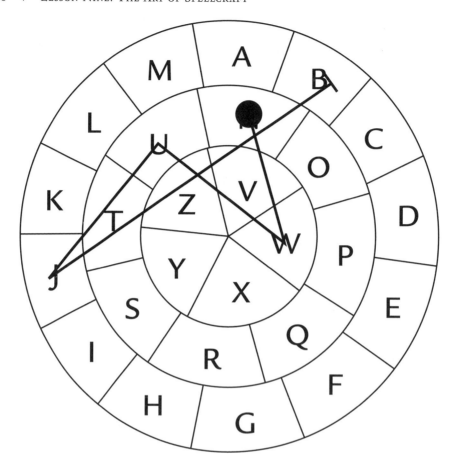

Figure 41: *Complete Sigil*

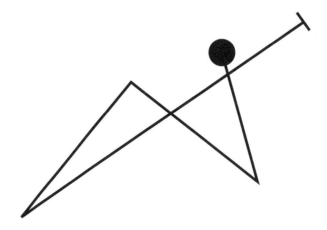

A traditional magickal symbol and phrase still used by witches and magicians is the old abracadabra. Although most people think of it as a joke, when written in a specific way, it is said to prevent and cure disease of all kinds.

ABRACADABRA

ABRACADABR

ABRACADAB

ABRACADA

ABRACAD

ABRACA

ABRAC

ABRA

ABR

AB

A

CORD MAGICK

Cord magick uses various types of cording as a focus for magick. Cords figure prominently in traditional initiation ceremonies, but can be used in everyday magick. The first type of cord magick I was exposed to was permanent cord magick. Three heavy cords of various colors, matching your intentions, are tied together, braided, and tied with at least three knots down the length. At each knot, an intention is tied in. This magick is for general purposes, not specific, timed actions. You could make a cord for protection, happiness, success, or all three, depending on the colors you mix together. Then the cord is decorated with charm bags, tarot cards, colored feathers, crystals, and anything else that symbolizes your intention.

The second type of cord magick is less pretty, but more useful for specific acts of magick. Like candle spells, it is very powerful. A few people have come to me saying they didn't believe in magick until they learned how to do this, and it worked so well, they decided to become witches.

Figure 42: Witch's Cords

Get a piece of string whose color matches your intention. Then braid nine knots in it, while focusing on your intention and saying this poem.

By the knot of one
The spell's begun.
By the knot of two

It comes true.

By the knot of three

It shall be.

By the knot of four

It's strengthened more.

By the knot of five.

It may thrive.

By the knot of six

This spell I fix.

By the knot of seven

With the stars of heaven.

By the knot of eight,

This spell is fate.

By the knot of nine

This thing is mine.

Keep the cord someplace special, perhaps on your altar, until it has done its work. Several variations of this spell exist, so feel free to adapt it your needs. For removing spells, knots can be untied, or the cord can be cut into pieces and then burned.

Sympathetic Magick

Sympathetic magick is ritually acting out whatever you want to occur. Through the Law of Correspondence (As above, so below), when you act something out in the magick circle, the microcosm, it will occur in the macrocosm, the world. If you want it to rain, doing magick by sprinkling out water symbolically acts out a rainfall. Witches dancing around the field on brooms were enacting the power of sympathetic magick. The brooms between their legs were fertility symbols, and the jumping symbolized the direction and how high they wanted the crops to grow. You can cut a thread as an act of separation. You can place someone's name in a bottle to contain their harmful energy.

The most popular form of sympathetic magick is the poppet, or voodoo doll. A symbolic representation of a person is made, such as a doll, but modern people often use photographs now as well. Ideally the poppet should be made from cloth the recipient has held or worn, invoking the Law of Contagion (ITOW, chapter 8). You can fill it with herbs and stones to match your intention. The icon is named after the person in the ritual. Energy is directed to the doll and whatever happens to the doll is sent to the person who embodies it. Usually healing energy is sent, regardless of popular Hollywood movie images of pain and curses.

I often use photos, and place crystals, metals, candles, and herbs on the photo to directly send these energies to the person in need of healing, love, or prosperity, but only if I have that person's permission to do the magick.

When the magick is completely done, another ritual is done to cut the energetic tie between the image and the person. I cut the air around it with my athame. Then the doll is dismantled and the contents buried.

Poetic Magick

Spells are often passed down as poetry and song. This is another powerful tool both for memory and making magick. Coming from the Eastern tradition of mantra and chant, it is quite likely ancient witches used poetic words of power to make magick. Since these traditions were destroyed, we must reclaim and rebuild our own magickal songs, stories, and power chants.

Certain chants are just for raising power, or celebrating the seasons, but there is no reason why you cannot make your own verse to fulfill specific intentions. This chant is said to grant wishes from the Goddess of the Moon, and was given to me by another witch. Although probably of modern origin, and not the ancient roots it is claimed to have, it still works wonders.

> Gracious Lady Moon
> Ever in my sight
> Kindly grant the boon
> I ask of thee tonight.

Entire spells can be phrased in the form of poetry. Just make sure you get all the important points of your spell in it. Don't suffer an unwanted intention for the sake of making something rhyme. Try this poem for a new job.

> Goddess of the Moon
> Goddess of light
> Please bring me my perfect job

One where I am happy and right
God of the Sun
God of the day
Please bring me this success
With your golden rays

Use magickal verse to inspire your own pagan poetry and share it with others.

ASTROLOGICAL SPELLCRAFTING

Learning the magickal correspondences of astrology was the most important step I took in truly learning magick. People will often be amazed at how I remember what herb is good for a particular spell, or how to use crystals, colors, or symbols. I wish I could say I have an excellent memory, but for details, I don't. I do love to understand systems though, and astrology gave me a system to craft my own spells.

Each planet and sign is related to specific sphere of influence, and timing your rituals to catch helpful alignments of the sky greatly increases your chances of success. Just as people each have Sun signs, Moon signs, and astrological birth charts, everything is influenced by astrology. Due to their nature, shape, color, and even chemical composition, herbs, stones, metals, and tools are all influenced, or ruled, by a planet or sign. If you want to bring more of a particular astrological energy into your ritual because you want its fortunate influences on the type of magick you are doing, you use items that are ruled by that sphere.

If you want to do a love spell, think about what astrological forces should be called upon. Immediately Venus springs to mind, as the planet of love. You could enhance that with Mars for passion and/or Mercury for communication. As for signs, Taurus and Libra are ruled by Venus. Scorpio influences sexuality and intensity. Cancer rules the home, if you are looking for a relationship to settle down into a home life. Decide what appeals to you, find the most appropriate time, and pick items for your spell that are ruled by the powers you are using.

Just as people have many astrological influences, most of these tools are influenced by more than one planet and sign, leading to some confusion and discrepancies among magickal books. Just as no one person is dominated by a single influence, no tool is exclusively dominated. A good witch can bring out the hidden powers of all tools. Many traditional herbalists and healers only work with a few tools and bring out all the power and benefits of those few tools they know intimately, since each can have many functions. Different techniques bring out different energies of the herbs. A potion might have different energies than a tincture or ointment. Magick often harvests one part of the plant, and medicine another, so different parts of the plant can have different powers and correspondences. In the reconstruction of our almost-lost magickal lore, many of these facts are overlooked, and the information is simply compiled together.

Vervain, for example, is one of my favorite herbs. Although ruled by Venus in most books, it is used for love, protection, healing, communication, and to enhance all magick. Sounds like more than just Venus to me. Some herbalists associate it more with Mercury and not Venus. In the end, it has many powers, as do most herbs. Each plant spirit is separate and distinct. A witch builds a relationship with these sprits. For stones, clear quartz can be use for any magickal purpose, though most resources list it as a stone of the Sun and/or Moon. You could, in fact, list all planets and signs for clear quartz.

Quite a few herbs come in seemingly conflicting pairs of correspondences. Often herbs of the Sun will also be coruled by the Moon. Herbs of Venus are often coruled by Mars. Yarrow is ruled by both Venus, traditionally, and Mars from a modern look. Yarrow's energy deals with boundary and flow, from the blood to the aura. It helps our aura's ability to attract what we desire and improve our psychic awareness, Venusian and water characteristics, but it also protects us like a warrior, creating a psychic barrier to those forces that would harm us, using Martian and fire powers.

Most modern correspondences are derived from Hermetic, Kabalistic, and Sanskrit texts, along with medieval herbology and alchemy, accounting for many conflicts between associations. Some correspondences are drawn from the mythology of the goddesses and gods that are associated with a particular planet, and may at first seem to be random, but upon further inspection, there is often great wisdom in the old myths. For example, due to its fiery, light nature and its typical color, amber is usually associated with the Sun and male energy. But to the Norse, they associated it with Freya, a goddess of love, fertility, and magick, who corresponds with the broader Venus archetype. Although amber does have a projective quality to it at times, it can also be used in magick with a magnetic, receptive qualities. Amber can be used to absorb illness and unwanted energy, clearing it from the body, a much more feminine, Venusian trait than our typical solar correspondence, even though amber doesn't match the green color scheme of Venus (though some forms of amber are green).

Here are some astrological correspondences drawn from my Book of Shadows. They come from traditional sources, modern sources, and my own experience and interpretations. Take them, adapt them, and make them your own. Since most witches often use a small number of favorite stones and herbs, I've also included some tools beyond my usual repertoire of favorites, by talking to other practitioners, so you have a broader palette of tools from which to choose. It also encourages me to venture out of my safe box and gather more knowledge and build more relationships with the natural world.

Sun

Day: Sunday

Zodiac: Leo

Colors: Yellow, gold, orange

Metal: Gold

Stones: Amber, ametrine, cat's-eye, citrine, diamond, carnelian, golden calcite, Herkimer diamond, pipestone, pyrite, orange calcite, quartz, ruby, sunstone, tiger's-eye, topaz, yellow calcite

Herbs: Agrimony, alfalfa, allspice, almond, angelica, ash, banana, bay, birch, borage, buttercup, cactus, calendula, caraway seed, celandine, centaury, chamomile, cinnamon, citron, copal, daisies, eyebright, frankincense, ginseng, goldenrod, goldenseal, goldthread, heliotrope, High John the Conqueror root, hops, juniper, marigold, mistletoe, mullien, mustard, oak, oats, orange, peony, pimpernel, pineapple, rosemary, rue, saffron, sage, shepherd's purse, storax, St. John's wort, sundew, sunflower, tansy, tarragon, tea, thyme

Moon

Day: Monday

Zodiac: Cancer

Colors: Silver, light blue, pale yellow, orchid, lavender

Metal: Silver

Stones: Amethyst, aquamarine, beryl, cat's-eye, chalcedony, Herkimer diamond, moonstone, mother-of-pearl, pearl, quartz, rainbow moonstone, sapphire, sea salt, selenite

Herbs: Adder's tongue, agrimony, aloe, angelica, anise seed, apple, ash, benzoin, birch, broom, cabbage, cactus, camphor, carnation, cedar, chickweed, clary sage, cleavers, coconut, cucumber, cypress, dill, dittany, fir, grape, honeysuckle, hyacinth, jasmine, larkspur, lemon, lemon balm, lemon grass, lemon verbena, lettuce, lily, lily of the valley, loosestrife, whirled magnolia, maple, milkweed, mistletoe, moonflower, money plant, mugwort, mushroom, myrrh, myrtle, onion, orris root, parsley, peach, pear, peony, perriwinkle, poplar, poppy, pumpkin, rowan, sandalwood, sea weed, sesame seed, silverweed, spearmint, star anise, turnip, water lily, watercress, white oak, white rose, willow, wintergreen, witch hazel, wormwood, yarrow, yerba mate, yew

Mercury

Day: Wednesday

Zodiac: Gemini, Virgo

Colors: Orange, gray, blue

Metal: Mercury, aluminum, electrum

Stones: Agate, alexandrite, azurite, carnelian, chrysocolla, howlite, kyanite, merlinite, mica, mottled jasper, orange calcite, Picasso stone, snowflake obsidian, turquoise, unakite

Herbs: Alfalfa, almond, bayberry, bittersweet, broom, buckwheat, calamint, caraway, carrot, cascara, cedar, celandine, celery, chamomile, cinquefoil, coltsfoot, daffodil, dill, echinacea, elecampane, eucalyptus, fennel, fern, flax, gentian, hazel, honeysuckle, horehound, Jacob's ladder, lady's slipper, lavender, lemon verbena, liquorice, lobelia, lungwort, mace, meadowsweet, morning glory, mulberry, mullien, mushroom, myrtle, oats, papyrus, parsley, parsnips, passion flower, pecan, peppermint, pistachio, Queen Anne's lace, sage, sandalwood, sassafras, savory, skullcap, slippery elm, uva-ursa, valerian, walnut

Venus

Day: Friday

Zodiac: Taurus, Libra

Colors: Green, pink, rose, copper

Metal: Copper

Stones: Amber, aventurine, azurite, chrysocolla, chysoprase, emerald, green calcite, jade, kunzite, lapis lazuli, loadstone, malachite, peridot, pink, calcite, rose, quartz, rhodochrosite, rhodonite, serpentine, sodalite, tourmaline (green, pink, watermelon), turquoise

Herbs: Adam and Eve root, African violet, alder, apple, ash, aster, avocado, basil, balm of Gilead, bedstraw, bean, bergamot, bleeding heart, bloodroot, boneset, bugleweed, burdock, catnip, celery, cherry, chickpea, cocoa, coltsfoot, columbine, cosmos, crocus, cumin, cypress, daffodil, daisies, damiana, dittany, echinacea, elder, fern, fleabane, foxglove, gardenia, geranium, heart's-ease, heather, hibiscus, hollyhocks, horehound, hyacinth, hydrangeas, jasmine, jewelweed, juniper, kava-kava, lady's mantle, lady's slipper, lily of the valley, lime, lovage, marshmallow, meadowsweet, moneywort, motherwort, orchid, oregano, orris root, pansy, parsley, passion flower, pear, pennyroyal, peony, periwinkle, plantain, plum, poppy, primrose, radish, ragweed, red clover, red raspberry, rice, rose, sarsaparilla, self-heal, slippery elm, spearmint, spiderwort, star anise, strawberry, sweet pea, sycamore, tansy, thyme, tulips, vanilla, vervain, vetivert, violet, watermelon, wheat, woodruff, yarrow

Mars

Day: Tuesday

Zodiac: Aries

Colors: red

Metal: Iron, steel

Stones: Apache tear (a form of obsidian), bloodstone, carnelian, diamond, fire opal, flint, garnet, hematite, lava, mochi balls, obsidian, pipestone, red aventurine, red calcite, red jasper, rhodochrosite, rhodonite, ruby, sardonyx

Herbs: Adam and Eve root, agrimony, all-heal, allspice, asafoetida, barberry, beech, beets, benzoin, betony, blackberry, bleeding heart, blood root, cashew, cattail, cayenne, cherry, chili pepper, chives, coriander, curry, damiana, deerstongue, dragon's blood, ephedra, flax, galangal, garlic, geranium, ginger, hawthorn, hemlock, High John the Conqueror root, holly, honeysuckle, horseradish, male fern, mandrake, marjoram, mastic, mustard, nettles, onion, orchid, paprika, peppercorn, pine, quince, radish, ragweed, raspberry, red oak, red pepper, red rose, rhubarb, rue, sassafras, snapdragon, spinach, strawberry, sweet briar, tarragon, thistle, tobacco, tomato, woodruff, wormwood, yarrow, yerba mate

Jupiter

Day: Thursday

Zodiac: Sagittarius

Colors: Blue, purple, violet, lavender

Metal: Tin, pewter

Stones: Amethyst, ametrine, apatite, blue calcite, blue lace agate, blue tiger's-eye, blue tourmaline, labradorite, lapis lazuli, lepidolite, merlinite, sapphire, sodalite, sugilite, turquoise

Herbs: African violet, agrimony, asparagus, betony, bilberry, bluebell, blueberry, borage, cardamom, carnation, cedar, chestnut, cinnamon, cinquefoil, clove, currant, dandelion, dock, dograss, fig, henna, hyssop, jasmine, juniper, lavender, lemon balm, lilac, lime, lungwort, maple, milkweed, milk thistle, mistletoe, moneywort, money plant, mulberry, mustard, narcissus, oak, oakmoss, onion, perriwinkle, pine, red clover, sage, sandalwood, sarsaparilla, sumac, sweet briar, sweet cicely, tonka bean, violet, wallflower, yellow dock

Saturn

Day: Saturday

Zodiac: Capricorn

Colors: Black, brown, wine, mustard, magenta

Metal: Lead, pewter, zinc

Stones: Alum, Apache tear, aragonite, black coral, black quartz, black tourmaline, bone, brown jasper, coal, garnet, hematite, howlite, jet, obsidian, onyx, salt, serpentine, smoky quartz, snowflake obsidian, star sapphire

Herbs: Aconite (monkshood), amaranthus, barley, beech, belladonna, bindweed, bistort, bluebell, boneset, buckthorn, burdock, carnation, comfrey, cornflower, cramp bark, cypress, datura, dodder, elder, elm, fern, fleabane, fumitory, garlic, heart's-ease, hellebore, hemlock, hemp, henbane, horsetail, Irish moss, ivy, kava-kava, knotweed, laurel, lobelia, mandrake, mastic, morning glory, mullein, myrrh, nightshade, onion, pansy, patchouli, pine, poke, potato, quince, rowan, rue, skullcap, shepherd's purse, Solomon's seal, tamarind, tansy, tobacco, vetch, Virginia creeper, witch hazel, yew

Uranus

Day: No traditional day; possibly Sunday or Wednesday

Zodiac: Aquarius

Colors: Dazzling white, lavender, electric blue

Metal: Uranium, chromium, white gold

Stones: Angelite, aqua aura quartz, aquamarine, feldspar, fire opal, howlite, labradorite, merlinite, quartz, rainbow moonstone, rutulated quartz, sapphire, zircon

Herbs: Allspice, angelica, anise seed, birch, burdock, chicory, cinnamon, clove, coffee, copal, curry, elecampane (elfwort), ginseng, kola nut, linseed, nutmeg, pimpernel, pine, purple loosestrife, Queen Anne's lace, rowan, sage, sassafras, sesame, spikenard, unicorn root, valerian, walnut, wisteria

Neptune

Day: No traditional day; possibly Monday or Friday

Zodiac: Pisces

Colors: Sea blues, sea greens, gray, all incandescent and opaque colors

Metal: Platinum, pewter

Stones: Amethyst, aquamarine, bloodstone, blue aragonite, blue tourmaline, calcite (all colors), celestite, coral, gem silica lithium, green tourmaline, jade, kyanite, lepidolite, mother-of-pearl, pearl, petalite, petroleum products (oils and plastics), sea salt, sea shell, watermelon tourmaline, turquoise

Herbs: Adam and Eve root, African violet, agaric, alder, aloe, apricot, ash, blue flag, cabbage, catnip, cedar, celery, chives, copal, cucumber, elm, fennel, fig, fir, grape, hemp, hops, Irish moss, jack in the pulpit, jade tree, jewelweed, jonquil, lavender, lemon, lemon grass, lettuce, lotus, lovage, magnolia, mastic, milkweed, morning glory, moss, mugwort, mushroom, narcissus, onion, papaya, passion flower, peach, pear, plum, poppy, pumpkin, sea weed, skunk cabbage, soapwort, sweet pea, violet, water lily, watercress, watermelon, willow, wisteria, yerba mate, ylang-ylang

Pluto

Day: No traditional day; possibly Tuesday

Zodiac: Scorpio

Colors: Black, dark red, rust, indigo

Metal: Plutonium, manganese, chromium, carbon steel

Stones: Alexandrite, Apache tear, black coral, black quartz, black tourmaline, dark opal, diamond, hematite, Herkimer diamond, jet, kunzite, labradorite, moldavite, obsidian, onyx, ruby, snowflake obsidian, unakite

Herbs: Aconite (monkshood), agaric, artichoke, asafoetida, basil, bayberry, belladonna, birch, blackberry, black-eyed susan, blackthorn, burdock, catalpa, cattail, chrysanthemum, cohosh (black and blue), damiana, datura, dogwood, dragon's blood, elder, eucalyptus, foxglove, fumitory, ginseng, hawthorn, heather, hemlock, holly, kava-kava, lifeverlasting, lobelia, mandrake, mistletoe, morning glory, nightshade, woody, orchid, pansy, patchouli, pine, pitcher plant, pomegranate, rhododendron, rosemary, rowan, rye, saw palmetto, slipper elm, sundew, toadflax, tobacco, unicorn root, vanilla, Venus flytrap, wormwood, yew, yucca

Although many of these correspondences are considered standard, many are not practical in the use of magick. I don't know about you but I have neither access to, nor the inclination to use, plutonium in my Pluto magick (vanilla beans are more my speed). Many of the plants of Saturn and Pluto are poisonous and difficult to obtain and use. A safer substitute might be a better choice. Some, like lady's slipper and sundew, are somewhat an endangered species and should not be harvested in the wild. They are included for historic knowledge, rather than full use.

If you don't find correspondences by planet useful, you can also look at the zodiac sign correspondences. Many correspondences will overlap with the planetary ruler, but some do not. In theory, you can use any plants or stones from the sign's ruling planet to invoke that sign's energy.

Aries

Ruler: Mars

Colors: Red

Birthstones: Ruby, garnet, diamond

Herbs: All-heal, beets, benzoin, betony, blackberry, cattail, cayenne, damiana, dragon's blood, male fern, marjoram, nettles, paprika, peppercorn, quince, radish, red pepper, red rose, spinach, sweet briar, tarragon, thistle, wormwood, yarrow, yerba mate

Taurus

Ruler: Venus

Colors: Green, pink, copper, red-orange

birthstones: Emerald, malachite, rose quartz,

Herbs: Apple, balm of Gilead, bedstraw, bean, bergamot, bugleweed, cocoa, cumin, cypress, dittany, foxglove, gardenia, geranium, heather, hibiscus, horehound, hyacinth, lady's mantle, lily of the valley, lovage, marshmallow, moneywort, motherwort, oregano, orris root, parsley, plum, potato, primrose, red clover, red raspberry, rice, rose, self-heal, slippery elm, star anise, strawberry, sweet pea, vervain, vetivert, yarrow

Gemini

Ruler: Mercury

Colors: Orange, blue, multicolor patterns

Birthstones: Agate, carnelian

Herbs: Almond, caraway, carrot, cedar, celery, cinquefoil, coltsfoot, daffodil, dill, elecampane, eucalyptus, fennel, fern, flax, gentian, hazel, horehound, Jacob's ladder, lemon verbena, liquorice, lobelia, lungwort, mace, meadowsweet, mulberry, papyrus, parsnips, passion flower, pecan, peppermint, pistachio, sage, sandalwood, sassafras, savory, skullcap, valerian, walnut

Cancer

Ruler: Moon

Colors: Silver, lavender

Birthstones: Beryl, moonstone, pearl

Herbs: Adder's tongue, agrimony, anise seed, birch, cabbage, camphor, clary sage, cleavers, coconut, fir, honeysuckle, jasmine, larkspur, lemon, lemon balm, lemon grass, lettuce, lily, loosestrife, whirled magnolia, milkweed, moonflower, moneyplant, mugwort, mushroom, myrrh, myrtle, onion, orris root, poplar, poppy, pumpkin, rowan, sandalwood, sesame seed, spearmint, sundew, watercress, white rose, willow

Leo

Ruler: Sun

Colors: Yellow, gold

Birthstones: Amber, citrine, diamond, topaz

Herbs: Almond, angelica, bay, buttercup, calendula, celandine, copal, daisy, eyebright, frankincense, ginseng, goldenrod, hawthorne, heliotrope, hops, marigold, mullien, oats, orange, peony, pimpernel, rosemary, rue, saffron, sage, St. John's wort, sunflower, tansy

Virgo

Ruler: Mercury

Colors: Green, gray

Birthstones: Agate, sapphire

Herbs: Alfalfa, caraway, carrot, cascara, cedar, chamomile, cinquefoil, dill, elecampane, fennel, fern, flax, gentian, lavender, lemon verbena, licorice, meadowsweet, myrtle, oats, passion flower, pistachio, sassafras, savory, valerian, vervain

Libra

Ruler: Venus

Colors: Turquoise, green, blue, pink

Birthstones: Peridot, jade, ametrine, watermelon tourmaline

Herbs: Adam and Eve root, apple, aster, bergamot, bleeding heart, burdock, catnip, cherry, chickpea, elder, heart's-ease, heather, hibiscus, hollyhock, hyacinth, hydrangea, jewelweed, kava-kava, lady's mantle, lady's slipper, lily of the valley, lime, lovage, marshmallow, meadowsweet, orris root, pansy, pear, pennyroyal, peony, plantain, primrose, radish, ragweed, rose, sarsaparilla, spearmint, spiderwort, star anise, strawberry, tansy, thyme, tulips, vervain, violet, yarrow

Scorpio

Ruler: Pluto, Mars

Colors: Black, scarlet, dark red

Birthstones: Diamond, obsidian

Herbs: Agaric, artichoke, asafoetida, basil, belladonna, blackberry, black-eyed susan, blackthorn, bloodroot, catalpa, cattail, chrysanthemum, cohosh (black and blue), damiana, datura, dogwood, dragon's blood, elder, foxglove, fumitory, ginseng, hemlock, horseradish, lobelia, mandrake, morning glory, nightshade, woody, pansy, patchouli, pomegranate, rye, saw palmetto, toadflax, tobacco, vanilla, wormwood, yew

Sagittarius

Ruler: Jupiter

Colors: Blue, purple, striped patterns

Birthstones: Sapphire, lapis lazuli, turquoise

Herbs: African violet, blueberry, borage, cardamom, cedar, chestnut, cinnamon, cinquefoil, clove, dandelion, dock, echinacea, fig, henna, hyssop, jasmine, juniper, lavender, lemon balm, lilac, milk thistle, money plant, mulberry, mustard, oak, oakmoss, pine, red clover, sage, sandalwood, sarsaparilla, sumac, tonka bean, violet, wallflower, yellow dock

Capricorn

Ruler: Saturn

Colors: Black, brown

Birthstones: Garnet, jet, onyx

Herbs: Aconite (monkshood), belladonna, bindweed, bistort, bluebell, boneset, buckthorn, comfrey, cornflower, cramp bark, elder, elm, fern, fleabane, garlic, heart's-ease, horsetail, Irish moss, ivy, knotweed, laurel, lobelia, mandrake, mastic, myrrh, nightshade, patchouli, poke, rowan, shepherd's purse, Solomon's seal, vetch, witch hazel, yew

Aquarius

Ruler: Uranus

Colors: Dazzling white, lavender, electric blue, magenta

Birthstones: Opal, aquamarine

Herbs: Allspice, angelica, anise seed, chicory, clove, coffee, copal, curry, elecampane (elfwort), kola nut, lady's slipper, nutmeg, pimpernel, purple loosestrife, Queen Anne's lace, sage, sesame, spikenard, unicorn root, valerian, walnut, wisteria

Pisces

Ruler: Neptune

Colors: Sea green, sea blue, violet

Birthstones: Amethyst, aquamarine

Herbs: Agaric, alder, apricot, blue flag, cabbage, catnip, cucumber, dogwood, fig, grape, hemp, hops, Irish moss, jonquil, lavender, lemon, lemon grass, lettuce, lotus, lovage, morning glory, mugwort, mushroom, narcissus, onion, passion flower, plum, poppy, pumpkin, sea weed, skunk cabbage, soapwort, water lily, watercress, watermelon, wild lettuce, willow, yerba mate, ylang-ylang

MATERIA MAGICKA

Medicinal herbalists often create a *materia medica*, an easy, information-filing system on various herbs, actions, and illnesses. I learned to create a materia medica from my herbal studies, using 8 x 5 index cards, creating a recipe box–like file with all the needed information at my fingertips.

Witches who are also herbalists have used materia medica systems to keep tract of their herbal lore in both magick and medicine. While most witches keep such information in their Book of Shadows, along with the spells they create, having a separate card file system can be quite helpful to find data at a glance.

I suggest making your own materia magicka file system, based on the medical model, but using information that is most pertinent to your craft. My friend Christine Tolf, an herbal witchcraft teacher, was the first to suggest this to me, and I love it.

Divide your materia magicka into several different categories. You can have one card per herb, listing the herb, its Latin name (since many herbs have the same folk name, but are completely different plants), its element, planet, sign, and a few brief lines about its magickal and medicinal uses. You can do the same thing with crystals and stones. There are great resources you can research such information in, such as *Cunningham's Encyclopedia of Herbal Magick* and *Cunningham's Encyclopedia of Crystal,*

Gem & Metal Magic (both Llewellyn Worldwide), Paul Bereyl's *A Compendium of Herbal Magick* and *The Master book of Herbalism* (both Phoenix Publishing), *A Salem Witch's Herbal Magick* (Celtic Crow Publishing) and *Power of the Witch* (Delta Publishing) both by Laurie Cabot, and Aleister Crowley's *777* (Weiser). The most important thing is to note your own experiences. Was the research information right in your experience, or did you have a different experience with the herb? What does your intuition and experiments tell you? Soon you will have your own personal magickal encyclopedia, along with your Book of Shadows. This foundation will serve you in subsequent studies, and in your lifetime.

Plant: _____
Latin Name: _____
Elements: _____
Planet: _____
Signs: _____
Magickal Uses: _____
_____
_____
_____
Personal Experiences: _____
_____
_____
_____
_____
Medicinal Uses: _____
_____
_____
_____
Warnings: _____
_____
_____

Figure 43: Plant Card

Stone: _____

Chemical Composition: _____

Usual Colors: _____

Hardness on Mohs Scale: _____

Active/Receptive: _____

Elements: _____

Planets: _____

Signs: _____

Magickal Uses: _____

_____

_____

_____

Healing Uses: _____

_____

_____

Personal Experiences: _____

_____

_____

_____

_____

Warnings: _____

_____

_____

Figure 44: Stone Card

EXERCISE 33

Materia Magicka

Pick ten herbs and create materia magicka cards for them. Research them, meditate with them, experiment with them, and use them in magick. Record your experiences both on the cards for quick reference, and in your Book of Shadows.

Pick ten stones and do the same research for them. As you continue your studies and learn about new magickal helpers, add to this database. If you are computer savvy, and prefer a digital material magicka, please do so. Do whatever it takes to do the work and research with the most amount of fun for you.

CRAFTING YOUR OWN SPELLS

Astrological spellcrafting is just one way to make your own magick. If you don't like working with astrology, pick another model. You can base correspondence around the elements without getting into the signs and planets. The chakras make an excellent correspondence system, since they already correspond with elements, color, stones, and body parts. In a later course book in this series, we will explore correspondence systems and focus on the Tree of Life. Every tradition and magick system has its own way of organizing and collecting information. Astrology is just one way. Find a method of remembering and relating information that works for you.

Use this introductory grimoire as a basis for your own spell casting. While you can do exactly what I describe, I suggest you consult other books on spell casting, and draw upon many ideas to craft your own spells. I very rarely follow a spell right from the book without making changes. Sometimes I simply don't have the ingredients and have no time to get them. Other times, I like part of the spell, but want to make it suit my own unique personality. Feel free to substitute. Be creative. Once you understand the science of spellcraft and apply it, you realize there are no set rules to the art.

When you have created a spell, record it in your Book of Shadows. You can also add it to your materia magicka, in a separate spell recipe section, particularly if you feel you will use it often and need to find it quickly for yourself, or to share with others.

PROTECTION AND BINDING

Protection spells are some of the most important first spells to learn. Contrary to popular opinion, they don't make you invincible and deflect punches or falling objects, but they do seem to naturally take you out of harm's way. By seeming coincidental, you are not put in the path of harm. Your intuition guides you. Events seem to conspire to keep you free from harm. If you deliberately put yourself in this path, then you have neutralized the magick by lack of real-world follow-up.

Protection magick also bolsters your spiritual defenses, increasing your psychic resilience. You are protected from harmful energies from other people and entities. They cannot cross the boundary around you or the place where you have cast your protection spell.

Wards are protection spells based on a location, such as a home or business, that are designed to protect the area from harm on all levels, even when the spell caster is not present. Bindings are specific acts of protection magick, when you feel someone is wishing you ill, intentionally or otherwise. They bind the harm the person is directing to you, so it will not harm you in any way.

Moon: Usually waning, close to the Dark Moon.

Elements: Earth, fire (sometimes water)

Planets: Saturn, Mars

Signs: Capricorn, Aries, Cancer

Protection Potion

Protection potion can be used in mundane cases, when you are traveling, before you leave your home or any other time you feel danger might cross your path. Most often, it is used as part of the magick circle ritual, to anoint yourself, or to cleanse objects of harm.

As with all potions, decide where you will create it. You can be in the kitchen, or anywhere else, depending on what your heating method will be. Make sure you have everything on hand. Charge each of these ingredients for protection as you mix them into a base mixture of water and sea salt.

2 cups of spring water

2 tablespoons of sea salt

1 teaspoons frankincense

1 teaspoons myrrh

½ teaspoon vervain

½ teaspoon dragon's blood

½ teaspoon juniper berries

½ teaspoon patchouli

½ teaspoon iron powder or 9 iron nails

1 pinch of wolf's hair

Let it brew for your ritual, and when it cools, strain out and bottle. You can use Solomon's seal, nettles, or mandrake as a substitution for any herbal ingredients. If you have difficulty with the iron powder/nails, whole cloves or cactus needles are a substitute. If you make the potion in an iron pan or cauldron, you may not need to add it, but in general, iron containers should only be used to brew protection potions, not other types of potion, since the iron will neutralize and ground many forms of magick. Faeries are notoriously wary of cold iron. Wolf hair can also be difficult to obtain, though some witch shops are supplied hair from wolf sanctuaries during shedding season. Wolf hair is used because wolf magick is about protecting the clan. Dog hair from a powerful, wolf-like dog can be used as a substitution.

Protection Charm

This protection charm is something you can carry with you in your pocket or purse, hang in your home, or keep in your vehicle. You will need:

1 onyx

2 tablespoons of sea salt or kosher salt

Solomon's seal root (one whole root or 1 tablespoon of powder)

Horsetail (one whole top or 1 tablespoon of powdered herb)

1 tablespoon of yarrow

1 pinch of St. John's wort

1 pinch of tobacco

While in a magick circle, charge each ingredient for protection and mix them together. Carry the powder in a black bag with the following symbol written on it:

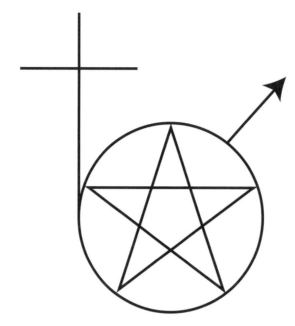

Figure 45: Protection Symbol

I like to paint the symbol in white paint on the inside of the bag, so that no one knows it is there but me. Even in secret, it still works. The symbol doesn't have to be visible at all.

If your bag is too small for all the herbs, you can use several small bags, just make sure each bag has its own stone and symbol in it. I made a large batch of this powder and made several bags at one time for my friends and family to keep in their cars (since we all travel so much).

Witch's Bottle Spell

The bottle spell is one of the most powerful binding spells I've ever worked. It should only be done when you feel a specific person is directing harm toward you magickally, psychically, or physically. Through this ritual, you are symbolically bottling their harm toward you, binding it from taking form in the world, and preventing this person from directing unwanted energies to you. Many people then store the bottle in the freezer (to cool down the situation) or bury it in the earth to ground the energy in the healing energies of the Earth. For this spell you will need:

1 bottle or jar that has a cork or lid

Black thread

Paper

Black pen

White candle

9 iron nails (you can substitute whole cloves, hawthorne spikes, or cactus needles)

Sea salt

1 tablespoon each of five protection or binding herbs. I suggest using these five, but there are many variations of this spell.

    Frankincense

    Myrrh

    Vervain

    St. John's wort

    Comfrey

You can use a variety of other herbs such as yarrow, mandrake, Solomon's seal, garlic, nettles, dragon's blood, rue, corriander, pine, oak, mistletoe, sage, cedar, mugwort, or nightshade, to name a few. If you lack any of these herbs, you can use a few tablespoons of protection potion.

Prepare a spell that says, "I, *(state your name)*, ask in the name of the Goddess, God, and Great Spirit, ask to completely and immediately bind and neutralize all harm from *(state the name of the person you seek to bind)* toward myself, my family, friends, and all in my circle. I ask this be correct, for the highest good, and harming none. So mote it be." Write the words down with black ink on white paper.

In a magick circle, as close to the dark of the Moon as possible, read the spell above and roll the paper up. Tie the paper tube with the black thread and place it in the bottle. Fill the bottle halfway with the sea salt, charged for binding harm. The salt will absorb and neutralize harm. Charge the nails and put them in the bottle. Iron grounds harm, like a lightning rod. Some witches drive one nail through the paper, but I don't. Charge each of the herbs and put them in the bottle. Top it off with more salt if needed, and seal the bottle. Charge the white candle for protection and light it. Seal the bottle with a counterclockwise circle of wax around the edge. The widdershins movement is to dispel harmful energy. As long as your bottle remains sealed, your binding is in effect. Release the circle and put the bottle someplace where it will remain safe. Let the candle burn down.

Binding spells will only take hold if you take responsibility for your part in the drama, and if your cause is just. I know of one witch who did this spell on a lover's current wife, when the wife had no knowledge of the affair, let alone harm toward anyone. The bottle was placed in a coffee can and filled with plaster, to keep it from opening. Yet, the plaster split open and the bottle broke. If you don't abuse this magick, it will serve you well for the rest of your life.

Home Protection Spell

Protection spells that are oriented around a location, rather than a person, are called wards or warding spells. Most witches cast a warding spell around their home, to protect it from physical harm, intrusion, theft, and violence, as well as psychic harm and unwanted energies and spirits. Usually the spell is repeated occasionally, perhaps near certain seasonal Sabbats.

Whenever I meditate or do magick in a new location, I cast a psychic ward, casting a protection shield much like the protection shields shown in chapter 9 of ITOW. When in my own home, I combine such visualization techniques with ritual work. I do mine in the fall. For this home ward, you will need:

    1 acorn for every room in your home

    1 black candle

Make a protection incense consisting of the following:

    1 teaspoon of frankincense

    1 teaspoon of myrrh

    1 teaspoon of orris root

    1 teaspoon of oak bark

    1 teaspoon of juniper berries or leaves

    1 pinch of dragon's blood

Grind all ingredients together in a mortal and pestle if you are a traditional witch, or an electric hand grinder if you are a modern witch.

Bowl of sea salt

1 tablespoon of lavender

1 tablespoon of frankincense

1 tablespoon of myrrh

1 tablespoon of patchouli

1 tablespoon of rowan berries (or juniper berries if rowan is not available)

First cleanse your home both physically and magickally. Then, in a magick circle, close to the Dark Moon, bless your black candle for protection and light your protection incense. You can use the self-igniting charcoal to use homemade incense. Pass the acorns through it, and charge them all for protection. Mix your bowl of salts and herbs together, consecrating each for protection. Visualize your entire home surrounded by a crystal shield of light, like a giant diamond. It lets helpful energy in and out, but blocks and neutralizes all unwanted energies, inside or out.

Release your circle and go to every room. Smudge the room with your incense. Put an acorn in each room, traditionally on the windowsill, but it can go anywhere it will be undisturbed. When you are done with all the room inside, go outside with your bowl of herbs, and sprinkle the mixture around your home or building clockwise. If you can make three rings, that is the best, but try to make at least one, depending on how big your yard is, and how much mixture you made. If you are in an apartment or otherwise can't do this step, that's fine. You can take the mixture and place it in a bowl someplace hidden in your home. In fact, even if you did make your three rings outside and have some left over, you can do this. The mixture will absorb and neutralize harm, and will need to be released at least every year. Your home now has a powerful ward. If any incense is left, you can use it as a general protection incense for any ritual you do.

HEALING

Healing magick is at the heart of the craft, since so much of our history has been of healers. Healing magick works on the body, emotions, mind, and soul, seeking to bring a person into true balance and not just mask the symptoms of the illness. Witches ask, "Why there is imbalance or injury? What is the gift it brings?" Only then can the mental, spiritual, and emotional be brought into alignment.

I have worked successfully with people in healing severe physical ailments when they are willing to get in touch with the mental, emotional, and spiritual roots of the illness. Sometimes healing is quite magickal, and after one spell or session there is a cure. Other times, the progress is slow and steady. Healing spells can be done on the waxing or waning Moon. You can banish illness during the waning, and promote health during the waxing. I recommend doing sessions for both.

Particularly with healing magick, always ask permission to do the magick. If you can't get verbal permission due to distance or an inability to respond (i.e., someone is unconscious), you can quietly meditate, ask to connect with the higher self of the recipient, and ask permission. If you are unsure, use a pendulum. Techniques of psychic healing and diagnosis, found in ITOW, can be used in conjunction with ritual magick.

Moon: Waning to banish illness. Waxing to bring health.

Elements: All, though it depends on where the root of the imbalance is.

Planets: Mercury, Sun, Venus, Saturn

Signs: Virgo, Taurus, Leo—all signs rule a body part, so if that part is afflicted, work with that sign.

Healing Potion

Healing potions can be made for specific illnesses, using herbs ruled by signs that relate to that part of the body. I like to have on hand a general, all-purpose healing potion that can be used on myself, on my jewelry and charms, and on candles, as well as given in small vials to those of my friends and family who are ill. A basic formula I've used is:

2 cups of spring water

2 tablespoons of sea salt

1 tablespoon of self-heal

1 tablespoon of vervain

½ tablespoon of ginseng

½ tablespoon of nettle

1 pinch of white oak bark

1 piece of gold jewelry

1 clear quartz

Brew on the waxing Moon, charging each for healing. Strain out and remove the gold and quartz before bottling if you wish.

Healing Tea

I like this simple, soothing healing herbal tea for when I am sick. Although many different herbal teas can be concocted for a variety of symptoms and ailments, based on a knowledge of medicinal herbalism, I suggest this general tonic tea for health. Once you have a comfort level with herbs, I highly suggest a deeper study of medicinal herbal lore.

1 part elder berries

1 part nettles

1 part hawthorne berries

1 part orange peel

1 part lemon peel

Make it in whatever quantity you want, and blend it in a magick circle. Then take one tablespoon of herb to one cup of boiling water to make the tea itself when you are feeling under the weather, or if you simply want to maintain health and balance.

Healing Candle Spell

I love doing candle magick for healing. Whenever I feel something coming on, from a simple cold to a more serious illness, I first sit and meditate. I ask to understand the root of the imbalance and bring myself into balance. Sometimes illness has great, deep spiritual messages. Other times, it simply is a part of yourself, your body, mind, or heart that wants to rest, and is forcing you to slow down and be quiet. When I meditate and speak with my spirit guides, I often get the answer, but sometimes I don't. The important thing is to put the intention out for understanding on some level.

Then I take a green candle and carve the following on it:

Figure 46: Healing Symbols

I love rune magick, and find it quite powerful. I also carve the astrological symbol of Taurus to bring myself back into balance with my nature (as Taurus is also my Sun sign). I think of Taurean energy as healthy and hearty. Then I anoint the entire candle with a healing potion. If I'm feeling up to it, I will cast a circle and charge the candle. If not, I will simply charge the candle for my own healing, saying something like, "I ask, in the name of the Goddess and God, to be completely and immediately healthy, for the highest good, harming none. So mote it be." If the Moon is waning, I might ask to banish illness. Then I light the candle and let the magick begin.

For simple illnesses, I use a taper or votive. If I am doing a spell for someone in critical long-term need, I will usually use a pillar or seven-day jar candle, if available. If you can't get the kind that the candles can come out of the jar, I paint the symbols on the outside of the glass.

Stone Healing Spell

Laying on stones is an ancient art of healing. This is best done when the recipient is present for the ritual, and can lay down with stones placed on the body. But if not available, a photo can be used. For the stones, you can use chakra stones, colored gems based on the seven chakras (see ITOW, chapter 11). I like to use three to seven white beach/river stones, polished by the water.

Cast your circle, and have the recipient lie down in the center. Cleanse and consecrate the stones for healing. Put them on the body where there is illness or imbalance. Feel the stones placing their power to heal in the body, while absorbing any illness. Keep them on from five to thirty minutes. I hold my wand over the afflicted body part, over the stones, doing counterclockwise circles first to remove illness, and then clockwise circles to restore health. I also like to count the recipient down to a meditative state, and suggest healing imagery and colored light to bring health, so they are actively involved in the ritual (ITOW, chapter 15). Use this in conjunction with candles spells, petitions, and potions. Healing is an intuitive art. Follow your instincts.

Remove the stones and release the circle. Cleanse the stones before using them again.

Poppet Healing Spell

Poppets are a simple act of folk magick that can yield very powerful healing results. I usually reserve them for those in need of long-term healing. Start by making a doll to resemble the one in need of healing. If you can make it out of a piece of old clothing, or use their own hair, fingernail clippings, or any other personal objects to embellish it or stuff it, so much the better. I also stuff the doll with healing herbs, such as chamomile, angelica, peppermint, mugwort, sunflower seeds, copal, hyssop, yarrow, orange peel, lavender, echinacea, goldthread, burdock, dandelion, ginger, cayenne, oats, corn, rice, and frankincense. I like to use a stone for the heart, such as clear quartz, citrine, or rose quartz.

While in the magick circle, name the doll after the healing recipient. You can place pins in the areas in need of healing. Cleanse and the bless the pin for healing, and anoint it with healing potion. Or, you can lay stones directly on the doll. Keep the doll on your altar, and send it light, touch it, and do your healing work on the doll daily. Place your healing power objects on it. I will often put my ring or necklace on it. The energy will be sent to the recipient, through its sympathetic link. If you don't want to use a doll, you can use a photo, but I prefer the poppet. When your work is done, cast another circle, and ask to release the link between the person and doll. Cut the air around the doll with your athame, cutting the energy link. Cleanse the doll. With respect, take the doll apart, and bury its components. The work is done.

PROSPERITY

Prosperity magick includes all money and career spells. Sometimes we use this discipline for fast cash for something we desire, while other times we focus on expanding our base of prosperity and power. Money magick is the one time when newly aspiring witches often ask me if this is wrong or if this is black magick. They can't believe that spiritual powers can be used for such blatant self-gain. It is no different than wanting health, love, or happiness. Money is just an energy, just a symbol for work and effort that we exchange for things, both necessities and luxuries. It's a form of barter, in a world where direct barter has little value. We have been conditioned by institutions that control the money and power that acquiring money is wrong or greedy, yet that is all they do. Some spiritual traditions feel that seeking money derails you from the spiritual path. I understand that, but it's hard to say to someone who doesn't have food, clothing, or shelter first.

True prosperity flows from fulfilling our life's purpose. When we do, all resources we need will be at our disposal. Magick and meditation help us figure out what we truly are here to do. Witches seek to live in balance and equality. We use what we need to be comfortable. We don't seek to be poor. We don't seek to be rich. We seek to be balanced. In your seeking, if you explore the powers of the material world, it may just be a part of your path, and in witchcraft you have the freedom to explore anything as long as you are not harming yourself or others.

Moon: Waxing

Elements: Earth, fire

Planets: Jupiter, Venus, Sun

Signs: Sagittarius, Taurus, Leo, Capricorn

Money Spell

This spell is done when you need funds. Realistically, it is best to spell for the actual result, not the money itself, but at certain times, an influx of cash, regardless of the source, is the solution to your situation.

During the waxing Moon, while in a magick circle, take a lodestone, a natural magnet, or a simple household magnet, and anoint it with the oil of patchouli, vanilla, juniper, or yarrow. Wrap a dollar bill around it and tie it together using green string/yarn. Release the circle. If you are working on a long-term investment, bury the talisman somewhere to the north of your home, like you are planting a seed. If you need immediate cash, burn the bill around the magnet, then carry the magnet with you.

Prosperity Change Jar

My favorite long-term prosperity spell is a family money jar. Get a large jar, preferably of green or blue glass. Charge it on the waxing Moon, in a circle, to increase your immediate family's fortune a hundredfold for every currency that is placed in it. Place prosperity herbs at the bottom of it. You don't have to measure it out. I just take small handfuls of yellow dock seed, dandelion root, cinnamon bark, mustard seeds, red clover tops, and a tonka bean. I also put in a piece of lapis lazuli, all charged for prosperity. I have every member of the family place a copper penny into the jar to include them all in the spell and to bring in the magnetic powers of Venus. Then, all my spare change goes into the jar. The more I put in, the more I receive prosperity and abundance. When full, I roll the change and do the spell again.

Money Oil

Make this oil on the waxing Moon. Anoint yourself for prosperity, or use it in additional spellwork.

  ⅛ cup base oil

  1 penny

  1 nickle

  1 dime

  1 quarter

  1 shredded dollar

3 whole cloves

5 drops of frankincense oil

3 drops of orange oil

3 drops of lavender oil

1 drop of cinnamon oil (you can replace with chips of cinnamon instead, since
  cinnamon oil can be caustic to sensitive skin)

Cleanse the money and consecrate for abundance. Add them to the base oil. Charge each oil as you add it to the base, while in a magick circle. Strain out the currency. Bottle in dark glass and keep it away from heat and light.

Alternately, if you want a water-based potion, try this:

2 cups of spring water

2 tablespoons of sea salt

1 teaspoon of cinnamon

1 teaspoon of cloves

1 teaspoon of frankincense

1 pinch of cinquefoil

1 pinch of yarrow

½ teaspoon of lemon balm

½ teaspoon of lavender

1 pinch of dandelion seed or root

1 pinch of yellow dock seed or root

Prosperity Charm

A talisman to attract prosperity and fortune can be made by plotting the word "prosperity" on the witch's wheel. Take PROSPERITY and cross out the repeated letters, giving you OSEITY. On the witch's wheel, it gives you the symbol:

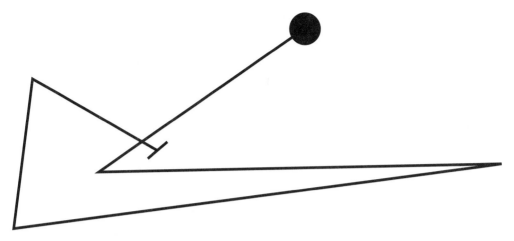

Figure 47: Prosperity Symbol

Draw this on a piece of wood in blue or purple ink. I like to get an oak branch, remove its bark, and cut a small piece, perhaps three or four inches long, and draw the symbol on it. I then tie three pieces of string/yarn together (green, blue, and purple), and in the magick circle, braid them together, with three knots. As I make each knot, I think about the type of prosperity I wish to attract. Then I tightly wrap the string/yarn around the wood clockwise, and tie it into place. If the end won't stay fixed, I glue it. Carry around the charm to fulfill your prosperity goal. Once you have achieved your magick, burn the charm and release it back to the universe.

Sweet Blessing Spell

To bring a new job or promotion in your life, or any sweet blessing, try this act of folk magick. It uses the powers of Venus and flowing sweet water to bring blessings back into your life. You will need:

Bowl or cauldron—a copper cauldron is best

Honey

Milk

Orange juice

Cloves

Cinnamon

In a magick circle, ideally on the first Friday of the waxing Moon, bless each of the ingredients for prosperity, money, and blessings from the Goddess and God, and stir them together. The honey and milk is for sweetness, a Venusian trait to attract blessings, and used often as an offering to both faery folk and the gods. Orange juice represents the solar success principles, while cloves and cinnamon are for the protective and expansive qualities of Jupiter. Release the circle and pour the mix into the nearest body of flowing fresh water, such as a stream or river. Do not use a lake, swamp, or ocean. You want something that moves. You must pour the offerings out the same day you do the magick circle. Repeat this ritual for every Friday of the waxing Moon, until the Moon goes full. By the next Full Moon, a boon should be granted to you, a blessing of prosperity, good fortune, or new opportunity to advance your career.

Łove

Love magick is one of the most-asked-about disciplines. When I teach a workshop on either love or money magick, it is always filled. People are always seeking what they lack, and true love magick can only come from a place of love. If you can't generate the feeling of perfect love in a ritual, or have love and compassion for yourself, even for just a few moments, you probably can't do a successful love spell. Similar energies gather together. They have the same vibration, so often "like attracts like." If you have no love, you can attract no love.

Love magick comes in many forms. There is love of self, romantic love, family love, and lust magick. To the witch, all of these loves are acceptable. You can do magick for a lifetime partner, or to meet someone right here, right now. As long as you harm none, including yourself, you are fine. Just make sure you are honest with yourself and what you really want.

For the ethics of love magick, most witches believe you shouldn't cast spells for specific people, feeling this might manipulate or tamper with their free will. This isn't a rule, but a suggestion from personal experience. Some laugh off the idea of manipulation, since we do so many things to influence others on a daily level. If you wear a special perfume, send flowers, or cook a meal, you are "manipulating" the person deeper into the relationship, but nobody has a problem with that. But with magick, there is a modicum of self-preservation when it comes to love magick.

Ideally, you can cast a love spell for someone specific, but hold the concept that it be for the highest good, harming none. That sentiment can be hard to hold if you are already hung up on a specific person. Some witches tell stories of casting love spells and sparking an interest, but they fall in love with their spell's target far harder and longer than the recipient of their affection. I've seen it happen. If you don't really mean "for the highest good" but only say it, it doesn't always work. Sometimes it happens for the highest good, to show you the power of magick, and to be careful what you wish for because you will get it. Sometimes asking for the person who is "correct and right for me at this time" is better than doing magick for a specific person in the long run.

Moon: Waxing to gain or improve a love; waning to release a relationship

Elements: Water, fire, earth, air—depends on the type of love

Planets: Venus, Mars, Sun, Neptune

Signs: Libra, Leo, Scorpio

Love Oil

I love love potions. I love the herbs of love. I love their scents. And I love wearing them. Love potions and oils can be used to generate the feeling of love, not only romantically, but self-love. I feel good when I wear them. They uplift me. You can use them as a daily perfume or cologne, or anoint candles and other charms in love magick. Here is a basic love oil.

⅛ cup of base oil

3 drops of rose oil (use rosewood or rose geranium if rose oil is too expensive)

4 drops of ylang-ylang

2 drops of hyacinth

Love Charm

For quite a while in my dating life, I was carrying a little red bag around my neck, with a variation of this formula, made on the last Friday before the Full Moon.

Rose quartz

2 teaspoons rose petals

½ teaspoon yarrow

½ teaspoon raspberry leaves

1 teaspoon damiana

1 teaspoon dragon's blood

1 teaspoon mandrake

½ teaspoon orris root

9 drops of rose oil

5 drops of patchouli oil

Although the charm worked as directed, and I had lots of dates, I should have been more specific about what I wanted—a long-term relationship. This spell can also be used with that intention. You simply have to be clear in your intention. I suggest writing out a petition spell, burning it and adding its ashes to the contents of your red bag.

Rekindling Love

Some magick is not for attracting new relationships, but re-igniting current ones. This spell is best done by invoking the energy of Mars or Pluto, rather than Venus, but having helpful aspects to Venus can always enhance it. If you use the planetary hours, pick the day of Mars, Tuesday, with the hour of Venus. Again, do this with the waxing Moon. If done on the waning Moon, it will lower your sex drive and passion. Like most spells, this is enhanced if done in a magick circle.

Steep the following herbs together in boiling water. You are brewing it for its power, not its taste or smell.

2 cups of water

½ teaspoon of damiana

½ teaspoon of basil

½ teaspoon of oregano

½ teaspoon of saw palmetto

½ teaspoon of red raspberry leaf

½ teaspoon of red rose petals

Anoint a red candle with this mix and charge it to rekindle your passion. Then take an article of jewelry from both you and your partner, and anoint them. Place the jewelry in the light of the candle until the candle burns down, and then return the articles.

Even if you don't wear the jewelry regularly, the energy will still be sent to both you and your partner.

If you have anything left of your infusion, anoint your bedroom and home with it. Anoint door and window frames. Anoint the headboard of your bed. Anoint the doorknobs. Fill the space with this new, passionate energy.

Release Ritual

Sometimes the most important love spells we do are not to attract a new love or deepen an existing love, but to release an old or lost love. Rituals of the heart can be healing as well as passionate. If you wish to heal your heart from a break-up and move on from a past relationship, take something that symbolizes the relationship. It can be a photo, a gift, or simply your names written together on a piece of paper. On a waning Moon, in a simple ritual circle (preferably outdoors), place the item in your flame-proof cauldron. Sprinkle yarrow in the cauldron to help create a boundary. Read this spell written from a petition paper.

> I *(state your name)*, ask in the name of the Goddess and God, to completely release from *(state the name of the person you wish to release)*, for the highest healing good, harming none. I wish to take the blessings and lessons of the experience, and move on to the next phase of my life path. So mote it be.

Place the petition in the cauldron. (Sprinkle it with a high-proof alcohol to really release it.) Throw in a match and let it burn, releasing the link. Take your athame and turn to each direction, making a sweeping motion in front of you, cutting all cords. Do the same motion above you, and below you, near the feet. Imagine the Goddess or God cutting the ties that bind you, and healing you and your past love. You can do the aura cleansing and decording meditation in chapter 11 of the ITOW during this spell as well. When done, release the circle and take real-world actions to move on in your life.

Lifemate Love Spell

This is my favorite love spell, and I share it with those who are really ready to find a life partner. It is the spell I used to find my own partner and I was taught, beyond a shadow of a doubt, the power of love magick. It is best done by those who have done a lot of exploration and are looking for a stable commitment. You will need:

1 live red rose

Vase

Spring water

Sugar

Dragon's blood

On the last Friday before the Full Moon, or any waxing Moon day with beneficial aspects to Venus, cast a circle and meditate with the rose. Pour your heart out to it. Tell it all the things you want in a partner, and how you envision your life with a partner. I wouldn't get specific about who, or what superficial qualities, but express the essence of what you want in a partnership. Call upon the spirit medicine of the rose to make your magick.

Bless a pinch of sugar (white or brown), and place it in the water of the vase. If you can obtain water from a special spring or well, so much the better, but any pure water will do. Then place a pinch of dragon's blood in the water for power. Put the rose into the vase, raise the cone of power, release the circle, and leave the rose on the altar for three days. As the rose begins to wilt, take the petals apart, dry them, place them in a green, pink, or red bag or box, and put them someplace special. You can carry it with you, but I chose to keep them under my mattress. If you are ready to meet your love, you will meet within three months.

MISCELLANEOUS MAGICK

The following spells don't fit in the typical categories of magick, but make useful additions to your magickal grimoire.

Psychic Potion

This psychic potion is used to enhance your intuitive abilities. I used it often when reading tarot at psychic fairs. It gave me a definite boost in my abilities and helped soothe my nerves as I began doing this work. I use it now to help students with their own psychic and intuitive work.

2 cups of spring water

2 tablespoons of sea salt

½ teaspoon vervain

½ teaspoon star anise

½ teaspoon lemon balm

½ teaspoon of lavender

3 pumpkin seeds saved from last Samhain

1 piece of silver jewelry

1 moonstone crystal

1 pinch of black cat hair

Ideally this should be made on the Full Moon. Good aspects to Jupiter, Neptune, and Pluto help as well. When you are done, strain out the silver and moonstone before you bottle it. Anoint your third eye and/or throat chakra before doing psychic work.

If you prefer a psychic tea to drink, try this recipe:

1 tablespoon mugwort

1 tablespoon of lemon balm

1 tablespoon of anise seed

1 amethyst stone

3 cups of water

Brew the tea and place the bowl under the light of the Full Moon. Retrieve before sunrise, strain, and drink one cup three times during the day. This will boost your psychic ability and dreams for the day, and lasts through the entire moon cycle.

Grounding Bag

This charm is a powerful tool for those people who are more likely to be spacy, unbalanced, and ungrounded. It forces your energy to be present, centered, and in the moment. Many people involved in the craft and New Age practices are often otherworldly, and have a hard time focusing on the physical world. This magick helps those walking between the worlds to come back when they have difficulty. Anyone who is weak in their connection to the earth element can benefit greatly from it.

While in a magick circle, near the dark of the Moon, either waxing or waning, but far from the Full Moon, charge each of these items, and place them in a black or brown bag.

1 smoky quartz

1 amber

1 black tourmaline

1 tablespoon of dandelion root

1 tablespoon of burdock root

1 pinch of coffee or tea

4 drops of patchouli oil

The roots are very grounding, along with the dark stones. The amber is energetic, without being too high energy. The coffee or tea is added because the energy of caffeine can actually ground the body by placing your energy in the body when you are floating. It doesn't make you peaceful and still when taken internally, but can bring you back to the physical. Carry this charm with you when you need the blessings of solid ground.

Invisibility

When witches talk about invisibility spells, people think of movie magick invisibility, literally bending light so no one can see you. Although I have had friends who believe it is possible, noticing that certain plants can seemingly go invisible when they don't want to be found, my experience with invisibility has been less dramatic.

Invisibility spells are those that keep you unnoticed by others. You do not disappear, but people don't register your presence, and you can move about unhindered. You become a face in the crowd, or part of the background and don't catch someone's attention. The trouble with such spells is to either clearly define the time frame of the spell, or the target group. One well-placed spell to protect you from bill collectors can also have you continually passed over for a promotion at work because all your hard work isn't noticed.

To make this magick, you can simply use intention through instant magick (ITOW, chapter 6), but I like to carry this charm around with me:

Figure 48: *Invisibility Charm*

I carry it in a black bag along with a combination of the herbs aconite, fern, heliotrope, mistletoe, or poppy, because these herbs are said to confer invisibility.

ELEMENTAL INCENSE

Some of the magickal items you create will not be focused on a specific intention, but will hold an energy to help you connect with a realm or force. One popular tool is to use incense for each of the four elements. You can also make incense, potions, and oils for connecting to deities, planets, and signs using their correspondences. Here are recipes for elemental incense. They are divided by parts, so you can make as much or as little as you desire following these proportions. I suggest making small amounts at first, and adjusting them to your taste.

Fire Incense
    2 parts frankincense
    1 part cinnamon
    1 part dragon's blood

1 part red sandalwood (use regular sandalwood if red is not available)

1 part rosemary

Air Incense

3 parts sandalwood

1 part lavender

1 part juniper

1 part sage

Water Incense

2 parts myrrh

2 part orris root

1 part star anise

1 part mugwort

1 part rose petals

Earth Incense

2 parts myrrh

1 part patchouli

1 pinch of mandrake root

You can add drops of essential oil to the mix if you desire. Just make sure they are essential, since synthetics will smell like burning plastic when used. Let the incense sit in an airtight jar for at least three weeks before using, to have the scents mingle together. Use them when meditating on the four elements individually, or in combination. If you have a large ritual space, you can create an altar for each element in the four quarters, and use four different incenses for them.

CREATIVITY SPELL

This spell can be used to boost your creative abilities for music, art, and writing. It helps you become a gateway for the sacred art to manifest through you. All art is very magickal, and this working helps the artist become in touch with the power of the sacred.

The spell is very simple and intuitive. Besides your regular ritual tools, all you need paper and a writing instrument. I prefer a crayon or marker for this. Cast your circle and meditate in the center of the circle. Ask for creativity, and in the dark, eyes closed, draw on the paper. Let your hand flow unfettered, without judgment. Just let yourself be an instrument. Let your intuition guide you. When done, you don't even have to look at what you created. Simply fold it up, and burn it like a petition spell. Raise the cone of power. You will have unlocked your creative potential and moved through any blocks you have had.

Power Powder

Power powder is made up of magickal catalysts, substances that enhance magickal formulas. Usually just a small amount of any of these ingredients is added to other spells. When you really want a spell to work, you can use this powder, sprinkling it in other formulas, burning as incense, or spreading it around the circle to increase the energy.

Mix all of these ingredients under the light of the Full Moon.

1 obsidian stone

1 part mandrake root

1 part dragon's blood

1 part orris root

1 part wormwood

1 part nightshade or belladonna

1 part elder flower or berry

1 part oak bark

1 part mistletoe

1 part rosemary

1 pinch rabbit hair

If you want a really powerful mix, you can add small pieces of amber and jet to the mix. Seal in a bottle, and let it sit for a month. If you do choose to burn it, don't inhale. The fumes will be less than pleasant and less than healthy for you. Use only a small amount at a time. Take the obsidian out before you burn it.

EXERCISE 34

Create and Cast a Spell

Meditate upon an intention you have for a spell. If you are in need of anything, or simply want it, reflect on your desire. I suggest doing a divination to make sure there are no hidden surprises to this desire. Then create a spell around the desire. Go beyond the petition spell format, and use one or more of the techniques above. Partner with your nature magick allies. Make your ritual and perform it at the appropriate time. Record it in your Book of Shadows and materia magicka. Wait for the results to come to you.

Homework

- Do Exercises 33–34.

- Continue regular altar devotional and any other regular meditative practice.

- Practice divination techniques.

- Continue journaling regularly.

Tips

- Don't try to incorporate everything into one spell. Use the tool and techniques that are appropriate right now. You will have time to try everything you want eventually.

- If you feel too intimidated to do a spell on your own, try doing one directly from the book and see how it works. As you gain confidence, you will gain the ability to make your own spells.

- What if you don't have a desire? Really meditate on it. Be clear with yourself. Are you trying to be selfless and deny yourself, or are you truly content? If you are content, that's great. I have reached a point that I don't do a lot of spellwork for gain because I am happy where I am at the moment, but many people equate having no needs, or even lacking, with being spiritual, and that is not true on the path of the witch. If you are saying you don't want anything but are lying to yourself, then you are doing more harm than avidly seeking your pursuits. The point of magick and wish fulfillment is spirituality. You truly understand in a personal reality, not just a philosophical level, that we are all connected and all our thoughts and words have an effect in the world.

LESSON TEN
TURNING THE WHEEL

The Wheel of the Year is one of the strongest foundation stones on the path of the witch. Many basic books start with the Wheel of the Year rituals and traditions. Although the history and images are powerful, if you have no experience in ritual, energy, or meditation, the Wheel of the Year will hold little deep significance. Like many religions, its rituals will be void of true meaning and experience for the practitioner. One of my first experiences was attending a large public Samhain circle in Salem, Massachusetts. While it piqued my interest, and was very special, it was not as life changing as my first Full Moon circle where I participated.

Anyone can give you a book of ritual to follow by rote. The rituals of witchcraft are not static. Like the seasons and times, they change, but the wisdom that underpins each holiday is eternal. With an understanding of magick, ritual design, and the Wheel itself, you have the freedom to create your own circles of celebration.

The Wheel of the Year consists of eight seasonal holidays. Four are solar in nature. Four are agricultural. There is a modern pagan nostalgia for some idealized golden age, where these rituals were practiced just as they are today. Unfortunately, modern scholarship doesn't support this. Although most ancient, tribal, and Earth-based cultures seem to acknowledge the change of seasons through a variety of rituals, our current modern version of the Wheel of the Year is an amalgam of several different cultures, borrowing concepts from all over the ancient world, with a bit of divine inspiration from the Goddess and God. Personally, I think we are blessed to have such an ethnically rich tradition, and do not seek out the "pure" forms of these rites. Very little survived from these cultures, due to both persecutions of the religion and lack of writing. I highly doubt there ever was a "pure" form, since each village or tribe had their own way of celebrating the seasons.

Though modern scholars and pagans often disagree on the facts of the ancient world, both having a bias toward the information, it appears that much of our modern seasonal practices are borrowed from the European traditions. Though some believe the rituals are strictly Celtic in origin, their names and symbols show influence from the Teutons and Mediterraneans. The concepts themselves, minus the ethnic coloring, can be found in wisdom traditions of the world.

The Celts are best known for the four agricultural holidays, or four fire festivals, marking the growing and waning seasons of the sacred land so strongly traced in their myths. The fire festivals are all involved in purification and transformation. The year can be divided into two basic cycles, growing and dying. The growing season really began with the festival of Beltane, in May, while the dying season started with the Celtic new year, Samhain (pronounced "Sow-wen"). It seems funny to start the year with the dying season, but some believe the Celts also measured the day starting with sunset, not sunrise.

Between the two points were added Imbolc, in the winter, to prepare for the spring, and Lammas, the first harvest, to reap before the dying season. All are intimately tied to the cycle of green life.

Although the ancient Celts were aware of the solar cycles, it seems that the northern tribes of the Teutons, the Germanics and Norse, were more concerned with the solar changes. Many other cultures marked the solar year, from the Greeks and Romans to the Egyptians. Current tribal cultures in both Africa and the Americas mark the passage of the solar holidays. In the modern Wheel of the Year, they carry the names Yule, for the winter solstice; Ostara, for the vernal equinox; Litha, for the summer solstice; and Mabon, for the autumnal equinox.

While certain cultures used agriculture and others used the Sun's movement, modern pagan reconstructionist had a hard time deciphering who used what. As the rise of Christianity came to full power, the pagan celebrations were outlawed, somewhat unsuccessfully. Many pagans would convert to Christianity, but would not give up their rituals completely as dancing with animal masks and other magickal rites were outlawed. The church started to absorb pagan holidays to gain more willing converts. The rituals would be Christianized and sanitized for the church, and after many generations, people forgot the original meaning of the rituals. Most modern holidays are relics of a pagan past, including Christmas, Easter, and Halloween.

To the church there was little difference between pagan cultures, so differences were not noted. As modern pagans try to trace the roots of the past, they find a tangled knot in time when all holidays seem blended together with few cultural distinctions. It was easy to assume they all held the same importance in the ancient world, but they probably didn't, depending on the time and place.

For modern pagans, I think each spoke in the Wheel is important, although we all have our own favorite holidays that resonate with us personally. The modern holidays can be looked on as symbolic truth, like any mythology. Through the horrible persecutions of the past come the opportunity to reap the harvest of world wisdom, rather than any one single culture reconstructed as before. We can never go back into the past, so we must create the new traditions of the witch together. The Burning Times sought to annihilate the witch's tree, but it seems all it did was create more and more branches.

The Story of the Goddess and God

The reconstruction of the Wheel is a modern interpretation of these ancient events. In this reweaving of the lore, we created a simplistic story of the year, the story of life and creation, be it the creation of the universe, the world, or another year. It is the story of the Goddess as Maiden, Mother, and Crone. It is the story of the God as God of Light and God of Shadow, for the waxing and waning year. The God is son, lover, king, and protector.

Woven into this simple story is the myths of many other gods and goddesses. Their particular stories relate to a particular holiday. At first this made little sense to me. Why was the story of Lugh told in August, while the story of Mabon told in September? They didn't connect. One story didn't flow into the other to tell the story of the year. How can one goddess, the Morgan, be involved in Samhain and Brid be called on Imbolc? Shouldn't they be the same goddess? Why was Persephone's story told on the spring equinox, when it was named after the Teutonic goddess Ostara?

Remember that each goddess is an expression of the Great Mother. She has many names and faces. Specific goddesses can share an aspect of her wisdom. Through learning their stories, we learn world wisdom. Perhaps the ancient followers of the Morgan has a story of her for each of the seasons. Perhaps the daughters of Brid had their own telling of the seasons. But now, we have only fragments of stories, often recorded by Christian scholars who did not understand the religious significance of the myths to pagans. They were recorded simply because they were good stories, and often Christianized in the process, as the gods became heroes and saints.

Now we witches have no true scripture. We need none. We have our scripture, in the changing colors of the leaves, in the seasonal shifts and weather patterns. We have it in the movement of the Sun, Moon, and Earth with the stars. Here is eternal wisdom that no one can burn and take from us. Without a book of scripture, we cannot hear the answer from another. We have rituals to guide us into finding the answer for ourselves.

The story of the Goddess and God vary from traditions to tradition, coven to coven. Here is one version I learned, but it is not the only one. As you practice and learn, the gods will reveal their own stories and meaning to you, and that will be the story you live by and teach to others. The events of the story are not necessarily linear and logical. They are not fact, but poetic, symbolic, and mythic truth. They are not any less true than fact, but exist in another plane intersecting with ours.

At the winter solstice, the Goddess, the Great Mother of the Universe, gives birth to the God, as the child of golden sunlight. From his birth, the world begins to grow warmer and the days grow longer.

Through Imbolc, the Mother nurses the Son as he grows into power. The Goddess returns to the world, from the Underworld, at the vernal equinox, and, with her power, resurrects the land after winter.

She returns as the Maiden of the Spring. The God grows into power and starts manifesting his power on Earth, as the growing world, transforming his mantle from Solar Child to Green God.

At Beltane he reaches young adulthood. Both Goddess and God are in their green prime. The young lovers consummate their union. There is joy throughout the land.

By summer solstice, the God has grown into his role as King of the Land, and the Goddess manifests as Queen. The King has reaches the peak of his power and is challenged by his own shadow, the Dark King and Horned God of the waning year. The shadow arises from the Underworld and defeats the God of Light.

At Lammas, the first harvest, the defeated God, both solar and green, is sacrificed for the good of his people, to feed his people as the grain harvest. He is cut as the grain is cut and sent to the Underworld. The Horned God begins his reign as father and protector during the winter months.

The festival of Mabon is his journey to the Underworld, and the Goddess grows older, missing her King and following him into the Underworld. As she withdraws her power the land begins to turn color and wither.

At Samhain the Horned God rules the year, and Goddess, in her grief, opens the gateway between the worlds to be with her partner and husband in the Underworld.

By the next solstice, she realizes that the essence of the God is within her womb. He battles his small shadow and is victorious, being born into the world as the Sun once again. The Horned God of Shadow returns to the Underworld, awaiting the next duel. The cycle begins again.

Most of the stories of the Wheel are from Celtic sources, since they are a favored lore of modern reconstructionists. Teutonic traditions also make their way into the names and holidays. If you favor traditions other than northern European, you can often be hard pressed to find complete equivalents in your myths. Some traditions relate the Greco-Roman gods to the story of the Wheel. Stories of Persephone, Apollo, and Dionysus fit in well to the seasons for me, and since they are the ones most people are familiar with, I often tell them at public circles.

Although I love Egyptian and Sumerian myth, these ancient Middle Easterners did not celebrate the year in quite the same cycles. You can adapt these godforms and call upon them at the appropriate times for ritual, or you can research the ancient calendars of others cultures and adapt these dates to fit in the modern year and seasons where you live. As long as you celebrate with an open heart and respect to all, there is no right or wrong way to call upon the divine.

WHY DO WE CELEBRATE?

Early on my path as teacher, I was giving a lecture at a New Age center introducing the topic of Wicca. I described the Wheel of the Year as the cycle of celebrations and told stories about the gods and goddesses. At the end, someone asked a really great question. "Why do you celebrate the holidays?" she asked. "Perhaps the ancient people felt that if they didn't, the Sun wouldn't rise, or the crops wouldn't grow, but we know that's not true now. Most of these traditions died out. The world didn't end. The Sun still rose the next day. So why do you do it?"

I was stumped for a moment. I never thought task why we do these rituals. Strangely enough, I never questioned it, like I questioned so many things. For many new pagans the idea of giving up holidays like Christmas can be very difficult, so the Wheel represents a return to both celebration and the original ideas behind the holidays. But my workshop participant was asking a far more existential question. I took a moment before I answered her.

"Do we know the Sun will rise tomorrow? Do we know it for a fact?" I said. "We assume the Sun is going to rise, the Moon will change, and the seasons will shift, but we don't know that. The balance of life on this planet is fairly delicate, and with the way humanity treats the environment, as well as threat of wars and man-made disasters, we don't know if the Sun will rise, or if we will be here to see it rise another day. Celebrating the Wheel of the Year brings us back into relationship with the Earth, with the cycles of nature. Only by actively participating in this relationship will we heal the imbalances. Only then can we truly count on the rise of the Sun, stars, and grain. Celebrating the Wheel of the Year is not only a symbolic act of celebration, but a magickal commitment to sustain life on this planet—all forms of life, including human. Without it, we spiral out of balance, and on to the path of destruction."

Celebrating the Wheel has many blessings and responsibilities. We, humans in general but witches in particular, are caretakers and stewards, partner to the cycles of nature. We are loyal members of the Earth tribe and work in partnership with the Mother and Father. We work together, like any good clan.

Witches are said to turn the Wheel of the Year. Without flowing with the cycles and seasons of life, humanity disrupts them. Through ritual we acclimate to the seasons, and turn with them, in our own personal rhythms. True, the seasons will change without our acts, but will they change as easily? Will we be prepared for them? Probably not. Those who keep the old ways also help keep the balance. The more people live in balance, the more the entire world will be healed.

Those who celebrate the cycles easily move into the flow of the universe. They live in the moment, and live more fully, accessing all the blessings and joy life has to offer, and move through the pains as well, recognizing more easily the transience of the world. Nature is change.

Such celebrants adjust to the changes more easily, both inner and outer change. If you flow with the darkness, both physical and inner personal darkness, you learn not to fear it, but realize it is a part of life. Those with seasonal affective disorder will more easily adapt to the changes in light and temperature when truly celebrating and adjusting to the cycle, rather than raging against it. I know my own allergies dramatically decreased with regular meditation, ritual, and seasonal celebration. I became more in tune with the rhythms of the plants.

Witches celebrate on these days because they represent alignments of energy, from astrological energies to those of the Sun and Earth. Each holiday is flavored with a particular theme, and associated with goddesses and gods who embody those themes. Each day opens a special gateway of knowledge, power, and healing, and their blessings are only available at those times of year. Meditations, rituals, and spells are particularly powerful on those days.

The Sabbats give you a chance to come together as a community. Some come together mystically as our circle, beyond space and time, touches every circle in the world. Others physically come together, celebrating in groups from traditional covens to large, pagan gatherings. Such group worship helps remind you of those who walk on the path, even if you are usually a solitary, and helps fill you with a sense of love, community, and solidarity in a world that often views witches as different from the "normal" world.

Lastly, folk wisdom tells us that every time a witch celebrates an entire cycle of the Wheel, or an entire lunar year, that witch's power increases and expands, as a blessing from the Goddess. I'm personally not sure if this is a blessing from the Goddess, or it simply represents a greater sense of self-awareness and knowledge in ritual and energy work from committing to these powerful rituals. The increase in magickal power may simply be a byproduct of putting so much time into the craft.

How Do We Celebrate?

Witches mark the Wheel of the Year in many ways. Some witches on the go do simple acts of magick and devotion to mark the passing of the year. When I worked in the city and had little time to devote to my craft, I often spent my lunch break on Sabbat days outside, in the park, doing a quick, quiet, little ritual or meditation to be a part of the day's energy and thank the gods for my blessings.

Most witches, alone or in a group, usually celebrate through a magick circle. The work of the circle is the celebration itself, but the temple space is created through the traditional circle casting. The circle is the foundation for Moon rituals, Sun rituals, and seasonal rituals. It is the foundation stone of most modern witchcraft.

The altar is decorated with colors associated with the holiday. Food, flowers, grains, and other offerings appropriate to the day are placed on the altar. Certain herbs and trees are linked with the holidays and used in magick and blessings during the Sabbat. Although many books show the ritual significance of certain herbs for certain days, look to see what is in bloom in your area during the holiday. That is what embodies the energy of the day for you. Most traditional lore on Wiccan holidays is from the UK, but living in New England, I notice that different things are in bloom at different times here. Unless you save and dry them for the holidays, certain flowers won't be fresh for your holiday. If you live in a different climate, use what works in your area.

The quarters are called with the holiday elements in mind, perhaps calling on deities or animals associated with the myths of that celebration. Those deities are often called to the center of the circle as well. Instead of traditional spellwork, a storyteller may expound upon the myths, or a guided meditation will be given based on the ritual themes. Some covens act out myths in ritualized drama. Others use folk magick rituals to connect with the theme of the day. Ritual themes can also include the astrology of the day, since the four solar holidays occur when the Sun is shifting from one sign to another. The fire festivals always occur in fixed astrological signs. Fixed signs correspond with the middle of a season. Each brings its own sign and planet lore, as well as astrological correspondences to the mix. Often you will be more familiar with the Christianized version of the holidays, and you can feel free to reclaim the pagan elements of those holidays in your own practice.

MAGICK

Should magick be done on the Wheel of the Year celebrations? It depends on your tradition. The use of spells on the Sabbat days, as they are often known, to differentiate them from Moon rituals known as Esbats, is a controversial point for some. There is certainly nothing wrong with it. They are powerful times of the year. Some covens debate the ethics of it, feeling that the Moons should be reserved for magick, and the eight holidays for worship and celebration. I guess it depends on the type of magick and what your personal feelings are. Usually my coven doesn't do much personal spellwork on the holidays, but if we do magick, it is with the intention of healing the world, creating peace, harmony, and awareness in the communities around us. We also do more introspective meditations and rituals on the holidays, particularly during the dark half of the year.

Historically, it seems that the holidays were a strong time for folk magick among pagan people. Only in modern times does it get the sense of the Judeo-Christian sabbath of rest and worship. Like so many other things, on this point you must figure out what practice rings true to you. I don't usually practice personal spells on the holidays, but I know if I'm called to do so, I have no moral problem with it. Magick is a part of everyday life, including holiday celebrations. Magick doesn't always have to be about spells, but the magick of participating in the cycles of life. If that calls you to do spell-work at that time, then so be it. The greatest magick on the Sabbats is partnering with life and turning the Wheel of the Year as you honor the gods and the forces of the universe. Beyond that, do what thou will and let it harm none.

TIMING

Four of the eight holidays, the two solstices and two equinoxes, are universally marked by astrological movements. The Sun moves from a mutable sign, which ends a season, into a cardinal sign, which begins the next season. Cardinal energy initiates. These holy days are recognized by many cultures and traditions across the world. The four fire festivals are more loosely defined. Usually they are traditionally noted at the first or second day of a month dominated by the fixed astrological signs—February (Aquarius), May (Taurus), August (Leo), and November (Scorpio), or the last of the previous month. Though recognized by most, these dates are oriented with the Gregorian calendar, and have little bearing on the cycles and seasons. One could argue since they are agricultural, you could find your clues when to celebrate based on the land around you. Beltane would come earlier to warmer climates and later to colder areas.

To measure the cross-quarter days more accurately through astrology, you should look on an astrological ephemeris to find when the Sun moves fifteen degrees into the fixed sign. You can find this information on an astrological ephemeris for the Sun. Although I'm a stickler for astrology, I actually prefer celebrating on the more common fixed day, rather than figuring out the degree the Sun enters. I like to know that most witches are celebrating the same holiday on the same day I am. In ancient times all of these holidays were celebrated with festivals that would last days, so it is difficult to tell what went on when. In our modern world, we seem to only take one day to mark a special time.

In traditional pagan cultures, these holidays could be week-long celebrations, not just single-day events. Because these festivals were held over long intervals, modern pagans have quite a bit of leeway in choosing when to celebrate. Most traditions feel you have a range of plus or minus three, five, or even seven days before and after the holiday to celebrate and still partake in the energies.

If you are doing magick on these rituals, and want to catch the peak of the energy, you would plan the ritual to start slightly before the astrological alignment, but sometimes that can be difficult. If doing a solar ritual, and the Sun changes signs at night where you are located, you might be lacking the appropriate magickal feel. Do it the day before.

Often the night before is a favorite time, particularly for rituals on the dark half of the year. Twilight is a very magickal time for the solstices. For lighter rituals, daytime rites are quite common, particularly for the spring. I lead public rituals at a Boston area bookstore, and we consistently celebrate the Saturday evening before or after the ritual. We have to take into account people's work schedules and when is best for the overall community to gather. You need to be practical as well as magickal. In the end, it is your choice as to when, where, and how you keep the Wheel of the Year.

The question of seasons arises when celebrating in the Southern Hemisphere. If you are oriented to the seasons, you will reverse the holidays. Your Beltane will come in October/November and your Samhain in April/May. If you are celebrating the cosmic cycles as expressed in astrology, you could keep them the same. Each sign contains the shadow of its opposite. The axis of Beltane and Samhain, Taurus and Scorpio, are about life, sex, and death. Each contains the essence of the other. The two holidays are more similar than many people give them credit, when contemplated in astrological terms. Think about how the Full Moon is in the opposite sign the Sun is occupying. Each contains the other. Neither practice of celebration, astrological or seasonal, is wrong. You simply have to find out what works best for you and any group you participate in when you find yourselves in the Southern Hemisphere.

ŁOCATION

Ideally, the Sabbats are celebrated outside, in close communion with the forces of nature. While this is the ideal, this isn't always the practical solution, depending on your own living space, location, access, and comfort level. You can have just as meaningful a ceremony alone in your living room or backyard as you can with a large festival in the middle of the woods. Each is different, but neither is more or less significant. As modern people, we have to weave these rituals into our modern lives and bring the magick into daily life. I have led rituals year round in a bookstore's attic teaching space and had wonderful experiences. The heat is on in the winter and the cooling system is on during the summer. Without it, many people would be very uncomfortable in that space, but we have wonderful, healing, and powerful rituals nonetheless. Don't feel that you have to hike out into the deep woods unless you feel called to do so. If you do feel called to do so, and have the access and opportunity to do it, then don't disregard the call. Such rituals can be quite magickal. I've had wonderful experiences alone, in a group, indoors, outdoors, home, work, public parks, deep forest, and historic sacred sites. Each is unique and individual as the moment in time and those who gather together. If you are worried about the energy at your place of celebration, concern yourself more with the energy you are bringing to the celebration. Celebrate the seasons wherever you can, and bring their magick into noticing the cyclical changes throughout the year, in between the holidays.

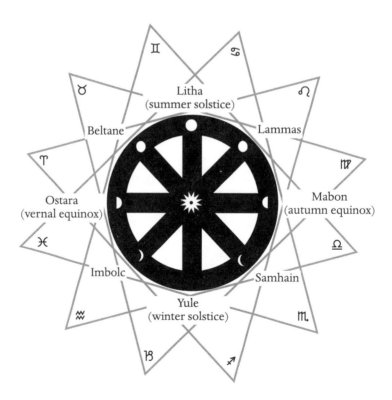

Figure 49: Wheel of the Year

Yule—Winter Solstice

Date: Near December 21

Ritual Theme: Rebirth of the Sun God, return of the old God to the Underworld

Astrology: Sun moves from Sagittarius to Capricorn

Lunar Correspondence: Dark of the Moon

Deities: Solar Child, Sun King, Great Mother, Underworld/Horned God, Oak King & Holly King, Saturn/Chronos, Bel, Mabon, Pryderi, Taliesin, Cerridwen, Balder, Apollo, Horus, Set

Altar: Evergreen decorations, pine cones, oak, holly, mistletoe, white candles

Colors: Red, green, white, black

Herbs: Herbs of Saturn, Capricorn, and the Sun. Traditional herbs include holly, mistletoe, pine, oak, fir, birch, chamomile, cinnamon, frankincense, myrrh, wintergreen, nutmeg, clove, ivy, blessed thistle, hyssop, and rosemary.

The winter solstice marks the rebirth of the Sun. On this holiday, the night is the longest in the entire year, but from this point forward, the Sun's power begins to wax. The Sun waxes and wanes, like the Moon, but over the yearly cycle. The two solstices are the turning points.

On this day, the aspect of the God as the force of life is reborn. As the Sun waxes, it brings more warmth, triggering the cycle of rebirth in the land. Even though we have just entered winter, there is hope. The days grow longer and the promise of renewal is there. This starts the season of light rituals.

In some traditions, the God is viewed as a child, and the Universal Mother gives birth to the young Sun King. Others see the God of Light, as the Oak King, rise up out of the Underworld and combat the God of Darkness, the Horned God or Holly King, and take his place as ruler for half of the year.

As the Sun enters Capricorn, Saturn and Capricorn have ties both to the old and young. Usually seen as the stern patriarch figure, these energies can be about handing off responsibility to the next generation. The figure of Saturn has been transformed into modern times as Father Time or the Grim Reaper with his sickle, but hands off the year to our image of Baby New Year, like the old god giving the reins to the new child god.

Traditional Christmas celebrations mimic the ancient pagan customs of Yule. Since so many cultures see this time as the birth of the god of light, the Christian church moved the celebration of Jesus' birthday closer to the solstice. Evergreen trees are decorated to show the promise of the Goddess and God to preserve life, as the trees are green even in the winter months. Pine cones hold the spiral of the Goddess within them. Yule logs are another traditional pagan blessing. Many of the yuletide drinks are like pagan potions of solar energy, to warm you in the winter.

Druid traditions call this day Alban Arthuans. Mistletoe plays a prominent role in Druidic rituals, cut with a golden sickle from an oak tree and used in magick and medicine. In the Norse traditions, mistletoe wood was the weapon to slay Balder, the Norse Sun god, signaling the start of the end of the world. His mother decreed that forever more the herb shall only be used in acts of love, starting the tradition of kissing under mistletoe. Mistletoe is hung in a house to protect it from lightning.

In Roman times, the feast was celebrated with the Saturnalia, a festival in honor of the god Saturn, who ruled the last golden age. During this time, things were turned upside down. Slaves lived like royalty. Master waited on their slaves. Gifts were exchanged. It was a great party to release pressures from the growing season and the stress of entering the winter.

To celebrate the winter solstice, focus on the rebirth of the sunlight in your life. Invite the God of Light into your circle, and into your life. Light candles to indicate the dawning of the light in darkness. Your chalice can be filled with an infusion of safe solar herbs, to drink in the light as part of the Great Rite. You can exchange magickal handmade gifts with those in your circle. You can meditate on the light, drawing the Sun's power not only into your body, but through you, and into the Earth Mother. Do healing for your inner child, and play with the light of the inner child. The Sun card from the major arcana of the tarot can be an excellent focus for your work. You can do magick for health and protection in the remaining winter months. Bring blessings, merriment, and festivities to your home by exploring the energy of the child of the Sun.

Imbolc
Date: Usually February 2
Ritual Theme: Awakening the Goddess through a festival of lights; home and child blessing

Astrology: Sun in Aquarius

Lunar Correspondence: Waxing crescent

Deities: Fire/Solar Goddess, Brid/Bridget, Hestia/Vesta, Freya, Sekhemet

Altar: Ring of candles, grain dolly and bed, grain cross, purification tools

Colors: Orange, white, aqua, lavender, magenta

Herbs: Herbs of Aquarius and Uranus. Traditional herbs include heather, holly, pine, ivy, willow, sage, clove, nutmeg, almond, angelica, bay, basil, benzoin, grains, and nuts.

Imbolc is the festival most commonly associated with the goddess Brid, also known as Bridget. She is a triple goddess of fire and light, as her three aspects involve healing, poetry, and smithcraft. Christians later called this holiday Candlemas because wreaths and crowns of candles are used to celebrate. It is a festival of growing light, to tide us over between Yule and the coming spring. With more light comes more hope. It is also known as St. Bridgit's Day, or Oimelc. Traces of the ritual can be found in our modern Groundhog Day.

At this time of year, the young God is growing stronger. The Goddess still slumbers in the winter, below the earth, after giving birth to the God. His growing light begins her process of awakening. We aid the process and turn the Wheel of the Year with our own light, gently coaxing the Goddess to awaken.

The Sun is in the sign of Aquarius. Though an air sign, it is about communication. The Age of Aquarius is often said to be an age of light and a time of spiritual awakening. Aquarian energy holds the experience of intuition and direct knowing of the divine. The communication is not necessarily by words, but the "waves" of Aquarius are waves of energy, of psychic light. Witches know the power of light to heal and transform. This energy is about community, the global community, and the greater good. At this time of year, ancient pagans were concerned with the community surviving the end of the winter. Aquarius helps awaken on many levels.

"Imbolc" as a term is said to refer to the lactation of the herd. The ewes of the sheep herd begin producing milk in preparation for the birth of the new sheep. There is hope and renewal for the tribe. In this sense, Imbolc is a fertility ritual, and Brid is a goddess of fertility. Milk or cream is symbolically poured into the Earth, or left as a offering to the fey folk. The home is physically and ritually cleared, like an early spring-cleaning, to prepare for the new life, even if the new life is simply the birth of spring. Children are blessed and spells of health and protection are done. Celtic witchcraft traditions have the making of Brid's cross out of grain stalks, hung for protection, or Brid's bed, a dolly made of grain or cord, dressed and ritually laid in a bed. Your grain stalks can be saved from your Lammas ritual, since the two are opposite points in the Wheel. As you care for it, the Goddess will care for and protect you. You are caring for the young child God as the Mother awakens. As you honor the light and child, you nourish that within yourself and your family.

To celebrate Imbolc, you can do a thorough spiritual cleansing of your home, and make protection charms to be hung for the next year. Magick for creativity and healing is powerful at this time. I have done rituals where we started in darkness and everyone involved lit a candle, creating a ring of light to wake the Mother. Songs, chants, and drumming can be done for the same intention. Any rituals to personally awaken to new knowledge or point of view is wonderful at this time. Care for your inner light and fan the flame to make it grow despite the winter cold.

Ostara—Vernal Equinox

Date: Near March 22

Ritual Theme: Resurrection of the land through the awakening of the Earth Maiden

Astrology: Sun moves from Pisces to Aries

Lunar Correspondence: First quarter

Deities: Maiden Goddess, Agricultural Goddess, Solar God, War God, Ostara, Kore/ Persephone, Demeter, Bel, Apollo, Horus, Ares/Mars, Freya and Frey

Altar: Seeds, pots of soil, colored eggs, red candles

Colors: Red, white, black

Herbs: Herbs of Aries and Mars; all early spring flowers. Traditional herbs include alder, almond, clover, flax, nettles, cattail, fern, rose, rose hips, iris, tansy, violets, lilac, marjoram, crocus, tulip, daffodil, dogwood, magnolia, and sunflower seeds.

The spring equinox is named after Ostara, or Ostre, the Teutonic goddess of spring. Sacred to her are seeds and eggs, both sources of life central to spring rebirth. Not many clear myths survive about this goddess. Modern pagan lore has similar stories to Persephone. As Persephone is retuned to the world every spring, to be with her mother the grain goddess Demeter, she returns to the Underworld to join her husband Hades in the fall. Ostara returns to the earth in the chariot of an unnamed Sun King, only to return to him in the fall. As long as the goddess is present on the earth, things will grow. When she leaves, the land dies, to be resurrected again. The myths of Ostara are preserved in the Christian tale of Easter. Some use the equinox to honor Mary, and call this day Lady's Day. To Druidic traditions, it is known as Alban Eiler.

At this time, the Goddess is awoken and returns from the Underworld. She is reborn as the flower maiden. As she walks the earth, it begins to bloom, as seen by the first few flowers and bulbs rising from the warming earth. The God no longer is sheltered in the crib of Brid's bed, but rises with power in the sky daily.

As the Sun turns from Pisces, the last water sign of merging and dreams, we leave the frozen dreaminess of winter's edge and enter Aries, the fiery, warrior energy. Aries begins and initiates. Astrologically, this is the beginning of the year, with a new influx of energy to start the Wheel rolling and begin a new cycle with a warming, fiery energy. Like the ram, Aries energy charges forward into the future.

When we celebrate Ostara, we are celebrating our own rebirth and must now take action. What have you wanted to do? What have you been waiting to accomplish? Put your energy into the world. Like Aries, how can you take charge? How can you be your own leader in life and take the initiative in your world? It is a time to overcome fears and simply do. Celebrate. Manifest. Make magick in your life.

Celebrations of Ostara include blessing and planting seeds and bulbs. They can be tied into spellwork. As you plant grows, your intention is fulfilled. Your meditations can involve planting the inner seeds of personal development and growth, or the seeds of peace for the world itself. You can meditate on the warrior spirit of Aries, and invoke your own personal spiritual warrior and leader to work with you. Egg decorating is also popular. The variety of colors and symbols used in your magickal eggs can hold specific intention. Drawing runes or animal totems on the eggs is a powerful way to invoke their blessing as a part of your ritual. When you celebrate Ostara, invoke the power of rebirth into yourself and the land.

Beltane

Date: Usually May 1; Beltane Eve sometimes celebrated the day before

Ritual Theme: Fertility of the land through the joining of the young Goddess and God, sexual passion, handfastings

Astrology: Sun in Taurus

Lunar Correspondence: Waxing gibbous

Deities: Young Fire/Sun God, young Green God, Maiden Goddess, Bel, Mabon, Pryderi, Pan, Apollo, Dionysus/Bacchus, Aphrodite/Venus, Balder, Freya

Altar: Spring flowers, flower wreaths, many candles or cauldron for a small fire

Colors: Green, white, black

Herbs: Herbs of Venus and Taurus; all flowers blooming in May. Traditional herbs include lily of the valley, rose, hawthorn, apple, heather, yarrow, meadowsweet, rosemary, broom, tulips, all-heal, tansy, elder, almond, cinquefoil, juniper, woodruff, marsh marigold, corn flower, and ivy.

Beltane translates to "the fire of Bel." Bel is an ancient Celtic god with few true stories remaining. Some associated him with the Eastern Baal figure, and he is implied to be a god of solar light and fire. Some relate him to the Greek god Apollo, implying later Greeks borrowed Bel from the Celts and formed the myths of Apollo.

Beltane is the ritual of first union between the Goddess and the God. The God usually manifests as solar god, but here we see his solar light absorbed by the vegetation, transforming him into the Green God, called the Green Man or Jack of the Green. He is grown into his power on earth, and into sexual maturity. The Goddess is the maiden of the land, receiving the seed of the God to fulfill the promise of the harvest.

As a fire festival, Beltane is about both sexuality and purification. The Celts would create two large fires of sacred wood to act as a focus for their purification rites. The herd, and even people, would pass between these fires to purify them from the last vestiges of winter illness. Other rituals of purification involve water, and the washing of hands and feet with spring water or herbal waters to cleanse, clear, and heal.

Fertility rituals were common on Beltane, with a free expression of sexuality in many tribes. Children born roughly nine months later from this time would be considered very blessed, special children to be cared for and fathered by the entire tribe.

No shame was attributed to mother or child without a husband. Pagans would dance around the Maypole. The men would create the pole from a tree and the women would dig the hole. Ribbons and cords were tied to the top, often with a flower wreath. Dances weaving the ribbons in and out and around the pole would commence, slowly lowering the wreath to the ground. The dance itself is the dance of union, with the pole and wreath symbolizing sexual union of the Goddess with the God of the Green. Couples would often have their year-and-a-day commitment at this time of year, or handfastings. Modern couples often use this first ritual as an engagement prior to a vow of longer commitment.

The pole is also symbolic of the World Tree of the shaman, and the dance of life around it. As time went on, and the tradition was more Christianized, the sexual elements of the holiday were forgotten and the dance became little more than a dance done in churchyards on a holiday renamed May Day.

The sign of Taurus is the energy of Beltane. Taurus is ruled by Venus, the planet and goddess of love and fertility. Taurus is about the material world, and on one hand, is about pleasing the senses through touch, taste, smell, and sound. It is also about prosperity, as its color is green, the green of the grass is the green of prosperity. Both are stored energy.

To celebrate Beltane, focus on your own passion and how you express that passion. Do something fun and spontaneous as a part of your ritual. Use flowers, song, dance, and movement. Meditations can be moving meditation, or inner workings focusing on uniting your inner God and Goddess together in fertile passion, to ensure your own creativity and vitality in the year. Light a fire or use lots of candles to invoke the power of Bel. I have used two, small, cauldron fires with wood and incense to walk between for purification and healing. If you have a group, try a Maypole dance. Find your own inner creative spark and passion in this holiday of pleasure and love.

Litha—Midsummer—Summer Solstice

Date: Usually June 21

Ritual Theme: God and Goddess preside as King and Queen of the Land, defeat of the Light God, opening to the faery realm

Astrology: Sun moves from Gemini into Cancer

Lunar Correspondence: Full Moon

Deities: Divine King and Queen, Solar/Grain God, Dark God, Mother Goddess, Holly King, Titania and Oberon, Thor and Sif, Odin and Frigga, Isis and Osiris, Horus and Set

Altar: Statue of the Goddess and God as Queen and King, faery statues or pictures, crowns, flowers in bloom

Colors: Gold, yellow, green, brown

Herbs: Herbs of the Sun, Gemini, and Cancer. Traditional herbs include St. John's wort, rosemary, sunflower, mugwort, vervain, heather, hemp, lavender, mint, cinquefoil, cedar, juniper, rue, oak, meadowsweet, chive, thyme, and rose.

The festival of Litha is more commonly known as the summer solstice or Midsummer's. Many traditions celebrate on Midsummer's Eve, rather than the day of the solstice. Druidic traditions call it Alban Heruin. Midsummer is the peak of solar power, the Sun's equivalent to the Full Moon. Though the Sun's energy is constant, it is the perception of the light on Earth in the North Hemisphere that peaks at this time. The day is the longest, and night is the shortest.

The theme of the divine couple, at the peak of their power, is constant at Litha. The Goddess is the Queen of the Bountiful Garden. Her love for the king and all of us is reflected in the lush greenery of the land. Her love makes the harvest grow. She is the Divine Mother providing nourishment with the growing plants. The energy of the land builds to its crescendo. The God is matured into his role as Divine King of the Land. He is the caretaker and protector. The solar and green attributes are merged into one, as he is both Solar King and Grain Lord bearing fruit.

Although he is at the peak of his power, all he can do now is wane. Tradition says he must face his shadow. The shadow of the God is the Dark Lord and Underworld King. He is the Horned God and the Holly King. The God of Light faces the God of Shadow, and is defeated, as is preordained on this day. He relinquishes control of the year to the Dark God. This shift is symbolic of the shadows we must all face. They are not evil, simply another side of us that we must look at as part of our development and growth. There can be no growing season without the waning season. Death makes life that much sweeter.

Astrologically, we move from the lighter and more social and jovial sign of Gemini to the influence of Cancer. Cancer is the ocean mother, the womb and the tomb, as embodying by the protective shell of the crab. It signals the start of our going within time, like the crab. The movement of energy is no longer direct, but moves from side to side as does a crab. Ruled by the Moon, which seems strange on this solar holiday, Cancer urges us to look within and take stock of our emotions and family relationships.

As the Sabbat is associated with the longest day, it is actually the longest twilight period, between day and night, at sunset, that is most magickal. The liminal points of the day—dawn, noon, sunset, and midnight—are the times between times, and the most magickal. Gateways open and folklore says this is the most appropriate time to connect with the faery realm. On this day in particular, the realm to the fey is suppose to open and communion with that realm, and the king and queen of the faery, is possible. Unlike many modern popular stories of happy, little, winged fairies, the faery realm is a realm of nature, and not always happy and friendly. You must treat all beings with great respect and manners, and never assume anything.

In the Christian calendar, this feast is associated with St. John, and St. John's wort, a very magickal, solar-oriented plant. If you look down on it from above, it forms a cross of equal arms, like the solar cross of the Sun or Earth, for protection. Rituals of Litha are for gathering solar strength to face your dark half and the dark half of the year. Potions, herbs like St. John's wort, charms, and crystals are used to absorb solar light to be drawn upon for later times in the year. When planning rituals for Litha, incorporate your sense of inner sovereignty to the ceremony. My coven has a mock "battle" between the High Priests, as representing Holly and Oak King. One leads the rituals for six months, and then we switch at the winter solstice. Meditations can involve speaking with your Shadow, finding your inner Sun, or communing with your own divine couple as the Goddess and God or faery king and queen. Bring out the peak of your powers and energy at this time, like the peaking Sun.

Lammas—Lughnassadh

Date: Usually August 1
Ritual Theme: Sacrifice of the Grain God, funeral feast, first harvest—grain
Astrology: Sun in Leo

Lunar Correspondence: Waning gibbous

Deities: Solar God, Grain God, Sacrificed God, Earth Mother, Lugh, Tailltiu, Lleu,
Arianrhod, Taliesin, Cerridwen, Macha, Aphrodite and Adonis, Inanna and Tammuz,
Odin

Colors: Gold, green, gray, black

Herbs: Herbs of Leo and the Sun; all grains such as wheat, barely, rye, hops, and corn.
Traditional Lammas herbs include frankincense, rosemary, sunflower, caraway, fenu-
greek, bilberry, blueberry, hollyhock, oak, sage, goldenrod, Queen Anne's lace, comfrey, marigold, and calendula.

Lammas is the first harvest, when the first grains are ready to be harvested. The ceremonial gathering is followed with a great celebration, as the grain is a fulfillment of
the promise of safety and health for the winter months, given by the Goddess and
God to the tribes.

The God of Grain and Light, defeated at the previous holiday, willingly plays the
role of sacrificed king found so often in pagan lore. If the land does not do well, the
king and his relationship to the Goddess, who truly gives him the authority to rule, is
in question. In certain areas and times in the past, the king would give his life to renew
the land. This divine link between king and Goddess is hinted at in the mythos of King
Arthur, though most Christian scholars who record the myth only touch upon the
power of the Goddess. The Good God, as the ultimate king figure, gives his life so
that his people may live, knowing he will be reborn once again. Symbolically, he is
killed by the cutting of the grain. In his place rules the Dark God, to guide and protect
us in the winter months.

In the Irish pagan traditions, the first harvest is associated with Lugh, the skilled
god of the Tuatha De Danann, who is associated with the Sun and grain. Named
Lughnassadh, the funeral feast of Lugh, many modern pagans feel this story referred
to Lugh's own death as the Sun King, but in fact, the story is about his foster mother,
Tailltiu, an Earth goddess who clears the Irish fields of stones so that planting may be
done. Her task exhausts her so much that she expires. The harvest is in her honor, and
her funeral feast. Like an Irish funeral, this is a time to celebrate the life of the one
who has passed, and it is commemorated with sports and games, often called the

Tailltean games. Games of contest, like archery and racing, are said to be reminiscent of Lugh's victory over the leader for the Fomorians, Balor. The festival is much like a feast, with storytelling, food, and spirits to be shared. Although the holiday name truly refers to his mother, I feel that the overall spirit of the holiday is the passing of the lord, and feel this the symbolic myth and truth, if not the literal. Some call the day Lunasa, but despite the word "Luna," it has nothing to do with the Moon.

The Irish goddess Macha, as warrior and queen, is also associated with Lammas. As part of the Triple Goddess, she is often seen as the Crone of the harvest, though in this story she is the Mother. Although associated with crows, she is also the goddess of horses, and her equine nature plays a prominent role in this tale. Her mortal husband boasts of his divine wife, saying she can run faster than the king's horses. The king challenges him to prove it, and Macha, pregnant with twins, is forced to run. She is victorious, gives birth, and curses the men of Ulster to know the pangs of childbirth during the time of their greatest need. The curse is fulfilled in the story of Cuchulain, the Irish wolfhound, often considered an avatar of Lugh.

Lugh's Welsh equivalent is Lleu, who is also associated with this time of year by modern pagans. His mother is Arianrhod, goddess of the silver wheel of rebirth, and his uncle and caretaker is the Druidic magician Gwydion. Another Welsh figure, Taliesin the bard, has solar attributes, due to his magick and knowledge. His "mother" is the goddess Cerridwen. He starts his life as her servant, Gwion Bach, and accidentally tastes the potion of knowledge meant for Cerridwen's son, gaining great magick. Through a shapeshifting duel between Cerridwen and Gwion, he takes the form of a seed, and she a chicken, eating the seed and giving birth to him nine months later as the child of solar light and knowledge. Thus she becomes mother to all bards.

The Sun is in Leo, the sign of the lion and the Sun King. Leo is the sustained power of the Sun. We know that even though it is waning, this is the hottest month, and we recognize and honor the gifts the light has brought us all year. Out of the three harvest festivals of the waning year, this is the most joyous and brightest.

To celebrate Lammas, save some of your corn husks and grain to be made into Brid's bed and dolly. I often weave grass and grain together in a small doll, and burn it in my cauldron, as a symbolic sacrifice of the grain god. Although sacrificial, Lammas rituals should also be fun. Use games and sports as a part of your celebration if you wish. Meditations can be on the personal sacrifice for the greater good. What do you give up for the good of others, like the Good God, or Lugh's mother? What seeds do you save and plan to plant in the future? On this holiday, amid your celebration, contemplate offering things up to the community and the divine.

Mabon—Autumnal Equinox

Date: Near September 21

Ritual Theme: Journey to the Underworld, balance of light and dark, second harvest—fruit, thanksgiving

Astrology: Sun moves from Virgo to Libra

Lunar Correspondence: Last quarter, New Moon

Deities: Child God/dess, Earth/Grain Mother, Mabon, Modron, Demeter/Ceres, Kore-Persephone/Proserpina, Pryderi, Rhiannon, Inanna and Tammuz

Altar: Apples, grapes, fruit, cider, wide fallen leaves

Colors: Orange, bronze, gold, red, green, black, wine, purple, pastels

Herbs: Herbs of Virgo, Libra, and Venus; all fruits and wines. Traditional herbs include apple, grape, walnut, passion flower, honeysuckle, caraway, dogwood, milkweed, myrrh, sage, and pomegranate.

On the autumnal equinox, the spirit of the God as the force of life that was sacrificed on the first harvest is now traveling to the Underworld. As he withdraws from the land, the life force of the Goddess follows him, signaling the end of the growing season and beginning of the fall. The leaves start to change color, as part of the Goddess' beautiful mourning for the God.

In modern witchcraft traditions, the autumn equinox is named after the Celtic god Mabon, even though the fire festivals played a more significant role in the Celtic culture. Although very little of his story survives in a complete form, Mabon is often referred to as the Celtic male Persephone. His strong connection to his mother and their story is very similar to Persephone and Demeter. Mabon is the young son of the Earth mother Modron. He ventures forth into the Underworld, losing touch with his mother. She follows him under, withdrawing her life force from the material world, causing the end of the growing season. They are reuniting and make their way back to the world by the vernal equinox, and bring the growing season again.

Modron and Mabon's story is much like the story of the goddess Rhiannon and her son Pryderi. Pryderi is stolen and his mother Rhiannon is blamed, put into chains until he returns much later. It is symbolic of many stories of the Goddess being imprisoned for a time in the Underworld.

The feast is called the second harvest, or fruit harvest, for after the grains the fruit comes to ripen. Druids call this day of the fruit harvest Alban Elved. The fruit is the sweetness of life. The spirit of the fruit, such as apples or grapes, is used to create an alcoholic beverage. Apples are symbolic of the Celtic otherworld of Avalon, the fabled paradise land of milk and honey, where souls go to rest. Grapes are connected to the Greek god Dionysus. He is the god of both ecstasy and madness. He is a god of love and fear, dying twice and traveling freely to the Underworld. Some myths have him trade places with Apollo in influencing the light and dark halves of the year.

Such fruit spirits are used in moderation to "open the gates" between worlds. Just as the in-between points of the day are times when the gates open, sunrise and sunset, the Wheel of the Year holidays are when the gates open as well. With the harvests, the gateways to the Underworld open wider and wider until Samhain, because life force is withdrawn from the world and into the Underworld. The use of ritual and such "spirits" like wine, ale, oils, and incense help open the gates to enter the Underworld like the God and Goddess.

Astrologically, the Sun is entering Libra as it leaves Virgo. Virgo is the harvest, as Libra is the scales. It represents the power of balance. Both equinoxes are about balance, but this time, in particular, is about finding balance between all polarities before entering the dark of winter. Libra's lesson is learning balance in all relationships, including your relationship with yourself. You must make sure your needs are met as well as others when you are in relationship. You must find a balance within yourself before you can give to others.

All the harvests, but Mabon in particular, are considered a form of pagan thanksgiving. We are thankful of all the blessings and gifts in our life. In ancient times, it was literally the harvest and the land's fertility. For modern people, it includes both the bounty of food, but also all our blessings in life, from friends, family, job, home, and all pleasures. My friend Kat loves traditional Thanksgiving celebrations, but does it on Mabon, rather than on the traditional American Thanksgiving, cooking a Mabon turkey.

Rituals of Mabon involve both giving thanks, getting into balance, and entering the Underworld. Some rituals enact a pageant at the equinoxes with a procession of those playing the roles of the Goddess and God entering the Underworld in the autumn and returning in the rituals of spring. My rituals often involve meditation or shamanic journey into the Underworld to find what I need to keep my balance in the winter. My intentions and thoughts focus on the blessings of my life and giving thanks to the Goddess and God for these blessings.

Samhain

Date: Usually October 31

Ritual Theme: Death and rebirth, Celtic new year, God and Goddess in the Underworld, honoring the ancestors, third harvest—meat

Astrology: Sun in Scorpio

Lunar Correspondence: Waning crescent Moon

Deities: Death God, Death Goddess, Horned God, War Goddess, Underworld King and Queen, Morgan, Dagda, Cernunnos, Dis Pater, Pan, Hades/Pluto and Persephone/Proserpina, Hel, Osiris, Ereshkigal

Altar: Pumpkins, gourds, leaves, acorns, animal horn, crow feathers, plates of food, photos/mementos of the ancestors, black candles, scrying mirror

Colors: Black, orange, scarlet, brown

Herbs: All herbs of Scorpio and Pluto; all poisonous and hallucinogenic herbs, as well as roots and rhizomes. Traditional herbs include apple, pomegranate, pumpkin, oak, ginger, sarsaparilla, ginseng, mushroom, mandrake, wormwood, mullien, almond, hazel, hemlock cones, garlic, and yew.

Samhain is by far the holiday most closely associated with witchcraft. Although I love all the holidays, Samhain is the one I enjoy the most. To me, it just sums up so much of the essence of the witch, being a state between worlds, involving change, death, and transformation, yet not fearing it. The traditions of Samhain were castrated by the Christians and left as a children's holiday as Halloween, but still the spirit survives in it through the ghastly image of the green-faced witches and ghouls. It is one of the most powerful times of the year for the witch, so, of course, the church made sure to do its best to rob it of power, injecting fear and childishness into it so others will not find its power.

Samhain was replaced by a mix of ancient and modern traditions. Many of the traditions were created to discourage pagan practices and to instill fear, such as wearing costumes. The church knew Samhain is not about their Heavenly Kingdom, so, in their simple mythology, the veil could only lead to Hell. Instead of receiving loving communication from the ancestors, the veil could allow demons and devils to escape. Lights to guide the way of the ancestors returning for a visit became the carved images to scare away monsters. Samhain, like sexuality, magick, and personal ritual, are gates to power that the church discouraged the general population from finding and using it to escape its oppression.

On this day, folklore tells us the veil between the worlds is the thinnest. There are many reason for this thinning. Ultimately, there is a lot of travel from this world to the realm of the dead. The God has traveled from the harvest and claims his role as the Underworld God, learning the lessons of shadow as he awaits his rebirth, leaving the Horned God to rule the land. The Goddess grows old in her mourning, becoming the Crone, the Death Goddess, and has retreated to the Underworld to be with her consort. Following the Goddess to the Underworld, plants are withdrawing their life force. The leaves turn and the herbs wither. And lastly, in the ancient world, this is the last harvest, the meat harvest, meaning most of the herd animals are slaughtered and either smoked or salted to preserve them, so the tribe would have sustenance in the winter months. In a manner of speaking, this is the Animal Lord, the Horned God of death, providing for the tribe, as the Green God has provided for his people in the first two harvests.

This day is the Celtic new year, and is commemorated with the story of the good god, the arch-Druid and all-father known as the Dagda. He journeys to the Underworld so that the Tuatha De Danann, the children of Danu, can be victorious against their enemies, the Fomorians. There he meets the Morgan, the goddess of war and death, often associated with the Triple Goddess in the form of Anu, Babd, and Macha. To gain the power of victory over death in battle, the giant gods mate in the river between worlds, symbolizing the veil between worlds being penetrated. Celtic witches say this mating occurs each Samhain, uniting the worlds of life and death through the sexual union of the Goddess and God.

The Sun is in the fixed sign of Scorpio. Scorpio's key word is transformation. It is the power of death and rebirth. Scorpio is well-known as one of the most psychically powerful signs, but also a sign of deep emotional power. Scorpio is the creative power of sexuality, as demonstrated by the Dagda and Morgan. Scorpio reveals that which is hidden, and destroys that which doesn't serve so one may ascend the expanding spiral of awareness. Scorpio is the sign of the phoenix, the spirit bird that dies to rise from the ashes and be reborn, as we all do.

Samhain is the feast of the ancestors. Pagans honor those who have passed before them. Ancestor reverence is a key part of many pagan traditions, believing the ancestors, both genetic and spiritual, help guide and protect us. As the veil thins, they can reach out from their place of rest and regeneration to remain in contact with the family. As they have fallen to the Underworld, they, too, will rise again, in this world or another, like the phoenix of Scorpio. Plates of food are left out for the dead, as well as altars made specifically for the dead. Candles are lit to guide their way to this world and back again. Some traditions will hold an entire supper in silence, putting out places and food for the dead, and then the food is left outside, for both animal and earth to consume after the dead feast on the love used to prepare it. Giving candy to children is like giving offerings to the ancestors of the past reincarnated as the children of the present.

Because of enhanced psychic and magickal ability on this day, rituals often encourage the use of scrying with crystals, black mirror, or pools of water, to gain insight of the future and aid from the ancestors. Tarot, runes, and other divination is particularly successful on this night, too. Shamanic journey to face the shadows of the Underworld, visit with the ancestors, and heal deep wounds from those who have passed unexpected are all excellent workings on this night.

When planning your own Samhain ritual, keep these points in mind. Use the power of death as a tool for rebirth, as it is the new year. Some witches make their new year resolutions on this day, rather than on January 1. Some witches bury the ashes of their year's previous spells, held in an ash pot on the altar all year long. They are released to start the year anew. Honor the ancestors. Honor death. Turn the Wheel of the Year with the gods and goddesses of the Underworld as you prepare for the light to wax again.

Many witchcraft books contain rituals on the Wheel of the Year holidays, from suggestions to fully written rituals. I suggest obtaining such resources to your magickal library, to have them on hand when creating your own ritual. I suggest *Celebrate the Earth: A Year of Holidays in the Pagan Tradition* by Laurie Cabot with Jean Mills (Delta), Scott Cunningham's *Wicca: A Guide for the Solitary Practitioner* (Llewellyn), and *The Witch's Circle* by Maria K. Simms (Llewellyn). My own book, *City Magick* (Weiser), contains simple rituals for those living in an urban environment.

EXERCISE 35

Turn the Wheel

Reflect on the next Wheel of the Year holiday. Write, plan, and perform a simple ritual circle to honor the holiday. It doesn't have to be long and complex or involve anyone but you. Simply do something to mark the day and strive to celebrate all eight feast days in your life.

HOMEWORK

- Complete Exercise 35.

- Continue regular altar devotional and any other regular meditative practice.

- Practice divination techniques.

- Continue journaling regularly.

- Celebrate the Moon through ritual.

Tips

- Experience the holidays before you try to intellectualize them too much. If you try to make it work as one coherent story in one single culture, you will have difficulty, unless you receive divine inspiration and understanding from the gods. Learn all you can about the holidays, but in the end, experience and enjoy.

- There is no right way to celebrate, just as there is no right way to eat a good meal, unwrap presents, or spend an evening with friends. These celebrations are magickal, but don't let the worry of getting it "right" prevent you from celebrating the season. Marking the holiday is the most important aspect of it. How you mark it is up to you.

Lesson Eleven
Weaving the Web

Community is one of the strongest aspects of the craft, but also one of its biggest weaknesses. It is quite an amazing experience to find others of similar mind, walking on a similar path. There is a sense of kinship, of coming home. Until fairly recently, with the boom of modern witchcraft books, most people are brought into the craft by another, and introduced to a formal coven or informal circle of witches. There is a sense of community and tradition, of forging a vital link to the past while heading into the future.

The Broom Closet

For eclectic solitary witches, it can be hard to find a sense of community, or once it's found, it is hard to find a long-lasting sense of community. Although more commonly accepted as the years go by, it can still be quite difficult to be a public witch.

Many witches are concerned about their physical safety and the safety of their family. Some fear repercussions at the workplace. Witches fear social stigma not only for themselves, but also for the children. It can be hard to grow up when one or both parents are publicly pagan.

Witches who are not public about their practice are considered in the "broom closet" (as it is affectionately known), while those of who are public are "out" of the broom closet. There are many pros and cons to public life as a witch. For many of us it is a personal affirmation of who we really are, and a comfort to share that with the world. Many other practitioners are private, and feel no need to be public. But such feelings can make the craft a hard and lonely path unless you already have a peer group.

Personally I feel it is important not only to claim the word "witch," but also to be public about it. I have talked to many people searching for a personal spirituality, of European descent, and have heard comments like, "It's too bad our ancestors didn't have any medicine men." Well, we did. They were called witches, or the equivalent. And they were driven to near extinction. "Witch" is the medicine man, healer, and ceremonial leader. If we want to have these traditions recognized in the greater culture, than we must have some visible presence.

I've been asked why don't we change the word. "Witch" comes with too much baggage. If you change the word, then you will open more people to the religion. I understand the sentiment, but it's like asking someone who is black to stop using the words "black" or "African" because those words come with false stereotypes. Perhaps my "witchiness" is not on my skin, but it is who I am and I reclaim it by using the word. I used to explain my path to friends in stages—starting with the term "Earth religion" when asked my faith. Then I said "pagan," which most people didn't understand. Then I said "Wiccan," since that word defuses some fear, but again, is not understood. Finally I said I am a "witch." More often than not, friends said, "Oh, why didn't you just say so?" So perhaps it was a bigger deal in my mind than others. Though I use the word "witch" and "Wiccan" somewhat interchangeably, I prefer the word "witch," and my practice is "witchcraft."

If you choose to be an out witch, then use some common sense and have some concern for your safety, but don't be paranoid. Take into account the community you live in and what you mean by public. Public doesn't necessary mean calling a press conference and announcing it to local newspapers and television. And I wouldn't make a big statement at the local fundamentalist Bible study class. Going public can simply mean wearing your witchy jewelry and not hiding it when in public. You may be asked questions, so make sure you have some intelligent and simple answers when someone asks about your pentacle and refers to it as a satanic symbol. Be sure you can explain that it is not and why it is not, if the person cares to listen. Practice composure. People may upset you with their ignorance, but most people don't mean it intentionally. Show them the poise, balance, integrity, and love of a true witch, even when they upset you. That will go much further in breaking false stereotypes of the witch, and showing that we are real people with a living tradition.

In any situation of being in the closet, one witch should not "out" another witch. Don't assume that someone is public. If you see someone at a gathering of witches and pagans, and then bump into them at the supermarket, don't assume you can publicly talk about the craft there and then. If this person is publicly wearing a pentacle or other obvious sign, then perhaps you can, but when in doubt, ask. Stay silent if the person is with someone else. You don't want to out someone as a witch to their friend or family member who is unaware of it. Be respectful. Just because it is not a big deal to you doesn't mean the attitude is shared by everyone. Coming out is a personal decision for everyone and you should never take that away.

Several organizations exist to help pagans with legal issues due to their paganism and to help educate the public on the basics of witchcraft, breaking the old Halloween stereotype of the green-faced, wart-nosed, hag witch. If you are in need of such assistance, or want to offer that assistance, web weave with others involved in these movements, such as the Witch's League of Public Awareness, among others.

WITCH WARS

Unfortunately as wonderful and loving as the teaching of witchcraft can be, and as welcoming the community can be, there are often problems within the community. Due to its very nature as a personal, nondogmatic tradition, it attracts many strong personalities. Often people are attracted to it because they are in need of personal healing, and not all are lucky enough to find the teachers, healers, and lessons that bring this balance. Sometimes personal squabbles blow up into community conflicts between groups, creating what some silly folk call "witch wars." There are no bloodied weapons or guns. There are only bad feelings and hopefully not often the foolish one who works against the Law of Three. I actually had one person tell me she was "willing to accept the karmic consequences" to get back at another. In the end, it is sad that often our worst enemy is ourselves, both individually and as a community.

As I write this it is my fervent hope that such things will wither away to nothing. Personal disputes will be kept personal, and will be resolved with love and guidance and not blown out of proportion. With the forces that we call upon, with the very dynamic and magickal lives we lead, it is easy to blow the smallest things into monumental events. Harsh words are suddenly perceived as grand curses. In the end, its really just two kids in the sandbox.

One of the reasons why witches often have such disputes, beyond personal ego, is the belief that their way, tradition, or ritual, is the "right" way to do things. Symbols vary from culture to culture, as to methods of training and a sense of "true" legitimacy to the word witch. If one is particularly zealous, or taught by a zealous priestess or priest, there may be little room in the personal cosmology for difference. In the end, all aspects of witchcraft are a symbol system, a paradigm, not an absolute truth. Those who can work in many paradigms are not threatened when something comes up to challenge their favorite paradigm. I am a witch, but I can talk to someone about the paradigms of Hermetic magick, Christianity, psychology, or Eastern philosophy. I don't necessarily agree with all of them on all points, but I can see the similarities between them far outweigh the differences. In the end, the intention is the most important part.

In witchcraft, the differences are even more minute. Healthy debate, and understanding why someone thinks or believes a certain way, is wonderful. I'm always interested more in the "whys" of something and too often only receive the answer, "I don't know why. That's the way my teacher did it." Here are some points that are debated in the craft. Think about each and see how you feel about them. Be open to other points of view.

I wish I knew about them before I started working in the community. No one really told me that others would feel differently, or so strongly, about them. Most of my teachers didn't present other points of view, and most of the books I read were in harmony with what I was taught. It wasn't until I broadened my research and saw how many books conflicted with each other, and met many other pagans who also conflicted with each other, did I understand there were other ways to do things.

I used to call this list "Ten Things Witches Disagree On" but realized it is probably much more than just ten things. But this is a good place to just reflect on your own thoughts and beliefs, and realize that others may feel differently. That's okay. In witchcraft, we are all entitled to our own experience and opinion. These topics are provocative to some, but in the end, I honestly don't care what you believe. I just want you to be aware and have both knowledge and experience to find a way that works for you personally.

Witches Are Made vs. Witches Are Born

This is the old argument regarding who is a legitimate witch. Some feel witches are "made" through initiation rituals, passing the lineage and title from one witch to another. Others feel legitimate witches are born that way, and no one can "make" you a witch. You either are or you aren't. But how you are born to it causes some disagreement. Many feel witchcraft is hereditary, and a witch gives birth to children who are witches. The power and ability are passed through the bloodlines. Others feel a soul comes into this world born a witch, and will be lead to the right experience and teachers to bring that out. Personally, I feel whether you feel witches are made or witches are born, both acts are through the Goddess and God. No one can make you a witch but the Goddess and God, but perhaps they will work through a priestess, priest, and ritual. No one can be born a witch if not born through the love of the Goddess and God, regardless of genetics.

Elemental Correspondences

Witches often disagree as to what tool represents what element, and what direction such tools should be placed. People also discuss the best way to arrange an altar, what direction it should face, how big it should be, and what size. We discussed some elemental and tool correspondences in Lesson Five, but the discussion could be lengthened. In the end, as long as you have all four elements, a tool for each, and place one in each direction, you will be good. I've experimented with all combinations and all work, but some work better for me than others.

Should Magickal Tools Be Used in the Mundane World?

Ask a group of witches if tools should be used outside of the ritual circle, and you will get a wide range of strong opinions. Folk and kitchen witches might use their ritual blades to make food, while a more ceremonial style witch would say that an athame should never be used to cut anything physical, and such ritual blades shouldn't even be sharp. Should a cauldron be used for things that are not specifically magickal? Many would argue that all acts with a cauldron are magickal, from spellwork to cooking dinner. Can you really divide your mundane life from your magickal? At first, there is a healthy boundary between the two, but as you practice more and more, every act becomes an act of worship, ritual, and magick.

The Validity of Traditional Witchcraft and Eclectic/Solitary Witchcraft

We live in an unusual time where there are many different traditions of witchcraft. All draw one the wisdom of the past. The earliest modern reconstructions are much more structured in form, such as the Gardnerian and Alexandrian traditions. One must be initiated after formal study to claim lineage in these traditions. Others are more eclectic, based on personal inspiration and study. The availability of many books on the subject opens up a once-forbidden topic. Both are wonderful and consist of different branches to the tree of the witch. Unfortunately, some think it is an either/or proposition. Many traditionalists feel that the eclectics are not true witches and lack the necessary skills and knowledge to properly practice the craft. In some cases, they are right. Modern eclectics look to traditionalists as dogmatic dinosaurs who lack a sense of freedom. They feel the traditionalists should move out of the way. Again, in some cases, they have a point. But both have wonderful things to offer. I know my own personal path would be nothing without both of these traditions and points of view.

The Validity of Self-Initiation

To continue the debate on the traditional vs. the eclectic, as well as who are the legitimate witches, the topic of self-initiation comes to mind. Thirty years ago, most witches were initiated into a formal tradition and coven. Now, most who identify as a witch have had little formal training and no traditional initiation by another. Some would argue they are not really witches. Solitary traditions, made very popular by Scott Cunningham's *Wicca: A Guide for the Solitary Practitioner*, are incredibly widespread and deeply meaningful for many modern witches. I believe in them highly, but then again I don't come from a traditional point of view myself.

Witch Queens and Kings

In some traditions, covens are very structured. If a person reaches the rank of High Priestess or High Priest, that witch "hives off" from the coven, forming their own coven, and giving the original coven space to take new members. Any High Priestess who has four covens hive off from her original coven is often known as a Witch Queen as a sign of respect, and often wears the ceremonial garter belt as a symbol of this. Less frequently is a High Priest referred to as a Witch King, though Alex Sanders was known as such among his tradition. While originally meant as a sign of respect, some priestesses and priests have let it go to their head. Others have harshly criticized these titles, and sometimes any titles, as flagrant displays of ego not befitting a spiritual leader and teacher. In the end, you can call yourself and have covens call you anything you want, but respect must be earned. We should all give respect to our elders until their actions, not their titles, give us a reason not to be respectful. We should be respectful of all, regardless of title or rank, witch or non-witch.

Politics

By the end of the twentieth century, the pagan community has definitely dug its way into politics. Some politics are regional and include the petty politics of the aforementioned "witch wars." If you come from a certain coven or tradition, you are suppose to not talk to, visit, or shop with certain people or places. That is not the type of politics I am talking about. I'm talking about regional, national, and global politics. Many witches are involved in political movements, usually involving civil rights, environmental awareness, and military reduction. Some are actively involved in public protests, while others are quietly working behind the scenes. Some witches are fully for political action, and on the far end, believe that every witch should be involved in these movements. Other witches are more conservative, and feel that demonstrating under the banner of witchcraft or paganism is lumping together a large group of people in the public eye, who may not necessarily share the same views.

The New Age Movement

When I talk about witchcraft to someone who is not aware of the history, a common question is, "So, that's a New Age thing, right?" People assume witchcraft is New Age because our books are in the New Age section in the bookstore, since they don't fit in with other mainstream religion sections. I usually reply, "Actually it's more like the Old Age. The ideas are pretty ancient, but so are most ideas you would call New Age anyway." People are surprised by that statement, having no idea there is a true history to these ideas. The New Age refers to the change of astrological ages, from the Age of Pisces to the Age of Aquarius, which is touted as a new golden age of peace and enlightenment. No one can pin down exactly when the New Age begins. Some say it is already here, while others place it in the near or distant future. Although the revival of witchcraft, magick, tarot, astrology, numerology, meditation, herbalism, and psychic skills can all be classified as part of the New Age resurgence, many who identify with being a "New Ager" have nothing to do with witchcraft, and may even be fearful of it. Many New Age philosophies are very Christian-oriented and have erroneous beliefs about witches. Sometimes modern witches' attitudes and reactions play into those stereotypes. Many witches chalk up those identified as New Agers as "fluffy bunnies" with no real understanding of metaphysics or healing, being ungrounded in the physical world. Certain New Agers often play into the flaky, ungrounded stereotype. Those in the mainstream often lump us all together because we do have many similarities. Both are fonts of wisdom, having something to offer to the world.

The Roots of the Craft

Witches will disagree on from where the craft springs. What was the first source of witchcraft? Usually their opinion will be biased by the cultural tradition they practice.

Those with a strong Celtic slant will say it came from the Celts first, though the concept of the witch can be found in other cultures, predating their contact with the Celts. The Druids are often cited as the source of witchcraft, as their traditions devolved into the practices of the cunning man and woman of medieval Europe. Egyptian mages will cite ancient Egypt as the birthplace. Shamanic witches will look to the Stone Age. I think the root of witchcraft is decided by how you define witchcraft. Narrower definitions bring us to a more definitive source, while broader definitions, like my own interpretation, encompass the world's traditions.

Witch and Wiccan

The words "witch" and "Wiccan," as well as "witchcraft" and "Wicca," are hotly debated with conflicting opinions. Both have the same root meaning. Wicca, with a capital *W*, is technically the modern revival of the practice of witchcraft. Some use "witch/witchcraft" to denote the practice of spells, while reserving "Wicca/Wiccan" to refer to the religion. Others use "Wicca/Wiccan" to denote formal traditions, such as Gardnerian and Alexandrian, while solitary or eclectic practices are simply "witchcraft." Others use the two interchangeably, depending on the situation. "Wicca" is often a less-frightening word than "witchcraft." Some practitioners just prefer one word to another, and that's fine, too. Use the words and titles that mean the most to you. Personally, I think reclaiming any form of the word "witch" or "Wiccan" is very important to our culture and history.

WEB WEAVING

The term "web weaving" refers to making connections in the pagan community. By making such connections, you strengthen the web that weaves us all together. I'm not sure where the expression originates, but I heard it first in the work of Silver Raven-Wolf. Having a personal affinity for spiders, I love the image.

Meeting other pagans can be difficult at times, unless you are at a specifically pagan shop or social gathering. Those places tend to make the best spots for chance meeting. If you meet someone in public, you can look for pagan-appropriate jewelry, such as a pentacle, rune, or a Goddess symbol, but such accoutrements do not necessarily make a pagan. As you have found out through your studies, witchcraft is more than a fashion statement. Such items have become fashionable in certain subcultures, and many wear them with no idea of their meaning in witchcraft. Sometimes a few well-placed words can determine if the person is a pagan. Key codewords among us are things such as "Blessed be," a general blessing used as a hello, goodbye, or anything in between. "Merry meet" is a usual welcome, as well as "Merry part" or "Merry meet, merry part, and merry meet again" for a farewell. Other subtle clues include saying "Goddess bless you!" instead of "God bless you!" when someone sneezes. Some replace the popular exclamation "Oh my God!" with "Oh my gods!" All are subtle yet powerful ways of stating your difference among others who have the ears to listen without wearing a sign that says "witch" around your neck. Most witches I know are quite subtle about their craft, even though they are publically open about it.

Exercise 36

Web Weaving

This is not a formal academic exercise, but is an exercise to stretch your personal boundary. For this lesson, I want you to do some act of web weaving beyond your normal, everyday contact. If you have a group of practitioners or pagan friends, you will already have a community connection. I want you to explore beyond that. If you are a solitary, I want to you take a step in making contact with others. It can be a new e-mail pen pal you found online, or visiting a store or public ritual group that is new to you. Expand your horizons. You never know who you might meet!

Homework

- Complete Exercise 36.

- Continue regular altar devotional and any other regular meditative practice.

- Practice divination techniques

- Continue journaling regularly.

- Celebrate the Moon and Wheel of the Year through ritual.

Lesson Twelve
Coven Working

If you learned your craft in a traditional coven, you would be learning to do rituals and spellwork in the context of group as well as a solitary. The lessons are purposely planned for those who are in a solitary practice, but everything can easily be adapted for group work. You may have a study partner through this work, and now be wondering how the rituals may be different when there is more than one person involved.

Covens

Group work is an incredibly rewarding and incredibly demanding prospect, depending entirely on the group. Groups of witches are traditionally known as covens, and usually consist of three to thirteen members. In such traditional covens, there is usually a High Priestess as the leader, assisted by a High Priest. For some the leadership roles are reversed, or split equally. The High Priest and High Priestess train the other members of the coven, acting as both clergy and teachers to the group. Members start as initiates and after a year-and-a-day study, with the leaders' approval, may take an initiation as a first-degree witch. Those who wish to take on the role of a priest or priestess within the group continue to study for at least another year and a day to earn the initiation of the second degree. The final degree in this three-tier system is High Priestess and High Priest, and may take many years to complete.

Some traditions are very strict, and will allow only one High Priest or Priestess in the coven. Once you attain that rank, you are asked to leave and start your own group, allowing the original coven to take on new members at the initiate level. This process is called "hiving off" and has some practical considerations. There is no confusion about leadership, keeping no more than one High Priestess or High Priest per coven, and it keeps fresh blood in the coven while preventing the group from getting too large. Social groups over twelve or thirteen members become unwieldy, from covens to business committees.

Other traditions are less formal. There is no requirement to hive off, and respect is simply given to the elders of the group while the elders give others the opportunity to grow and lead. Certain traditions require a new applicant to start at the initiate level, even if they have had previous experience or initiation, because it is a new tradition and they must learn it from ground up. Others respect previous training and will allow the new member to join at the appropriate rank.

Many modern covens, mine included, are nonhierarchical and have no ranking system. Such groups often dislike the word "coven," and use the term "circle," though it can get confusing with the main ritual known as the magick circle. Many witches feel the new Age of Aquarius is one of nonhierarchy, of lateral relationships, based on sisterhood and brotherhood, and to hold to the tiered system is a throwback to the hierarchy created in the Age of Pisces and the Christian church. I agree, but realized that a nonhierarchical system has its advantages and drawbacks.

Through I train my students in a five-tier system, based on the elements, and many are somewhat equivalent to the traditional ranks of Wicca, this has no bearing on membership in the coven. Those with knowledge and skill are respected regardless of the tradition. Leadership, for both ritual and other work, is rotating. Everyone, from the most experienced to least, has a turn at guiding the group. The term "High Priestess" or "High Priest" is reserved for the members who are leading the ritual on a particular meeting. The title is then passed to whoever is leading the next ritual or meeting.

The advantages of rotating authority are learning to work as a group and make group decisions. It is quite a good ego challenge for those of us used to leading and being in charge. I know it gives me quite a better view on being a good member, and that helps me be a better leader when it is my turn again. The disadvantage is a lack of focus or direction at times. Group decisions often take much longer to make when there is no clear leader pointing the way. Task-oriented people are forced to focus on the process, not the accomplishments.

Some groups are very structured, hierarchical or not, with explicit bylaws, rules, and traditions. Ongoing groups often keep a group Book of Shadows or group tools to be used by all. Less-formal groups do not have such things spelled out, but work in a moment-by-moment manner, going freely with the flow of things. Situations are handled as they arise.

GROUP CONSCIOUSNESS

When one works in a group, from a several week class to a long-term coven, a group consciousness develops. The group shares an identity, a group thoughtform. In magick, this is a particularly powerful dynamic, since all members are familiar with working with thoughtforms through ritual.

Truly, the sum of the group is much more than its individual parts. Things can be accomplished in the group that might be impossible to achieve individually. Energy in a group grows exponentially, not linearly. The more members you have, the more potential power you have to do your workings.

This rule only holds true to a certain extent, until it starts work against you. A small group of focused, magickal individuals can work miracles at times. But a larger group that is fractious or unfocused may yield worse results than a single individual. I would rather have a few witches who know their stuff and share a similar goal, than a fractured, squabbling group of one hundred witches, regardless of their individual training or power. I believe this is why covens are often limited to thirteen. More than that, and the social dynamic becomes hard to guide into a cohesive whole. Too many differences outweigh the similarities for specific spellwork.

Group minds do form naturally, but for a magickal group, they are best when they are guided and facilitated by the group itself. For a truly effective and fun group, intimacy must be built. Personal egos and guards must be lowered to achieve this intimacy. My coven did an intimacy act by sharing a secret or something special with the group that most people didn't know. They were silly, but personal, things, like doing housework naked when no one is around. We also meet regularly, twice a month, and our rituals focus on the Wheel of the Year holidays rather than the Moons, which we all celebrate privately. We do craft and community projects together, as well as teach each other about new topics, with a rotating leadership. Over time, we developed this intimacy through our friendship, and many members spend quite a bit of time together outside of coven work. Intimacy is a process, and can't be forced or rushed.

Naming the group and coming up with group symbols, colors, flowers, stones, totems or other correspondences also help build a powerful consciousness among people. Covens often use crests or other symbols to reflect their purpose and character. One technique I find powerful with any long-term group is the astral temple.

Exercise 37

Astral Temple

1. Decide who will guide this group meditation. Choose someone who can speak and participate in the exercise at the same time. The guide should read this meditation, embellishing it as needed, while visualizing with the group. As a group, you can discuss what will be created together before meditating, and be guided by the leader of the meditation to create a group visualization, or let your intuition guide you, and see what you come up with together and intuitively. These images are just symbols for the wonderful group energy you are creating on the astral plane.

2. Relax the group. Count the group down to a meditative state.

3. Everyone stands before the World Tree, the great tree with its roots in the Underworld and branches in the heavens. You stand before the World Tree. See its power. Feel its bark. Smell the fresh earth beneath it. Hear the wind through its branches. Imagine the group forming a circle around the tree.

4. As a group, rise up into the branches, climb up the tree and go into the branches. Rise above the clouds into the world of the stars. Here in the night sky, you gather in the ethers upon a cloud with the Moon shining down upon you.

5. Together build a temple. It can be a castle, tower, pyramid, or anything else you decide as a group. Make it out of stone, crystals, wood, metals, and light. Make it harmonious and healing, a safe haven for all members of the group. Design it with the theme, purpose, or name of the group in mind.

6. When done, take some time to enjoy the group energy. Play, have fun, and explore the astral temple.

7. Return back down the World Tree, and stand at the base of the trunk. Thank the World Tree. Step back through the screen of your mind's eye and let the World Tree gently fade from view.

8. Return the group to normal consciousness, counting up, giving clearance and balance. Do any necessary grounding.

When the coven does meditations, dream work, or any other type of psychic work, use this astral temple as the group's inner temple or launching pad for future work. You can visit it alone in your solitary meditation, or choose times to meet together astrally when you are not capable of getting together physically.

GROUP RITUALS

When working with a group in ritual, there are some technical specifications that are quite traditional in witchcraft. If you go to a public ritual, they may follow such techniques. They are by no means mandatory, but each has a practical purpose when doing this work. I choose to follow some and not others.

Purification
When a space is set, cleanse it as you normally would. Before people enter the space, cleanse or smudge them in some ritualistic manner to keep the space in a purified state before any spellwork. My coven's circles usually have a gate, or entry to the circle, and as people enter, a member will smudge with incense or anoint with water.

Response
In most groups, if someone says "So mote it be," "Blessed be," "Hail and welcome," or "Hail and farewell," the group repeats it in unison. This is a way to build the group energy by everyone focusing on the same works and intent.

Hand Holding

Traditionally, those in the circle will hold hands when possible, to keep a flow of energy. In a large circle, the High Priestess and/or Priest will be in the center, while others are holding hands around them. The hand-holding position is much like that of a séance, the right hand is on top of your neighbor's left hand. Everyone's left hand has the palm facing up and the right hand has the palm facing down. Metaphysics tells us that the left hand absorbs energy, while the right projects. Even if you are left-handed naturally, in the circle, this group dynamic takes affect. With this hand motion, the circle is strengthened.

People will ask me why this is since the circle is cast clockwise, yet the energy of the hands is counterclockwise. I feel the circle is many fields of energy, both clockwise and counterclockwise. The outer edge may be clockwise, the energy inside the circle is multidimensional. I remember learning altar set-up from Laurie Cabot's training and books, and she recommends two quartz points on the altar, one pointing toward you on the left, going to the left hand, and one point away from you, on the right. The motion mimics the handholding, creating a counterclockwise swing inside of the clockwise motion. When my altar is lacking these crystals, I notice a difference.

If someone is holding hands in the circle and must step into the circle for part of the ritual, the two members to the sides of this witch can either come together and hold hands, or extend their hands and, with their will, continue the energy circuit.

Hands are usually held at the beginning of the circle casting, raising the energy, sometimes with spellwork, and when releasing the circle. I like to end my circles with hugs and a "Blessed be" to all.

Gender

In many traditions, the ideal mix is to have an equal number of men and women in the circle, with perhaps one more female to male if you have an odd number (such as thirteen), and alternate the genders while standing the circle, so it goes female/male/female. This poses some problems for those who identify differently than their biological gender. I believe we each have male and female in us and have found such mixes don't matter that much to me. We each add a blend of male and female energy. Most circles I attend have a larger number of women than men anyway.

Figure 50: *Altar with Crystals*

Chalice

During the Great Rite, the chalice water or wine is consecrated. Some traditions only the High Priestess and High Priest share in it. Others pass it to the coven members and in more open traditions it is passed to coven members and guests as well. In some, the High Priest/tess brings the chalice to each person in the circle, while others pass it from person to person, always going clockwise around the circle. Words said at this time are often "Blessed be" or "Blessings of the Goddess upon your heart" or "May you never thirst." Either during the Great Rite, or at the end of the circle, if cakes are blessed, they are shared with similar blessings, such as "Blessings of the God upon your body" or "May you never hunger."

Protection Blessing

My tradition anoints everyone in the ritual with protection potion, upon both wrists and sometimes upon the third eye, back of the neck, or other chakra points. Like passing the chalice, it can be done by each member in the circle, or the High Priest or High Priestess, going around clockwise. I usually say, "I use this potion to protect you from all harm on any level, and return love on the source of the harm. So mote it."

Group Visualization

When doing group ritual, it is powerful to guide the group through similar images and symbols. If everyone is visualizing fire and the archangel Michael in the southern quarter at the same time, then group connection will be that stronger. Many covens take time to build strong group images, available to everyone in the working.

Spellwork

If the group is doing spellwork, it is considered the best magickal etiquette to discuss and read spells before entering the circle. If any member feels that a particular spell is not quite ethical, the group can decide the spell is not appropriate for the group and should be done by the individual solitarily. No one should be part of a group energy doing spells that she or he doesn't agree with. At the very least, if the group decides to proceed, that member should be excused from the ritual. If someone doesn't agree with a spell, they are only going to add unwanted energy to the working and weaken it, intentionally or otherwise. Most covenmates who object to a spell are doing so out of love and concern, perhaps seeing a way the spell is not for your highest good, or could potentially backfire. Listen to their critique with an open heart, and if you are the criticizer, then speak firmly, but gently.

Raising the Energy

Chanting, dancing, visualization, and simple ritual actions are great ways to bring the energy together and raise it to a higher level for your ritual. Some do a visualization spiraling the energy through the chakras of the members, starting at the root and making seven rings around. You should only do this with a group you are intimate with and feel strongly they are clear and centered. This is a variation of the "spiral dance," although most typically in America the spiral dance refers to an actual dance-like movement.

Keep in mind the comfort levels of those attending. If you are working with a group that doesn't like to sing, chanting might not be your tool. If you are working with those who are physically inhibited, injured, or elderly, dancing may not be your tool. Keep your participants in mind when planning the ritual.

Cone of Power

When a spell is read and the cone of power is released, typically all members will raise their arms to add to the energy and release it. All will form the God Position and reflect. At this time, group members may get a psychic flash or message about someone else's spell. If you do receive such information, share it with the member of the circle it pertains to, after the circle. Usually spells are released individually, in several cones, but some covens release all spells in one cone of power at the end.

Charging

Traditions will often place special objects on the altar to absorb the perfect energies of circle, even though they have nothing to do with the specific ritual. Members and guests can place rings, necklaces, stones, or herbs on the altar. Some traditions give members a few moments at the end, before or after spellwork, to hold the object and consecrate it. Others assume the energy of the circle will banish unwanted energies and infuse it with a general blessing of the Goddess and God.

Feasting

Many pagan traditions uphold the idea of celebration through food after the ritual. Post-ritual parties and potlucks are common after the Wheel of the Year celebrations, initiations, and rites of passage, but they will often occur after Moon Esbats and other rituals.

Many groups will have a particular person in charge of group dynamics, and do things during the ritual and before to help smooth the group consciousness. Counting the group into a meditative state, reading inspiring poetry, and guiding group visualization and energy work all contributes to the overall effectiveness and love of the circle. If the group is eclectic, from many different backgrounds and traditions, whoever leads the ritual should describe the basic outline and what is asked of each member. Some groups all face the direction to call the quarters, others only the High Priestess and High Priest do, while the remaining members hold hands in the circle. When you raise the cone of power, everyone may hold hands, or do it individually, in unison. Each tradition is a bit different, and there is no right or wrong to it. As long as you remember the fundamental principles of magick, the art can be varied to your tastes and the tastes of the group.

Many traditions bar guests who are not initiated into the tradition, while others will welcome guests with open arms. Some require the guest already be a witch from another tradition, while more eclectic circles will welcome non-witches who are interested. Someone should explain the basics of the circle and proper etiquette to those not familiar with the tradition. It is customary for guests to bring an offering or token to the ritual or for the group to share in after the circle.

Covens also go through great changes. People leave for a variety of reasons. New people come. Groups go through growing pains and this is the way of life. Such changes are not necessarily personal. I prefer to mark all those changes with ritual, to speak to both the universe and this group mind. If a member is leaving, do a farewell ritual, even if he or she chose to not be part of it. If a new member joins, do a welcoming ritual. If a coven disbands, do a dissolving ritual that releases the group consciousness you have created. Likewise, when forming a group, do a group dedication or creation ritual. Be imaginative in your work and build your group consciousness together.

If you have the opportunity, I highly suggest that you experience group working, even if it is only a few times. It can be a larger public group circle, or working with a more intimate group. Sometimes participation in such groups opens a new door, or really affirms the path we are already walking.

Homework

- Do Exercise 37 if you have a group to work with that plans on staying together for future work. If you don't, return to this exercise in the future if the time and situation is right.

- Continue regular altar devotional and any other regular meditative practice.

- Practice divination techniques.

- Continue journaling regularly.

- Celebrate the Moon and Wheel of the Year through ritual.

Lesson Thirteen
Second Initiation

The last ritual you will perform for this year-and-a-day course is initiation. The second-degree mark of traditional witchcraft is the role of priest and priestess. Although this system is based on five tiers, rather than the usual three, the second degree is still initiation into the role of the priestess or priest.

With these twelve previous lessons, you have learned the art and ritual of the craft. You have developed your relationship with the forces of the divine as embodied by nature. You have developed your personal relationship with the gods and goddesses. You have studied the cycles of the universe. You have made magick. You have celebrated the seasons. You have done all that is necessary to be a full priestess or priest of the craft.

The true test of this last lesson goes on for a lifetime. Anyone can learn rituals by rote and do spells out of a book, but not everyone can incorporate the path of the witch into daily life, making it the spiritual foundation needed for even further study and awareness. To do this, you must strive to live a magickal life. See the magick in everything, and realize you have a hand in shaping your world. Become conscious, and

403

consciously create with your thoughts, words, and deeds. A true priestess or priest starts to take rituals and spells and make every part of life a ritual of devotion and a spell of transformation. We start in this path with very divided boundaries, separating magickal time from mundane time, and separating magickal tools from mundane ones. Once you truly walk the path, you realize that at times the boundary is necessary for daily living, but in essence, it is artificial. Everything, everyone, and every time is sacred and magickal. A priestess and priest know this, and start incorporating this view into every action of life. We know the reality of magick in all things.

Initiation truly means a new beginning—a challenge or trial that makes us stronger and takes us to a new place in life. Use this lesson to mark the changes already within you, to solidify them into helpful, healing traditions to last a lifetime.

PREPARATION

This whole course has been your preparation for initiation. In most teachings, a year and a day is taken for this purpose. The year is for study, and the day is for reflection and ultimately the ritual itself. Many take a second magickal name at the second initiation, either discarding the first name, or adding to it. A vigil is often kept, staying up overnight in a sacred space, to be granted knowledge of your new name. You can see chapter 17 in ITOW for more about magickal names.

If you completed your training before the year is over, and even if you didn't, I highly suggest looking at other books on modern witchcraft, to understand other rituals and traditions. An eclectic witch must always be highly educated on many traditions and techniques. Although I don't agree with all the material in these books, they offer an excellent spectrum of ideas and traditions.

> *The Witches' Bible* by Janet and Stewart Farrar (Phoenix Publishing)
> *Buckland's Complete Book of Witchcraft* by Raymond Buckland
>   (Llewellyn Publications)
> *To Stir a Magick Cauldron* by Silver RavenWolf (Llewellyn Publications)
> *Wiccan Magick* by Raven Grimassi (Llewellyn Publications)
> *Celebrate the Earth* by Laurie Cabot (Delta Press)

Before going on to the self-initiation ritual, make sure you review the previous lessons and take the self-test in appendix I. You should be able to answer the majority of those questions before completing this course, or at the very least know where to look for the answers.

Complementary Training

After completion of second-degree training, many witches focus on a complementary skill to aid them in being a priest or priestess in the pagan community. The skills of healing, ranging from medicinal herbalism to energy healing techniques such as reiki, are very popular among us. I explored many aspects of healing, from crystals to flower essence, and then went back to learn medicinal herbology to complement my magickal plant knowledge.

Divination skills at a professional level, including astrology, runes, tarot, or exploring other psychic gifts, makes a natural progression from your own personal divination skills learned in this manual. Many witches are quite talented in handcrafts, and make ritual tools for the community, infusing their magick into the creation of it. Many will only buy rituals tools for witches made by witches. Some create intricate rituals tools and jewelry. Others make magickal products to share the magick with the world.

Scholarly witches study the history of witchcraft from an anthropological view, adding to and clearing up misconceptions about witchcraft. They catalog the various traditions of our modern history, and peel back the layers of our collective past. You can be a public educator, teaching others; even informally, by example, what real witchcraft is. Others parlay that role into freedom fighter for civil rights and religious freedom. Whatever your skill or calling I suggest research and training in such a skill. They will come in quite handy later on the path.

Traditional Second Initiation Rituals

Initiation rituals vary in many different traditions. In more formal schools, the ritual of the second degree is one "of the spirit," meaning it was a spiritual rebirth. Through sacred drama, covens would enact such rebirths, usually using a resurrection theme to symbolize the dark night of the soul. Stories of the goddess Inanna or Persephone, with their initiatory descent to the Underworld, are popular, as well as the myths of Osiris, Tammuz, Dionysus, and other sacrificed gods.

Initiates often wear cords of purple and silver. Sometimes binding and blindfolding is used at the second level, with a reaffirmation of the vows from the first level. Many are asked to take vows of secrecy or vows to the Wiccan Rede. Ritual tools are gathered prior to the ceremony, particularly the four elemental tools of the wand, athame, chalice, and pentacle. They are reconsecrated during the initiation.

The coven members review the eight ways of raising power (ITOW, chapter 5) are reviewed in dramatic form, along with the Threefold Law. The fivefold kiss, a symbolic homage paid by the Goddess and the God, can be given by the High Priest or Priestess. The kiss can be done two ways, either kissing the five points of the pentagram on the body (head, outstretched arms/hands, legs/feet) or at five body points (feet, knees, belly, chest/heart, and lips). Each point comes with a blessing. Typically a ring, such as a pentacle ring, is given to newly anointed second-degree witch, as a symbol of passing the power to the next generation, and offering a magical blessing.

While all of these rituals are quite wonderful and loving for a second initiation, you are out of luck if you are a solitary witch or prefer not to work with a coven. To me, you have already passed the formal initiation of the second level. If you have cast a circle successfully, you have passed the hardest part of the course. The successful creation of sacred space and the ability to do ritual is the most important aspect of being a priestess or priest. Even if you have done it before, learning all the parts well, and developing relationships with all the divine powers deepens your experience.

When you have a developed, living relationship with all the powers gathering in a circle, your life will never be the same. You will be empowered to be your own intermediary between this world and all others. You will need no other priest or priestess to do this for you. Through the creation of sacred space with your will, you are forever changed and empowered in a way undreamt of by most people.

İNITIATION RITUAL OF THE PRIESTESS AND PRIEST

This initiation ritual is simply to deepen your experience and formalize your commitment to the path of the priestess and priest. Although the ritual is given below, a true test of your readiness would be to revise it, and work it to your own personal tastes and traditions.

This version is a variation of the ritual I perform at the end of my Witchcraft II: Building the Outer Temple class. You can perform this ceremony by yourself, and simply state things as written, or if you are practicing with a fellow on the path, you can guide, ask, anoint, and initiate each other, as sisters and brothers on the path.

For this ritual you will need:

- Full altar, and in particular, your four elemental tools

- Robe or other ritual garb. If you want a special cord belt or sash to mark your second initiation, I suggest green for the element of earth, for we are creating sacred space in the physical world. (Green will complement the fire grade's red cord of ITOW.) You can also choose the traditional purple and/or silver.

- Ring symbolic of the second degree

- Cleansing/consecrating incense

- Anointing potion/oil—make your own using your magickal knowledge

- Intention paper from Exercise 5

- New craft name if you choose to take one

Prepare yourself and your space. For initiations, ritual bathing before the ceremony is not only appropriate, but it is recommended. Make this ritual special and put a lot of time, effort and thought into it. When done, you can do most of the ritual skyclad or don your ritual robes. If wearing robes, I would save the cord belt for after the anointing. Have your altar set and begin.

Cast the circle.

> We cast this circle in to protect us from all forces that come to do us harm.
> We charge this circle to allow only the most perfect energies for this work, and block out all other energies.
> We charge this circle to create a space beyond space, a time beyond time, a temple of perfect love and perfect trust, where the highest will is sovereign.
> We create a temple of initiation.
> So mote it be.

Call the quarters. I prefer to call upon both totems and divinities. Change the quarter calls and presentation to the directions to suit your own preferences and energies.

> To the north, I call upon the element of earth. I call upon the great Stag. I call upon horned father Cernunnos. Please bring your blessing to this initiation. Guide and guard us in this circle. Hail and welcome.

> To the east, I call upon the element of fire. I call upon the great Red Fox. I call upon Lord Lugh of the Long Arm. Please bring your blessing to this initiation. Guide and guard us in this circle. Hail and welcome.

> To the south, I call upon the element of air. I call upon the dark Crow. I call upon Mother Macha of the Feathered Cloak. Please bring your blessing to this initiation. Guide and guard us in this circle. Hail and welcome.

> To the west, I call upon the element of water. I call upon the loving Dolphin. I call upon Cerridwen of the Cauldron. Please bring your blessing to this initiation. Guide and guard us in this circle. Hail and welcome.

Evoke the Great Divine.

> I call upon the Two Who Move As One in the love of the Great Spirit, the Goddess, and God, to aid me in this initiation. I call upon the divine in all their forms and faces most perfect for this ritual. I ask for your guidance and blessing on the path of the priest/tess.

> I call upon my highest spirits guides and guardians to be present.
> Hail and welcome.

Name the work.

In the name of the Goddess and God, in all spirits of love and trust, I ask for my initiation as a priest/tess of the craft, for the highest good, harming none. I have studied the path for a year and a day, and know its ways. I seek to truly live the wisdom of the witch. So mote it be.

Reflect on your training. Take out your intention paper from the beginning of the year. Read it and think about if you have fulfilled your intention. Your intentions may have changed along the way, or you may have superseded them. When done with your reflection, burn the paper like a spell in your cauldron.

The vows to accept the gifts and responsibilities of the craft in accord with the Wiccan Rede.

I vow to accept the gifts of magick which are my birthright as a witch, and vow to use my magick in accord with the Goddess, God, and Great Spirit. I use them in accord with the Rede of the Witches: do what thou will and let it harm none.

At this point, I suggest reading "The Charge of the Goddess" or any other suitably in-spirational piece of poetry. It can be something of your own devising, as an offering to the divine.

The Great Rite, drawing down the Moon, and drinking from the chalice: these rit-ual can be done at anytime. Full Moons are traditional, but all phases of the Moon Goddess are sacred and worthy of initiation rituals.

As the sword is to the grail, the blade is to the chalice, truth is to love. I draw together the power of the Goddess and God, their sacred love in the power of creation. I drink it in as their priest/tess. I ask for the blessing and nourish-ment of the Goddess and God. With their love, I will never thirst. Blessed be.

Presentation to the four quarters. Start by facing the north. Hold your earthen tool to the north.

To the north, to the element of earth, and to the god Cernunnos. I am *(name or witch name)*, **your daughter/son. Please allow me on this path and give me your support and blessing. I hold the stone/peyton, a symbol of the foundation of the earth and the sacredness of the world. Continue to teach me the ways of earth. I honor you and give you my honor, time, and commitment. Blessed be.**

Feel your body and your tool fill with the blessings of this quarter. Turn and face the east, holding your wand.

To the east, to the element of Fire, and the god Lugh. I am *(name or witch name)*, **your daughter/son. Please allow me on this path and give me your support and blessing. I hold the wand, the symbol of the will and the guiding light of the soul. Continue to teach me the ways of fire. I honor you and give you my honor, time, and commitment. Blessed be.**

Feel your body and tool fill with the blessings of this quarter. Turn and face the south, holding your athame.

To the south, to the element of air, and to the goddess Macha. I am *(name or witch name)*, **your daughter/son. Please allow me on this path and give me your support and blessing. I hold the athame, the symbol of the truth and the power of the word. Continue to teach me the ways of air. I honor you and give you my honor, time and commitment. Blessed be.**

Feel your body and tool fill with the blessings of this quarter. Turn and face the west, holding your chalice.

To the west, to the element of water, and to the goddess Cerridwen. I am *(name or witch name)*, **your daughter/son. Please allow me on this path and give me your support and blessing. I hold the chalice, the symbol of love and the vessel of healing. Continue to teach me the ways of water. I honor you and give you my honor, time, and commitment. Blessed be.**

Feel your body and tool fill with the blessings of this quarter. Face the center of the altar.

To the Goddess, God, and Great Spirit, above, below, around, and within me.I am (*name or witch name*)**, your daughter/son. Please allow me on this path and give me your support and blessing. I hold the pentacle within my body,my arms, my legs, and my head, symbol of magickal balance and harmony.I am earth, water, air, fire, and spirit. Continue to teach me the ways of spirit. I call you and give you my time, honor, and commitment. Blessed be.**

Feel yourself fill with the perfect trust and perfect love of the divine. Repeat the Goddess and God meditation, Exercise 6, to deepen your relationship with the divine. Make sure you have permission and blessing of the gods to go forward. If you don't, this circle can be a circle of celebration and preparation for when you are truly ready. When done, return yourself to the center of the circle and prepare yourself for your anointed blessing.

Get out your anointing oil or potion. Draw invoking pentagrams on each part of the body. If you are working skyclad, it can be done on the skin, and then robes are worn after the blessing, or you can do this on or above the robes.

> *Feet*—**Blessed be these roots to grow strongly in love with the Earth and the Mother.**
>
> *Belly*—**Blessed be this cauldron of fire to burn brightly with the guidance of the gods.**
>
> *Heart*—**Blessed be this heart, my inner temple, to hold the waters of love.**
>
> *Throat*—**Blessed be this throat to draw the breath of life and the love of the Father.**
>
> *Crown*—**Blessed be this crown to know the divine spirit in all things.**

Anoint your ring and wear it, symbolizing you taking on the role of priest/tess.

In the name of all those gathered here today, I am a priest/tess in the craft of the witch. I accept all responsibilities and blessings of this path. So mote it be.

You can close the ritual however you want. You can do a circle of light and healing and raise a cone of power, or not. It is up to you. You are skilled enough now to make that decision on your own.

Release the quarters.

To the north, I thank and release the element of earth. I thank the great Stag and the horned father Cernunnos for their aid and blessings in this initiation. Hail and farewell.

To the west, I thank and release the element of water. I thank the loving Dolphin and the crone mother Cerridwen for their aid and blessings in this initiation. Hail and farewell.

To the south, I thank and release the element of air. I thank the dark Crow and the dark mother Macha for their aid and blessings in this initiation. Hail and farewell.

To the east, I thank and release the element of fire. I thank the great Red Fox and the good god Lugh for their aid and blessings in this initiation. Hail and farewell.

I thank and release the Goddess, God, Great Spirit, and all spirits who gather in perfect love and perfect trust. I thank you all for your guidance and blessings. Stay if you will, go if you must. Hail and farewell.

Release the circle

I cast this circle, this temple of initiation, out into the cosmos as a sign of our rites. The circle is undone, but never broken. So mote it be.

Your initiation as a priestess or priest is complete. Congratulations! Many blessings upon you for completing such a training course. You have all the tools of a traditional witch for spellcraft, and if you have also completed ITOW, you also have all the inner tools necessary for making magick.

The third book in this series, *The Temple of Shamanic Witchcraft*, will explore the shamanic branch of witchcraft, tracing our roots back to core shamanic techniques. Through it, a witch learns to walk between the worlds, commune with spirits, develop relationships with power animals, and use shamanic healing techniques for personal balance and to help others. Diving into the element of water, we face the shadow self hiding beneath our surface. We heal and transform ourselves, reborn through the Goddess to truly be centered in our personal power.

Appendix I: Self-Test

You can answer these questions in your Book of Shadows, or on a separate piece of paper if you need more room.

1) Briefly define the following words or phrases.

amulet:

astrology:

athame:

boline:

Charge of the Goddess:

charm:

circle:

cone of power:

correspondences, magickal:

coven:

deosil:

divination:

drawing down the Moon:

elements:

Esbats:

Hail & welcome / Farewell:

High Priest / High Priestess:

perfect love and perfect trust:

plane of forces:

polytheism:

potion:

priest/priestess:

quarters:

ritual:

Sabbat:

scourge:

skyclad:

So mote it be:

talisman:

thoughtform:

tools:

wand:

watchtowers:

widdershins:

2) What is the role of a priest or priestess in modern witchcraft?

3) Briefly recount your favorite pagan myth. Why is it your favorite?

4) What is your favorite element, and why?

5) What is your least favorite element? Why?

6) Describe everything on your altar and what it symbolizes.

7) What is your favorite way to cleanse yourself, your space, and your tools? Why?

8) What is sacred space? What is the magick circle?

9) What elements do you use to correspond to each direction? Why?

10) What is a spell and how does it work?

11) Explain the Law of Three and the Wiccan Rede.

12) Explain the cycle of the Moon and how it affects magick.

13) Name the days of the week and what planet is associated with each day.

14) Pick a planet or sign and explain its magickal significance.

15) How do you use magickal timing in your rituals?

16) Pick one stone, metal, or herb, and describe how it is used magickally.

17) Tell the story of the Wheel of the Year and the changes of the God and Goddess.

Appendix II: Chants

The following are chants used for entering an altered state, creating group consciousness, celebrating, and to raise power for spellwork. Each is associated with a Wheel of the Year holiday if you choose to use them for your celebrations. Recordings of these chants can be found on *The Outer Temple of Witchcraft CD Companion*.

YULE

Holly King

God of Holly and Withering
Give your crown to the Oak King
God of Leaf and Growing Light
Welcome back your golden light
Prince of Fire warm our souls
Melt away winter's cold
Yule comes with the Wheel
Fill with fire and we are healed

© Christopher Penczak

Draw Down the Sun

Draw down the Sun
Draw down the light
Welcome the God
Banish the night

Warming the heart
Warming the soul
Healing us all
Making us whole

© Christopher Penczak

ÎMBOLC

Brid, Triple Goddess

Triple Goddess
Maiden, Mother, Crone
With your light
Bless our hearts and homes

Goddess Fire
Healer, poet, smith
Bless us please
With all your gifts

© Christopher Penczak

ØSTARA

Rise, O Goddess

Rise, O Goddess
Bless the seed
Rise, O Goddess
Fulfill our need
Rise, O Goddess
Queen of Spring
Rise, O Goddess
With your king

© Christopher Penczak

BELTANE

The Fires of Bel

Come let's light the fires of Bel
Come let's light the fires of Bel
And ask for the blessing from the goddess of the well
Come let's light the fires of Bel
Come let's light the fires of Bel
Wipe away the anger and the sadness and the shame
Come let's light the fires of Bel
Come let's light the fires of Bel
And dance in the light and the love of Beltane

© Christopher Penczak

LITHA

Oak King

God of Oak and Growing Things
Give your crown to the Holly King
God of Horn and Waning Light
Guide us all through the night
Shadow come and show the way
Open gates to the fey
Litha comes but once a year
Fill with fire and banish fear

© Christopher Penczak

LAMMAS

Lammas Blessing

Goddess of the Earth
God of the Sun
And from you
All life comes

Son, Lover,
King, and Death
With your love
We are blessed

© Christopher Penczak

Lord Lugh

O Lord Lugh
We call to you
Please bring your gifts
As we pledge our hearts to you

© Christopher Penczak

MABON

Modron, Mabon

Modron, Mabon
Mother and son
Turning the Wheel
Your time has come

Goddess of the Earth
God of the Vine
With your love
Come the harvest wine

© Christopher Penczak

SAMHAIN

Gods of Life, Gods of Death

Earth and air, fire, and water
Goddess, Crone, Mother, and Daughter
God of Light, God of Dark
In this space, open our hearts

Perfect love and perfect trust
Return to you, all things must
Gods of life, gods of death
With your love, we are blessed

© Christopher Penczak

Bibliography

Andrews, Ted. *Animal Speak: The Spiritual & Magical Powers of Creatures Great and Small.* Llewellyn Publications, St. Paul, MN, 1993.

Awiakta, Marilou. *Selu: Seeking the Corn Mother's Wisdom.* Fulcrum Publishing, Golden, CO, 1993.

Beyerl, Paul. *A Compendium of Herbal Magick.* Phoenix Publishing, Inc., Custer, WA, 1998.

———. *The Master Book of Herbalism.* Phoenix Publishing Inc, Custer, WA, 1984.

Brink, Jan. "Astrological Glossary" class notes. Unicorn Associates, Arlington, MA, 1997.

Cabot, Laurie. *A Salem Witch's Herbal Magic.* Celtic Crow Publishing, Salem, MA, 1994.

———, with Jean Mills. *Celebrate the Earth: A Year of Holidays in the Pagan Tradition.* Dell Publishing, New York, NY, 1994.

———, and Tom Cowan. *Love Magic.* Dell Publishing, New York, NY, 1992.

———, with Tom Cowan. *Power of the Witch.* Dell Publishing, New York, NY, 1989.

———. "Witchcraft As a Science I and II" class handouts and lecture notes. Salem, MA, 1993.

Conway, D. J. *The Ancient & Shinning Ones.* Llewellyn Publications, St. Paul, MN, 1993.

———. *Celtic Magic.* Llewellyn Publications, St. Paul, MN, 1991.

———. *Moon Magic.* Llewellyn Publications, St. Paul, MN, 1995.

Cooper, Phillip. *Basic Magic: A Practical Guide.* Samuel Weiser, Inc., York Beach, ME, 1996.

Crowley, Vivianne. *Wicca: The Old Religion in the New Age.* Aquarian Press. San Francisco, CA, 1989.

Cunningham, Scott. *Cunningham's Encyclopedia of Crystal, Gem, & Metal Magic.* Llewellyn Publications, St. Paul, MN, 1992.

———. *Cunningham's Encyclopedia of Magical Herbs.* Llewellyn Publications, St. Paul, MN, 1985.

———. *The Complete Book of Incense, Oils & Brews*. Llewellyn Publications, St. Paul, MN, 1989.

———. *Wicca: A Guide for the Solitary Practitioner*. Llewellyn Publications, St. Paul, MN, 1988.

Daniels, Estelle. *Astrological Magick*. S. Weiser, York Beach, ME, 1995.

Davidson, Gustav. *A Dictionary of Angels, Including the Fallen Angels*. The Free Press, New York, NY, 1967.

Denning, Melita, & Osborne Phillips. *Planetary Magick*. Llewellyn Publications, St. Paul, MN, 1989.

Farrar, Janet and Stewart. *Spells and How They Work*. Phoenix Publishing Inc., Custer, WA, 1990.

———. *The Witch's Goddess: The Feminine Principle of Divinity*. Phoenix Publishing Inc., Custer, WA, 1987.

———. *The Witch's God: Lord of the Dance*. Phoenix Publishing Inc., Custer, WA, 1989.

———. *The Witches' Bible: The Complete Witches Handbook*. Phoenix Publishing Inc., Custer, WA, 1996.

Gaiman, Neil. *The Sandman: Kindly Ones* trade paperback. Vertigo/DC Comics. New York, NY, 1996.

Grist, Tony and Aileen. *The Illustrated Guide to Wicca*. Sterling Press Publishing Company, New York, NY, 2000.

K, Amber. *Covencraft: Witchcraft for Three or More*. Llewellyn Publications, St. Paul, MN, 1998.

Kraig, Donald Michael. *Modern Magick*. Llewellyn Publications, St. Paul, MN, 1988.

Medici, Marina. *Good Magic*. Fireside Publishing. New York, NY, 1988.

Melody. *Love Is In the Earth: Kaleidoscope Pictorial Supplement Z*. Earth-Love Publishing House, Wheat Ridge, CO, 1995.

Myers, Stuart. *Between the Worlds*. Llewellyn Publications, St. Paul, MN, 1995.

Pajeon, Kala and Ketz. *The Candle Magick Workbook*. Citadel Press, New York, NY, 1992.

Paterson, Helena. *The Handbook of Celtic Astrology*. Llewellyn Publications, St. Paul, MN, 1994.

Penczak, Christopher. *City Magick: Urban Rituals, Spells, and Shamanism*. Weiser, York Beach, ME, 2001.

———. *The Inner Temple of Witchcraft: Magick, Meditation and Psychic Development*. Llewellyn Publications, St Paul, MN, 2002.

———. *Spirit Allies: Meet Your Team from the Other Side*. Weiser, Boston, MA, 2002.

Peschel, Lisa. *A Practical Guide to the Runes*. Llewellyn Publications, St. Paul, MN, 1989.

Rainbird, Ariadne, & David Rankine. *Magick Without Peers: A Course in Progressive Witchcraft for the Solitary Practitioner*. Capall Bann Publishing, Berks, UK, 1997.

RavenWolf, Silver. *To Stir a Magick Cauldron: A Witch's Guide to Casting and Conjouring*. Llewellyn Publications, St. Paul, MN, 1995.

Rhodes, J. Philip. *Wicca Unveiled*. *The Complete Rituals of Modern Witchcraft*. The Speaking Tree, Glastonbury, Somerset, Great Britain, 2000.

Roderick, Timothy. *Dark Moon Mysteries*. New Brighton Books, Aptos, CA, 2003.

Starhawk. *The Spiral Dance: A Rebirth of the Ancient Religion of the Great Goddess*. HarperSanFrancisco. New York, NY, 1989.

Telesco, Patricia. *The Urban Pagan*. Llewellyn Publications, St. Paul, MN, 1995.

Thorsson, Edred. *The Book of Ogham*. Llewellyn Publications, St. Paul, MN, 1994.

———. *Northern Magic: Mysteries of the Norse, Germans & English*. Llewellyn Publications, St. Paul, MN, 1992.

Tolf, Christine. "Herbal Witchcraft: Ethics, Methods and Musings from the Witch of Lichenwood"—class notes. 2002.

Valiente, Doreen. *An ABC of Witchcraft Past & Present*. St. Martin's Press, Inc. New York, NY, 1973.

Walker, Barbara G. *The Women's Dictionary of Symbols and Sacred Objects*. HarperSanFrancisco, New York, NY, 1988.

Whitcomb, Bill. *The Magician's Companion*. Llewellyn Publications, St. Paul, MN, 1993.

Willis, Tony. *Discover Runes*. Sterling Publishing Co., Inc., New York, NY, 1993.

Ziegler, Gerd. *Tarot: Mirror of the Soul*. Samuel Weiser, Inc., York Beach, ME, 1988.

Index